ACT®

ELITE 36

2nd Edition

The Staff of The Princeton Review

PrincetonReview.com

Penguin Random House

The Princeton Review
24 Prime Parkway, Suite 201
Natick, MA 01760
E-mail: editorialsupport@review.com

ISBN: 978-1-101-88200-9
eBook ISBN: 978-1-101-88205-4
ISSN: 2373-9614

The Princeton Review is not affiliated with Princeton University.

Editor: Aaron Riccio
Production Editors: Kathy Carter and Becky Radway
Production Artist: Deborah Silvestrini

Printed in the United States of America on partially recycled paper.

10 9 8 7 6 5 4 3 2

Second Edition

Editorial

Rob Franek, Senior VP, Publisher
Casey Cornelius, VP Content Development
Mary Beth Garrick, Director of Production
Selena Coppock, Managing Editor
Meave Shelton, Senior Editor
Colleen Day, Editor
Sarah Litt, Editor
Aaron Riccio, Editor
Orion McBean, Editorial Assistant

Random House Publishing Team

Tom Russell, Publisher
Alison Stoltzfus, Publishing Manager
Melinda Ackell, Associate Managing Editor
Ellen Reed, Production Manager
Kristin Lindner, Production Supervisor
Andrea Lau, Designer

Contributors

Project Managers
Zoe Gannon
Kathryn Menefee

Authors
Brian Becker
Jonathan Edwards
Melissa Hendrix
Bobby Hood
Amy Minster
Elizabeth Owens
Alice Swan

Reviewers
Clarissa Constantine
Cara Fabre
Teresa Schuberg
Michelle McCannon
Leah Murnane

National Content Director, High School Programs
Jonathan Chiu

Contents

Register Your

1 Go to **PrincetonReview.com/cracking**

2 You'll see a welcome page where you can register your book using the following ISBN: 9781101882009.

3 After placing this free order, you'll either be asked to log in or to answer a few simple questions in order to set up a new Princeton Review account.

4 Finally, click on the "Student Tools" tab located at the top of the screen. It may take an hour or two for your registration to go through, but after that, you're good to go.

If you are experiencing book problems (potential content errors), please contact EditorialSupport@review.com with the full title of the book, its ISBN number (located above), and the page number of the error. Experiencing technical issues? Please e-mail TPRStudentTech@review.com with the following information:

- your full name
- e-mail address used to register the book
- full book title and ISBN
- your computer OS (Mac or PC) and Internet browser (Firefox, Safari, Chrome, etc.)
- description of technical issue

Book Online!

Once you've registered, you can...

- Access and print out additional drills and their corresponding answers and explanations

- Find any late-breaking information released about the ACT

- Sort colleges by whatever you're looking for (such as Best Theater or Dorm), learn more about your top choices, and see how they all rank according to *The Best 380 Colleges*

- Check to see if there have been any corrections or updates to this edition

The **Princeton** Review®

Part I
Orientation

Chapter 1
Introduction to the ACT

The pursuit of a perfect or near-perfect ACT score is an impressive goal. Achieving that goal requires a thorough command of the material and strategies specific to the ACT. To begin your quest, know everything you can about the test. This chapter presents an overview of the ACT, advice about when to take it, and how to report your scores.

WELCOME

So you think you can dance, ahem, score a 34 or better? We're all for it. The Princeton Review supports all students who want to do their best. We've written this book specifically for students who are in a position to score at the very highest levels. We believe that to achieve a perfect or near-perfect score, you have to know as much as possible about the test itself. Even more, however, you need to know about yourself as a test taker.

You may be familiar with many of the basic facts about the ACT already, but even if you think you are, we encourage you to read through the following to be sure you know every single thing you can about the test you're going to conquer.

FUN FACTS ABOUT THE ACT

All of the content review and strategies we teach in the following lessons are based on the specific structure and format of the ACT. Before you can beat this test, you have to know how it's built.

Structure

The ACT consists of four multiple-choice, timed tests: English, Math, Reading, and Science, always given in that order. The ACT Plus Writing also includes an essay, with the Writing Test given after the Science Test. (ACT calls them tests, but we may also use the term "sections" in this book to avoid confusion.)

English	Math	Reading	Science	Writing
45 minutes	60 minutes	35 minutes	35 minutes	40 minutes
75 questions	60 questions	40 questions	40 questions	1 essay

Scoring

You'll earn one ACT score (1 to 36) on each test (English, Math, Reading, Science) and a composite ACT score, which is an average of these four tests. Usually, when people ask about your score, they're referring to your composite ACT score. The composite score falls between 1 and 36. The national average is about 21.

If, for example, you scored 31 on the English, 30 on the Math, 29 on the Reading and 30 on the Science, your composite ACT score would be 30.

Students receive subscores in English, Math, and Reading that range between 1 and 18. These scores provide you with more detail about your performance, but they are not actually used by colleges or universities.

The ACT includes an optional essay, known as the Writing Test. Visit **ACT.org** for detailed information about how your ACT Writing Test will be scored. The Writing Test is scored on a scale of 1–36, but this score won't be factored in to your composite. This is not to say that the Writing Test is unimportant, but rather that the Writing Test is not quite as important as the other four sections in your dogged pursuit of a 36 composite.

It's All About the Composite

Whether you look at your score online or wait to get it in the mail, the biggest number on the page is always the composite. While admissions' offices will certainly see the individual scores of all five tests (and their subscores), schools will use the composite to evaluate your application, and that's why, in the end, it's the only one that matters.

The composite is an average. When you're shooting for a 34 or higher, you need the best performance from both your strengths and weaknesses. You can't neglect your strengths and focus all your time on your weaknesses. In Chapter 3, we'll discuss in more detail how to think about the scores on the four multiple-choice tests and how to set your goals for your score.

> Use your best subjects to lift the composite as high as possible.
> Don't let your weakest subjects pull the composite down.

The higher your strongest scores, the less pressure on your weaker scores. While you can't afford for your weaknesses to drag the composite too far down, it's easier to earn a perfect score on your best subjects than it is to earn a perfect score on your weakest subjects.

Thus, when you divide your time among the four subjects, focus as much time and effort on your strengths—if not more—as you spend on your weaknesses.

Content

At the beginning of each section, we'll thoroughly review the content and strategies you need for each test. Here is an overview of each test.

English Test

The English Test consists of five passages, accompanied by 14–16 questions per passage and four answer choices per question. Some words or phrases are underlined in the passage, and the accompanying questions ask whether the underlined portion is correct as written or whether one of the three alternatives listed would be better. The questions test conventions of usage mechanics (grammar, punctuation, sentence structure) and rhetorical skills. Other questions are marked by a boxed number embedded in the passage and ask about overall organization and style.

Math Test

The Math Test features 60 questions with five answer choices per question. The easier questions *tend* to come in the first 20 questions, but the test writers can mix in easy, medium, and difficult problems throughout. The bulk of the difficult questions are found in the last 15–20 questions. Content is drawn from pre-algebra, elementary algebra, intermediate algebra, plane geometry, coordinate geometry, and trigonometry.

Reading Test

The Reading Test consists of four passages, accompanied by ten questions per passage and four answer choices per question. The passages always appear in the same order: prose fiction (sometimes known as "literary narrative"), social science, humanities, and natural science. Within the four categories, ACT selects excerpts from books and articles to create one long or two shorter passages.

Science Test

The Science Test consists of six or seven passages, a total of 40 questions, and four answer choices per question. The number of questions per passage will vary, but it is usually 5, 6, or 7 questions. The order of the passages varies from test to test. Most passages are accompanied by figures, such as charts, tables, and graphs. The content is drawn from biology, chemistry, physics, and the Earth/space sciences (astronomy, geology, and meteorology). As on the Reading Test, at least one of these passages will consist of two different passages and will require students to compare and contrast to a certain extent.

Writing Test

The Writing Test consists of one essay designed to measure your writing skills. The prompt defines an issue and presents three perspectives on that issue, and you must write an essay that offers your analysis of the three perspectives while generating your own. The Writing Test is given four subscores (ranging from 1–6) by two graders, and their total scores are factored into the 1–36 scale. The score from the Writing Test is not included in the ACT composite score, but it will be part of your ELA subscore (an average of your English, Reading, and Writing scores).

The Writing Test is optional. Not all schools require it, but most do. If you're looking for a high composite score, the schools you're applying to almost certainly require the Writing Test. Take it.

Answer Choices

Odd-numbered questions come with answers that are A/B/C/D (A–E on Math), and even-numbered questions come with answers that are F/G/H/J (F–K on Math). ACT designed the letter choices to alternate to help students avoid making mistakes while bubbling in their answers.

THE ACT SCHEDULE

In the United States, Canada, and U.S. Territories, the ACT is offered six times a year: September, October, December, February, April, and June. The February test is not offered in international locations or in New York. Some states offer an ACT as part of their state-mandated testing. For students who live in those states, the state-mandated test offers an additional testing opportunity, and you can use the score from the state test for college admissions.

Your Schedule

Take the ACT when your schedule best allows. Many high-scorers take their first ACT in the fall of their junior year. If you have more commitments in the fall from sports, plays, or clubs, then plan to take your first ACT in the winter or spring.

Many counselors advise waiting to take the ACT until spring because students may be unfamiliar with some advanced math concepts before then. Students in an honors track for math, however, will have covered all of the content by the end of sophomore year at the latest. Even if you aren't in honors-track math, there are likely only 3–4 questions that will be unfamiliar to you, and those questions won't pull your score down if you bank all the others. We recommend taking your first ACT as early as your schedule allows.

REGISTERING FOR THE ACT

Go to **ACTstudent.org** and create your free ACT Web Account. You will start at this portal to view test dates, fees, and registration deadlines. You can research the requirements and processes to apply for extended time or other accommodations. You will also start at **ACTstudent.org** to access your account to register, view your scores, and order score reports.

You must register yourself for any national test date. For state-mandated ACT administrations, most schools register their students for that exam only.

The fastest way to register is online, through your ACT Web Account. You can also obtain a registration packet at your high-school guidance office, online at **ACTstudent.org/forms/stud_req**, or by writing or calling ACT at the address and phone number below.

ACT Student Services
2727 Scott Blvd
P.O. Box 414
Iowa City, IA 52243-0414
319.337.1270

Bookmark **ACTstudent.org**. Check the site for the latest information about fees. The ACT Plus Writing costs more than the ACT (No Writing), but ACT also offers a fee waiver service. While you can choose four schools to send a score report to at no charge, there are fees for score reports sent to additional schools.

Registration Tips

You have options about ACT's survey, score reports, copies of your test, and cancelation. We have recommendations on each.

ACT Survey

The registration process includes ACT's survey on your grades and interests, but you are not required to answer these questions. To save time, you can provide only the required information, which is marked by an asterisk.

Score Reports

When you register, do not supply the codes for any schools on your application list. Wait until you are happy with your score and no longer plan to take the ACT before you choose the scores to send to your schools. Any extra fees are worth this flexibility.

Test Information Release

If you take your first—or second—ACT on a date that offers the Test Information Release, choose this option when you register. Six to eight weeks after the test, you'll receive a copy of the test and your answers. This service costs an additional fee and is available only on certain test dates. You can order the Test Information Release up to three months after the test date, but it's easier to order it at the time you register. It's a great tool to help you prepare for your next ACT, as you'll be able to review all of your answers, right and wrong.

Through the 2014–2015 school year, the Test Information Release program has been offered for the December, April, and June tests. ACT may offer this program for different test dates in the future. Check **ACTstudent.org** when you register.

How Many Times Should You Take the ACT?

We would be thrilled if you review the content in this book, take the ACT for the first time, and earn the 34 or better you seek. But if you don't hit your target score in your first ACT, take it again. In fact, we recommend that you enter the process planning to take the ACT two or three times. Nerves and anxiety can be unpredictable catalysts, and for many students, the first experience can seem harder than what you've seen in practice. Perception is reality, so we won't waste your time explaining that it only *seems* harder and different. That's why we recommend taking your first ACT as soon as your schedule allows. Get that first experience with a real test over with as soon as possible, and leave yourself enough time to take the test again. Subsequent administrations won't seem nearly as hard and daunting as the first.

If you have scored 34+ in practice but not on a real test after your third try, take it again. We don't recommend going into the process planning to take the test every time it's offered, but we do support a goal of trying to achieve on a real test what you've done in practice. By April of your senior year, you won't care how many times you took the ACT.

But before you take the test again, evaluate what has suppressed your composite. If your composite has stayed flat because some scores have improved while others have fallen, then take more full-length ACT practice tests in one sitting. Take the practice tests in an environment as similar to a proctored test as possible. Take it outside of your house, such as in a library or empty classroom (but not a noisy coffeeshop). Time yourself, including the break, exactly as a real proctor would.

If one or two scores are stuck and are bringing your composite down, consider what you will do differently before taking the test again. Dedicate yourself to trying new strategies that you first thought you didn't need.

Maximum ACT Administrations
For security reasons, ACT will not let you take the exam more than twelve times. But we certainly hope no one is dismayed by this restriction. There are certainly better things to do with your time on a Saturday morning, and we don't believe any college will consider "taking the ACT" an extracurricular activity.

Score Choice, Super Composite, and Deletion

Our goal for you is to have one ACT official score report with a 34 or better, but that is not the only way to apply. Know your options about score choice, the super composite, and deletion of a score.

Score Choice and the Super Composite

We recommended above that you do not send your scores until you have taken your last ACT and are ready to apply. Choose your best composite score to send to your schools. ACT will send only the score reports you choose, and they do not provide a "Super Composite," an average comprised of your best performance on each test from multiple administrations. However, many schools—and the common application—do super score. The common app asks you to report your best score, and test date, for each individual test and then has you calculate your super composite. Submit all of your score reports that support the super composite.

If you have a super composite of 34 or better from two or three tests, we recommend sending all the score reports, even to schools that do not explicitly ask for a super composite. In the worst-case scenario, the school will take only your top score. If you have one score report with a composite better than all your rest, and super scoring will not yield a higher score, we recommend sending only your highest score.

Deletion and Full Disclosure

Some schools require you to submit every ACT score regardless of super scoring. We trust that if these schools ask for every score report, they are looking for *improvement* and will use only your best scores.

You do have an option to delete scores from a particular test date. You must request in writing that ACT delete the test date from your records.

> ACT Institutional Services
> P.O. Box 168
> Iowa City, IA 52243-0168
> USA

Do Your Research
Use *The Princeton Review's Best 380 Schools* to find out which schools require a release of all scores.

We recommend this option only if you take a test and score well below your scores *and* you know you're applying to schools that require that you release all scores. For all other schools, you can send only the score reports you want them to see.

HOW TO PREPARE FOR THE ACT

The following lessons cover the content and strategies for the English, Math, Reading, Science, and Writing Tests. Review all lessons, even in the subjects that you already believe are your strengths. We want to make sure you're thoroughly prepared, and we'll risk boring you a tad to cover content you may know. But we won't waste your time. All of the content and strategies we cover are necessary.

As we noted above, the easiest path to your best score is to maximize your strengths. Find every point that you can from your strengths even as you acquire new skills and strategies to improve your weaknesses.

Some lessons include skill-reinforcement drills, and every section is followed by a full-length practice test in that subject. Take the practice test after you've completed all the lessons.

Practice, Practice, Practice

To achieve a perfect or near-perfect ACT score, you have to practice as much as possible. For additional materials, we recommend you practice with real ACT tests as much as possible and use Princeton Review practice tests to supplement.

ACT publishes *The Real ACT Prep Guide*, which we think is well worth the price for the five real tests it contains (make sure you buy the 3rd edition). There are also up to four additional tests that ACT makes available for purchase, even if some are offered only to schools. Check to see if your school offers these extra tests for practice. In addition, in the registration bulletin and at **ACT.org/aap/pdf/Preparing-for-the-ACT.pdf**, ACT publishes a free practice ACT.

For more practice materials, The Princeton Review publishes *1,460 Practice ACT Questions*, which includes six tests' worth of material. We also publish additional practice tests in *Cracking the ACT, Math and Science Workout for the ACT,* and *English and Math Workout for the ACT.* We also recommend contacting your local Princeton Review office to investigate free practice test dates and follow up sessions. Visit **PrincetonReview.com** for more information.

TEST TAKER, KNOW THYSELF

To earn a perfect or near-perfect score on the ACT, it's not enough to know everything about the test. You also need to know yourself. Identify your own strengths and weaknesses. Stop trying to make yourself something you're not. You do not need to be a master of English, Math, Reading, or Science to earn a top score on the ACT. You do need to be a master test taker. Stop the part of your brain that wants to do the question the *right* way. All that matters is that you get it right. *How* you get the question right doesn't matter. So, don't waste time trying to make yourself into the math or reading genius you thought you needed to be.

Read more in the next chapter about the overall strategies, and read through all the lessons in individual subjects that follow. Be willing to tweak what you already do well, and be willing to try entirely new approaches for what you don't do well.

Summary

- o The ACT is always given in the same order: English, Math, Reading, Science, Writing.

- o Sign up for the ACT Plus Writing Test.

- o Take your first ACT as soon as your schedule allows.

- o Order the Test Information Release if it's available for your test date.

- o Plan to take the ACT 2–3 times.

- o Take the ACT again if you do not achieve the best score you've hit in practice.

- o Know your options about score choice, super composite, and deleting a score.

- o Practice on real ACTs as much as possible.

- o Use Princeton Review practice materials to supplement your practice.

Chapter 2
Strategy

To earn a perfect or near-perfect ACT score, you need strategies specific to the ACT. In this chapter, we'll provide an overview of the universal strategies. Each test on the ACT demands a specific approach, and even the most universal strategies vary in their applications. In Parts II through VI, we'll discuss these strategies in greater detail customized to English, Math, Reading, Science, and Writing.

THE BASIC APPROACH

The ACT is significantly different from the tests you take in school, and, therefore, you need to approach it differently. The Princeton Review's strategies are not arbitrary. They have been honed to perfection, based specifically on the ACT.

Enemy #1: Time

Consider the structure of the ACT as we outlined in Chapter 1. The Math Test consists of 60 questions to answer in 60 minutes. That's just one minute per question, and that's as good as it gets. The English, Reading, and Science Tests all leave you with less than a minute per question. How often do you take a test in school with a minute or less per question? If you do at all, it's maybe on a multiple-choice quiz but probably not on a major exam or final. Time is your enemy on the ACT, and you have to use it wisely and be aware of how that time pressure can bring out your worst instincts as a test taker.

Enemy #2: Yourself

There is something particularly evil about tests like the ACT and SAT. The skills you've been rewarded for throughout your academic year can easily work against you on the ACT. You've been taught since birth to follow directions, go in order, and finish everything. But treating the ACT the same way you would a school test won't necessarily earn you a perfect or near-perfect score.

On the other hand, treating the ACT as a scary, alien beast can leave our brains blank and useless and can incite irrational, self-defeating behavior. When we pick up a #2 pencil, all of us tend to leave our common sense at the door. Test nerves and anxieties can make you misread a question, commit a careless error, see something that isn't there, blind you to what is there, talk you into a bad answer, and worst of all, convince you to waste time on a question that you should approach strategically.

Work Smarter, Not Harder

When you're already answering *almost* every question right, it can be difficult to change your approach. But to answer *every* question right, you have to do something different. You can't just work harder. Instead, you have to work smarter. Know what isn't working. Be open-minded about changing your approach. Know what to tweak and what to replace wholesale. Know when to abandon one approach and try another.

The following is an introduction to the general strategies to use on the ACT. In Parts II through VI, we'll discuss how these strategies are customized for each test on the ACT.

ACT STRATEGIES

Personal Order of Difficulty (POOD)

If time may run out before you finish a section, would you rather it run out on the hardest questions or the easiest? Of course, you want it to run out on the ones you are less likely to get right.

You can easily fall into the trap of spending too much time on the hardest problems and either never getting to or rushing through the easiest. You shouldn't work in the order ACT provides *just because* it's in that order. Instead, find your own Personal Order of Difficulty (POOD).

Make smart decisions quickly for good reasons as you move through each test.

Now

Does a question look fairly straightforward? Do you know how to do it? Do it *Now*.

Later

Will this question take a long time to work? Leave it and come back to it *Later*. Circle the question number for easy reference to return.

Never

If you're trying for a perfect or near-perfect score, there may be no questions that fall into the *Never* category for you. But even one random guess may not hurt your score, particularly if it saves you time to spend on Now and Later questions you can definitely answer correctly.

The Best Way to Bubble In

Work a page at a time, circling your answers right on the booklet. Transfer one page's worth of answers to the bubble sheet at one time. It's better to stay focused on working questions rather than disrupt your concentration to find where you left off on the bubble sheet. You'll be more accurate at both tasks. Do not wait to the end, however, to transfer all the answers of that test on your bubble sheet. Go a page at a time on English and Math, and a passage at a time on Reading and Science.

Pacing

The ACT may be designed for you to run out of time, but you can't rush through it as fast as possible. All you'll do is make careless errors on easy questions that you should get right and spend way too much time on difficult ones that you're unlikely to answer correctly. Let your Personal Order of Difficulty (POOD) help determine your pacing. Go slowly enough to answer all the Now questions correctly, but quickly enough to get to the number of Later questions that you need to reach your goal score.

In Chapter 3, we'll teach you how to identify the number of questions you need to reach your goal score. You'll practice your pacing in practice tests, going slowly enough to avoid careless errors and quickly enough to reach your goal scores.

Process of Elimination (POE)

Multiple-choice tests offer one great advantage: They provide the correct answer right there on the page. Of course, the correct answer is hidden amid three or four incorrect answers. However, it's often easier to spot the wrong answers than it is to identify the right ones, particularly when you apply a smart Process of Elimination (POE).

POE works differently on each test on the ACT, but it's a powerful strategy on all of them. For some question types, you'll always use POE rather than waste time trying to figure out the answer on your own. For other questions, you'll use POE when you're stuck. ACT hides the correct answer among wrong ones, but when you cross off just one or two wrong answers, the correct answer can become more obvious, sometimes jumping right off the page.

POOD, Pacing, and POE all work together to help you nail as many questions as possible.

BE RUTHLESS

The worst mistake a test taker can make is to throw good time after bad. You read a question, don't understand it, so read it again. And again. If you stare at it really hard, you know you're going to just *see* it. And you can't move on, because really, after spending all that time it would be a waste not to keep at it, right?

Wrong. You can't let one tough question drag you down, and you can't let your worst instincts tempt you into self-defeating behavior. Instead, the surest way to earn a perfect or near-perfect ACT score is to follow our advice.

- Use the techniques and strategies in the lessons to work efficiently and accurately through all your Now and Later questions.
- Know when to move on. Use POE, and guess from what's left.
- If you have any Never questions, use your LOTD.

In Parts II through VI, you'll learn how POOD, Now/Later/Never, and POE work on each test. In Chapter 3, we'll discuss in greater detail how to use your Pacing to hit your target scores.

Summary

o Don't let your own worst instincts work against you on the ACT. Work Smarter, Not Harder.

o Identify your own Personal Order of Difficulty (POOD). Let time run out on the most difficult questions.

o Pace yourself. Don't rush through Now and Later questions only to make careless errors.

o Use Process of Elimination (POE) to save time, when you're stuck, or out of time.

o If time does run out, never leave any blanks on your bubble sheet. Use your Letter of the Day (LOTD).

o Be Ruthless. If one strategy isn't working, switch immediately to another.

Chapter 3
Score Goals

To hit a perfect or near-perfect score, you have to know how many raw points you need. Your goals and pacing for English, Math, Reading, and Science will vary depending on the test and your own individual strengths.

SCORE GRIDS

On each test of the ACT, the number of correct answers is converted to a scaled score of 1–36. ACT works hard to adjust the scale of each test at each administration as necessary to make all scaled scores comparable, smoothing out any differences in level of difficulty across test dates. Thus, there is no truth to any one test date being "easier" than the others, but you can expect to see slight variations in the scale from test to test.

This is the score grid from the free test ACT makes available on its website, act.org. We're going to use it to explain how to pick a target score and pace yourself.

Scale Score	English (Raw Score)	Math (Raw Score)	Reading (Raw Score)	Science (Raw Score)	Scale Score
36	75	59–60	40	40	36
35	73–74	57–58	39	39	35
34	71–72	55–56	38	38	34
33	70	54	—	37	33
32	69	53	37	—	32
31	68	52	36	36	31
30	67	50–51	35	35	30
29	66	49	34	34	29
28	64–65	47–48	33	33	28
27	62–63	45–46	32	31–32	27
26	60–61	43–44	31	30	26
25	58–59	41–42	30	28–29	25
24	56–57	38–40	29	26–27	24
23	53–55	36–37	27–28	24–25	23
22	51–52	34–35	26	23	22
21	48–50	33	25	21–22	21
20	45–47	31–32	23–24	19–20	20
19	42–44	29–30	22	17–18	19
18	40–41	27–28	20–21	16	18
17	38–39	24–26	19	14–15	17
16	35–37	19–23	18	13	16
15	33–34	15–18	16–17	12	15
14	30–32	12–14	14–15	11	14
13	29	10–11	13	10	13
12	27–28	8–9	11–12	9	12
11	25–26	6–7	9–10	8	11
10	23–24	5	8	7	10

PACING STRATEGIES

Focus on the number of questions that you need to hit your goal scores.

It's All About the Composite

To score a 34 composite, you could score a 34 on each test.

$$
\begin{array}{r}
34 \\
34 \\
34 \\
+\ 34 \\
\hline
136
\end{array}
\qquad\qquad 136 \div 4 = 34
$$

You can see that, to score a 34, you need a total of 136 points, a sum that any combination of the four individual scores could achieve. In fact, you really only need a total of 134 total points, and a score of 33.5 rounds up to a 34.

How can you earn 134 points?

$$
\begin{array}{r}
36 \\
36 \\
32 \\
+\ 30 \\
\hline
134
\end{array}
\qquad
\begin{array}{r}
35 \\
35 \\
35 \\
+\ 29 \\
\hline
134
\end{array}
\qquad
\begin{array}{r}
36 \\
36 \\
36 \\
+\ 26 \\
\hline
134
\end{array}
$$

In all cases, your strengths relieve the pressure on your weaknesses.

Even a perfect score does not require perfection across the board. To earn a 36, you need a total of 142 points.

$$142 \div 4 = 35.5, \text{ and } 35.5 \text{ rounds up to a } 36.$$

$$
\begin{array}{r}
36 \\
36 \\
36 \\
+\ 34 \\
\hline
142
\end{array}
\qquad\qquad
\begin{array}{r}
36 \\
36 \\
35 \\
+\ 35 \\
\hline
142
\end{array}
$$

Don't pressure yourself to be perfect on all four tests. The highest possible score on your strongest subjects leaves you some flexibility on your weakest subjects.

Raw Score

Use the score grid to identify exactly how many questions you need to answer correctly to hit your goal scores.

English

For English, there is no order of difficulty of the passages or their questions. The most important thing is to finish, finding all the Now questions you can throughout the whole test.

Math

Pace yourself on Math to make sure you nail every question you know how to answer. Missing one or two of the very hardest questions won't hurt your score, but making several careless errors on Now and Later questions definitely will.

Reading

When it comes to picking a pacing strategy for Reading, you have to practice extensively to figure out what works best for you.

You could spend more time on three out of the four passages and earn 30 raw points. As long as you leave enough time on the fourth passage to answer 5 questions correctly, you would have a total of 35 raw points and a scaled score of 30. Or you could leave 1–2 tough questions on every passage—using smart POE to increase your chances when you have to guess and move on—and you could still earn 35 raw points and have a scaled score of 30.

Which is better? There is no answer to that. True ACT score improvement will come with a willingness to experiment and analyze what works best for *you*.

Science

In the Science lessons, you'll learn how to identify your Now and Later passages. To earn at least a 30 scaled score, you have to work all seven passages.

Our advice is to be aggressive. Spend the time you need on the easiest passages first, but keep moving to get to your targeted raw score. Use POE heavily to increase your chances of guessing correctly when you do have to guess and move on. Identify Never questions on Now Passages and use your LOTD. Find the Now questions on even the toughest passage.

PACING CHARTS

Improvement comes in stages. Revisit this page as you practice. Record your scores from the practice tests that are placed at the end of each subject's section. Set a goal of 1–2 points improvement in your scaled score for each subsequent practice test until you hit your goals. Identify the raw score (the number of correctly answered questions) needed in order to reach the desired scale score.

Practice Materials
For practice, use real ACT exams in *The Real ACT Prep Guide*, the free exam on ACT's website, and Princeton Review titles such as *1,460 Practice ACT Questions*.

English Pacing

Scale Score	Raw Score	Scale Score	Raw Score	Scale Score	Raw Score
36	75	27	62–63	18	40–41
35	73–74	26	60–61	17	38–39
34	71–72	25	58–59	16	35–37
33	70	24	56–57	15	33–34
32	69	23	53–55	14	30–32
31	68	22	51–52	13	29
30	67	21	48–50	12	27–28
29	66	20	45–47	11	25–26
28	64–65	19	42–44	10	23–24

Remember that in English, your pacing goal is to finish.

Prior Score (if applicable): _35_

Practice Test 1 Goal: _36_

# of Questions Needed: _75_

Practice Test 1 Score: _34_

Next Practice Test Goal: _36_

# of Questions Needed: _75_

Next Practice Test Score: _____

Math Pacing

Scale Score	Raw Score	Scale Score	Raw Score	Scale Score	Raw Score
36	59–60	27	45–46	18	27–28
35	57–58	26	43–44	17	24–26
34	55–56	25	41–42	16	19–23
33	54	24	38–40	15	15–18
32	53	23	36–37	14	12–14
31	52	22	34–35	13	10–11
30	50–51	21	33	12	8–9
29	49	20	31–32	11	6–7
28	47–48	19	29–30	10	5

If your prior score in Math is at least a 33, work all 60 questions. If you are running out of time, use smart POE on the hardest questions.

If your prior score is under 33, add 5 questions to your targeted raw score to identify how many questions to work. This will give you a cushion to get a few wrong—nobody's perfect—and you're likely to pick up at least a few points from your LOTDs. Track your progress on practice tests to pinpoint your target score.

Prior Score (if applicable): _35_

Practice Test 1 Goal: _36_

# of Questions Needed: _59_

Practice Test 1 Score: _____

Next Practice Test Goal: _36_

# of Questions Needed: _59_

Next Practice Test Score: _____

Reading Pacing

Scale Score	Raw Score	Scale Score	Raw Score	Scale Score	Raw Score
36	40	27	32	18	20–21
35	39	26	31	17	19
34	38	25	30	16	18
33	—	24	29	15	16–17
32	37	23	27–28	14	14–15
31	36	22	26	13	13
30	35	21	25	12	11–12
29	34	20	23–24	11	9–10
28	33	19	22	10	8

Experiment with Reading, using different pacing strategies to find the one that is most likely to earn you the most points. Identify first how many questions you need.

Prior Score (if applicable): _35_

Practice Test 1 Goal: _36_

# of Questions Needed: _40_

Practice Test 1 Score: _____

Next Practice Test Goal: _36_

# of Questions Needed: _40_

Next Practice Test Score: _____

Science Pacing

Scale Score	Raw Score	Scale Score	Raw Score	Scale Score	Raw Score
36	40	27	31–32	18	16
35	39	26	30	17	14–15
34	38	25	28–29	16	13
33	37	24	26–27	15	12
32	—	23	24–25	14	11
31	36	22	23	13	10
30	35	21	21–22	12	9
29	34	20	19–20	11	8
28	33	19	17–18	10	7

Be aggressive on Science. Get to every Now question you can on all of the passages.

Prior Score (if applicable): 33

Practice Test 1 Goal: 35

# of Questions Needed: 39

Practice Test 1 Score: 34

Next Practice Test Goal: 35

# of Questions Needed: _____

Next Practice Test Score: _____

Summary

o   The composite score is rounded up from .5.

o   Identify how many raw points you need to hit your target score. A scaled score of 34 needs a total of 134 raw points. A scaled score of 35 needs a total of 138 raw points. A scaled score of 36 needs a total of 142 raw points.

o   Earn the best possible scores that you can in your strongest subjects to relieve pressure on your weaker subjects.

o   Use the score grid in this lesson to track your improvement from practice to practice.

o   Practice on real ACTs as much as possible.

o   Use Princeton Review practice materials to supplement your practice.

Part II
ACT English

Chapter 4
Introduction to the
ACT English Test

To pursue a perfect or near-perfect score on the English Test, you have to apply a basic approach to correctly answer every question that tests an identifiable rule. But you must also be able to crack the trickiest questions. Even for the most difficult questions, you do not need to know every rule of English grammar that you either forgot or never learned. Review the rules that are tested the most frequently and use appropriate strategies on the questions, and you can target a perfect score on the English Test. This chapter will teach you the 5-Step Basic Approach and provide a Grammar Glossary that includes both the few terms you need to know and some additional terms we included just in case you were curious.

WHAT'S ON THE ENGLISH TEST

The English Test tests your editing skills: your ability to fix errors in grammar and punctuation and to improve the organization and style of five different passages. In this chapter, you'll learn the 5-Step Basic Approach to use on the questions.

On the English Test, there are five prose passages on topics ranging from historical essays to personal narratives. Each passage is typically accompanied by 15 questions for a total of 75 questions to answer in 45 minutes. Portions of each passage are underlined, and you must decide whether these are correct as written, or whether one of the other answers would fix or improve the selection. Other questions will ask you to add, cut, and re-order text, while still others will ask you to evaluate the passage as a whole.

HOW TO CRACK THE ENGLISH TEST

The Passages

As always on the ACT, time is your enemy. With only 45 minutes to review five passages and answer 75 questions, you can't read a passage in its entirety and then go back to do the questions. For each passage, work the questions as you make your way through the passage. Read from the beginning until you get to an underlined selection, work that question, and then resume reading until the next underlined portion and the next question.

The Questions

Not all questions are created equal. In fact, ACT divides the questions on the English Test into two categories: Usage and Mechanics and Rhetorical Skills. These designations will mean very little to you when you're taking the test. All questions are worth the same, and you'll crack most of the questions the same way, regardless of what ACT calls them. Many of the rhetorical skills questions, however, are those on organization and style and will come with actual questions. We'll teach you how to crack those in Chapter 6.

For all the questions accompanied only by four answer choices and with no actual question, use our 5-step Basic Approach.

Step 1. Identify the Topic

When you reach an underlined portion, read to the end of the sentence and then look at the answers. The answers are your clues to identify what the question is testing. Read through the following example.

Canadian author Alice Munro, has won
<u>   1   </u>
wide acclaim for her collections of short

stories.

1. A. ~~NO CHANGE~~
   Ⓑ. ~~author, Alice Munro~~
   C. author Alice Munro
   D. author, Alice Munro,

Do any of the words change? No. What is the only thing that changes? Commas. So what must be the topic of the question? Commas.

Always identify the topic of the question first. Pay attention to what changes versus what stays the same in the answers.

Step 2. Use POE

You may have already identified the correct answer for Question 1, but hold that thought. To earn the highest possible English score, you have to use Process of Elimination (POE). If you fix a question in your head and then look for an answer that matches your fix, you will invariably miss something, such as a new comma added or a comma taken away. Instead, once you've identified an error, always begin by eliminating the choices that do not fix it.

For Question 1, the comma is unnecessary and should be deleted. Cross off the choices that leave it, (A) and (D).

~~1. A. NO CHANGE~~
   B. author, Alice Munro
   Ⓒ. author Alice Munro
~~D. author, Alice Munro,~~

Now compare the two that remain, (B) and (C). Do you need the comma after *author*? 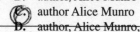 No, you don't need any commas, so (C) is the correct answer. You could easily have missed the new comma and picked (B), however, if you had just been looking for an answer that did not have a comma at the end. POE on English isn't optional or a back-up when you're stuck. Make it your habit to first eliminate wrong answers and then compare the ones that are left.

Let's move on to the next step.

Confused by commas?
Review the rules for commas in the next chapter.

Step 3: Use the Context

Don't skip the non-underlined text in between questions. You need the context to help you choose answers that are both clear and consistent with the rest of the passage. Take a look at this next question.

Munro received the 2009 Man Booker International Prize for her lifetime body of work. In 2013, she <u>will win</u> the Nobel Prize in Literature for her work as "master of the contemporary short story."

2. **F.** NO CHANGE
   G. won
   H. wins
   J. would win

Don't forget to apply the first two steps. First, look at the answer choices to see that the verb is changing, specifically verb tense. How do you know which tense to use? Use the non-underlined verb *received* to identify the need for the past tense. Then you can eliminate the answer choices that don't use past tense, (F) (future tense) and (H) (present tense).

2. ~~F. NO CHANGE~~
   G. won
   ~~H. wins~~
   J. would win

Vexed by verbs?
Review all the rules for verbs, including tenses, in the next chapter.

Next, compare the remaining answers to each other. Choice (J) uses the past tense of the helping verb *will*, but there are no clues in the non-underlined portion that would justify such a shift. Choice (G) is correct because it's consistent with the other past tense verb, *received*.

Don't skip from question to question. The non-underlined text provides context you need.

Let's move on to the next step.

Step 4: Trust, But Verify Your Ear

For the first two questions, you may have identified the correct answers right away because they sounded right. If you had that thought, it turned out you were right, but don't depend exclusively on your ear.

Your ear is a pretty reliable tool for raising the alarm for outright errors and clunky, awkward phrasing. You should, however, always verify what your ear tells you by going through Steps 1 and 2. Always use the answers to identify the topic and use POE heavily.

You also have to be on the lookout for errors your ear *won't* catch. Using the answers to identify the topic will save you there as well.

Let's try another question.

The Swedish Academy was unable to reach Munro before announcing <u>their choice</u> for the 2013 award.

3. A. NO CHANGE
   B. it's choice
   C. they're choice
   D. its choice

Perplexed by pronouns?
Review all the pronoun rules in the next chapter.

Your ear likely found no problem with the sentence as written. Looking at the answers identifies the topic as pronouns, so you need to confirm or correct the pronoun used. *Their* is a plural possessive pronoun, but it replaces the singular *Swedish Academy* and is therefore incorrect. Cross off (A) and (C). Since you need a possessive pronoun, cross off (B) as well. Choice (D) is the correct answer.

Let's move on to the last step.

Step 5: Don't Fix What Isn't Broken
Read the following sentence.

A master of the short form, Munro <u>uses sparse prose to capture the boundless</u> universal truths of the human condition.

4. F. NO CHANGE
   G. writes with few yet well-chosen words
   H. adapts a style
   J. makes a strong impression built on few words

Even if it sounds fine to your ear, go to Step 1 and identify the topic. In this case, the changes do not make the topic obvious because so much changes. You can't confirm what you can't identify, so leave "NO CHANGE" as an option and ask yourself the following questions:

Does one of the answers fix something you missed?

Does one of the answers make the sentence better by making it more concise?

If the answer to both questions is *No* for all three other answers, the answer is NO CHANGE, which is the correct answer here. Choices (G) and (J) express the same sentiment as *uses sparse prose* but (ironically) with many more words. Choice (H) is roughly the same length as (F), but it doesn't identify the specifics of the style.

NO CHANGE is a legitimate answer choice. Don't make the mistake of assuming that all questions have an error that you just can't spot. If you use the five steps of our Basic Approach, you'll catch errors your ear would miss, and you'll confidently choose NO CHANGE when it's the correct answer.

GRAMMAR GLOSSARY

This is not an exhaustive list of grammar terms, but it's also more than we think you need. In fact, the only terms you really need to know are *subject, pronoun, verb, conjunction,* and *preposition.* Some other terms we included because we use them to explain how to spot and fix some of the more difficult questions on the ACT. We included still others just because you may be curious or think you have to know them. For example, you don't need to know what *predicate* or *subjunctive* means, but we included them to provide a comprehensive list of terms.

If you're not curious, you have our blessing to focus only on the big terms.

Active Voice: The construction used when the subject acts and the object receives. *The dog **chases** the car.* The dog is the subject, and the car is the object. See the contrast in *passive voice.*

Adjective: A descriptive word that always modifies a noun or a pronoun. *Pretty, vast, quick, yellow, bad*

Adverb: A descriptive word that always modifies a verb, adjective, or other adverb. *Hopefully, always, quickly, however*

Article: A short word that identifies a noun. *The, a, an*

Case: The function or behavior of a pronoun in a sentence. The three cases are *objective, possessive,* and *subjective* (or *nominative*). See *object pronouns, possessive pronouns,* and *subject pronouns.*

Clause: A group of words with a subject and a verb. See more under *dependent clause* and *independent clause.*

Comma Splice: Two complete ideas linked incorrectly by a comma. *The dog chased the car, I chased the dog.* One fix would be *The dog chased the car, **and** I chased the dog.*

Compound Noun: A noun made up of two elements that acts as a single noun. Depending on the item, the two elements that make up a compound noun might be linked with either a hyphen or space between them, or they can be merged as one word. *Swimming pool, baby-sitter, whiteboard*

Conjunction: A word that joins words, phrases, or clauses together. See more under *coordinate conjunctions* and *subordinate conjunctions.*

Coordinate Conjunction: A word used to link elements of equal importance: adjectives, adverbs, nouns, phrases, or—with the help of a comma—even independent clauses. The acronym FANBOYS can help you remember the seven coordinate conjunctions: *for, and, nor, but, or, yet, so.*

Dependent Clause: An incomplete idea that contains a subject and a verb. The presence of a subordinate conjunction or a relative pronoun acting as a conjunction makes the clause dependent. A dependent clause is also known as a subordinate clause. *Because the dog chased the car, while the car was moving, when the dog chases brooms*

FANBOYS: The seven coordinate conjunctions. *For, and, nor, but, or, yet, so*

Future Perfect: A tense used to describe a future event that will be completed at a definite later time before a second event occurs. *I **will have cleaned** the whole house before the dog destroys the vacuum.* The helping verbs *will* and *to have* work with the past participle of the main verb to form the future perfect.

Future Perfect Progressive: A tense used to describe a future event that will be ongoing when a second event occurs. *By 5 pm, I **will have been cleaning** all day.* The helping verbs *will, to have,* and *to be* (its past participle *been*) work with the present participle to form the future perfect progressive.

Future Progressive: A tense used to describe an ongoing event in the future. *I **will be cleaning** all day tomorrow.* The helping verbs *will* and *to be* (the base form of *be*) work with the present participle to form the future progressive.

Gerund: The *-ing* form of the verb used as a noun. ***Drooling** is a sign of rabies.*

Idiom: An expression whose form and meaning can be determined by neither grammatical rules nor the usual definitions of its elements. The ACT usually tests idioms that involve a preposition. *Different from, in order to, focus on, argue over*

Independent Clause: A complete idea that contains a subject and a verb. *The dog chased the car. The car is moving. The dog chases brooms.*

Infinitive: The base form of the verb with *to* in front. *To bark. To run. To clean.* The presence of an infinitive does not meet the requirement of a verb needed to make a clause. An infinitive is like a car up on blocks, but a main verb in a clause is a car in drive. *The dog learned **to bark.** The dog wants **to run.** I need **to clean** the mess.*

Irregular Verb: A verb with a past participle that doesn't follow the usual pattern that regular verbs do of adding *-ed* at the end. See more under *past participle* and see *regular verb* for contrast. *The dog **ran** down the street. The dog has **run** away before. The dog **ate** the roast beef. The dog has **eaten** our dinner.*

Misplaced Modifier: Any kind of description that is in the wrong place in a sentence and at best creates confusion and at worst describes the wrong item. *I made a sweater for the dog **with pom-poms and sequins**.* The meaning would be clearer with *I made a sweater **with pom-poms and sequins** for the dog.* **Running** *down the street, **a car** almost hit me.* The meaning would be correct with either changing the item that the phrase describes or moving the phrase and changing it into a clause. **Running** *down the street, I was almost hit by a car.* Also correct would be *A car almost hit me when I was running down the street.*

Modifier: A word, phrase, or clause that describes something.

Noun: A person, place, thing, or idea. *Benjamin Franklin, Chicago, mother, dog, car, freedom*

Object: The receiver of the action, or the end of a prepositional phrase. *The dog chased **the car**. She gave **the dog** to me.*

Object Pronoun: A pronoun that replaces a noun as the object in a sentence. *Me, you, him, her, whom, us, them*

Passive Voice: The construction used when the subject receives the action and the object, if present, performs the action. *The car **is chased** by the dog.* The car is the subject, and the dog is the object. In passive voice, the helping verb *to be* works with the participle of the main verb, and the preposition *by* is used when the performer of the action is included as the object. See the contrast in *active voice.*

Past Participle: Past participles work with the helping verb *to have* to form the perfect tenses. *The dog **has chewed** the upholstery. The dog has **broken** the heirloom vase.* For regular verbs, the past participle is the *-ed* form of the verb and is indistinguishable in form from the simple past. *The dog **chewed** the upholstery.* For irregular verbs, the form of both the past participle and the simple past follows no predictable pattern, and they are usually different forms. *The dog **broke** my heirloom vase.* See more at *irregular verb.* Past participles can also function as adjectives. *The **chewed** upholstery can be replaced, but the **broken** heirloom vase can't.*

Past Perfect: A tense used to make clear the chronology of two events completed at a definite time in the past, one before the other. *I **had just calmed** the dog when the doorbell startled him.* The helping verb *to have* works with the past participle of the main verb to form the past perfect.

Past Perfect Progressive: A tense used to make clear the chronology of two events in the past, one of which is ongoing. *I **had been cleaning** for several hours and was ready to relax.* The helping verbs *to have* (in the past tense) and *to be* (its past participle *been*) work with the present participle of the main verb to form the past perfect progressive.

Past Progressive: A tense used to describe an ongoing action in the past tense. *The dog was snoring.* The helping verb *to be* works with the present participle of the main verb to form the past progressive.

Phrase: A group of words without a subject and a verb. *In most homes, snoring like a sailor*

Possessive Pronoun: A pronoun that indicates possession. *My, mine, your, yours, her, hers, his, its, whose, our, ours, their, theirs*

Predicate: The part of the sentence that provides information about the subject. The simple predicate is the verb. *The dog **is chewing** all of my shoes.* The complete predicate includes all the words that say something about the subject. In other words, everything but the subject. *The dog **is chewing all of my shoes.***

Preposition: A little word that describes relationships of time or place between words. *About, at, behind, between, by, in, of, off, on, to, with*

Prepositional Phrase: A group of words that begins with a preposition and ends with an object, almost always a noun or pronoun. *By the car, on the table, between you and me*

Present Participle: The *-ing* form of the verb, used with the helping verb *to be* to form the progressive tenses. *The dog **is drooling** on my leg.* Present participles can also function as adjectives. *I love a **drooling** dog.*

Present Perfect: A tense used to describe an event that began in the past and continues into the present, or to describe an event that was completed at some indefinite time before the present. *The dog **has lived** with me for 10 years. The dog **has attended** obedience school.* The helping verb *to have* works with the past participle of the main verb to form the present perfect.

Present Perfect Progressive: A tense used to describe an ongoing event that began in the past and continues into the present, or to describe an ongoing event that was completed at some indefinite, recent time before the present. *I **have been trying** to train the dog for 10 years. The dog **has been behaving**.* The helping verbs *to have* and *to be* (its past participle *been*) work with the present participle of the main verb to form the present perfect progressive.

Present Progressive: A tense used to describe an ongoing event. *The dog **is attending** obedience school.* The helping verb *to be* works with the present participle of the main verb to form the present progressive.

Pronoun: A word that takes the place of a noun in a sentence. *She, me, it, those, ours, who, that*

Regular Verb: A verb that uses *-ed* at the end to form its past participle. *The dog **listened** to my commands. I have **trained** the dog.* See more at *past participle* and see *irregular verb* for contrast.

Run-on Sentence: Two complete ideas linked incorrectly with no punctuation. *The dog chased the car I chased the dog.* One possible fix would be *The dog chased the car,* **and** *I chased the dog.*

Sentence Fragment: An incomplete idea left incorrectly on its own as a full sentence. *Because everyone recommends that dogs should be trained right away.* One possible fix would be *Because everyone recommends that dogs should be trained right away, I sent her to puppy class.*

Subject: The performer of the action in a sentence that is in active voice. *The* **dog** *chases the car.* **She** *gave the dog to me.* The receiver of the action in a sentence that's in passive voice. *The* **car** *was stolen. The* **car** *is chased by the dog.*

Subject pronoun: A pronoun that replaces a noun as the subject in a sentence. *I, you, she, he, who, we, they*

Subjunctive Mood: A type of sentence used to express wishes, recommendations, and counterfactuals. *I wish I* **were** *an Oscar Mayer Wiener. I recommend he* **study** *the basics. If I* **were** *a rich man, I would give all my money away.* In contrast, most sentences are in the indicative mood. *The dog* **was** *hungry. I* **run** *marathons.* The imperative mood is used for commands. **Eat** *your vegetables!* **Sit!**

Verb: A word that expresses an action, a feeling, or state of being. *Attend, be, calm, came, chase, chew, clean, drool, give, have, live, ring, run, snore, steal, train*

Verbal: A word derived from a verb that doesn't function as a verb in a sentence. Infinitives, participles, and gerunds are all verbals. *The dog was a challenge for me* **to train.** *The* **training** *class meets every Wednesday.* **Training** *a dog requires patience. A* **trained** *dog is a good dog.*

Tense: The form of the verb that tells the time of an event (*past, present, future*). *I* **chased** *the dog. I* **chase** *the dog. I* **will chase** *the dog.* These examples can also be referred to as the simple past, simple present, and simple future. The perfect and progressive tenses provide more information about the duration and status of events within each of the three timeframes of past, present, and future.

Summary

- Identify what the question is testing by changes in the answer choices.

- Use POE heavily.

- Don't skip the non-underlined text: Use it for context.

- Trust your ear, but verify by the rules.

- NO CHANGE is a legitimate answer choice.

Chapter 5
The 4 C's

The English Test is not a grammar test. It's also not a test of how well you write. In fact, it tests your editing skills: your ability to fix errors in grammar and punctuation and to improve the organization and style of five different passages.

The topics in this chapter represent the rules tested most frequently. Questions on these topics should be in your "correct" column every time. The changes in the answer choices make the topics tested easy to identify, and simple rules to master make the errors easy to fix. While your ear may get most of these most of the time, learning *why* will help you get all of them correct every time.

THE 4 C'S: COMPLETE, CONSISTENT, CLEAR, AND CONCISE

You'll never be asked to identify a particular rule by name on the ACT. While we'll use some specific grammar terms to explain the most common rules, we advocate adopting a common sense approach to English: Use the 4 C's.

Good writing should be in *complete* sentences; everything should be *consistent*; the meaning should be *clear*. The best answer, free of any errors, will be the most *concise*. All of the rules we'll review fall under one or more of the C's. But even when you can't identify what a question is testing, apply the 4 C's and you'll still get the most difficult questions right.

While the idea of English grammar makes many of us think of persnickety rules that are long since outdated, English is actually a dynamic, adaptive language. We add new vocabulary all the time, and we let common usage influence and change many rules. Pick up a handful of style books and you'll find very few rules that everyone agrees upon. This is actually good news for studying for the ACT: You're unlikely to see questions testing the most obscure or most disputed rules.

This is not an exhaustive review of English grammar. It is an overview of the most common rules tested on the English Test. We focus on the rules we know show up the most AND that we know you can easily identify. The end of Chapter 4 includes a Grammar Glossary that defines the common grammar terms that we use in this chapter. If you're unsure of any terms, consult the glossary in Chapter 4.

QUIZ I: COMPLETE

Work the brief passage and then read the rules that follow, even if you answer all of the questions correctly. You may have a nuanced ear that can identify the right answer, or you may have internalized these rules and know how to use them correctly without being able to articulate *why* your choices are correct. However, in the pursuit of a perfect or near-perfect score on the English Test, the more you know *why*, the more you can count on answering questions correctly every single time.

The Homer Laughlin China Company of Newell, West
Virginia, introduced affordable, brightly colored dinnerware
called Fiesta in 1936, and continues to manufacture the ceramic
dishes today. Serious collectors and casual fans alike are

drawn to the simple shapes and colorful glazes, because it
is sold as open stock, Fiesta allows buyers to assemble their
collections by the piece instead of by sets. The ceramic dishes
are also prized for their range of colors. Some of the original
glazes were made with detectable amounts of uranium oxide,

which created the brilliant color effects, until the government,
redirected all commercial uses of uranium toward development
of the atom bomb during World War II. The dishes began to
decline in popularity after World War II, dropping out of favor
entirely by the late 1960s. In 1973, the company discontinued
the line. Almost immediately, collectors began buying pieces at
garage sales and in secondhand shops. When Homer Laughlin
China Company noticed the surge in interest for vintage Fiesta
pieces. The company relaunched the line with new glazes in
1986, the company's 50th anniversary. The range

of colors available today includes: Scarlet, Peacock, Tangerine,
Sunflower, and Lemongrass.

1. A. NO CHANGE
   B. called Fiesta, in 1936, and continues to manufacture the
      ceramic dishes today.
   C. called Fiesta in 1936 and continues to manufacture the
      ceramic dishes today.
   D. called Fiesta, in 1936 and continues to manufacture the
      ceramic dishes today.

2. F. NO CHANGE
   G. colorful glazes, because it is sold as open stock Fiesta
   H. colorful glazes. Because it is sold as open stock Fiesta
   J. colorful glazes. Because it is sold as open stock, Fiesta

3. A. NO CHANGE
   B. brilliant color effects until the government,
   C. brilliant color effects until the government
   D. brilliant color effects, until the government

4. F. NO CHANGE
   G. pieces, the company relaunched
   H. pieces; the company relaunched
   J. pieces the company relaunched

5. A. NO CHANGE
   B. includes Scarlet, Peacock, Tangerine, Sunflower, and
      Lemongrass.
   C. includes Scarlet, Peacock, Tangerine, Sunflower and
      Lemongrass.
   D. includes: Scarlet, Peacock, Tangerine, Sunflower and
      Lemongrass.

Some vintage pieces are radioactive because of the glaze, other
original colors command hefty prices on online auction sites.
Collectors will even pay top dollar for some of the modern

colors if the colors have been retired: Lilac pieces sell for

hundreds of dollars. Dismissing all Fiesta as too expensive, but
Homer Laughlin China has stayed true to its roots with brand-
new sets for sale in department stores for modest prices.

6. **F.** NO CHANGE
   G. Some pieces
   H. Because vintage pieces
   J. Although some vintage pieces

7. Which of the following alternatives to the underlined portion would NOT be acceptable?

   A. retired, Lilac pieces
   B. retired; Lilac pieces
   C. retired. Lilac pieces
   D. retired—Lilac pieces

8. **F.** NO CHANGE
   G. While many people think that all Fiesta is too expensive,
   H. Many people think that all Fiesta is too expensive,
   J. Having dismissed all Fiesta as too expensive,

The answers are 1. (C), 2. (J), 3. (D), 4. (G), 5. (B), 6. (J), 7. (A), and 8. (H). Now read all about Complete and Incomplete Ideas to learn why, and learn how to crack questions on sentence structure and punctuation.

COMPLETE

Many questions on the English Test involve sentence structure and punctuation. The correct structure and punctuation all depend on whether the ideas are complete or incomplete.

A complete idea can stand on its own, whether it's the entire sentence or just one part. In grammatical terms, it's an independent clause, consisting of a subject and a verb.

Complete ideas can be statements (*I finished my paper*), commands (*Leave me alone!*), or questions (*Why are you bothering me?*). Each example contains a subject and a verb. In the first example, the subject is *I* and the verb is *finished*. In the second example, the understood subject is *you*, and the verb is *leave* (I'm telling *you* to leave me alone), and in the third, the subject is *you* and the verb is *are bothering*.

Incomplete ideas can't stand on their own. They're missing something, either the subject and verb, the main idea, or the rest of the idea. In grammatical terms, they can be phrases (*in the evening, to get a good grade*), dependent clauses (*although I finished the paper, when I study*), or a subject with a verb that needs an object (*I broke*). But you don't need to get into the grammar weeds with terms like *dependent clause* if you're not already well-versed in those terms. An incomplete idea is missing something. It's unfinished. It's . . . incomplete.

On the ACT, questions on both sentence structure and punctuation depend on identifying complete and incomplete ideas.

STOP!

Complete ideas have to be separated with the correct punctuation. If complete ideas are two major roads meeting at an intersection, then they need a red light or stop sign in between to prevent an accident. Stop punctuation can be used *only* in between complete ideas.

> STOP Punctuation
> Period (.) Semicolon (;) Question mark (?) Exclamation point (!)

For the record, semicolons can be used to separate items on a very complicated list, but ACT almost never tests this. Exclamation points and question marks show up only occasionally.

Here's How to Crack #2

Choices (H) and (J) use a period after *glazes*, identifying the topic as STOP punctuation. Draw the vertical line to the right of *glazes*.

> *Serious collectors and casual fans alike are drawn to the simple shapes and colorful glazes,* | *because it is sold as open stock, Fiesta allows buyers to assemble their collections by the piece instead of by sets.*

Read from the beginning of the sentence to the vertical line. The idea is complete. Read from the vertical line to the end of the sentence. The idea is complete. Eliminate (F) and (G) because two complete ideas must be linked with STOP punctuation. Compare the two choices that are left. Choice (J) is correct because it provides the comma (H) lacks. Why is the comma needed? Read on.

GO!

If complete ideas are major roads that need red lights and stop signs at the intersection of the ideas, incomplete ideas are minor roads that *don't* need a red light or stop sign. Incomplete ideas need green lights, maybe a blinking yellow, or best of all, no traffic signals or signs at all.

> ### GO Punctuation
> No punctuation (nothing, nada, zilch) or Comma (,)

Let's go back to the traffic analogy. Imagine a road with a stop sign at every block. Those stop signs prevent accidents, but when rush hour hits, traffic backs up. Punctuation functions the same way. Use it to prevent accidents, but don't slow down ideas and make the sentence longer than necessary.

Here's How to Crack #1

There is no STOP punctuation in any of the answers to help divide the ideas. The complete idea *The Homer Laughlin China Company of Newell, West Virginia, introduced affordable, brightly colored dinnerware called Fiesta in 1936* links with the incomplete idea *and continues to manufacture the ceramic dishes today.* (Notice the incomplete idea is missing a subject). There is no need to slow down, so use NO punctuation at all until the end of the sentence. Therefore, (C) is the correct answer.

Use the 4 C's: Be *Concise*. Use punctuation only to avoid accidents.

Here's How to Crack #4

Choices (F) and (H) use STOP punctuation, so draw the vertical line right after *pieces.* The vertical line will always help identify intersections and make POE much faster.

> *When Homer Laughlin China Company noticed the surge in interest for vintage Fiesta pieces. | The company relaunched the line with new glazes in 1986, the company's 50th anniversary.*

From the beginning of the sentence to the vertical line, the idea is incomplete. From the vertical line to the end of the sentence, the idea is complete. Eliminate (F) and (H) since STOP punctuation can be used only between two complete ideas. Compare (G) and (J). The incomplete idea introduces the complete idea, so a comma is needed. Therefore, (G) is the correct answer. The same construction of *incomplete, complete* in Question 2 also requires a comma. Use a comma only when necessary, and it's necessary when an incomplete idea introduces a complete idea.

Commas

Commas work like blinking yellow lights: They slow down but do not stop ideas. Since the goal is to be concise, use a comma only for a specific reason. On the ACT, there are only four reasons to use a comma.

STOP

A comma by itself can't come in between two complete ideas, but it can when it's paired with one of the FANBOYS: *for, and, nor, but, or, yet, so.* A comma plus any of these is the equivalent of STOP punctuation. These words also impact direction, which might influence the correct answer.

> *Many people think that all Fiesta is too expensive,* **but** *Homer Laughlin China has stayed true to its roots with brand-new sets for sale in department stores for modest prices.*

FANBOYS

For the record, FANBOYS are called coordinate conjunctions. All conjunctions link things, but FANBOYS specifically come in between two ideas and are never part of either idea.

**Comma versus
No Comma**
When in doubt, choose an
answer with no comma.

GO

A comma can link an incomplete idea to a complete idea, in either order. When the incomplete idea comes first, a comma is always needed. When the complete idea comes first, use a comma only if the incomplete idea is a modifying phrase.

> *Almost immediately, collectors began buying pieces at garage sales and in secondhand shops.*

> *The popularity of the dishes began to decline after World War II, dropping out of favor entirely by the late 1960s.*

Lists

Use a comma to separate items in a list.

> *affordable, brightly colored dinnerware*

Affordable and *brightly colored* both describe *dinnerware*. If you could say *affordable and brightly colored,* then you can say *affordable, brightly colored.* In a list of two items, use either *and* or a comma between the two items.

When you have three or more items in a list, always use a comma before the *and* preceding the final item. This is a rule that not everyone agrees on, but if you apply the 4 C's, the extra comma makes your meaning *Clear.* On the ACT, always use the comma before the *and.*

> *The range of colors available today includes Scarlet, Peacock, Tangerine, Sunflower, and Lemongrass.*

Here's How to Crack #5, Part I

Eliminate (C) and (D) because neither one uses a comma before the *and* at the end of the list.

Unnecessary Info

Use a pair of commas around unnecessary info.

If information is necessary to the sentence in either meaning or structure, don't use the commas. If the meaning would be exactly the same but less interesting, use a pair of commas—or a pair of dashes—around the information.

Here's How to Crack #3

Some of the original glazes were made with detectable amounts of uranium oxide, which created the brilliant color effects, until the government, redirected all commercial uses of uranium toward development of the atom bomb during World War II.

Note the comma in the non-underlined portion of the sentence, just before *which*. The first comma opens the detour to unnecessary info, so use the changes in the answer choices to identify when the detour ends. The entire idea *which produce the brilliant color effects* could be removed without changing the meaning of the sentence. Eliminate (B) and (C), then compare (A) and (D). The extra comma after *the government* in (A) would make *until the government* unnecessary, but it is needed because *the government* is the subject of *redirected* in the non-underlined portion. Choice (D) is correct because commas are used only where they are needed. Too many commas in one sentence is like hitting the gas...then the brakes...then the gas...then the brakes again, which would ruin any drive—or sentence.

Colons and Single Dashes

Colons and single dashes are very specific pieces of punctuation, and they are very flexible. They can link a complete idea to either an incomplete idea or another complete idea. The complete idea must come first, and the second idea will be a definition, explanation, or list. Since colons and single dashes are always used with at least one complete idea, use the Vertical Line Test whenever they appear in the text or in the answer choices.

Here's How to Crack #5, Part II

Draw a vertical line after *includes*.

The range of colors available today includes: | Scarlet, Peacock, Tangerine, Sunflower, and Lemongrass.

The idea from the beginning of the sentence to the vertical line is incomplete, so a colon can't be used. Therefore, (A) and (D) can be eliminated. But recall that (C) and (D) have already been eliminated because both lack a comma before the *and*. Applying POE with the rules for commas and colons leaves only (B), the correct answer.

Here's How to Crack #7

First, note that there is an actual question above the four answer choices, and the question directs you to choose the alternative that is NOT acceptable. For the negative questions (phrased with EXCEPT, LEAST, or NOT), the sentence is always correct as written, and you can use it as a standard of comparison. Because STOP punctuation appears in several answer choices, draw a vertical line after *retired*.

Collectors will even pay top dollar for some of the modern colors if the colors have been retired: | *Lilac pieces sell for hundreds of dollars.*

The idea from the beginning of the sentence to the vertical line is complete, and the idea from the vertical line to the end of the sentence is complete. A colon or a single dash, as in (D), can go in between two complete ideas, as can the STOP punctuation in (B) and (C). A comma by itself is GO punctuation and can never be used between two complete ideas. Thus, (A) is NOT acceptable, and is the correct answer.

Conjunctions

Punctuation isn't the only way to link ideas. In some of the more difficult questions, you have to change ideas by adding or deleting a conjunction.

Here are some of the more common conjunctions you may see.

> although, as, because, if, since, that, until, how, what, which, while, when, where, who, whom

Proper grammarians would object to calling *how, what, which, when, where, who, whom* conjunctions, but the technical terms aren't important. It's not as if ACT makes you name any part of speech, and all that matters is that those words, when they are used in a statement instead of a question, act just like conjunctions by making an idea incomplete. For an example, look at how we used *when* in the last sentence or *how* in this sentence.

Here's How to Crack #6

Look at the answer choices to identify the topic as conjunctions. Check the entire sentence to see whether the ideas in it are correctly joined. *Some vintage pieces are radioactive because of the glaze* is complete, and *other original colors command hefty prices on online auction sites* is also complete. The two complete ideas, however, are incorrectly linked by a comma (GO punctuation). Since you can't fix the non-underlined punctuation, fix the idea by making it incomplete and therefore correct with GO punctuation. A conjunction makes an idea incomplete. Eliminate (F) and (G). Compare (H) and (J). Both add a conjunction, but *although* and *because* indicate different directions (we'll discuss that more in the next section). Since the two ideas in the sentence show a contrast—*some vintage pieces* and *other pieces*— (J) is correct.

Subjects and Verbs

The minimum requirements of a complete idea are a subject and verb. Just as some difficult questions fix the error by adding or deleting a conjunction, so too some questions add or delete a subject and verb to fix.

Here's How to Crack #8

Only (G) uses a conjunction, which is your clue to read the sentence to determine whether all ideas are linked correctly. In the non-underlined portion, *but* immediately follows the underlined comma in each choice. Because *but* is STOP punctuation, the ideas on either side have to be complete. In the non-underlined portion, *Homer Laughlin China has stayed true to its roots with brand-new sets for sale in department stores for modest prices* is complete. In (F), *Dismissing all Fiesta as too expensive* is incomplete because it lacks a subject and a verb. Similarly, *Having dismissed all Fiesta as too expensive,* in (J), also lacks a subject and verb and is therefore incomplete. In (G), *While many people think that all Fiesta is too expensive,* there is a subject and a verb, but the presence of the conjunction *While* makes the idea incomplete. Choice (H) is correct because *Many people think that all Fiesta is too expensive* adds a subject and verb to make the idea complete.

QUIZ II: CONSISTENT, CLEAR, CONCISE

Work the brief passage and then read the rules that follow, even if you answer all of the questions correctly. You may have a nuanced ear that can identify the right answer, or you may have internalized these rules and know how to use them correctly without being able to articulate *why* your choices are correct. However, in the pursuit of a perfect or near-perfect score on the English Test, the more you know *why*, the more you can count on answering questions correctly every single time.

After years of disastrous, cataclysmic experimental attempts at baking sweet things, I decided it was time to learn in a formal setting. I investigated a community college and a grocery store

1. A. NO CHANGE
   B. disastrously experimental attempts at baking pies, cookies, and cakes,
   C. disastrous attempts at baking,
   D. disastrous attempts at baking many different desserts,

and saw that it offered several classes, from the basics to the

2. F. NO CHANGE
   G. the store
   H. this
   J. she

most advanced concepts. Some of the cities best chefs taught

3. A. NO CHANGE
   B. cities'
   C. citys
   D. city's

the classes. Unfortunately, the most established chefs taught classes in the mornings, which didn't fit my schedule. Only one

4. Which of the following alternatives to the underlined portion would be LEAST acceptable?
   F. Moreover,
   G. However,
   H. Sadly,
   J. DELETE the underlined portion and capitalize "the."

of the basic classes were taught in the evening. The instructor

5. A. NO CHANGE
   B. was
   C. are
   D. have been

was a pastry chef whom began her career on a reality cooking competition show.

6. F. NO CHANGE
   G. who began
   H. who begun
   J. who was beginning

The answers are 1. (C), 2. (G), 3. (D), 4. (F), 5. (B), and 6. (G). Now read all about Verbs, Pronouns, Apostrophes, Transitions, and Concise to learn why, and learn how to crack these questions every time on every test.

VERBS

A verb expresses an action, feeling, or state of being. The form of a verb depends on the number of the subject—singular or plural—the time of the event, and the presence of helping verbs. Whenever you spot the verb changing among the answers, use these three steps along with your Basic Approach.

1.   **Identify the subject.** The verb must be consistent with its subject: singular subject with a singular verb, and plural subject with a plural verb.
2.   **Check the tense.** The tense must be consistent with the setting and the participle. Use the context of the non-underlined portion to determine if the verb should be past, present, or future.
3.   **Be concise.** Pick the shortest answer free of any errors.

Subject-Verb Agreement

Verbs have to be consistent with their subjects. Singular subjects take singular forms of the verb, and plural subjects take plural forms of the verb.

Your ear can alert you to many, if not most, subject-verb agreement errors. As a general rule, singular verbs end with *s* and plural verbs do not.

If you struggle to identify the subject flip the statement into a question.

> *The list of famous chefs impresses students.*

> Q: *What impresses students?*

> A: *The list.*

Be particularly careful of prepositional phrases that separate the subject from the verb and can easily fool your ear into identifying the subject incorrectly. In the example above, the subject *list* is singular and is modified by the prepositional phrase *of famous chefs*. Notice that the singular subject *list* uses the singular form of the verb *impresses*, but the plural noun *chefs* in between could easily cause a careless error.

Prepositional Phrases
Prepositions are little words that show a relationship between nouns. Some examples include *at, between, by, on, of, to,* and *with*. A prepositional phrase modifies a noun. Examples include **on the stove, the notebook of recipes, tasting like dust**.

The changes in the answers identify the topic as verbs.

> *Only one of the basic classes were taught in the evening.*

Identify the subject: *one.* The prepositional phrase *of the classes* is there to trick you into thinking that the subject is plural. Eliminate (A), (C), and (D) because they are all plural. Choice (B) is correct because the verb *was* is singular to match the singular subject.

Verb Tense and Irregular Verbs

The tense of the verb marks the time of the event in the past, present, or future. Tenses come in different forms. The simple, progressive, and perfect tenses provide information about the duration, completion, or frequency of the event.

Simple uses the verb by itself, with the helping verb "will" added for the future tense. Simple tenses identify the general timeframe of events, or they are used with specific mentions of time.

> *I **studied** yesterday. I **study** weekends. I **will study** tomorrow.*

Progressive uses a present participle paired with the helping verb "to be." The helping verbs "will" and "to be" are also used for the future progressive. Progressive tenses reflect ongoing events within one timeframe, or events that are "in progress." Specific mentions of time can also be used with the progressive tenses.

> *I **was studying** when you called. I **am studying** today. I **will be studying** at the library tomorrow.*

Perfect uses a past participle paired with the helping verb "to have." The helping verb "will" is also used for the future perfect. Perfect tenses are used to describe events that are ongoing from past to present, were completed at an indefinite time, happened in a specific sequence in the past, or will be completed at a definite later time before a second event occurs. Often the perfect tenses are used with words like "already," "ever," "just," "never," "recently," and "yet."

> *I **had** never **studied** at Starbucks before you suggested it. I **have** already **studied** for the Latin final. I **will not have studied** yet by the time you arrive.*

Perfect progressive uses a present participle paired with the helping verbs "to have" and "to be." The helping verb "will" is also used for the future perfect progressive. Perfect progressive tenses describe the sequence of events when at least one of the events is ongoing.

> *I **had been studying** for days before you rescued me. I **have been studying** all day. I **will have been studying** for a month by the time I take the final.*

All verbs add the suffix *-ing* to form the present participle. Regular verbs add the suffix *-ed* for the simple past and for the past participle. Irregular verbs use idiosyncratic forms, and many use one form for the simple past and a different one for the past participle. Here is a short list of some of the most common irregular verbs.

Infinitive	Simple Past	Past Participle
become	became	become
begin	began	begun
break	broke	broken
come	came	come
drink	drank	drunk
drive	drove	driven
eat	ate	eaten
fall	fell	fallen
forget	forgot	forgotten
get	got	gotten
give	gave	given
go	went	gone
know	knew	known
lead	led	led
ring	rang	rung
run	ran	run
see	saw	seen
speak	spoke	spoken
take	took	taken
teach	taught	taught
write	wrote	written

On the ACT, most questions on tense test the need for past, or present, or future. The difference among tenses within the same timeframe is very nuanced, and it's rare for questions to require choosing the perfect or progressive over the simple.

More commonly, when the perfect and progressive tenses appear, the question usually requires choosing the past, present, or future tense of the helping verb, the correct subject-verb agreement of the helping verb, or the correct participle of the main verb.

The changes in the answer choices indicate verb tense and pronouns as topics. Let's look at the verbs first; we'll discuss the pronouns in the next section. *The instructor was a pastry chef whom began her career on a reality cooking competition show* is in past tense, as are the verbs in the rest of the answer choices. The past tense is consistent with the setting and the non-underlined verbs. The answer choices show different participles. *To begin* is an irregular verb. Without the helping verb *to have*, *begun* on its own is incorrect. Eliminate (H). *Began* is more concise than *was beginning*. Eliminate (J). To decide between *who* and *whom*, move on to pronouns.

PRONOUNS

Pronouns take the place of a noun and make your writing more concise. Whenever you spot pronouns changing among the answers, use these three steps with your Basic Approach.

1. **Find the original.** The pronoun has to be consistent in number and gender with the noun it replaces or with a pronoun already in use.
2. **Check the case.** Choose the correct pronoun based on its specific function in the sentence.
3. **Be clear.** Do not use a pronoun if it could possibly refer to more than one noun of the same number and gender.

Pronoun Agreement

Pronouns have to be consistent with the nouns they replace in number and in gender.

	Female	Male	Things
Singular	she, her, hers	he, him, his	it, its
Plural	they, them, their	they, them, their	they, them, their

Pronoun Case

Pronouns also need to be consistent with the function they perform in a sentence. There are three different cases of pronouns.

	1st person	2nd person	3rd person
Subject	I, we	you	she, he, it, they, who
Object	me, us	you	her, him, it, them, whom
Possessive	my, mine, our, ours	your	her, hers, his, its, their, theirs, whose

Here's How to Crack #6, Part II

The instructor was a pastry chef whom began her career on a reality cooking competition show.

We've already eliminated (H) and (J). The difference between the remaining choices is in the pronouns *who* and *whom*. Follow the steps for pronouns, and identify the original, which in this case is *the pastry chef*. Both choices agree with the original, so next identify the case the pronoun performs in this part of the sentence, the incomplete idea. In the incomplete idea, the pronoun is the subject of the verb *began*. Choice (G) is the correct answer.

Here's How to Crack #2

The changes in the answer choices indicate pronouns as the topic.

I investigated a community college and a grocery store and saw that it offered several classes, from the basics to the most advanced concepts.

It is singular, but it could refer to *community college* or *grocery store*, so eliminate (F). There is no reference to a woman in the sentence, so eliminate (J). *This* in (H) is ambiguous, leaving the meaning just as unclear as the pronoun *it*. Choice (G) is correct because it makes the meaning clear by identifying the grocery store as the host of the cooking classes.

APOSTROPHES

Just as pronouns do, apostrophes make your writing more concise. They have two uses, possession and contraction.

Possession and Contractions

To show possession with singular nouns, add *'s*, and with plural nouns, add just the apostrophe. For tricky plurals that do not end in *s*, add *'s*. For personal pronouns, *never* use an apostrophe: Use the proper pronoun.

A pronoun with an apostrophe is a contraction, which means the apostrophe takes the place of at least one letter. (*It's, you're,* and *you've* are all examples of contractions.)

Whenever you spot apostrophes changing among the answers, use these two steps with your Basic Approach.

1. **Confirm possession.** Look at the *next* word. Only nouns can be possessed. If the next word is a verb, preposition, conjunction, pronoun, or article, eliminate all choices with nouns and apostrophes or possessive pronouns.

2. **Check the number.** Determine if the noun is singular or plural or if the possessive pronoun replaces a singular or plural noun.

Here's How to Crack #3
The changes in the answer choices identify apostrophes as the topic.

Some of the cities best chefs taught the classes.

The *best chefs* follow *cities*, and they belong to the city. The sentence could be rewritten as *the best chefs of the city*, proof that *the chefs* belong to *the city* and that an apostrophe is needed. Eliminate (A) and (C). There is no proof that there is more than one city, so choose the singular *city's* in (D).

TRANSITIONS
If good writing is like a pleasant drive, then transitions are road signs, preventing you from getting lost and helping you make important turns. Good transitions are consistent with the flow of ideas.

Many words can act as transitions. Some are specific to the context, in which only one word will fit the precise meaning. But others are just slight variations telling you to *turn around* or *keep going*. Here's a partial list.

Turn Around
although, but, despite, even though, however, nonetheless, nevertheless, yet

Keep Going
and, because, finally, furthermore, moreover, since, so, thus, therefore

---

Whenever you spot transitions changing among the answers, use these three steps with your Basic Approach.

1. **Be consistent.** Read the sentences on either side of the transition to determine the context to choose a transition with the correct direction.
2. **Be concise.** Use a transition only when necessary.
3. **Be complete.** Read the full sentence to confirm that the ideas are linked correctly.

Good transitions make the meaning clearer, but they are necessary only if they help connect the ideas correctly. FANBOYS, conjunctions, and adverbs can all be used as transitions. Adverbs provide only direction, but as we discussed in the Complete section above, FANBOYS and conjunctions do more than provide direction. A conjunction may be needed to make one of the ideas complete. With a comma, one of the FANBOYS may be needed to link two complete ideas.

Here's How to Crack #4

First, note that there is an actual question above the four answer choices. *Which of the following alternatives to the underlined portion would be LEAST acceptable?* For the negative questions (phrased with EXCEPT, LEAST, or NOT), the sentence as written is always correct and you can use it as a standard of comparison.

> *Unfortunately, the most established chefs taught classes in the mornings, which didn't fit my schedule.*

Unfortunately works as a turn-around transition because the context shifts from something positive (famous chefs teach) to something negative (not on the narrator's schedule). Eliminate (G) and (H) because they are both turn-around transitions and therefore are acceptable. *Unfortunately* and the three other transitions in the answers are all adverbs, and there is no error in the way the ideas are linked. Therefore, the transition isn't necessary and could be deleted. Eliminate (J). *Moreover* is a keep-going transition and would be LEAST acceptable and is therefore the correct answer.

CONCISE

Good writing may be like a pleasant drive, but you're not on a joyride on the ACT. Get to your destination as fast as you can. Be Concise.

Eliminate the most concise choice *only* if it fails to correct an error or creates a new one. However, concise isn't just a strategy. The topic is frequently tested on the ACT. On concise questions, none of the answers are grammatically wrong, but three answers are unnecessarily wordy, featuring either redundant or irrelevant information.

Whenever you spot the use of the same word or phrase used in all answer choices, use these two steps with your Basic Approach.

1. Eliminate answer choices that have unnecessary information.
2. Eliminate answer choices that are redundant.

Here's How to Crack #1
The sentence as written is wordy and redundant.

> *After years of disastrous, cataclysmic experimental attempts at baking sweet things, I decided it was time to learn in a formal setting.*

Eliminate (A) because it is redundant. Eliminate (B) and (C) because they contain unnecessary information.

Now try these strategies on your own. Go online to your Student Tools and answer the Chapter 5 Drills.

Summary

o   Shoot for perfection on questions that test punctuation, verbs, pronouns, apostrophes, transitions, and whether the sentence is concise. These topics are heavily tested, are easily identifiable from changes in the answer choices, and follow relatively few rules in their correct usage.

o   Good writing should be *complete, consistent, clear,* and *concise.*

o   STOP punctuation includes a period, a semicolon, an exclamation mark, and a question mark. STOP punctuation can link only two complete ideas.

o   Whenever you see STOP punctuation in the text or in the answers, use the Vertical Line Test.

o   GO punctuation includes no punctuation and a comma. GO punctuation can link anything except for two complete ideas.

o   Use commas only when necessary.

o   Colons and single dashes must follow a complete idea but can precede a complete or incomplete idea.

o   Conjunctions make an idea incomplete.

o   Verbs have to be consistent in number with their subject and consistent in tense with the context of the sentence.

o   Pronouns have to be consistent in number, gender, and case, and clear in which nouns they replace.

o   Singular nouns take *'s* to show possession. Plural nouns that end in *s* take an apostrophe after the *s* to show possession.

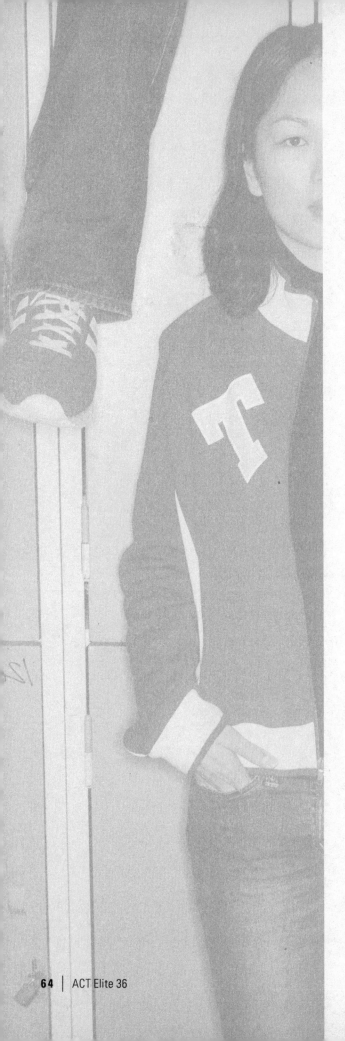

o   Possessive personal pronouns show posses-sion. Pronouns and verbs use apostrophes to form contractions.

o   Transition words provide directions and con-nections between ideas.

o   Be Concise.

Chapter 6
Rhetorical Skills

ACT categorizes the questions on the English Test as either Rhetorical Skills or Usage and Mechanics. For most questions, the basic approach used to crack them is the same, regardless of what ACT labels them. There are certain questions, however, that do require a different approach. In this chapter, we'll cover all the questions that come with an actual question and not just four answer choices. These are questions that many students find difficult and time-consuming, and they may be the main obstacle to getting a perfect or near-perfect score. We'll teach you how to crack questions that ask for wrong answers as well as questions on strategy and order.

Be on the lookout for E/L/N questions: expect as many as 3–4 *per passage*.

EXCEPT/LEAST/NOT

You know a question is tricky when the right answer is wrong. That is, if the question asks you to identify the choice that does NOT work, you have to cross off three answers that work and choose the one that doesn't.

The EXCEPT/LEAST/NOT questions, or E/L/N for short, hide in plain sight and therefore pose a challenge to spot. Because most "questions" on the ACT English Test feature only four answer choices and no actual question, it is easy to miss the presence of a bona fide question. Moreover, many of the topics on E/L/N will look familiar: STOP/GO punctuation and transition questions are two topics heavily tested in this format, so the four answers look pretty much the same as they always do—except that the first choice won't be NO CHANGE. NO CHANGE is almost never an option on E/L/N questions. When it's not, then the sentence is correct as written.

ACT English Test Categories

Not all EXCEPT/LEAST/NOT questions are rhetorical skills questions by ACT standards. An E/L/N question on STOP/GO, for example, would be counted as Usage and Mechanics. But when most of the "questions" are just four answer choices, the presence of a true question demands a different approach. Thus, we're addressing the E/L/N questions in this lesson, regardless of how ACT may categorize them.

It's very easy to get confused with E/L/N questions. Use an organized strategy.

1. Cross out NOT.
2. Use the sentence as written as the standard of comparison to evaluate the answer choices.
3. Write "Y" (for Yes) next to each choice that IS acceptable and "N" (for No) next to the one choice that is NOT acceptable.

The correct answer is the one choice with an "N" next to it.

―――――――――――○―――――――――――

[1]

The golden age of live television in the late 1950s and early 1960s witnessed the rise to prominence of a small band of actors, writers, and directors who worked on revolutionary shows such as *Playhouse 90*.

1. Which of the following alternatives to the underlined portion would be LEAST acceptable?
   A. increase in fame
   B. projection of fame
   C. rise to stardom
   D. rise to fame

Here's How to Crack #1

Cross out LEAST, and compare the answer choices to the sentence as written. The changes in the answer choices identify the topic as vocabulary and idioms, two of the most challenging topics ACT tests, either in regular or E/L/N format. Vocabulary requires selecting the precise word that fits with the context. An idiom is an expression whose form and meaning can be determined neither by grammatical rules nor the usual definition of its elements.

Choices (C) and (D) use the same idiom (*rise to*), and *stardom* and *fame* mean in context the same as *prominence*, so write "Y" next to both of them. Choices (A) and (B) use different idioms, but only the idiom *increase in* means the same as *rise to,* so mark "Y" next to (A) and "N" next to (B). Choice (B) is the correct answer because it is the one choice that is LEAST acceptable.

Look for changes in prepositions among the answer choices to identify idioms.

————————◯————————

While the vocabulary and idioms that appear on the ACT tend to be fairly common words and expressions, they rarely repeat. Thus, there is no way to prepare for the particular ones that will show up on your ACT. You'll either know them or you won't. Use your ear, read for the context, and lean on POE heavily.

Learn more about how to crack questions on vocabulary and idioms in Chapter 7.

STRATEGY QUESTIONS

Strategy questions come in many different forms, but they all revolve around the *purpose* of the text. Among the different types of strategy questions, expect to see questions asking you to add or replace text, determine whether text should be added or deleted, evaluate the impact on the passage if text is deleted, and judge the overall effect of the passage on the reader.

Add or Replace

Strategy questions that ask you to add or replace text always state a purpose for the proposed text. Identify the purpose and pick an answer that best fulfills it.

Let's see some examples.

Established stars and undiscovered talent

alike worked long hours reading scripts.
₂

2. Given that all the choices are true, which one most clearly indicates that the actors worked to improve their skills?
   F. NO CHANGE.
   G. honing their craft.
   H. constructing the set.
   J. skimming the want-ads.

Here's How to Crack #2

Identify the purpose stated in the question, and pick the choice that fulfills that purpose. In this case, the question asks for the choice that indicates that the actors worked to improve their skills. You don't even need to go back into the passage: Find an answer choice that describes improving skills. Choices (F), (H), and (J) say nothing about acting skills. Only (G), the correct answer, does.

[2]

Because of this frantic pace, accidents

happened frequently. David Niven once

revealed that during an early show,

he accidentally locked his costume in his
₃
dressing room two minutes before air time.
₃
As the announcer read the opening credits,

the sound of axes splintering the door to

Niven's dressing room could be heard in the

background. [4]

3. Given that all choices are true, which one provides the most specific and relevant information?
   A. NO CHANGE
   B. a casting agent approached him about auditioning for the role of James Bond.
   C. cast members improvised changes in dialogue.
   D. the producers announced that the program had been renewed.

Here's How to Crack #3

Identify the purpose stated in the question, and pick the choice that fulfills that purpose. In this case, the question asks for the choice that *provides the most specific and relevant information.* Read through to the end of the paragraph and use the context to find an answer that *provides the most specific and relevant information.* The preceding sentence indicates that *accidents happened frequently,* and the succeeding sentence describes *axes splintering the door to the dressing room.* Choice (A) is the best introduction because it provides an example of a specific accident and makes sense of why the door was broken down.

Lose

Another type of strategy question asks you to identify what the passage would *lose* if a particular sentence or phrase were deleted.

Lean heavily on POE for these questions. Look for the choice that best describes the deleted portion.

---

[2]

Because of this frantic pace, accidents happened frequently. David Niven once revealed that during an early show, he accidentally locked his costume in his dressing room two minutes before air time. As the announcer read the opening credits, the sound of axes splintering the door to Niven's dressing room could be heard in the background. 4

4. The writer is considering deleting the preceding sentence. If the writer were to make this deletion, the essay would primarily lose a statement that:
   F. explains the organization of the paragraph.
   G. adds a much needed touch of humor to the essay.
   H. explains how one accident was resolved.
   J. adds nothing since the information is provided elsewhere in the paragraph.

Here's How to Crack #4

Use POE heavily: The correct choice will accurately describe the sentence to be deleted. Choice (F) is incorrect because the sentence does not *explain the organization of the paragraph.* Choice (J) is incorrect because the information is NOT *provided elsewhere in the paragraph.* Choice (G) is possible, but (H) is better. The sentence relates how David Niven's costume was retrieved from behind a locked door. Choice (H) is correct because it provides the most specific description of the sentence.

Yes or No

Some strategy questions provide you with a choice to make. Should the author add something new to the passage? Two answers are *Yes,* and two answers are *No.* A variation can also ask whether some part of the passage be kept or deleted. Two answers are *Kept,* and two answers are *Deleted.*

Even when you have a strong feeling of *Yes* or *No,* or *Keep* or *Delete,* always consider the reasons in the answer choices carefully. The correct answer has to provide a reason that accurately describes the proposed text and its role in the passage.

[4]

Despite the undeniable risks of live performance—or perhaps because of—the results rank among the greatest achievements in American entertainment. Many of *Playhouse 90*'s productions were later remade, both for television and film, including *Requiem for a Heavyweight, Judgment at Nuremberg,* and *Days of Wine and Roses.* ⌐5⌐ Many critics maintain that none of the remakes could match the brilliance and electricity of the live performances displayed in *Playhouse 90.*

5. At this point, the writer is considering adding the following true statement:

> The theme song for *Days of Wine and Roses* was composed by Henry Mancini, who also wrote the theme song for *The Pink Panther.*

Should the writer add this sentence here?

A. Yes, because it explains how the film version of *Days of Wine and Roses* was different from the television version.
B. Yes, because it provides an important detail about one of the movies made from a *Playhouse 90* production.
C. No, because it doesn't clarify whether *The Pink Panther* was first performed on *Playhouse 90.*
D. No, because it distracts the reader from the main point of this paragraph.

Here's How to Crack #5

Evaluate the reasons in the answer choices carefully. The reason should correctly explain the purpose of the selected text. Choice (A) is incorrect because there is no information about how the movie was different, Choice (B) is incorrect because the composer of the theme song is not *an important detail.* Choice (C) is possible because the proposed text does not state whether *The Pink Panther* was performed on *Playhouse 90,* but (D) is better. Choice (D) is correct because the main point of the paragraph is on the quality of the productions that came out of *Playhouse 90,* and information on the composer of a score is irrelevant and a distraction.

ORDER

Just as strategy questions come in several different varieties, there are also several types of order questions. All order questions involve the correct placement of ideas. Some order questions will ask you to correctly place a modifier or a new sentence. Other questions will ask you to evaluate and possibly correct the order of sentences within a paragraph or the order of the paragraphs themselves.

To work order questions, use POE. Ideas should be consistent and the meaning should be clear, but that meaning can be difficult to understand until ideas are in their proper place.

Order of Modifiers

A modifier out of place will leave the meaning of the sentence at best vague and at worst incorrect. Try each placement given in the answer choices. When the modifier is placed in its proper position, it should make the meaning of the sentence clear.

Let's look at an example.

⎯⎯⎯⎯⎯⎯⎯◯⎯⎯⎯⎯⎯⎯⎯

[3]

[1] For both the experienced and inexperienced actors, the chance to perform attracted them on live television to appear on *Playhouse 90.*

6. The best placement for the underlined phrase would be:
   F. where it is now.
   G. after the word *actors*.
   H. after the word *perform*.
   J. after the word *attracted*.

Here's How to Crack #6

Use POE. Choices (F) and (J) are incorrect because placing *on live television* before *attracted* or after *them* makes it sound as if the performers were drawn to performing on *Playhouse 90* while they were already appearing on *live television*. Choice (G) is incorrect because placing *on live television* after *actors* makes it sound as if only actors who already were appearing on live TV were drawn to *Playhouse 90.* Choice (H) is correct because the placement of *on live television* after *perform* clarifies why the actors wanted to appear on *Playhouse 90.*

⎯⎯⎯⎯⎯⎯⎯◯⎯⎯⎯⎯⎯⎯⎯

Order of Sentences

If there is a question on the order of the sentences in a paragraph, all of the sentences will be numbered. While NO CHANGE is a possible answer choice, it's also possible the sentences should be in a different order.

Just as you shouldn't try to fix a grammatical error in your head, don't waste time on an order question trying to put all the sentences in a paragraph into the perfect order. Look for one pair of sentences that need to go back-to-back, or one sentence that clearly begins or ends the paragraph, and use POE.

Certain clues can help determine the proper order. Transition words may be used to indicate an introduction or a conclusion. A pronoun may refer to a noun in a different sentence; in this case, the sentence that contains the pronoun should immediately follow the sentence that contains the original noun. In other cases, the context of the sentence may establish a chronology of events.

Try an example. Sentence 1 now shows the correct answer from Question 6.

———————————○———————————

[3]

[1] For both the experienced and inexperienced actors, the chance to perform on live television attracted them to appear on
_____
7
Playhouse 90. [2] Each week, a new "teleplay" was created from scratch—written, cast, rehearsed, and performed. [3] *Playhouse 90* was truly a remarkable training ground for the young talents. [4] Such future luminaries as Rod Serling, Sidney Lumet, Paddy Chayefsky, Marlon Brando, and Patricia Neal worked on various productions. [5] In some weeks, the censors would find something in it objectionable, and the network would intervene mere hours before airtime, leaving the cast and crew to scramble quickly to adapt.

7. Which of the following orders of sentences makes the paragraph most logical?
   A. NO CHANGE
   B. 1, 3, 4, 2, 5
   C. 5, 4, 3, 2, 1
   D. 1, 4, 5, 3, 2,

Here's How to Crack It

Use the pronoun *it* in Sentence 5 to help determine the placement of that sentence. The pronoun has to refer to a noun in a sentence that immediately precedes Sentence 5. There is no singular noun in Sentence 4 that agrees with *it*, so eliminate (A) and (D). Sentence 5 can't begin the paragraph because the *it* has to replace a noun in a prior sentence, so eliminate (C). Choice (B) is correct because the *it* replaces the singular noun *teleplay* in Sentence 2. Moreover, the transition phrase *In some weeks* in Sentence 5 should follow the transition phrase *Each week* in Sentence 2.

———————————○———————————

AFTER THE PASSAGE

Questions 9 and 10 ask about the passage as a whole.

Some order and strategy questions routinely appear at the end and are always preceded by the announcement above.

Order of the Paragraphs

If there is a question on the order of the paragraphs in a passage, there will be a warning at the beginning of the passage, alerting you that the passages may or may not be in the correct order and identifying which question will ask about the order.

The following paragraphs may or may not be in the most logical order. Each paragraph is numbered, and Question 8 will ask you to choose where Paragraph 2 should most logically be placed.

On a question that asks about ordering paragraphs, use a similar approach to that used for order of sentences. Look specifically at the first and last sentence of the paragraph that needs to be placed, and identify any transition words or pronouns that make the order of events consistent and clear.

The passage in its entirety, with all corrected text, is reprinted and paired with an example of a question on the order of the paragraphs.

---

[1]

The golden age of live television in the late 1950s and early 1960s witnessed the rise to prominence of a small band of actors, writers, and directors who worked on revolutionary shows such as *Playhouse 90*. Established stars and undiscovered talent alike worked long hours honing their craft. 4

Because of this frantic pace, accidents happened frequently. David Niven once revealed that during an early show, he accidentally locked his costume in his dressing room two minutes before air time. As the announcer read the opening credits, the sound of axes splintering the door to Niven's dressing room could be heard in the background.

[3]

[1] For both the experienced and inexperienced actors, the chance to perform on live television attracted them to appear on *Playhouse 90*. [2] Each week, a new "teleplay" was created from scratch—written, cast, rehearsed, and performed. [3] *Playhouse 90* was truly a remarkable training ground for the young talents. [4] Such future luminaries as Rod Serling, Sidney Lumet, Paddy Chayefsky, Marlon Brando, and Patricia Neal worked on various productions. [5] In some weeks, the censors would find something in it objectionable, and the network would intervene mere hours before airtime, leaving the cast and crew to scramble quickly to adapt.

[4]

Despite the undeniable risks of live performance—or perhaps because of—the results rank among the greatest achievements in American entertainment. Many of *Playhouse 90*'s productions were later remade, both for television and film, including *Requiem for a Heavyweight, Judgment at Nuremberg*, and *Days of Wine and Roses*. Many critics maintain that none of the remakes could match the brilliance and electricity of the live performances displayed on *Playhouse 90*.

8. For the sake of the logic and coherence of this essay, Paragraph 2 should be placed:
   F. where it is now.
   G. before Paragraph 1.
   H. after Paragraph 3.
   J. after Paragraph 4.

Here's How to Crack #8

Note the pronoun in the phrase *this frantic pace* in Paragraph 2 means that the pace has already been described. Consider the placements for Paragraph 2 offered by the answer choices. Choice (F) is incorrect because *this frantic pace* has to be explained first, and because Paragraph 1 introduces the topic of *Playhouse 90*. For the same reason, Paragraph 2 can't come before Paragraph 1, so eliminate (G). Choice (J) is incorrect because the last sentence of Paragraph 4 doesn't mention the pace of the performances. Choice (H) is correct because the last sentence of Paragraph 3 describes the cast and crew scrambling *quickly*, and thus explains the *frantic pace*.

Grading the Passage

A question at the end that asks you to evaluate the passage as a whole is another type of strategy question. This type of question states the intended purpose of the passage and asks you to determine whether the author fulfills that purpose. Two answers are *Yes,* and two answers are *No.*

Even if you have a strong feeling toward *Yes* or *No,* consider the reasons in the answer choices carefully. The correct choice should offer a reason that both addresses the proposed purpose of the passage and describes the passage accurately.

The passage in its entirety, with all corrected text and in the correct order, is reprinted below and followed by an example of a strategy question that asks you to grade the passage.

The golden age of live television in the late 1950s and early 1960s witnessed the rise to prominence of a small band of actors, writers, and directors who worked on revolutionary shows such as *Playhouse 90*. Established stars and undiscovered talent alike worked long hours honing their craft.

For both the experienced and inexperienced actors, the chance to perform on live television attracted them to appear on *Playhouse 90*. *Playhouse 90* was truly a remarkable training ground for the young talents. Such future luminaries as Rod Serling, Sidney Lumet, Paddy Chayefsky, Marlon Brando, and Patricia Neal worked on various productions. Each week, a new "teleplay" was created from scratch—written, cast, rehearsed, and performed. In some weeks, the censors would find something in it objectionable, and the network would intervene mere hours before airtime, leaving the cast and crew to scramble quickly to adapt.

Because of this frantic pace, accidents happened frequently. David Niven once revealed that during an early show, he accidentally locked his costume in his dressing room two minutes before air time. As the announcer read the opening credits, the sound of axes splintering the door to Niven's dressing room could be heard in the background.

9. Suppose that one of the writer's goals has been to write a brief essay describing an influential program in television's history. Would this essay fulfill that goal?
A. Yes, because it explains that many future stars underwent valuable training working on *Playhouse 90*.
B. Yes, because it mentions that *Playhouse 90* had the greatest number of viewers in its time slot.
C. No, because it fails to mention any future stars by name.
D. No, because even though many future stars received their start on *Playhouse 90*, few ever returned to television.

Despite the undeniable risks of live performance—or perhaps because of—the results rank among the greatest achievements in American entertainment. Many of *Playhouse 90*'s productions were later remade, both for television and film, including *Requiem for a Heavyweight*, *Judgment at Nuremberg*, and *Days of Wine and Roses*. Many critics maintain that none of the remakes could match the brilliance and electricity of the live performances displayed on *Playhouse 90*.

Here's How to Crack #9

Identify *describing an influential program in television's history* as the purpose the writer was supposed to fulfill. The writer describes *Playhouse 90* as *revolutionary, a remarkable training ground,* and one of the *greatest achievements in American entertainment,* making a *Yes* likely. Review the reasons carefully. Choice (A) explains why the program was *influential* by pointing out the *future stars who underwent valuable training.* Choice (B) is incorrect because there is no information about viewership in the passage. Choice (C) is incorrect because several stars are mentioned by name. Choice (D) is incorrect because the passage never states that few stars *returned to television.* Choice (A) is correct because it agrees that, yes, the passage fulfilled the author's goal and provides a reason that describes the passage accurately.

Now try these strategies on your own. Go online to your Student Tools and answer the Chapter 6 Drills.

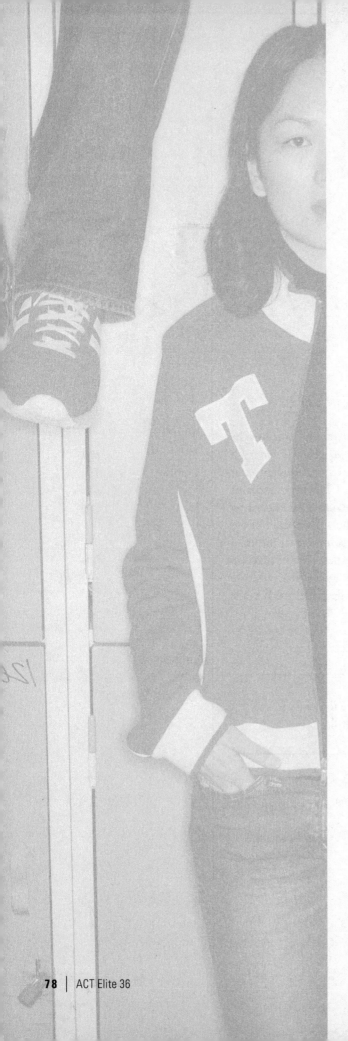

Summary

o   Questions that come with actual questions—not just answer choices—need a different approach.

o   For EXCEPT/LEAST/NOT questions, cross off the E/L/N word and use POE. Mark each choice that is acceptable with a "Y" and the choice that is not acceptable with a "N." The "N" is the correct answer.

o   Strategy questions all involve a purpose. Pick an answer that fulfills the purpose stated in the question. On strategy questions that involve making a decision, pick an answer that provides a reason that describes the passage accurately.

o   Order questions involve the correct placement of words, sentences, and paragraphs. Try the placements provided in the answer choices and lean on POE.

Chapter 7
Advanced English

The pursuit of perfection, or near perfection, on the English Test requires banking every point you can on questions on which you can identify the topic and apply a basic approach to fix, just as we've shown in the last two chapters. But it also includes answering correctly the idiosyncratic English questions. In this chapter, we'll show you how to spot and crack the most challenging questions on the English Test.

VOCABULARY

Vocabulary isn't heavily tested on the ACT, but questions do appear on the English Test that require you to choose the best word for the context of a sentence. In some examples, the words offered are close enough in meaning that in some contexts, they could be synonyms. In other examples, the words sound alike but have different meanings.

HOMOPHONES

Homophones are words that sound similar but have different meanings and/or spelling.

Common Homophones

The vocabulary that appears on the ACT rarely repeats, but below is a list of some common homophones that could appear on the test.

Accept: (verb) to take, receive, or agree to
Please accept *this gift.*

Except: (preposition) excluding
I like all types of fruit except *for pears.*

Access: (noun) a way or means of approach; (verb) the ability to approach
Lobbyists have access *to politicians. Please* access *the building through the back door.*

Excess: (noun) the amount or degree of one thing over another or over what is necessary
I have an excess *of Sharpie pens in case you want one.*

Aisle: (noun) a walkway between or along sections of seats
The usher walked down the aisle *of the theater.*

Isle: (noun) a small island
"So join us here each week my friends, you're sure to get a smile, from seven stranded castaways, here on 'Gilligan's Isle.'"

Affect: (verb) to act on or have an impact on, to produce an effect, change, or consequence; (noun) an expressed or observed emotional response
The closing of the assembly plant affected *the whole town. When Lindsay displayed a troubling* affect, *friends thought this odd response was a sign of mental illness.*

Effect:	(noun) a result or consequence produced by an agency or cause; (verb) to bring about or accomplish *The closing of the assembly plant had a negative* effect *on the whole town.* *The prisoners* effected *a dazzling escape when they rappelled down a 20-story building.*
Allusion:	(noun) a reference to something *Classic literature makes many* allusions *to Greek and Roman mythology.*
Illusion:	(noun) a false or misleading image of reality *My hope that I could raise my D to an A was just an* illusion.
Bare:	(adjective) without covering, unconcealed, or plain; (verb) to reveal or divulge *The* bare *facts of the case prove her guilt.* *I don't like to* bare *my legs in the middle of winter.*
Bear:	(verb) to hold up or support, to remain firm, or to produce; (noun) big, furry animal *The table can* bear *three hundred pounds of books.* *Smokey the* Bear *warns us against forest fires.*
Brake:	(noun) a device for slowing; (verb) to slow or stop by means of a brake *Hit the* brakes *before we crash!* Brake *the car before we crash!*
Break:	(verb) to smash, to split, to dissolve, or to divide into parts Break *the candy bar in half so we can each have some.*
Cereal:	(noun) edible grains *My favorite* cereal *is Froot Loops.*
Serial:	(noun) a program that is published in installments; (adjective) arranged in a series *I read every book in the "Tales of the City"* serial. *The newspaper wrote several articles about political corruption and later won an award for this* serial *story.*
Cite:	(verb) to quote; to mention in support, proof, or confirmation *Always* cite *your sources when you use a direct quotation.*
Sight:	(noun) the ability to see *I never let my dog out of my* sight *at the dog park.*
Site:	(noun) the position or location of something *This park is a great* site *for a picnic.*

Complement:	(verb) to complete; (noun) something that is used to complete or make perfect (noun) *The blue scarf* complements *the green sweater.* *Coffee is a* complement *to dessert.*
Compliment:	(noun) an expression of praise or admiration; (verb) to praise, to express admiration *We gave the chef many* compliments *after enjoying her delicious meal.* *Friends* complimented *me on my chic outfit.*
Die:	(verb) to cease living, to lose force or energy; (noun) a piece of machinery or single game cube *My call ended when the battery* died *on my cell phone.* *Some board games use a pair of dice, and others use a single* die.
Dye:	(verb) to change color; (noun) a coloring material *I* dye *my hair different colors to suit my mood.* *I use red* dye *to make Easter eggs.*
Flour:	(noun) finely ground grain *I'd love to make cookies, but I don't have any* flour, *butter, or sugar.*
Flower:	(noun) the blossom of a plant *Roses, tulips, and daisies are all beautiful* flowers.
For:	(preposition) expressing purpose or use; (coordinate conjunction) expressing a reason or cause *I shop at Mega Lo Mart* for *all my groceries and clothes.* *I shop at Mega Lo Mart,* for *it has the best prices for groceries and clothes.*
Four:	(noun) the number in between three and five *There are* four *quarters in a dollar.*
Hole:	(noun) an opening or gap through something *Dig a* hole *in the ground and bury your valuables in it.*
Whole:	(noun) an unbroken or undivided amount; (adjective) comprising the full quantity or amount *Two parts make a* whole. *I ate the* whole *pizza.*
Lead:	(noun) a heavy metal *Some pipes are made of* lead, *while others are made of copper.*
Led:	(verb/participle) the simple past and past participle of the verb *to lead,* which means to guide or show the way *I* led *the nature group on a walk through the forest.*

Morning:	(noun) the part of the day between midnight and noon *Call me in the* morning *when you wake up.*
Mourning:	(noun) an act or expression of sorrow *Traditionally, black clothing indicated a person was in* mourning *after the death of a loved one.*
Plain:	(adjective) lacking ornamentation, or clear *Plain bagels lack the salt, garlic, sesame seeds, and poppy seeds of the flavored varieties.*
Plane:	(noun) a flat or level surface, or an airplane *I watched the* plane *take off from the airport.*
Pray:	(verb) to offer praise or petition to a religious figure *Students* pray *to the ACT gods for a good score.*
Prey:	(noun) an animal hunted for food *The hungry lion chased its* prey *through the jungle.*
Principal:	(noun) a chief or head; (adjective) first or highest in rank *The* principal *of the school likes to meet every student.* *The* principal *violinist is considered the leader of the string section.*
Principle:	(noun) a fundamental law of truth, doctrine, or belief. *It would violate my* principles *to cheat on a test.*
Root:	(noun) the underground part of a plant; (verb) to implant, or to cheer for *The* root *of an aspen tree can be thousands of years old.* *"Root, root, root for the home team . . ."*
Route:	(noun) a course, way, or road for travel *If you want to avoid traffic, choose a* route *that avoids the expressway.*
Stationary:	(adjective) standing still, unmoving *Some people prefer riding a* stationary *bike at a gym instead of riding a bike on city streets.*
Stationery:	(noun) writing paper *Write your thank-you notes on your personalized* stationery.
Than:	(conjunction) used for comparisons *She is taller* than *I am.*
Then:	(adverb) next, subsequently *I made breakfast and* then *washed the dishes.*

To:	(preposition) expressing direction, movement, or intention *Walk* to *the store to* buy *groceries.*
Too:	(adverb) in excess, in addition, very *I have* too *much work to finish in* too *little time.*
Two:	(noun) the number in between one and three *Take* two *hours for lunch today.*
Waist:	(noun) the part of the body in between ribs and hips *Some pants sit below the* waist, *almost on the hips.*
Waste:	(verb) to consume, use, or spend recklessly *I* wasted *my lottery winnings at the slot machines.*

Strategy for Homophones on the ACT

The strategy for homophones depends on your familiarity with the pair or trio of words that is featured in the question. If you know both/all words well, you may be able to identify which is needed based on the meaning or the function.

- Use the context to identify the meaning of the word in the sentence. If the words are all the same parts of speech, substitute your own word and eliminate choices that don't match the meaning of your word.
- Use the context to identify the function of the word in the sentence. Eliminate choices that are the wrong part of speech. Eliminate choices that are verbs but that do not match the subject. Eliminate choices that are nouns but that are the wrong number (singular versus plural).
- Use POE aggressively, guess, and move on. You may not be certain which word means what or what word is which part of speech. Eliminate what you are confident is wrong, guess from what's left, and move on.

Try an example.

———————————○———————————

The increase in extreme weather patterns

effects countries all over the world.
<u> </u>
1

1. **A.** NO CHANGE
   B. effect
   C. affect
   D. affects

Here's How to Crack It

Affect and *effect* can be very confusing because they sound alike and have related definitions. Both words can be verbs or nouns, but the more common verb is *affect* (to act on or have an impact on, to produce an *effect*, change, or consequence) and the more common noun is *effect* (a result or consequence produced by an agency or cause). Even if you have trouble remembering which word is the verb, start by identifying the underlined word as the verb in the sentence, then identify the subject to check subject-verb agreement. The singular subject *increase* needs a singular verb, so eliminate (B) and (C). At this point you have a 50-50 chance of guessing the right answer if you don't know which one is correct. *Affect* is the verb that means *have an impact on*, so (D) is the correct answer.

SYNONYMS

Synonyms are words that are close enough in meaning that they can be substituted for each other in a sentence without changing the meaning. That makes vocabulary a great subject for EXCEPT/LEAST/NOT questions, which require you to identify the one word that does not work for the context.

Strategy for Synonyms on the ACT

The strategy for synonyms depends on your familiarity with the words. However, most words that appear are fairly common words.

- If the question uses the E/L/N format, apply the strategy you learned in Chapter 6. The sentence is correct as written, so you can use the original word as the point of comparison for the words in the answer choices. Write a "Y" next to each choice that could replace the original word and work with the context. Write an "N" next to the one choice that can't replace the original word. The "N" is the correct answer.
- If the question is in the regular format, use the context to identify the meaning of the word in the sentence. Substitute your own word and eliminate choices that don't match the meaning of your word.
- Use POE aggressively, guess, and move on. You may not be certain of some words. Eliminate what you are confident is wrong, guess from what's left, and move on.

Try an example.

Against the backdrop of an ink-black sky, the constellations twinkled above us.
2

2. Which of the following alternatives to the underlined portion would NOT be acceptable?
   F. sparkled
   G. shimmered
   H. glittered
   J. glared

Here's How to Crack It

Cross out NOT. Use *twinkled* as the point of comparison for the words in the answers. Write a "Y" next to the choices that could replace *twinkled* and work in the context of the sentence. *Twinkled, sparkled, shimmered, glittered,* and *glared* all mean to give off light. Choices (F), (G), and (H) could all replace *twinkled* because each provides the same meaning of giving off a pleasant, intermittent light that *twinkled* does. Write "Y" next to each choice. Choice (J) is the correct answer because *glared* can't replace *twinkled*. *Glare* is used to describe a light that is strong, harsh, and constant in quality.

IDIOMS

Idiomatic phrases are expressions whose form and meaning can be determined by neither grammatical rules nor the usual definitions of their elements. Therefore, you either know these phrases or you don't: they don't follow any rules.

Common Idioms

While the idioms that appear on the ACT rarely repeat, below is a list of some of the more common idioms. Even if you memorize every one of these, you may encounter a question on the ACT that tests an idiom not on the list.

Allow to:	I cannot *allow* you *to* leave the house without a jacket on.
Assert over:	The oldest sister *asserted* her power *over* her siblings.
Associate with:	No one wants to be *associated with* cheats and frauds.
Benefit from:	Everyone can *benefit from* rest and relaxation.
Bring about:	A bi-partisan effort can *bring about* real reform in the legislature.
Capable of:	You had no idea that I was *capable of* such an act.
Choose to:	I *choose to* ignore that criticism.
Complain about:	Don't *complain about* the food in front of the chef.
Create from:	The sculpture was *created from* discarded metal and rubber.
Decide to:	The guests *decided to* leave when the food ran out.

Demonstrated by:	The doctor *demonstrated* her concern *by* staying with the patient overnight.
Determined by:	The winner is *determined by* a simple majority.
Different from:	Apples are *different from* oranges.
Emerge from:	Diplomats *emerged from* the peace discussions feeling hopeful.
Exposure to:	*Exposure to* ultraviolet rays can be dangerous to your health.
Focus on:	Conservation efforts have *focused on* restoring the beachfront to its former glory.
Forbid to:	Invited guests were *forbidden to* reveal the location of the party.
Modeled on:	The new headquarters were *modeled on* the Parthenon.
Persuade to:	Nobody could *persuade* her *to* give up the search.
Problem with:	Many experts had *problems with* the theory.
Prohibit from:	Students are *prohibited from* wearing midriff-baring tops.
Refreshed in:	I left the spa *refreshed in* body and mind.
Regard as:	The members of the society are *regarded as* heroes in preservation circles.
Responsible for:	You are *responsible for* the outcome.
Responsibility to:	I have a *responsibility to* my fans.
Sit across from:	I *sat across from* a crying baby on the long bus ride.
Try to:	She *tries to* make everyone happy.
Typical of:	He is *typical of* most athletes.
Worry about:	I will never stop *worrying about* my grades.

Strategy for Idioms on the ACT

Your ear is your best tool for idioms. Many idioms use a preposition, and your ear can identify the wrong prepositions, if not the right one.

- Focus on the preposition, evaluating its use with the word in the idiom as well as the context of the sentence.
- Shut your eyes or look away from the example as you repeat each idiom in your head. Your eyes and brain will get in the way of your ear.
- Your ear may not identify the correct idiom, but it may identify the wrong ones.
- If the question uses the E/L/N format, cross off the NOT and use the sentence as written to compare the idioms in the answer choices. Write a "Y" next to each choice that could replace the original idiom and work with the context. Write an "N" next to the one choice that can't replace the original idiom. The "N" is the correct answer.
- Use POE aggressively, guess, and move on. You may not be familiar with the idiom. Eliminate what you are confident is wrong, guess from what's left, and move on.

Try an example.

———————————————○———————————————

Parents all over the world have

benefitted by Marion Donovan's invention
 $_{3}$

of disposable diapers.

3. **A.** NO CHANGE
    B. benefitted from
    C. benefitted in
    D. benefitted on

Here's How to Crack It

Use your ear as you work through the different choices, focusing on the prepositions. Your ear may more easily identify the wrong prepositions than the right one. *Benefited in* in (C) and *benefitted on* in (D) may sound more wrong than either *benefitted by* or *benefitted from*, allowing you to eliminate (C) and (D). You have a 50-50 chance of picking the right answer, so guess and move on. Choice (B) is correct because the idiom is *benefitted from*.

———————————————○———————————————

COUNTABLE AND UNCOUNTABLE NOUNS

Certain words can describe items that can be counted in individual units, and other words are used to describe items that can't be counted. Some examples of countable nouns are *dog, child, problem,* and *idea.* Some examples of uncountable nouns are *integrity, nutrition,* and *wisdom.*

Look for changes in prepositions among the answer choices to identify idioms.

Countable

If a noun has both a singular and plural form, it's countable. You can also tell a noun is countable if it is preceded by the indefinite articles *a* or *an*. A singular countable noun can't stand alone and needs an article in front of it.

> *A **child** gave me an **idea**. A **dog** was a **problem**. A **problem** gave me a **headache**.*

You can also tell a noun is countable if you can make it plural by adding an *s* or using the unique plural. Plural countable nouns can stand alone.

> ***Children** played with **dogs**. **Ideas** can cause **problems**.*

Use the following adjectives with countable nouns.

Few: She had *few* complaints after the great lesson.

Fewer: He made *fewer* careless errors on the last practice test.

Many: *Many* children shouted out the answer.

Number: A *number* of students complained about the curve.

Uncountable

Some nouns are uncountable. You can tell that a noun is uncountable when there is no plural form of the word. You can also tell that nouns are uncountable when you can't use the indefinite articles *a* and *an* in front of them.

> *I have **integrity**. He showed **wisdom**. Good **nutrition** is important.*

Use the following adjectives with uncountable nouns.

Amount: A record-breaking *amount* of snow fell this winter.

Less: I have *less* patience for such pranks than you do.

Little: We have *little* time to waste.

Much: You spent too *much* money on me.

---

10 Items or Less

That sounds right to your ear, doesn't it? Walk into most grocery stores, and the express lane will likely be marked by such a sign. But according to the counting rules, *10* items can obviously be counted, and the sign should read "10 Items or Fewer" (as the sign reads in Whole Foods). "10 Items or Less" is so embedded in our culture (there was both a movie and unrelated TV series with that title) that it doesn't sound wrong to most people. English is a fluid language, and it's possible the rules about the distinction will fade. But for now, follow the rules about countable and uncountable nouns on the ACT.

Strategy for Countable and Uncountable Nouns

- Look at the word that the adjective describes.
  - If the word is singular, say it in your head with *a* or *an* in front, or try to make it plural and say it in your head with an *s*. If the *a* or *an* works, it's countable. If the word can be made plural, it's countable.
  - If the word is already plural, it's countable.
- Eliminate choices that use the wrong adjective.
- Do not depend on your ear.

Try a few examples.

———————————◯———————————

Compared to Mediterranean cuisines,

Latin American cooking uses <u>less lemons</u>.
                                  4

4. **F.** NO CHANGE
   G. the least
   H. fewer
   J. lesser

Here's How to Crack It

If a noun is in plural form, it's countable. The only countable adjective is *fewer* in (H). Choices (F), (G), and (J) all use a form of *less,* which is an adjective used for uncountable nouns.

———————————◯———————————

———————————◯———————————

Experienced chefs recommend that

beginners use <u>few creativity and more fidelity</u>
                             5

when it comes to following the steps of the

recipe.

5. **A.** NO CHANGE
   B. least creativity and more fidelity
   C. lesser creativity and much fidelity
   D. less creativity and more fidelity

Here's How to Crack It

Try *a creativity* or *creativities.* Neither works, which confirms that *creativity* is uncountable. Eliminate (F) because *few* is a countable adjective. Compare the remaining choices. *Creativity* should be consistent with *fidelity.* Choice (B) is incorrect because *least* is a superlative, but *more* is a comparative word. Choice (C) is incorrect because *lesser* is a comparative word, but *much* is not a comparative word. Read more on superlatives and comparatives in the next section. Choice (D) is correct because *less* is used for uncountable nouns and it is consistent with *more.*

———————————◯———————————

Advanced Counting

Certain situations make the difference between countable and uncountable nouns more difficult.

Switch-Hitters

Some adjectives/adjectival phrases can be used with both countable and uncountable nouns.

Any: Are there *any* men in the book club? Do you have *any* milk?

Enough: I've read *enough* articles. I have *enough* time to go shopping.

More: I want *more* cookies. I need *more* air.

Plenty of: He had *plenty of* excuses. He has *plenty of* money.

Some: We have *some* questions for you. You need *some* water.

Time and Rate

Consider the following example.

> *I'll be there in 20 minutes or* less.

Minutes can be counted, but the meaning of the sentence is more about the amount of time rather than the number of minutes.

On the ACT, the correct answer uses *less than* for constructions about time or rate, regardless of whether the noun is countable.

> On questions that involves rate or time, use *less than*.

The act was repealed less then a decade later.
6

6. **F.** NO CHANGE
   G. less than
   H. fewer then
   J. fewer than

A decade indicates time, so the correct construction is *less than* (G). If you struggle to remember this rule, you can also apply the homophone strategy to *than* versus *then* and eliminate two wrong answers at least. *Than* is a preposition used with comparisons. *Then* is an adverb that means *next*. A good mnemonic (memory device) is to relate *then* with *next*, two words with an *e*. Relate *as* with *than*, two words with an *a* and both used for comparisons. Eliminate (F) and (H), and you have a 50-50 shot of guessing the correct answer before you move on. To repeat, the correct answer is (G) because *less than* should be used with time or rate.

HOT MESS

Some of the most challenging questions on the English Test underline most, if not all, of the sentence. It can be difficult to spot what the question is testing when *so much* is underlined, is changing, and sounds awful. Here's an example to clarify what Hot Mess questions look like.

7. Having been promoted brevet, or honorary, Brigadier
   General during the Civil War, George Armstrong Custer,
   Seventh Cavalry leader to the catastrophe at the Little Big
   Horn River, actually was a Colonel at the time of his death.

These questions usually involve picking the correct form of the modifiers and placing them in the correct location. Review the rules of modifiers and apply a strategy for tackling these, and Hot Mess questions aren't so bad.

First up, more information on modifiers.

Modifiers

A modifier is a word, phrase, or clause that describes something.

Adjectives modify nouns.

> *I gave a* meticulous *response.*

Adverbs modify verbs and adjectives, and some adverbs can modify other adverbs.

> *I responded thoroughly. The teacher appreciated my thoroughly meticulous response. She almost always likes meticulous responses.*

Placement of Modifiers

Adjectives should immediately precede the noun they describe. When two adjectives modify a noun, use *and* or a comma in between them.

> *I gave a* meticulous *and* thorough *response. I gave a* meticulous, thorough *response.*

When an adjective modifies a compound noun, do not use either *and* or a comma in between the adjective and the compound noun.

> *The teacher gave a difficult final exam.*

When adverbs modify verbs, they can be placed before or after the verb, *and* can even be separated from the verb by other elements of the sentence.

> *The teacher* quickly *graded the exams. The teacher graded the exams* quickly.

Misplaced Modifiers

A modifier in the wrong place describes the wrong item and creates ambiguity and confusion.

> ***Staring in panic at the final exam***, *my knees started to shake.*

Knees can't panic, stare, or take a final. A modifying phrase set off by a comma at the beginning or end of a sentence should be consistent with the subject of the sentence.

> ***Staring in panic at the final exam***, *I felt my knees start to shake.* That makes a lot more sense.

When adjectives are misplaced, they create a situation that is either wrong or makes no sense.

> *The **unfinished** student's exam earned an F.* Huh?

> *The student's **unfinished** exam earned an F.* That makes a lot more sense.

Adverbs have more flexibility in where they can be placed, but changing their placement can affect the meaning of a sentence.

> *She **almost** failed all of her exams.*

In other words, she got a D– on every exam.

> *She failed **almost** all of her exams.*

In other words, she got an F on most of her exams but earned a higher grade on at least one of them. Both sentences make sense, but the meaning changes depending on the placement of the adverb.

Strategy for Hot Mess Questions

1. Use the answer choices to compare the changes in the form and placement of modifiers.
2. Place modifiers as close as possible to the items they describe and apply comma rules correctly.
3. When a modifying phrase is offset by a comma at the beginning or end of a sentence, identify the subject and confirm the modifying phrase is consistent with the subject.
4. Use the 4 C's: Look for a *concise* choice that makes a *complete* sentence, is *consistent* with the rest of the passage, and makes the meaning most *clear*.

Use the strategy on an example.

───────────────○───────────────

8. Bill Gates, a <u>committed deeply vocal global philanthropist,</u>
   ⁸
   made his fortune as the founder of Microsoft.

   F. NO CHANGE.
   G. deep global philanthropist committed and vocal,
   H. committed global vocal deep philanthropist,
   J. vocal, deeply committed global philanthropist,

Here's How to Crack It

Consider each choice in comparison to the others, noting the form and placement of the modifiers. The adverb *deeply* in (F) and (J) changes to the adjective *deep* in (G) and (H), and the adjectives *committed, vocal,* and *global* move all around. The modifiers in (G) and (H) are all adjectives, but there are no commas separating them. Eliminate (G) and (H) because they do not follow comma rules. Compare (F) and (J). Choice (F) has no commas, but (J) uses a comma to separate *vocal* from *deeply committed* (adverb modifying an adjective), both of which describe *global philanthropist* (which is a compound noun) and is the correct answer.

───────────────○───────────────

Try another.

Brought by me to my favorite restaurants, all in Greektown, I started being taught by Beatrice how to cook the most popular Greek dishes.

9. **A.** NO CHANGE
    B. Bringing Beatrice to my favorite restaurants, all in Greektown, she started teaching me how to cook the most popular Greek dishes.
    C. Teaching me how to cook the most popular Greek dishes, Beatrice was brought by me to my favorite restaurants, all in Greektown.
    D. I brought Beatrice to my favorite restaurants, all in Greektown, and she taught me how to cook the most popular Greek dishes.

Here's How to Crack It

The sentence begins with an introductory modifying phrase in (A), (B), and (C). Choices (A) and (B) both use a modifying phrase that is not consistent with the subjects of their sentences, so eliminate both (A) and (B). The modifying phrase in (C) is consistent with the subject of the sentence. Compare (C) and (D). Choice (C) uses the passive voice (*Beatrice was brought by me);* (D) uses the active voice *(I brought Beatrice).* Choice (D) is correct because it is more concise.

Now try these strategies on your own. Go online to your Student Tools and answer the Chapter 7 Drills.

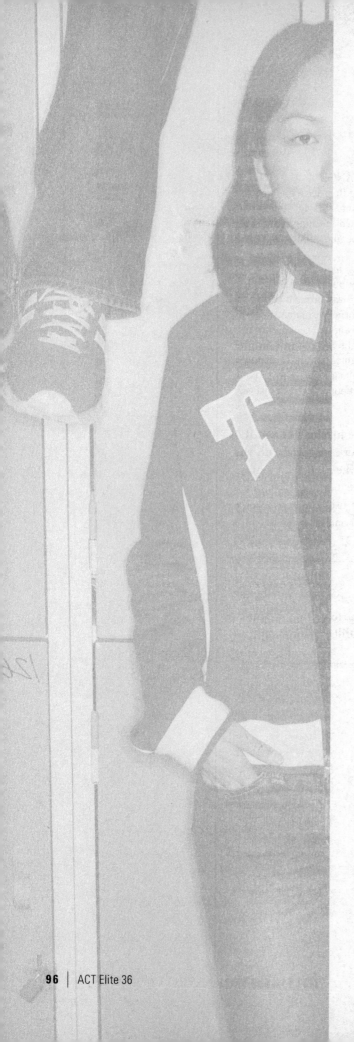

Summary

- Questions on vocabulary feature synonyms, closely related words, or homophones. Context determines the correct choice.

- Questions on idioms require choosing the correct preposition for the idiom. Studying the list of common idioms can help.

- Questions on countable and uncountable nouns follow rules regarding which adjectives work with which type of noun.

- Questions that underline most or all of a sentence usually require choosing the correct form and placement of modifiers.

Chapter 8
English Test

ENGLISH TEST

DIRECTIONS: In the five passages that follow, certain words and phrases are underlined and numbered. In the right-hand column, you will find alternatives for the underlined part. In most cases, you are to choose the one that best expresses the idea, makes the statement appropriate for standard written English, or is worded most consistently with the style and tone of the passage as a whole. If you think the original version is best, choose "NO CHANGE." In some cases, you will find in the right-hand column a question about the underlined part. You are to choose the best answer to the question.

You will also find questions about a section of the passage, or about the passage as a whole. These questions do not refer to an underlined portion of the passage, but rather are identified by a number or numbers in a box.

For each question, choose the alternative you consider best and fill in the corresponding oval on your answer document. Read each passage through once before you begin to answer the questions that accompany it. For many of the questions, you must read several sentences beyond the question to determine the answer. Be sure that you have read far enough ahead each time you choose an alternative.

PASSAGE I

Yélé Haiti and the Fugee President

Although rap and political office have not often met before, hip-hop artist, Wyclef Jean has made a career out of his close involvement with both. Referring to his charity foundation Yélé Haiti, Jean said in a recent interview, "Before you knew the foundation, you knew me from the Fugees." But "always," he adds, "my whole idea was to wear this flag [of Haiti] on my back and put my country on the map." Jean has done just that, as his music (as well as much of his public speech) have addressed the same issues that led him to enter his candidacy for Haitian president in 2010.

As Jean's 2006 song "If I Was President" would foretell many of the platforms on which he would run in 2010, long

before he had any idea that he would do so. Nevertheless, the song was a tremendous hit in the United States. Many listeners in the United States felt the song represented many of

1. A. NO CHANGE
   B. before, hip-hop artist Wyclef Jean,
   C. before, hip-hop artist Wyclef Jean
   D. before hip-hop artists, Wyclef Jean,

2. F. NO CHANGE
   G. address
   H. were addressing
   J. addresses

3. A. NO CHANGE
   B. When
   C. Although
   D. DELETE the underlined portion.

4. F. NO CHANGE
   G. The
   H. Notwithstanding, the
   J. Besides, the

they're concerns with the political climate of the day.
⎯⎯
5

    While Jean has always been politically active, his true awakening came after the massive earthquake in Haiti in 2010. His EP of the same year, *If I Were President: My Haitian Experience*, gave a stark portrayal of a nation that had been
⎯⎯⎯⎯⎯⎯⎯⎯⎯⎯⎯⎯
6

devastated by an earthquake, a devastation made worse for then
⎯⎯⎯⎯
7
President René Préval's weak response to the crisis. Jean felt that Préval had not done nearly enough to help Haiti emerge from the rubble. As a result, Jean led fundraising efforts in the United States, contributing most notably to "We Are the World 25 for Haiti," which one *Washington Post* critic called the worst
⎯⎯⎯⎯⎯⎯⎯⎯⎯⎯⎯⎯⎯⎯⎯⎯⎯⎯⎯⎯⎯⎯⎯
8
song of all time.
⎯⎯⎯⎯⎯⎯
8

[1] Jean is perhaps proudest of his charity Yélé Haiti, an organization that was founded in 2005 and organized to seek to
⎯⎯⎯⎯⎯⎯⎯⎯⎯⎯⎯
9
help Haiti's poor with its life.
⎯⎯⎯⎯⎯⎯⎯⎯⎯⎯
9

[2] Many credited this charity with hastening recovery efforts
⎯⎯⎯⎯⎯
10

5. A. NO CHANGE
   B. their
   C. there own
   D. its

6. F. NO CHANGE
   G. nation, that was being
   H. nation, it had been
   J. nation, moreover it had been

7. A. NO CHANGE
   B. by than
   C. by then
   D. for than

8. Given that all the choices are true, which one best concludes the paragraph and reaffirms Jean's commitment to Haitian improvement?
   F. NO CHANGE
   G. a song whose proceeds went to earthquake relief.
   H. which was sold digitally on iTunes.
   J. a remake of a song that had raised funds for Africa.

9. A. NO CHANGE
   B. organized a search for a way to help end the lives of poor Haitians.
   C. has sought to improve the lives of Haiti's poor.
   D. he organized it in order that he might aid poor Haitians with their lives.

10. F. NO CHANGE
   G. who credited
   H. crediting
   J. who were crediting

after 2004's, Hurricane Jeanne, tore through Haiti. [3] In the wake of Jeanne, Yélé Haiti provided scholarships to 3,600 students in Gonaïves alone. [4] This belief in the power of an

organization to support Haiti—both its infrastructure and its

residents—were the main motivations for Jean's candidacy for the 2010 Haitian presidential election. [5] Jean's activism,

however, is not limited to his musical contributions. [14]

Jean would have to withdraw from the 2010 election, but his musical activism has continued to the present day. Jean is now known as one of the most politically conscious artists in all of hip hop, and his work for the 2010 earthquake recovery in Haiti is continuing to fund the work being done there.

11. A. NO CHANGE
    B. 2004's Hurricane Jeanne
    C. 2004's Hurricane Jeanne,
    D. 2004's, Hurricane, Jeanne,

12. F. NO CHANGE
    G. their infrastructure and his
    H. its infrastructure and their
    J. their infrastructure and their

13. A. NO CHANGE
    B. was the main motivation
    C. were the main motivation
    D. having been the main motivation

14. For the sake of the logic and coherence of this paragraph, Sentence 5 should be placed:

    F. where it is now.
    G. before Sentence 1.
    H. before Sentence 3.
    J. before Sentence 4.

Question 15 asks about the preceding passage as a whole.

15. Suppose the writer's goal had been to describe charity fundraising in detail. Would this essay accomplish that goal?

    A. Yes, because the essay details the ways in which Jean's songs and albums were used to raise money for charities.
    B. Yes, because the essay suggests that Jean earned a good deal of money as a musician before starting the charity.
    C. No, because the essay primarily focuses on Jean's engagement with charitable, civic, and political affairs, not on the details of his charity fundraising.
    D. No, because the essay clearly indicates that Jean's charity had been discontinued in 2012.

Migrations by GPS

[1]

Every winter, the Egyptian vulture migrates from its summer home ☐16 to the warmer climes of southern Africa.

Because the vulture is so large, it flies overly large bodies of water as rarely as possible. Although these birds come from three different continents and migrate to a relatively

underdeveloped region, their face with extinction by the use of pesticides in all the regions through which they fly.

[2]

[1] Though the boom in agricultural pesticides has been good for farmers, it has indifferently caused significant harm to Egyptian vulture populations. [2] Estimates for the remaining number of vultures can be as low as 10,000. [3] The scientists placed GPS devices inside three vultures and have tracked the patterns of migration by following them from Turkey to

16. At this point, the writer is considering adding the following accurate information:

   in Europe, West Africa, and Asia

   Should the writer make this addition here?

   F. Yes, because it completes the sentence naming both the summer and winter homes of the Egyptian vulture.
   G. Yes, because it shows how the Egyptian vulture's endangered status is linked to its widespread habitat.
   H. No, because it provides an unnecessary detail about the habitat that is already implied in the vulture's name.
   J. No, because it suggests that the Egyptian vulture is a healthy enough species to migrate.

17. A. NO CHANGE
   B. over
   C. higher
   D. high

18. F. NO CHANGE
   G. then facing with
   H. the face for them of
   J. they are faced with

19. A. NO CHANGE
   B. indecisively
   C. industrially
   D. indirectly

20. F. NO CHANGE
   G. the birds' migration patterns
   H. them by means of a tracking device that gives positional coordinates
   J. the vultures as they were migrating with the devices on them

southern Africa and having mapped the routes. [4] Since 2012,
                        _____
                             21

a group of researchers, from University of Utah's Department
                        _____
                                         22
of Biology and its Sekercioglu Laboratory
_____
     22

has been conducting a study that will help to better understand
_____
        23
Egyptian vulture behavior and to save the species from

extinction. ⬚24

[3]

    The tracking devices download the vulture's positions
at certain intervals, showing that the vultures have traveled
through as many as seven countries in the Middle East. [A] The
scientists were fascinated to see, however, that the three birds
they captured took very different flight patterns. One bird, Igdir,
was crossing from the Arabian Peninsula to the Horn of Africa
within a month of observation. [B] Another, Aras, spent a much
longer time around the area which he was captured. As
                                _____
                                       25

the birds complete their migrations to Africa, the University
                                    _____
                                             26
of Utah website updates its maps and blogs to show the birds'
_____
     26
movements. [C]

21. A. NO CHANGE
    B. mapped
    C. mapping
    D. they would map

22. F. NO CHANGE
    G. researchers from University of Utah's Department of
       Biology,
    H. researchers, from University of Utah's Department of
       Biology,
    J. researchers from University of Utah's Department of
       Biology

23. A. NO CHANGE
    B. is conducting
    C. have been conducting
    D. been conducting

24. For the sake of the logic and coherence of this paragraph,
    Sentence 3 should be placed:

    F. where it is now.
    G. before Sentence 1.
    H. before Sentence 2.
    J. after Sentence 4.

25. A. NO CHANGE
    B. that
    C. where
    D. staying

26. F. NO CHANGE
    G. Africa the University of Utah website,
    H. Africa the University of Utah website
    J. Africa, the University of Utah website,

[4]

The researchers are interested in bringing public attention to the Egyptian vultures. [D] They believe that in doing so, they can bring attention to the risks of wide-scale pesticide use, which has reduced the population of Egyptian vultures to less
27
than 15,000 worldwide. The pesticides improve farms' produce,
27
but the collateral damage may outweigh the benefit. Vultures and other animals are essential to a thriving ecosystem, and the University of Utah scientists hope to save some of these
28
endangered species.
28

27. **A.** NO CHANGE
B. fewer as
C. less then
D. few than

28. **F.** NO CHANGE
G. prevent this outcome.
H. put an end to all of it.
J. improve life on Earth.

Questions 29 and 30 asks about the preceding passage as a whole.

---

29. The writer is considering adding the following sentence to the essay:

    These countries include Azerbaijan, Iran, Iraq, Syria, Jordan, Saudi Arabia, and Yemen.

    If the writer were to add this sentence, it would most logically be placed at Point:

    A. A in Paragraph 3.
    B. B in Paragraph 3.
    C. C in Paragraph 3.
    D. D in Paragraph 4.

30. Suppose the writer's primary goal had been to describe the role the Egyptian vulture plays in its ecosystem. Would this essay accomplish that goal?

    A. Yes, because it shows clearly how the Egyptian vulture improves the ecosystem of Yemen and Eastern Turkey.
    B. Yes, because it describes how the scientists' plans have succeeded in improving the ecosystem in Turkey.
    C. No, because it instead focuses on a plan to save the Egyptian vulture and does not detail the vulture's role within the ecosystem.
    D. No, because it instead concerns itself with the migratory patterns of the Egyptian vulture.

PASSAGE III

Mami Kudo Runs for Days and Days

Though it may seem a feat of nearly superhuman strength, the International Association of Ultrarunners (IAU) 24-Hour Run has been gaining popularity since its first European race in 1994. In this race, participants run as far as they can within a 24-hour period, with some running over 160 miles within the span.

Mami Kudo, who is now known as one of the great
"ultramarathoners," actually has a pretty normal life. Kudo is a
friendly bank teller by day, who, like many people, has
³¹

a passion for running. Even with her day job, however Kudo is
frequently invited to ultramarathons, and her relatively
³²

advanced age of 49 has misleaded much of her competitors into
thinking she is too old to win such races. Kudo may be older
³³
than many ultramarathoners, but her age didn't prevent

her from winning the race in 2009 and setting a new record; an
³⁴

31. Given that all the choices are true, which one provides the best transition between the preceding paragraph and this paragraph?
   A. NO CHANGE
   B. who also competes in 48-hour races and runs marathons, is Japanese.
   C. who has incredible stamina, was born and trains in Japan.
   D. a minor celebrity in her home country of Japan, likes to keep fit.

32. F. NO CHANGE
   G. job however Kudo,
   H. job however Kudo
   J. job, however, Kudo

33. A. NO CHANGE
   B. miss lead many
   C. misled many
   D. misled much

34. F. NO CHANGE
   G. record an
   H. record, an
   J. record. An

incredible distance of 158.6 miles. $\boxed{35}$

Ultramarathoners have a different set of skills from those of typical runners. Traditional runners must build muscle mass, whereas the ultramarathoners are much more concerned with

speed and pace and endurance. The rest, as with any such
$\overline{\text{36}}$

grueling activity, is all <u>psychological in the mind.</u>
$\overline{\text{37}}$

Combining all of these skills in perfect harmony, <u>Kudo set</u>
$\overline{\text{38}}$
<u>her first world record</u> in 2009 in Taipei.
$\overline{\text{38}}$

After <u>running for twenty-four straight hours;</u>
$\overline{\text{39}}$

Kudo had <u>shut the whole operation down:</u> nearly 160 miles.
$\overline{\text{40}}$
She would in fact break her own record the following year

35. Given that all the following statements are true, which one, if added here, would most specifically elaborate how Kudo uses her age to her advantage?

- **A.** Kudo's approach is actually very similar for the 24-hour and the 48-hour races.
- **B.** Kudo is actually not alone: the American who won the men's race in 2013 was 45.
- **C.** She knows that running is a mental sport above all, and much of her focus is on keeping a positive dialogue with herself.
- **D.** While younger runners burn themselves out by going too quickly too early, Kudo has learned through experience how to maintain a steady pace and outrun all of them.

36. The best placement for the underlined portion would be:
- **F.** where it is now.
- **G.** after the word *must*.
- **H.** after the word *build*.
- **J.** after the words *whereas the*.

37. **A.** NO CHANGE
- **B.** psychological.
- **C.** mental mind psychology.
- **D.** mental and psychological.

38. **F.** NO CHANGE
- **G.** here was set the
- **H.** behold the
- **J.** setting the

39. **A.** NO CHANGE
- **B.** running for twenty-four straight hours,
- **C.** running, for twenty-four straight hours;
- **D.** running, for twenty-four straight hours,

40. **F.** NO CHANGE
- **G.** reached a new plateau:
- **H.** called it a day and moved on:
- **J.** stopped running and fell into a blanket:

when she continued to work her day-job as a bank teller. In the
$\underline{\hphantom{when she continued}}$
41

latter, at Greeces ultramarathon in 2011, Kudo ran over 225
$\underline{\hphantom{latter, at Greece}}$
42
miles in the two-day span.

Even as her fiftieth birthday approached, Kudo showed no signs of stopping. In 2013, she won the 24-Hour Run World Challenge. In 2014, at a race to be held in Soochow, Kudo was
$\underline{\hphantom{at a race to be held}}$
43

heavily favored to win again, and Jon Olsen was favored to win
$\underline{\hphantom{heavily favored to win again}}$
44
the men's race.
$\underline{\hphantom{the men}}$
44

41. Given that all the choices are true, which one provides the most relevant and specific transition into the last sentence of this paragraph?

A. NO CHANGE
B. she outran the other women who race alongside her.
C. she added to her resumé the record in the 48-hour race.
D. an American, Jon Olsen, won the men's with a distance of 167.5 miles.

42. F. NO CHANGE
G. at Greece
H. at Greece's
J. at a greasy

43. Given that all the choices are true, which one clearly suggests that it is particularly noteworthy that Kudo is still favored for the 2014 race?

A. NO CHANGE
B. alongside the American Jon Olsen in the men's race,
C. though the Japanese team as a whole would likely win second place,
D. despite the more competitive field that the sport's popularity had attracted,

44. Given that all the choices are true, which one most effectively concludes the essay?

F. NO CHANGE
G. though the American Sabrina Little was expected to finish second.
H. further cementing her position as one of the greatest ultramarathoners of all time.
J. and ultramarathons will be run in more places in 2015.

Question 45 asks about the preceding passage as a whole.

---

45. Suppose the writer's primary goal had been to present an ultramarathoner's personal recommendations for training for long-distance running. Would this essay accomplish this goal?

A. Yes, because it emphasizes that Kudo was successful in both the 24-hour and the 48-hour races.
B. Yes, because it describes how Kudo is able to succeed despite being older than many other racers.
C. No, because it describes ultramarathoning and Kudo's achievements more than her personal recommendations.
D. No, because it suggests that Kudo's accomplishments are actually not so remarkable in the world of ultramarathons.

PASSAGE IV

That Really Gets My Goat

"Just chill out," the goat seems to say. Timidly, the horse nods and tries to keep its mind on other things. The horse trains nonstop, and he see nothing but his stable and the track for weeks at a time. "It's okay," the goat says with a look. This unlikely friend helps to calm the horse, keeping him from
<u>46</u>

going stir-crazy in the small pre-race stall. 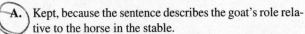 47 Sometimes,

because the horse insists on the presence of his "pet," the goat
<u>48</u>

will follow him all the way to the paddock. Kept calm before
<u>49</u>

the race, they are carrying the jockey to victory.
<u>50</u>

46. F. NO CHANGE
G. sees
H. has saw
J. have seen

47. The writer is considering deleting the preceding sentence. Should the sentence be kept or deleted?

A. Kept, because the sentence describes the goat's role relative to the horse in the stable.
B. Kept, because it suggests that the goat is still waiting for a response from the horse.
C. Deleted, because the sentence breaks from the paragraph's main focus on the horse and the goat.
D. Deleted, because the sentence is predicated on the idea that goats and horses speak to one another.

48. F. NO CHANGE
G. the horse insisted
H. the horse insists
J. the horse who insists

49. Which choice most vividly captures the relationship between the horse and the goat?

A. NO CHANGE
B. comes along for the ride.
C. follows the horse, follows him wherever he may go.
D. and the horse have a real bond.

50. F. NO CHANGE
G. the horse carries
H. they are carried by
J. the horse is carrying

The goat, an often unseen feature of a racetrack stable,
₅₁

became the unlikely companion to the racehorse, being that
₅₂
horse owners were surprised to see their horses relax when a goat was nearby. Some owners have tried other animals—pigs, dogs, and burros—but these owners always come back to goats, whose special bond with horses exceeds that of any of the other
₅₃
animals. Furthermore, goats have been so effective

that goats are still kept around stables even though they literally
₅₄
eat garbage. Trainer Marty Wolfson attributes his best twenty
₅₄
years of training to his goat Precious, whose calming influence on horses had enabled him to produce an impressive list of winners. When Marty and his wife bought a new farm with their earnings, it was only right that they should call it Precious Acres.

The stable goat has a long lineage in horse racing. Some suggest that the stable goat may have been used to calm horses before classical Greek chariot races. We don't really know. We can be much more certain, however, about it's more recent
₅₅
history. In fact, the phrase "to get one's goat" comes from early 1800s England, and it refers to the companionship

between racehorses and their goats. It was a classic ploy that
₅₆
was well-known for years at the racetrack: a trainer sneaks into
₅₆
a rival's stable and "gets the goat" of his horse. The horse will be so rattled that he won't have a chance in the next day's race.

---

51. Given that all the choices are true, which one provides material most relevant to the paragraph's focus?
- **A.** NO CHANGE
- **B.** one of the oldest mammals in the world,
- **C.** which is the most commonly eaten meat on the globe,
- **D.** known by its bizarre bleating sound,

52.
- **F.** NO CHANGE
- **G.** racehorse when
- **H.** racehorse; expectedly,
- **J.** racehorse, where

53.
- **A.** NO CHANGE
- **B.** abiding love of
- **C.** chilling effects on
- **D.** tending to

54. Which choice would best serve as a transition to the next sentence?
- **F.** NO CHANGE
- **G.** some of the biggest successes in racing history can be attributed to them.
- **H.** those who have tried to replace the goats with pigs have been disappointed.
- **J.** a lot of places still won't let goats run on the actual horse tracks.

55.
- **A.** NO CHANGE
- **B.** Its
- **C.** their
- **D.** our

56.
- **F.** NO CHANGE
- **G.** ploy that was tricky and sneaky at
- **H.** ploy at
- **J.** ploy, as in a plot or trick, at

Although the ploy has died out, the saying persists, and any

57. **A.** NO CHANGE
     B. the ploy dying
     C. dying
     D. having died

racehorse trainer will tell you that taking a horse's goat away
before a race, can have very bad consequences.

58. **F.** NO CHANGE
     G. away, before a race
     H. away before a race
     J. away, before a race,

We know that animals communicate with one another, but the case of the horse and the goat shows a curious instance of something more, like seriously way more, intimate. Some horse trainers refer to the goats as "mascots," but others refer to them as the horses' "best friends" or even "soul mates." Full of

59. **A.** NO CHANGE
     B. something of a more kind of intimate instance.
     C. instance of something more intimate.
     D. something, an instance, a moment, of more intimacy.

tenderness and affection, good horse psychologists noting these essential friendships and show us a side of that psychology that we may not have even suspected was there.

60. **F.** NO CHANGE
     G. good horse psychologists are saying how essential these friendships are
     H. these friendships are being called essential to good horse psychology
     J. these friendships are essential to good horse psychology

---

PASSAGE V

When my aunt, was a research chemist, gave me my first chemistry set, I set to work right away, hoping to get proficient enough that she'd start taking me along with her to work. She worked for a small pharmaceutical company, and her research always intrigued me, though I wasn't sure exactly what she did. I followed the directions closely, but I couldn't get the food-dye experiment quite right, and I couldn't make my copper pennies turn gold—as a chemist, I wasn't exactly Madame Curie.

61. **A.** NO CHANGE
     B. aunt,
     C. aunt was
     D. aunt who was

62. Which most effectively completes the sentence and uses sarcasm to emphasize that the experiments named in the sentence were, scientifically speaking, unimpressive?

     F. NO CHANGE
     G. I was still learning how to do it.
     H. I didn't have a very fancy chemistry set.
     J. my aunt was still much better than me.

My failed experiments didn't dissuade me, though. I took my aunt's advice; to keep tinkering away when success seems out of reach. [A] Keep working, keep reading, keep trying, and the successful experiments will come. The experiments

are there to build you're knowledge of the chemical world, in general. [B] Once you understand this world, the successful experiments will come to you. [C] The last piece of advice

frustrated me the most—it seemed so far out of reach, I whimpered to my aunt one day. "We all struggle at first," she

told me, as she sat next to me in my "laboratory" nearly defeated, I watched as she set up one of the simple experiments. She was so calm as she did it. [D] The table didn't shake as she snapped everything into place. She could even look at me as she shows what she was doing, whereas my eyes were completely fixed on those deft movements. Whenever I looked away from experiments, even to blink sometimes, the whole

thing went to pot.

63. A. NO CHANGE
    B. advice: Keep
    C. advice, like: keep
    D. advice, things like, keep

64. F. NO CHANGE
    G. your knowledge of the chemical world,
    H. your knowledge of the chemical world
    J. you're knowledge of the chemical world

65. The writer wants to emphasize that the narrator sees her aunt's advice as very difficult to implement. Which choice most effectively accomplishes this goal?
    A. NO CHANGE
    B. like the wrong advice,
    C. really frustrating,
    D. like a good point,

66. F. NO CHANGE
    G. "laboratory," near defeat,
    H. "laboratory." Near defeat,
    J. "laboratory," nearly defeated

67. A. NO CHANGE
    B. does
    C. is into
    D. explained

68. The writer wants to divide this paragraph into two in order to separate the list of chemistry principles from the anecdote that follows. The most logical place to begin the new paragraph would be at Point:
    F. A.
    G. B.
    H. C.
    J. D.

Once she had completed the experiment, she held up a small test tube of the red food dye that I had slaved for weeks to try to create. Nevertheless, she held up a tube of blue dye that she had made during the same experiment. The two colors,

69. A. NO CHANGE
    B. Then,
    C. Still,
    D. Notwithstanding,

right next to each other in this way complimented each other beautifully. My aunt showed me that most of the materials

70. F. NO CHANGE
    G. way complemented
    H. way, complemented
    J. way, complimented

were identical; with just a few different elements producing these starkly different hues. I had been combining all the

71. A. NO CHANGE
    B. identical,
    C. identical. There
    D. identical, they

elements haphazardly, but she had combine all the elements to

72. F. NO CHANGE
    G. she combine
    H. she'd had combined
    J. she'd combined

form the base and then allowed the coloring agent to intertwine with that base. In other words, once she created the foundation,

73. A. NO CHANGE
    B. mingle
    C. experiment
    D. react

then came all the little tweaks, that could begin to produce a world of many colors.

74. F. NO CHANGE
    G. tweaks that
    H. tweaks, that,
    J. tweaks that,

Question 75 asks about the preceding passage as a whole.

75. Suppose the writer's goal had been to demonstrate that conducting a successful experiment is as simple as following a few foundational principles. Does this essay accomplish that goal?

A. Yes, because it indicates that the narrator's aunt was able to create different colored dyes from a chemistry set.

B. Yes, because it shows that the narrator was able to implement the aunt's principles in creating her own successful experiments.

C. No, because it focuses more on the difficulties the narrator experienced despite following the principles of chemistry.

D. No, because it suggests that the narrator has little interest in following her aunt's career path as a research chemist.

Chapter 9
English Test:
Answers and
Explanations

ANSWER KEY

Passage I	Passage II	Passage III	Passage IV	Passage V
1. C	16. F	31. A	46. G	61. B
2. J	17. B	32. J	47. A	62. F
3. D	18. J	33. C	48. F	63. B
4. G	19. D	34. H	49. A	64. H
5. B	20. G	35. D	50. G	65. A
6. F	21. B	36. H	51. A	66. H
7. C	22. J	37. B	52. G	67. D
8. G	23. A	38. F	53. A	68. H
9. C	24. J	39. B	54. G	69. B
10. F	25. C	40. G	55. B	70. H
11. B	26. F	41. C	56. H	71. B
12. F	27. A	42. H	57. A	72. J
13. B	28. F	43. D	58. H	73. D
14. G	29. A	44. H	59. C	74. G
15. C	30. C	45. C	60. J	75. C

ENGLISH TEST EXPLANATIONS

Passage I

1. **C**   Two rules are being tested in this question. An introductory idea has to be followed by a comma. In this case, the introductory idea ends at the word *before*, so (D) can be eliminated. The words *Wyclef Jean* are essential to the sentence (that is, the sentence would not be complete without them), so there should be no commas around the words, eliminating (A) and (B). Only (C) has appropriately placed commas.

2. **J**   To determine the necessary verb in this sentence, find the subject. In this case, the subject is *music*, which requires a singular verb, thus eliminating (F), (G), and (H). Because it's in parentheses, *as well as much of his public speech* does not affect the number of the subject. There's no need to worry about the tense here because only one of the answers agrees with the subject.

3. **D**   The sentence as written does not give a complete idea. The only way to make this idea complete is to remove the word at the beginning, as (D) indicates. Whenever you see DELETE as an option, find a reason NOT to pick it. It is often correct, so unless you have a very good reason not to, go with DELETE.

4. **G**   Pick the most concise choice. Transition words are seldom necessary to a sentence, and the transition words in (F), (H), and (J) are not consistent with the meaning of the sentence.

5. **B**   The underlined pronoun refers back to the word *listeners*, which is plural, eliminating (D). The word is used possessively, as in *the concerns belonging to many listeners*, so the possessive plural pronoun *their* (B) is correct. Choice (A) is the contraction *they are*. *There* is the adverb or pronoun (it can be both) referring to place.

6. **F**   The sentence is correct as written. Choices (H) and (J) create two complete ideas joined by a comma, so those choices can be eliminated. Choice (G) is awkwardly stated and actually makes the meaning of the sentence unclear, so it too can be eliminated.

7. **C**   The correct idiom is *made worse by* rather than *made worse for*, thus eliminating (A) and (D). The word *then* is used in this sentence to mean *at that time*, so *then* is correct, as (C) has it. The word *than* in (B) is used for comparisons.

8. **G**   Identify the purpose of the correct choice as stated in the question, which asks for the choice that *reaffirms Jean's commitment to Haitian improvement*. The only choice that addresses anything relating to Haiti is (G), which refers to the Haitian earthquake. The other choices do not fulfill the purpose stated in the question.

9. **C**   Pick the most concise choice.

10. **F** A sentence must be a complete idea, and among these answer choices, only (F) gives a complete idea by supplying a verb for the subject *Many*. Choices (G) and (J) add the pronoun *who*, which acts here as a conjunction, begins an incomplete idea, and robs the subject *Many* of its verb. Without a form of the verb *to be, crediting* in (H) is not a verb.

11. **B** If you cannot cite a reason to use commas, don't use them. In this case, all the information is necessary to the meaning of the sentence, and there is no other reason to introduce a comma.

12. **F** Both pronouns in this sentence refer back to *Haiti*, a singular noun. Therefore, both pronouns should be *its*, as in (F).

13. **B** The subject of this sentence is *belief*, which requires the singular verb *was*, eliminating (A) and (C). Choice (D) creates an incomplete idea, so it too can be eliminated. Only (B) remains, correctly using the singular verb *was* and the singular noun *motivation*.

14. **G** Sentence 5 offers a link between Jean's musical contributions and his more explicit social and political contributions. It should be placed at the beginning of this paragraph because the previous paragraph talks about music and this one talks about Jean's charity.

15. **C** This essay would not accomplish the goal stated in the question because the essay is more concerned with an overview of Wyclef Jean's career in music and public affairs. Eliminate (A) and (B). Choice (D) mentions that the charity was discontinued in 2012, but this is never mentioned in the passage. Only (C) remains, which provides a reason that describes the passage accurately and explains why the stated goal was not met.

Passage II

16. **F** The non-underlined portion identifies the location of the summer home as *the warmer climes of southern Africa*. The proposed addition would present a useful counterpoint in adding the vulture's points of origin, so the writer *should* make the addition here, eliminating (H) and (J). Choice (G) can also be eliminated because it does not describe the proposed addition accurately. Only (F) remains, as it correctly states that the addition should be made and gives a correct reason for this addition.

17. **B** The Egyptian vulture flies *over* bodies of water, making (B) the correct answer. The other words provide adjectives and adverbs that do not work in this particular context.

18. **J** The sentence needs a complete idea, and a complete idea must have a subject and verb. Only (J) provides a subject and verb.

19. **D** There is a contrast in this sentence between the good that pesticides have done for farmers and the unintended negative consequences that the pesticides have had on vultures. Given this contrast, the words *indifferently, indecisively*, and *industrially* do not work in this sentence because they do not refer to these consequences. Only (D), *indirectly*, can work with the words *caused significant harm*.

20. **G** The four answer choices say essentially the same thing, so choose the most concise one that is grammatically correct.

21. **B** The earlier verb in this context is *have tracked*, so this verb should be consistent. *Mapped* in choice (B) works, with the helping verb *have* applying to both *tracked* and *mapped*.

22. **J** If you cannot cite a reason to use commas, don't use them. In this case, all the information is necessary to the meaning of the sentence, and there is no other reason to introduce a comma.

23. **A** The subject is *group*, a collective noun and therefore singular. Thus, the verb must be singular, which eliminates (C). Choice (D) is missing the helping verb *has*, which leaves the sentence incomplete. The action described in this sentence began in 2012 and continues into the present, so the present perfect is needed over the present tense in (B).

24. **J** Sentence 3 discusses the details of the experiment described in Sentence 4; therefore, Sentence 3 will need to come after Sentence 4, or at the end of the paragraph.

25. **C** The underlined pronoun refers back to *the area*, a place. Choose the pronoun *where* (C) over the pronouns that refer to things, *which* and *that*. *Staying* in (D) doesn't link the two parts of the sentence together the way the pronoun, acting as a conjunction, does.

26. **F** This sentence contains an introductory idea, *As the birds complete their migrations to Africa*, that must be followed by a comma, thus eliminating (G) and (H). Eliminate (J) because there is no reason to put a comma after the word *website*.

27. **A** *Less* is used for non-countable things, such as *the population*. *Fewer* is used for countable things, but the choice is moot in this question since there is no viable choice containing the word *fewer*. *Than* is used for comparisons, and *then* is used for time or progression. Choice (A) is therefore the only viable answer.

28. **F** Choice (F) is specific and makes the sentence the clearest. Choices (G) and (H) contain ambiguous pronouns (*this, it*) that damage the meaning of the sentence, and (J) changes the meaning of the sentence altogether.

29. **A** The first sentence of Paragraph 3 ends by mentioning *as many as seven countries in the Middle East*. The list of countries in the proposed sentence should therefore go after this mention of the *seven countries*, or at Point A.

30. **C** While the passage as a whole is about the Egyptian vulture, it does not describe the vulture's role within its ecosystem in any detail, which eliminates (A) and (B). Choice (D) is incorrect because the passage does more than just describe migration patterns. Choice (C) is correct because the reason provided describes the content of the passage accurately.

Passage III

31. **A** Identify the purpose of the correct choice as stated in the question, which asks for a choice that provides *the best transition between the preceding paragraph and this paragraph*. The next few sentences of the paragraph discuss Kudo's day job and her "normal" life, which makes (A) the best transition.

32. **J** The word *however* is important because it sets up a contrast with the previous sentence, but it is not *essential* to the meaning of this particular sentence. If *however* were to be removed, the sentence would still have the same meaning. Therefore, because the information is unnecessary, the word *however* should be surrounded by commas, as in (J).

33. **C** *Misleaded* is not a word, so (A) can be eliminated, and *miss lead* is a misspelling of the word *misled*, so (B) can be eliminated. *Many* is for things that can be counted, and *much* is for things that cannot. Since *competitors* can be counted, this sentence needs the word *many*, as in (C).

34. **H** Use the vertical line test. The first idea, *that didn't prevent the 45-year-old from winning the race in 2009 and setting a new world record*, is complete, but the second, *an incredible distance of 158.6 miles*, is incomplete. Therefore, STOP punctuation cannot be used in this sentence, and (F) and (J) can be eliminated. Because the first idea is complete and the second, modifying idea is incomplete, though, there should be some pause, as the comma in (H) provides.

35. **D** Identify the purpose of the correct choice as stated in the question, which asks for a choice that indicates *how Kudo uses her age to her advantage*. The only choice that addresses Kudo's age advantage at all is (D), which talks about *younger runners* and the *things* that Kudo's age and *experience* have allowed her to learn.

36. **H** The underlined portion cannot go where it is now because it creates a list with too many *and*s. *Speed* is not being used as a verb (nor would this answer make sense even if it were), so (G) can be eliminated, as can (J), which also does not make sense. The only possible placement comes from (H), which situates *speed and* in the sentence, *Traditional runners must build speed and muscle mass*. This also keeps the sentence parallel.

37. **B** Choose the most concise answer that works in the context.

38. **F** The modifying phrase *Combining all of these skills in perfect harmony* describes the first word after the comma, which must be Kudo. Choices (G), (H), and (J) all create a misplaced modifier.

39. **B** Use the vertical line test. The first idea, *After running for twenty-four straight hours* is incomplete, so the STOP punctuation in (A) and (C) must be eliminated. Choice (D) is wrong because the pair of commas would incorrectly make *for twenty-four straight hours* unnecessary to the sentence.

40. **G** Choose the most concise answer that works in the context. Choice (G) is the most concise and is consistent with the rest of the sentence, linking *plateau* to the mileage given after the colon.

41. **C** Identify the purpose of the correct choice as stated in the question, which asks for a choice that provides *the most relevant and specific transition into the last sentence.* The following sentence mentions *the latter,* so the correct choice must provide a clear connection to another race. Only (C) can work, as the last sentence discusses Kudo's performance in this 48-hour race.

42. **H** An apostrophe is needed to show the possessive relationship *Greece* has with its ultramarathon.

43. **D** Identify the purpose of the correct choice as stated in the question, which asks for a choice that *suggests that it is particularly noteworthy that Kudo is still favored.* Choice (D) is the most effective: although the field has grown more competitive, Kudo is *still* one of the best in it.

44. **H** Identify the purpose of the correct choice as stated in the question, which asks for a choice that *effectively concludes the essay.* Choices (F), (G), and (J) are true, but they do not connect to themes from earlier in the passage. Only (H) continues the discussion of Mami Kudo and talks about her impressive run as one of the greatest ultramarathoners of her time.

45. **C** There are no *personal recommendations* in this passage because none of it is told from Kudo's perspective, which eliminates (A) and (B); Choice (D) gives a reason that is untrue, especially given how much space in the essay is devoted to marveling at Kudo's achievements. Only (C) provides a correct answer and correct reason.

Passage IV

46. **G** The subject of this verb is *he,* so the verb must agree with its singular subject, eliminating (F) and (J). The past participle of *to see* is *seen,* eliminating (H).

47. **A** The sentence in question helps to explain the previous interaction in the paragraph, so it should be kept, eliminating (C) and (D). Choice (A) correctly states that the information should be kept and gives an accurate reason for why it should. Choice (B) reads the interaction too literally and is not supported by the information in the passage.

48. **F** The conjunction *because* is needed to make the first idea incomplete. Otherwise, two complete ideas are linked incorrectly by a comma.

49. **A** Identify the purpose of the correct choice as stated in the question, which asks for a choice that *most vividly captures the relationship between the horse and goat.* Choice (A) is correct because it shows the extent of that relationship in a specific way.

50. **G** The modifying phrase *Kept calm before the race* refers to the horse, so *the horse* must be the first words after the comma. Choices (F) and (H) create a misplaced modifier, while (J) switches the tense.

51. **A** Identify the purpose of the correct choice as stated in the question, which asks for a choice that *provides material most relevant to the paragraph's focus*. The paragraph talks about the goat's importance in the stable, so the underlined portion must refer to the goat's position in the stable.

52. **G** Use the vertical line test. In (H), both ideas on either side are complete, so the semicolon works. However, the transition word *expectedly* is not consistent with the information that the owners *were surprised*. Choice (G) is correct because the pronoun *when* acts as a conjunction and makes the second idea incomplete. With no punctuation (GO punctuation), *when* links the incomplete idea correctly to the complete idea. Choice (J) is wrong because *where* can be used to modify places only. Choice (F) is wrong because *being that* is an unclear way to link the two ideas.

53. **A** Choice (A) is correct because the word choice of *special bond* is consistent with the context of the passage.

54. **G** Identify the purpose of the correct choice as stated in the question, which asks for a choice that *would best serve as a transition to the next sentence*. The early parts of the paragraph discuss the goat's role within stables. The following sentence discusses one particular goat whose role at a stable was particularly notable. Choice (G) correctly links both.

55. **B** Choice (B) is correct because it is a singular possessive pronoun that refers to *the stable goat*, a singular noun. Choice (A) is the contraction *it is*, which cannot be used in this context. Choice (C) is plural, and while (D) is a possessive pronoun, it's in the plural form, which doesn't match the singular goat.

56. **H** Choose the most concise answer that works in the context.

57. **A** Choice (A) is correct because it is the only choice that provides a subject and verb needed to make the idea complete. *Dying* and *having* (B), (C), and (D) are participles, and without a form of the helping verb *to be*, are not verbs.

58. **H** If you can't cite a reason to use commas, don't use them. There's no need for commas in the underlined portion, so any choice with commas can be eliminated. Only (H) is left.

59. **C** Choose the most concise answer that works in the context.

60. **J** The modifying phrase *Full of tenderness and affection* has to refer correctly to the words after the comma. The context of the rest of the sentence makes clear that it refers to the *friendship*, which eliminates (F) and (G). Choice (J) is correct because it's more concise than (H).

Passage V

61. **B** In this portion of the sentence, the subject is *my aunt* and the verb is *gave*, so there's no reason to introduce another verb as (A), (C), and (D) do. Choice (B) is correct because it removes the verb and adds the necessary first comma needed to offset the unnecessary *a research chemist*.

62. **F**   Identify the purpose of the correct choice as stated in the question, which asks for a choice that *completes the sentence and uses sarcasm*. Choices (G), (H), and (J) may be true, but they are simple statements of fact rather than sarcastic remarks. Choice (F) gives a sarcastic remark that emphasizes how unsuccessful the experiments were.

63. **B**   Use the vertical line test. The first idea is complete, but the second idea is incomplete, which eliminates (A). Note that the colon in (C) is in a different place than the semicolon in (A). With the addition of *like*, the idea before the vertical line is now incomplete, which eliminates (C). A colon can follow only a complete idea. Choice (D) is incorrect because by changing the infinitive *to keep* to the command *keep*, the second idea is now complete. However, the comma is GO punctuation and can't link two complete ideas on its own. Choice (B) correctly uses a colon in between two complete ideas. When a colon separates two ideas, the second idea can be upper or lowercase.

64. **H**   The contraction *you're* cannot be used in this context because the possessive pronoun *your* should modify the noun *knowledge*, which eliminates (F) and (J). If you can't cite a reason to use a comma, don't use one. In this case, there is no reason to place a comma after the word *world*, so (G) can be eliminated.

65. **A**   Identify the purpose of the correct choice as stated in the question, which asks for a choice that emphasizes that the aunt's advice was *very difficult to implement*. Eliminate (B) and (D) because they are simply statements of whether the narrator agreed or disagreed. Choice (C) is closer, but it doesn't quite address the advice. Choice (A), *so far out of reach*, does the best job of showing that implementing the aunt's advice is beyond the narrator's ability.

66. **H**   Use the vertical line test. The first idea, *"We all struggle at first," she told me, as she sat next to me in my "laboratory,"* is complete. Evaluate the second idea in (H), the only one with STOP punctuation. *Near defeat, I watched as she set up one of the simple experiments.* The period works in between the two complete ideas, so (H) is correct.

67. **D**   This verb should be in the past tense to be consistent with the rest of the sentence and passage. Choices (A), (B), and (C) can therefore be eliminated, leaving only (D).

68. **H**   This question is a Strategy/Order combination. Identify the purpose as stated in the question, which asks for the place in the paragraph to separate the *list of chemistry principles from the anecdote*. The Order part of the question appears in the answer choices. The anecdote starts just after Point C, where the narrator mentions that she *whimpered to her aunt one day*, making (H) correct.

69. **B**   Choose a transition that is consistent with the meaning of the sentence. Choices (A), (C), and (D) suggest a contrast, but there is none in the passage. Only (B), *then*, shows a simple continuation from one event to another, as the passage itself contains.

70. **H** The word *complement* means "to complete" or "to go with"; the word *compliment* means "to say something nice." Therefore, *complement* is the correct word in this sentence, thus eliminating (F) and (J). Choice (H) is correct because the portion of the sentence, *right next to each other in this way*, is unnecessary to the meaning of the sentence and should therefore be set off with commas.

71. **B** Use the vertical line test. The first idea is complete, but the second idea is incomplete, which eliminates (A). Choice (B) is correct because a comma, as GO punctuation, can come in between a complete and incomplete idea. Choice (C) adds another word, but the word *There* does not create a complete idea, so STOP punctuation is still incorrect. Choice (D) adds the correct word but the incorrect punctuation, as now there are two complete ideas separated only by a comma.

72. **J** The correct past participle of *combine* is *combined*, so *had combine* cannot work, which eliminates (F). Choice (G) is caveman-speak, so it can't be used. Choice (H) is redundant because the word *had* is already contained in the contraction *she'd*. Only (J) can work because it contains the correct helping verb and the correct past participle.

73. **D** The correct word in this sentence is *react*, as it describes a chemical reaction between two different things. The words in the other choices are not consistent with the context.

74. **G** Choice (G) is correct because there is no need for a comma. If you can't cite a reason to use commas, don't use them.

75. **C** Choice (C) is correct because the reason describes the passage accurately. Choice (A) is wrong because, while the passage does state that the aunt was able to create different colored dyes, the narrator failed despite following the simple rules. Choices (B) and (D) are incorrect because the reasons given do not describe the passage accurately.

Part III
ACT Mathematics

Chapter 10
Introduction to the ACT Mathematics Test

The ACT Math Test is always the second section of the ACT.

If you're aiming for the highest scores on the ACT, you probably already have a broad range of math skills. In fact, you probably already know the math required to answer almost every question on the typical ACT Math Test. So why aren't you already scoring a 36 on Math?

A student with strong math skills is often accustomed to solving problems with what we might call "brute force brainpower": see a question, attack it, try methods to solve it until you find a solution, and then move on to the next question. While this approach can get you a pretty good score on the ACT Math Test, you'll need to refine this approach with a few strategies to get to the highest scores.

For instance, students sometimes underestimate the easy and medium questions, not taking them as seriously as the "hard" questions near the end. But to get the highest scores, you can't afford errors on *any* of the easy and medium questions. So, you'll need to watch out for traps on those questions that might lead you into careless errors. And, of course, you'll need good time management strategies, so that you can move through questions efficiently and ensure you have the time to get to the correct answer on the longer, tougher questions.

The first step is to make sure you understand the structure of the ACT Math Test and some fundamental strategies that will increase your test savvy. This chapter will discuss the types of questions you should expect and the ways you can use organizational strategy, estimation, and elimination skills to improve your efficiency and accuracy, and to earn a higher Math score.

WHAT TO EXPECT ON THE MATH TEST

You will have 60 minutes to answer 60 multiple-choice questions based on "topics covered in typical high-school classes." For those of you who aren't sure if you went to a typical high school, these questions break down into rather precise areas of knowledge.

The Math Test usually includes

33 Algebra questions

- 14 pre-algebra questions based on math terminology (such as integers and prime numbers), basic number theory (rules of zero, order of operations), and manipulation of fractions and decimals
- 10 elementary algebra questions based on inequalities, linear equations, ratios, percents, and averages
- 9 intermediate algebra questions based on exponents, roots, simultaneous equations, and quadratic equations

23 Geometry questions

- 14 plane geometry questions based on angles, lengths, triangles, quadrilaterals, circles, perimeter, area, and volume
- 9 coordinate geometry questions based on slope, distance, midpoint, parallel and perpendicular lines, points of intersection, and graphing

4 Trigonometry questions

- 4 questions based on basic sine, cosine, and tangent functions, trig identities, and graphing

---

WHAT NOT TO EXPECT ON THE MATH TEST

Unlike the SAT, the ACT does *not* provide any formulas at the beginning of the Math Test. This means you need to memorize those formulas so you can recall them quickly as needed throughout the ACT Math Test. Does this mean that the ACT Math Test is harder than the SATs Math section? Not necessarily: since the SAT includes those formulas at the beginning of each Math section, the SAT math questions need to be trickier than they might otherwise be. On the ACT, a question could simply test whether you know the formula, so the Math Test doesn't need to be quite as tricky.

A NOTE ON CALCULATORS

The ACT allows calculators on the Math section, but it prohibits, among others, the TI-89, TI-92, and TI-Nspire CAS models. Be sure to check which calculators are allowed before you take the test! Your calculator can definitely come in handy for complicated calculations; to be efficient on the test, you'll probably want to use a calculator occasionally. But be careful, especially on the early questions! Some of them are designed with "calculator traps" in mind—careless errors the test writers know you might make when you just dive into a problem on your calculator. Let's look at an example.

27. Given the function $r(s) = 5s^2 - s - 7$, what is $r(-4)$?

    A.   −91
    B.   −83
    C.   69
    D.   77
    E.   397

How to Solve It

This problem can be solved manually or with the calculator—whichever you prefer! But if you use a calculator, be careful with that −4. What you punch into your calculator should look something like this:

$$5(-4)^2 - (-4) - 7$$

When working with negative numbers or fractions, make doubly sure that you use parentheses. If not, a lot of weird stuff can happen, and unfortunately all of the weird, wrong stuff that can happen is reflected in the wrong answer choices. If you ran this equation and found 77, (D), you got the right answer. If not, go back and figure out where you made your calculator mistake.

Types of Calculators

Throughout the rest of the Math chapters, we discuss ways to solve calculator-friendly questions in an accurate and manageable way. Because TI-89, TI-92, and TI-Nspire CAS model calculators are not allowed on the ACT, we will show you how to solve problems on the TI-83. If you don't plan to use a TI-83 on the test, we recommend you make sure your calculator is acceptable for use on the test and that it can do the following:

- handle positive, negative, and fractional exponents
- use parentheses
- graph simple functions
- convert fractions to decimals and vice versa
- change a linear equation into $y = mx + b$ form

Use your calculator, but use it wisely. Be careful with negative numbers and fractions.

THE PRINCETON REVIEW APPROACH

Because the test is so predictable, the best way to prepare for ACT Math is with

- a thorough review of the very specific information and question types that come up repeatedly.
- an understanding of The Princeton Review's test-taking strategies and techniques.

In each Math chapter in this book, you'll find a mixture of review and technique, with a sprinkling of ACT-like problems. At the end of each chapter (except the Introduction to Math), there is a summary of the chapter and a drill designed to pinpoint your math test-taking strengths and weaknesses. In addition to working through the problems in this book, we strongly suggest you practice our techniques on some real ACT practice tests.

Let's begin with some general strategies.

Order of Difficulty: Still Personal Even For High Scorers

Why should a high-scoring student care about the order of difficulty on the ACT Math Test? If you've got the math skills to do all—or almost all—of the questions on the ACT Math Test, you may think the best approach for you is to dive straight in and do the questions in order. That's not necessarily the best approach, though.

The Math Test is the only part of the ACT that is presented in Order of Difficulty (OOD). What this means is that the easier questions tend to be a bit earlier in the exam, and the harder questions tend to be later. None of the other tests have an OOD, so they are all about Personal Order of Difficulty (POOD).

The Math OOD is helpful for planning how you will attack this part of the ACT. Just because the earlier questions are generally easier does not mean they are safe to move through quickly. Not every question near the beginning will be easy, and questions that are easy for one student may be difficult for another. Regardless, if you're aiming for the highest scores, you need to take every question seriously. It would be a shame to go get all those "hard" questions right, and miss the top score because you made careless errors rushing through the earlier questions.

So what makes a hard question hard? Is it hard because it's a long word problem, or because it tests an arcane concept that you haven't reviewed in years? Only the very hardest questions will be both. So even on the Math Test of the ACT, you still need to use your POOD to adjust your approach for different types of questions. Know what sort of questions tend to lead you into careless errors, and slow down on them. Work every step of the problem methodically, showing your work at every step.

Now, Later, Never

Hard questions generally take longer to work through than short questions. That's obvious, but as we've seen, the definition of an "Easy" question is a tough one to pin down. That's why you'll want to be careful with ACT's Order of Difficulty on the Math Test. The no-brainer approach is to open the test booklet and work questions 1 through 60 in order, but you can help to lock in the higher scores by outsmarting the test. You'll have a lot easier time drawing your own road map for this test rather than letting ACT guide you.

Of course, a lot of the easy questions will be near the beginning, but they won't all be. So, when you arrive at each question, you'll want to first determine whether it is a Now, Later, or Never question. Do the Now questions immediately: they're the freebies, the ones you know how to do and can do quickly and accurately. Skip any questions you think might take you a bit longer, or that test unfamiliar concepts—save them for Later. Make sure you first get all the points you can on the problems you know you can do, no matter what the question number.

Once you've done all the Now questions, go back to all the ones you left for Later. But you should be careful on these as well. For both Now and Later questions, don't rush and make careless errors. On the other hand, if you find yourself spinning your wheels on a question, circle the question number and come back to it at the end if you have time. Don't get stuck on a particular problem. In a 60-minute exam, think of how much it can cost you to spend 5 minutes on a single problem!

Finally, there's no problem with leaving a question or two behind in the Never category. But wait, what's a Never question for a top scorer? Sometimes a question might be on a topic that you simply didn't cover; maybe you missed the week your teacher taught matrices, or logarithms, or the unit circle. Or for whatever reason, you have no idea how to approach a problem. In that case, your time is likely better spent on other questions (and it's still possible to get a 34 or better on the Math Test even if you miss a question or two).

Note, of course, that you should **never leave a question blank** on the ACT, since there is no penalty for guessing. If you skip any questions, fill them in with a Letter of the Day: choose one pair of letters and bubble in all blanks this way. For example, always bubble in (A) and (F) or (B) and (G). This will maximize your chance of getting some of the guesses right.

Chapter 11
Plug and Chug

Questions on the ACT Math Test can be divided into two categories: word problems and Plug and Chug problems. Plug and Chug problems are questions that present you with math problems you can just manipulate and solve, while word problems require you to translate the words of the problem into math before you start solving.

Plug and Chug problems often test skills from the following areas:

- Math Fundamentals (vocabulary, number theory, prime numbers, factors, multiples, exponents, and roots)
- Plane Geometry
- Coordinate Geometry
- Trigonometry

This chapter covers the material you need to know in each of the areas above in order to earn the highest scores on the ACT Math Test.

MATH FUNDAMENTALS

Vocabulary

The ACT Math questions love to test vocabulary words. Make sure you're familiar with all of these definitions:

Absolute Value:	The distance from zero on the number line
Consecutive:	In increasing order
Decimal:	A way of expressing a fraction in which numbers are divided by ten, hundred, thousand, and other powers of ten
Difference:	The result of subtraction
Digits:	The integers 0 through 9
Distinct:	Different
Divisible:	An integer can be divided by another integer evenly, with no fraction or decimal left over
Even:	Divisible by 2
Exponent/Power:	A number that indicates how many times to multiply a base by itself
Factors:	Integers that multiply together to make a given product
Fraction:	A way of expressing the division of numbers by stacking one over the other

Greatest Common Factor:	The largest factor common to two numbers
Imaginary:	The square root (or other even root) of a negative number
Integers:	All real numbers other than decimals or fractions
Irrational:	A number that can be expressed as a decimal but not a fraction
Least Common Multiple:	The smallest multiple common to two numbers
Multiple:	The product of an integer and another integer
Negative:	Less than 0
Non-negative:	Zero or positive
Non-positive:	Zero or negative
Number:	Any number (including real, irrational, transcendental, and imaginary numbers)
Odd:	NOT divisible by 2
Opposite:	Two numbers with the same distance from zero on the number line, but one is positive and the other negative
Opposite Reciprocal:	The negative reciprocal
Order of Operations:	Parentheses (or "Brackets," outside the United States), Exponents, Multiplication and Division, Addition and Subtraction
Positive:	Greater than 0
Prime:	A number that has exactly two distinct factors: 1 and itself (1 is not prime)
Product:	The result of multiplication
Quotient:	The result of division
Real:	Any non-imaginary number (including zero, all positive and negative integers, fractions, decimals, roots, irrational numbers, and transcendental numbers)
Radical:	Another word for the $\sqrt{}$ sign
Rational:	A number that can be expressed as the ratio of two other numbers (a fraction)
Reciprocal:	The inverse of a number—flip the numerator and the denominator.
Remainder:	The number left over in long division when a number is not evenly divisible by another number
Sum:	The result of addition

Factors and Multiples

Factors and multiples are two sides of the same coin. Factors are integers that can be multiplied together to form a number; multiples result when an integer is multiplied by another integer.

A Good Rule of Thumb

- The positive factors of a number are always equal to that number or *smaller*.
- The positive multiples of a number are always equal to that number or *larger*.

For instance, the positive factors of 24 are 1, 2, 3, 4, 6, 8, 12, and 24. The first four positive multiples of 24 are 24, 48, 72, and 96.

The ACT Math Test will play around with this vocabulary and try to trip you up. For example, consider the following statements:

- x is a factor of 24
- 24 is evenly divisible by x
- when 24 is divided by x, the result is an integer
- when 24 is divided by x, there is no remainder
- 24 is a multiple of x

For each of the above statements, the possible values for x are the same: 1, 2, 3, 4, 6, 8, 12, and 24.

Also, be sure you are familiar with these definitions:

- Least Common Multiple: the lowest number that is a multiple of each of two other numbers
- Greatest Common Factor: the largest number that is a factor of each of two other numbers

Exercise (Vocabulary):

See exercise answers on page 142.

1. List the factors of 36.
2. List the first four positive multiples of 36.
3. Is 8 a multiple or a factor of 24?
4. What is the greatest common factor of 24 and 36?
5. What is the least common multiple of 24 and 36?

Prime Numbers

Many students learn that the definition of a prime number is something like "A prime number is a number that is divisible only by 1 and itself." This definition is a bit confusing, since it leaves open the idea that 1 might itself be a prime number. We need a more precise definition.

> A prime number is any number that has
> exactly two distinct factors (1 and itself).

This definition helps clear up why 1 is not a prime number: it has only one distinct factor.

It also helps with 0: Why isn't 0 prime? It has infinitely many factors.

> The prime factorization of a number is the reduction of a number to its prime factors. Find the prime factorization of a number by using a factor tree. Example:
>
>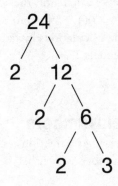

Exercise (Prime Numbers):

1. List the single-digit prime numbers.
2. What is the only even prime number?
3. What is the prime factorization of 45?
4. What is the sum of the prime factors of 45?
5. What is the sum of the distinct prime factors of 45?

See exercise answers on page 142.

Real vs. Imaginary Numbers

Many ACT Math Tests include a question or two about imaginary numbers. As long as you know the basics of imaginary numbers, you should be well-prepared for these questions.

Real numbers include every type of number except imaginary numbers. Real numbers include all the rational numbers (positive and negative integers, zero, and numbers with fractional or decimal components), as well as the irrational numbers (decimals that cannot be expressed as a fraction and transcendental numbers such as π and e).

> Imaginary numbers are numbers that cannot exist on the real number line. Imaginary numbers result when you attempt to take an even-numbered root of a negative number. The number $\sqrt{-1}$ is defined as the imaginary number i. All other imaginary numbers are expressed as a number multiplied by i.

You can use a calculator to easily deal with most problems involving imaginary numbers. On a Texas Instruments calculator, the second function of the decimal is i. For instance, try entering $(4 + i)(4 - i)$ in your calculator. The result will be 17. Or, if you prefer, you can do the calculations by hand: $(4 + i)(4 - i)$ equals $4^2 - i^2$, which equals $16 - (-1)$, which equals 17.

Rational vs. Irrational Numbers

A rational number can be expressed as a fraction—one integer divided by another. In decimal form, a rational number will either be a terminating decimal or a repeating pattern.

An irrational number cannot be expressed as a fraction, because the decimal portion continues forever without repeating.

Occasionally, the ACT Math Test asks you to determine whether a number is irrational. One way to check this on a Texas Instruments calculator is to attempt to convert the value to a fraction. Enter the value on the calculator and then access the >*Frac* command by hitting ENTER, then MATH>ENTER>ENTER. If the number can be converted to a fraction, then the number is rational.

Exponents

Exponents, at the most basic level, are used to indicate that a number is multiplied by itself. For example, $7^5 = 7 \times 7 \times 7 \times 7 \times 7$ (the number 7 multiplied by itself 5 times).

Basic Exponent Rules

You have likely already memorized a number of special exponent rules in order to deal with exponent problems. Most of these rules, however, derive from a few basic rules, so it's helpful to see how the rules all fit together. All the exponent rules stem from the basic "M^{A}D^{S}P^M" rules:

- When you *Multiply* two exponential expressions with the same base, *Add* the exponents.
- When you *Divide* two exponential expressions with the same base, *Subtract* the exponents.
- When you raise an exponential expression to a *Power* (another exponent), *Multiply* the exponents.

Exercise (Exponents):

Simplify the following expressions.

1. $(x^2)(x^3)$

2. $\dfrac{x^5}{x^3}$

3. $\left(x^3\right)^5$

4. $x^3 \times 3x^4$

5. $(3x^4)^3$

6. $\dfrac{15x^7}{5x^3}$

7. $\dfrac{(3x^3)(8x^5)}{(6x^4)}$

See exercise answers on page 142.

Special Exponent Rules

The special exponent rules are all straightforward variations of the basic exponent rules.

1. $\dfrac{x^5}{x^5} = 1$

2. $x^0 = 1$

Note that both of the expressions above simplify to 1. When the numerator and denominator are the same, they cancel out and leave 1 as the result. The $M^AD^SP^M$ rules tell you to subtract the exponents, leaving an exponent of zero. Thus, any number raised to an exponent of zero equals 1, since the top and bottom are equal and cancel out.

3. $\dfrac{y^3}{y^5} = \dfrac{1}{y^2}$

4. $y^{-2} = \dfrac{1}{y^2}$

Note that both of the above expressions simplify to $\dfrac{1}{y^2}$. The expression $\dfrac{y^3}{y^5}$ is equivalent to $\dfrac{y \times y \times y}{y \times y \times y \times y \times y}$. The three y's in the numerator cancel out with three of the y's in the denominator, resulting in $\dfrac{1}{y^2}$. The $M^AD^SP^M$ rules tell you to subtract the exponents, which also results in y^{-2}. Thus, when a negative exponent is applied to a number, it means simply to take the reciprocal of the number.

5. $x^1 = x$
6. $1^{635} = 1$
7. $0^{124} = 0$

Any number to the power of 1 equals itself.
1 to any power equals 1. 0 to any power equals 0.

---

8. $(-3)^2 = 9$
9. $(-3)^3 = -27$
10. $-3^2 = -9$

A negative number to an even power is positive; a negative number to an odd power remains negative. Note, however, that the exponent applies to the minus sign only if the minus sign is inside the parentheses.

11. $\left(\dfrac{1}{4}\right)^2 = \dfrac{1}{16}$

12. $\left(\dfrac{3}{7}\right)^2 = \dfrac{9}{49}$

Numbers between 0 and 1 (fractions) raised to a power become smaller. Numbers greater than 1 raised to a power become larger.

Roots

The rules for roots are similar to the rules for exponents. The M^{A}D^{S}P^M rules apply when two numbers with the same *base* are multiplied or divided. Separate rules apply when two numbers with different bases both have the same *exponent* and are multiplied or divided:

$$(x^2)(y^2) = (xy)^2$$

$$\frac{x^2}{y^2} = \left(\frac{x}{y}\right)^2$$

The same rules apply as long as the exponents are the same, even when the exponent is a root (a fraction):

$$(x^{\frac{1}{2}})(y^{\frac{1}{2}}) = (xy)^{\frac{1}{2}}$$

$$\sqrt{x}\sqrt{y} = \sqrt{xy}$$

$$\frac{\sqrt{x}}{\sqrt{y}} = \sqrt{\frac{x}{y}}$$

Note that these rules don't apply for adding or subtracting. Numbers can only be added together when both the base and the exponent are the same.

$$3x^2 + 4x^2 = 7x^2$$

$$3\sqrt{x} + 4\sqrt{x} = 7\sqrt{x}$$

Exercise (Roots):

1. $\sqrt{x} + \sqrt{x}$

2. $2\sqrt{x} + 4\sqrt{x}$

3. $x\sqrt{2} + x\sqrt{5}$

See exercise answers on page 142.

4. $\left(\sqrt{5x}\right)\left(\sqrt{3y}\right)$

5. $\left(\sqrt{x}\right)\left(\sqrt{xy}\right)$

6. $\left(4\sqrt{6}\right)\left(5\sqrt{54}\right)$

7. $\dfrac{\sqrt{108}}{\sqrt{3}}$

8. $\left(\sqrt{484} - \sqrt{324}\right)^{\frac{1}{2}}$

How Exponents Relate to Roots

Exponents generally make numbers get bigger: 4 squared is 16, and so on. But exponents make fractions smaller instead of bigger. Why is that? Because exponents don't simply make numbers *larger*. Rather, it's easier to think of exponents as a method for moving the value of a number toward or away from the number 1. Consider the following:

$$4^2 = 16$$

$$4^1 = 4$$

$$4^{\frac{1}{2}} = 2$$

$$4^0 = 1$$

$$4^{-\frac{1}{2}} = \frac{1}{2}$$

$$4^{-1} = \frac{1}{4}$$

$$4^{-2} = \frac{1}{16}$$

When an exponent is applied to a number that is greater than 1, an exponent moves the number *toward* or *away from* the number 1. An exponent greater than 1 moves the number *away from* 1; an exponent of 1 keeps the number the same; a fractional exponent moves the number *toward* 1; an exponent of zero makes the number *equal to* 1; and a negative exponent makes the number *less than* 1.

Consider the same sequence of exponents applied to a fraction:

$$\left(\frac{1}{4}\right)^2 = \frac{1}{16}$$

$$\left(\frac{1}{4}\right)^1 = \frac{1}{4}$$

$$\left(\frac{1}{4}\right)^{\frac{1}{2}} = \frac{1}{2}$$

$$\left(\frac{1}{4}\right)^0 = 1$$

$$\left(\frac{1}{4}\right)^{-\frac{1}{2}} = 2$$

$$\left(\frac{1}{4}\right)^{-1} = 4$$

$$\left(\frac{1}{4}\right)^{-2} = 16$$

For fractions (numbers less than 1), the exponent has the same, but opposite, effect: An exponent greater than 1 moves the fraction *away from* 1; an exponent of 1 keeps the fraction the same; a fractional exponent moves the number *toward* 1; an exponent of zero makes it *equal to* 1; and a negative exponent makes the number *greater* than 1.

So, exponents don't make numbers *larger* or *smaller*; they are a tool for moving numbers *toward* or *away from* the number 1.

EXERCISE ANSWERS

Exercise: Vocabulary
1. 1, 2, 3, 4, 6, 9, 12, 18, 36
2. 36, 72, 108, 144
3. factor
4. 12
5. 72

Exercise: Prime Numbers
1. 2, 3, 5, 7
2. 2
3. 3, 3, 5
4. 11
5. 8

Exercise: Exponents
1. x^5
2. x^2
3. x^{15}
4. $3x^7$
5. $27x^{12}$
6. $3x^4$
7. $4x^4$

Exercise: Roots
1. $2\sqrt{x}$
2. $6\sqrt{x}$
3. Can't be combined!
4. $\sqrt{15xy}$
5. $\sqrt{x^2 y} = x\sqrt{y}$
6. 360
7. 6
8. $(22 - 18)^{\frac{1}{2}} = (4)^{\frac{1}{2}} = 2$

PLANE GEOMETRY

The ACT Math Test includes about 14 questions covering plane geometry. While some of these questions will cover complex shapes or advanced formulas, it's helpful to realize that most of the questions will test the <u>same</u> basic shapes and rules. Harder geometry questions generally just combine simple rules and shapes in ways that make them hard to identify. *Noticing this pattern is the key to solving ACT geometry questions quickly and accurately.*

Attacking ACT Geometry Questions

High-scoring students have a tendency to start solving geometry problems in their head as they go. As soon as you see a geometric shape and some values, it's tempting to simply start calculating everything you can about the figure. As often happens on the ACT, though, *thinking* turns out to be a bad—or at least an inefficient—way to start off any given problem.

Instead, always attack geometry problems by using these simple steps, and you will be amazed at how much more directly—and simply—you will arrive at the solution.

Step 1: Know the Question

Read through the entire problem before you begin calculating. Underline the actual question. Leave the *thinking* until later.

Step 2: Let the Answers Help

Take a look at the answers. Sometimes the form of the answers provides a good clue about how to efficiently work the problem.

Step 3: Break the Problem into Bite-Sized Pieces

Start back at the beginning of the problem, and work through the problem piece by piece. Start by labeling all the information in the problem on the figure (or drawing the figure, if one isn't provided). Next, write down all the geometry formulas related to the problem, fill in the information you know, and let the formulas show you what to solve for next.

POE and Ballparking

Step 2 of the approach to geometry questions ("Let the Answers Help") is a key to POE and Ballparking on geometry questions. Ballparking's not just a tool to use if you aren't sure how to do a question—it's also a powerful way of getting through questions quickly and easily.

Why spend three minutes fighting through a question when it can be solved quickly and easily by simply looking at the answers and estimating from the figure? The time and brainpower you save on questions like this can be used to attack the hardest questions that you need some extra time to work through.

Scale Matters

Although the ACT says that geometry figures are "NOT necessarily drawn to scale," most of them usually are—at least enough to do some estimating. The exception is problems that are specifically testing rules about shapes: if a problem asks what *must be true* about the figure above, usually you can't trust the scale of the figure at all. The end of this chapter will include drills to test your ability to use POE and Ballparking on tough geometry questions.

How Big Is Angle *NLM* ?

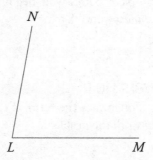

Obviously, you don't know exactly how big this angle is, but it would be easy to compare it with an angle whose measure you *do* know exactly. Let's compare it with a 90-degree angle.

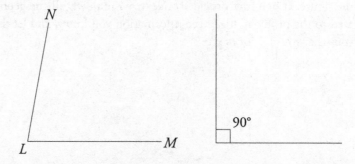

Angle *NLM* is clearly a bit less than 90°. Now look at the following problem, which asks about the same angle *NLM*.

———————○———————

1. In the figure below, *O*, *N*, and *M* are collinear. If the lengths of $\overline{ON}$ and $\overline{NL}$ are the same, and the measure of angle *LON* is 30° and angle *LMN* is 40°, what is the measure of angle *NLM* ?

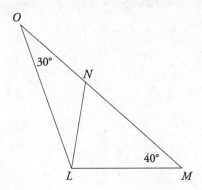

   A. 30°
   B. 80°
   C. 90°
   D. 110°
   E. 120°

Here's How to Crack It

Start with Step 1: Know the question. Underline "what is the measure of angle *NLM* ?" and even mark the angle on your figure. You don't want to answer for the wrong angle. Now move to Step 2 and let's focus on eliminating answer choices that don't make sense. We've already decided that ∠*NLM* is a little less than 90°, which means we can eliminate (C), (D), and (E). How much less than 90°? 30° is a third of 90. Could ∠*NLM* be that small? No way! The answer to this question must be (B).

In this case, it wasn't necessary to do any "real" geometry at all to get the question right, but it took about half the time. ACT has to give you credit for right answers no matter how you get them. Revenge is sweet. What's more, if you worked this problem the "real" way, you might have picked one of the other answers: As you can imagine, every answer choice gives some partial answer that you would've seen as you worked the problem.

———————○———————

Let's Do It Again

2. In the figure below, if $\overline{AB} = 27$, $\overline{CD} = 20$, and the area of triangle $ADC = 240$, what is the area of polygon $ABCD$?

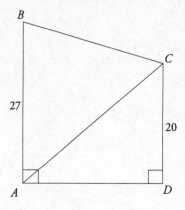

    F.   420
    G.   480
    H.   540
    J.   564
    K. 1,128

Here's How to Crack It

Start with Step 1: Know the question. Underline "what is the area of polygon *ABCD*?" This polygon is not a conventional figure, but if we had to choose one figure that the polygon resembled, we might pick a rectangle. Try drawing a line at a right angle from the line segment $\overline{AB}$ so that it touches point *C*, thus creating a rectangle. It should look like this:

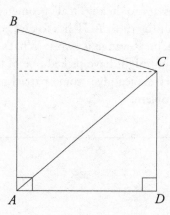

The area of polygon *ABCD* is equal to the area of the rectangle you've just formed, plus a little bit at the top. The problem tells you that the area of triangle *ADC* is 240. What is the area of the rectangle you just created? If you said 480, you are exactly right, whether you knew the geometric rules that applied or whether you just measured it with your eyes.

So the area of the rectangle is 480. Roughly speaking, then, what should the area of the polygon be? A little more. Let's look at the answer choices. Choices (F) and (G) are either less than or equal to 480; get rid of them. Choices (H) and (J) both seem possible; they are both a little more than 480; let's hold on to them. Choice (K) seems pretty crazy. We want more than 480, but 1,128 is ridiculous.

---○---

The answer to this question is (J). To get this final answer, you'll need to use a variety of area formulas, which we'll explore later in this chapter. For now, though, notice that your chances of guessing have increased from 20% to 50% with a little bit of quick thinking. Now what should you do? If you know how to do the problem, you do it. If you don't or if you are running out of time, you guess and move on.

However, even as we move in to the "real" geometry in the remainder of this chapter, don't forget:

> Always look for opportunities to Ballpark on geometry problems even if you know how to do them the "real" way.

GEOMETRY REVIEW

Often on an ACT geometry question, several answer choices can be eliminated based solely on the diagram provided (or by drawing the diagram described by the problem, if a diagram is not given). Sometimes you can even completely solve the problem just from the diagram.

One important feature of ACT geometry questions is that the "hard" questions don't necessarily test "hard" concepts; rather, they often combine several basic concepts together and disguise them so that it's hard to determine where to start, and so that multiple steps are required to come to a solution. The first step, of course, is to ensure you have mastered all the basic geometry rules tested by the ACT. We've divided our review into the following four topics.

1. Angles and lines
2. Triangles
3. Four-sided figures
4. Circles

ANGLES AND LINES

Here is a line.

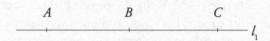

A line extends forever in either direction. This line, called l_1, has three points on it: *A*, *B*, and *C*. These three points are said to be **collinear** because they are all on the same line. The piece of the line in between points *A* and *B* is called a line **segment**. ACT will refer to it as segment *AB* or simply $\overline{AB}$. *A* and *B* are the **endpoints** of segment *AB*.

A line forms an angle of 180°. If that line is cut by another line, it divides that 180° into two pieces that together add up to 180°.

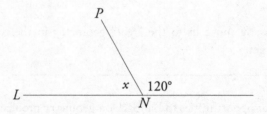

In the above diagram, what is the value of *x*? If you said 60°, you are correct. To find $\angle x$, just subtract 120° from 180°.

An angle can also be described by points on the lines that intersect to form the angle and the point of intersection itself, with the middle letter corresponding to the point of intersection. For example, in the previous diagram, $\angle x$ could also be described as $\angle LNP$. On the ACT, instead of writing out "angle *LNP*," they'll use math shorthand and put $\angle LNP$ instead. So, "angle *x*" becomes $\angle x$.

If there are 180° above a line, there are also 180° below the line, for a total of 360°.

When two lines intersect, they form four angles, represented below by letters *A*, *B*, *C*, and *D*. ∠*A* and ∠*B* together form a straight line, so they add up to 180°.

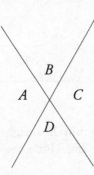

Angles that add up to 180° are called **supplementary** angles. ∠*A* and ∠*C* are opposite from each other and always equal each other, as do ∠*B* and ∠*D*. Angles like these are called **vertical** angles.

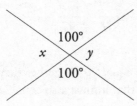

In the previous figure, what is the value of ∠*x*? If you said 80°, you're right. Together with the 100° angle, *x* forms a straight line. What is the value of ∠*y*? If you said 80°, you're right again. These two angles are vertical and must equal each other. The four angles together add up to 360°.

When two lines meet in such a way that 90° angles are formed, the lines are called **perpendicular**. The little box at the point of the intersection of the two lines below indicates that they are perpendicular. It stands to reason that all four of these angles have a value of 90°.

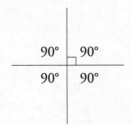

When two lines in the same plane are drawn so that they could extend into infinity without ever meeting, they are called **parallel**. In the figure below, l_1 is parallel to l_2. The symbol for parallel is | |.

When two parallel lines are cut by a third line, eight angles are formed, but in fact, there are really only two—a big one and a little one. Look at the diagram below.

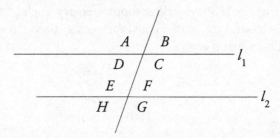

If $\angle A = 110°$, then $\angle B$ must equal 70° (together they form a straight line). $\angle D$ is vertical to $\angle B$, which means that it must also equal 70°. $\angle C$ is vertical to $\angle A$, so it must equal 110°.

The four angles $\angle E$, $\angle F$, $\angle G$, and $\angle H$ are in exactly the same proportion as the angles above. The little angles are both 70°. The big angles are both 110°.

Try the following problem.

1. In the figure below, line L is parallel to line M. Line N intersects both L and M, with angles a, b, c, d, e, f, g, and h as shown. Which of the following lists includes all the angles that are supplementary to $\angle a$?

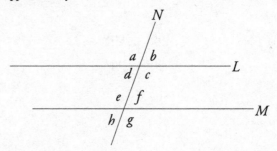

    A. Angles b, d, f, and h
    B. Angles c, e, and g
    C. Angles b, d, and c
    D. Angles e, f, g, and h
    E. Angles d, c, h, and g

Here's How to Crack It

An angle is supplementary to another angle if the two angles together add up to 180°. Because ∠a is one of the eight angles formed by the intersection of a line with two parallel lines, we know that there are really only two angles: a big one and a little one. ∠a is a big one. Thus, only the small angles would be supplementary to it. Which angles are those? The correct answer is (A). By the way, if you think back to the last chapter and apply what you learned there, could you have Plugged In on this problem? Of course you could have. After all, there are variables in the answer choices. Sometimes it is easier to see the correct answer if you substitute real values for the angles instead of just looking at them as a series of variables. Just because a problem involves geometry doesn't mean that you can't Plug In on it.

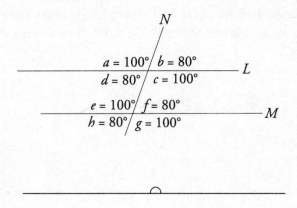

TRIANGLES

A triangle is a three-sided figure whose inside angles always add up to 180°. The largest angle of a triangle is always opposite its largest side. Thus, in triangle *XYZ* below, *XY* would be the largest side, followed by *YZ*, followed by *XZ*. On the ACT, "triangle *XYZ*" will be written as △*XYZ*.

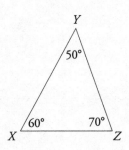

The ACT likes to ask about certain kinds of triangles in particular.

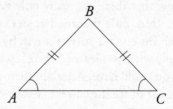

An **isosceles** triangle has two equal sides. The angles opposite those sides are also equal. In the isosceles triangle above, if $\angle A = 50°$, then so does $\angle C$. If $\overline{AB} = 6$, then so does $\overline{BC}$.

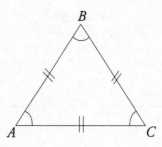

An **equilateral** triangle has three equal sides and three equal angles. Because the three equal angles must add up to 180°, all three angles of an equilateral triangle are always equal to 60°.

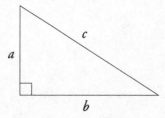

A **right triangle** has one inside angle that is equal to 90°. The longest side of a right triangle (the one opposite the 90° angle) is called the **hypotenuse**.

Pythagoras, a Greek mathematician, discovered that the sides of a right triangle are always in a particular proportion, which can be expressed by the formula $a^2 + b^2 = c^2$, where a and b are the shorter sides of the triangle, and c is the hypotenuse. This formula is called the **Pythagorean theorem**.

There are certain right triangles that the test writers at ACT find endlessly fascinating. Let's test out the Pythagorean theorem on the first of these.

$$3^2 + 4^2 = c^2$$
$$9 + 16 = 25$$
$$c^2 = 25, \text{ so } c = 5$$

The ACT writers adore the 3-4-5 triangle and use it frequently, along with its multiples, such as the 6-8-10 triangle and the 9-12-15 triangle. Of course, you can always use the Pythagorean theorem to figure out the third side of a right triangle, as long as you have the other two sides, but because ACT problems almost invariably use "triples" like the ones we've just mentioned, it makes sense just to memorize them.

The ACT has three commonly used right-triangle triples.

3-4-5 (and its multiples)

5-12-13 (and its multiples)

7-24-25 (not as common as the other two)

Don't Get Snared

- Is this a 3-4-5 triangle?

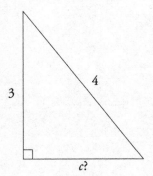

Pythagoras's *Other* Theorem
Pythagoras also developed a theory about the transmigration of souls. So far, this has not been proven, nor will it help you on this exam.

No, because the hypotenuse of a right triangle must be its *longest* side—the one opposite the 90° angle. In this case, we must use the Pythagorean theorem to discover side c: $3^2 + c^2 = 16$. $c = \sqrt{7}$.

- Is this a 5-12-13 triangle?

No, because the Pythagorean theorem—and triples—apply only to *right* triangles. We can't determine definitively the third side of this triangle based on the angles.

The Isosceles Right Triangle

As fond as the ACT test writers are of triples, they are even fonder of two other right triangles. The first is called the **isosceles right triangle**. The sides and angles of the isosceles right triangle are always in a particular proportion.

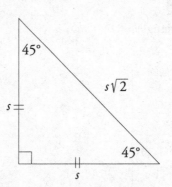

> **Be on the Lookout...**
> for problems in which the application of the Pythagorean theorem is not obvious. For example, every rectangle contains two right triangles. That means that if you know the length and width of the rectangle, you also know the length of the diagonal, which is the hypotenuse of both triangles created by the diagonal.

You could use the Pythagorean theorem to prove this (or you could just take our word for it). Whatever the value of the two equal sides of the isosceles right triangle, the hypotenuse is always equal to one of those sides times $\sqrt{2}$. Here are two examples.

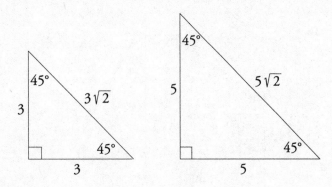

The 30-60-90 Triangle

The other right triangle tested frequently on the ACT is the **30-60-90 triangle**, which also always has the same proportions.

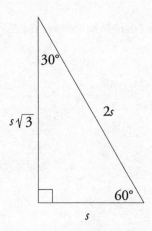

You can use the Pythagorean theorem to prove this (or you can just take our word for it). Whatever the value of the short side of the 30-60-90 triangle, the hypotenuse is always twice as large. The medium side is always equal to the short side times $\sqrt{3}$. Here are two examples.

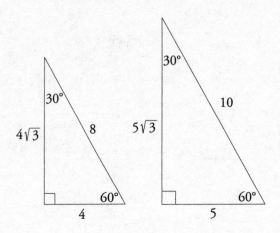

Because these triangles are tested so frequently, it makes sense to memorize the proportions, rather than waste time deriving them each time they appear.

Don't Get Snared

• In the isosceles right triangle below, are the sides equal to $3\sqrt{2}$?

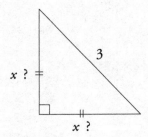

No. Remember, in an isosceles right triangle, in which x represents two of the triangle's sides, hypotenuse = the side $\sqrt{2}$. In this case, 3 = the side $\sqrt{2}$. If we solve for the side, we get $\dfrac{3}{\sqrt{2}}$ = the side.

For arcane mathematical reasons, we are not supposed to leave a radical in the denominator, but we can multiply top and bottom by $\sqrt{2}$ to get $\dfrac{3\sqrt{2}}{2}$.

- In the right triangle below, is x equal to $4\sqrt{3}$?

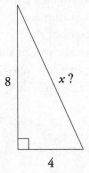

No. Even though it is one of ACT's favorites, you have to be careful not to see a 30-60-90 where none exists. In the triangle above, the short side is half of the *medium* side, not half of the hypotenuse. This is some sort of right triangle all right, but it is not a 30-60-90. The hypotenuse, in case you're curious, is really $4\sqrt{5}$.

Area

The **area** of a triangle can be found using the following formula:

$$\text{area} = \frac{\text{base} \times \text{height}}{2}$$

Height is measured as the perpendicular distance from the base of the triangle to its highest point.

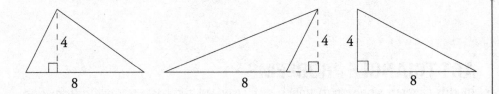

In all three of the above triangles, the area is:

$$\frac{8 \times 4}{2} = 16$$

Don't Get Snared

- Sometimes the height of a triangle can be *outside* the triangle itself, as we just saw in the second example.
- In a right triangle, the height of the triangle can also be one of the sides of the triangle, as we just saw in the third example. However, be careful when finding the area of a *non-right* triangle. Simply because you know two sides of the triangle does not mean that you have the height of the triangle.

Similar Triangles

Two triangles are called *similar* if their angles have the same degree measures. This means their sides will be in proportion. For example, the two triangles below are similar.

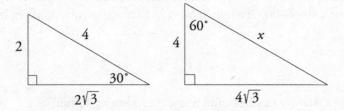

Because the sides of the two triangles are in the same proportion, you can find the missing side, *x*, by setting up a proportion equation.

$$\frac{\text{short leg}}{\text{hypotenuse}} \quad \overset{\text{small triangle}}{\frac{2}{4}} = \overset{\text{big triangle}}{\frac{4}{x}}$$

$$x = 8$$

ACT TRIANGLE PROBLEMS

In this chapter, we've pretty much given you all the basic triangle information you'll need to do the triangle problems on the ACT. The trick is that you'll have to use a lot of this information all at once. Let's have a look at a typical ACT triangle problem and see how to use the basic approach.

3. In the figure below, square *ABCD* is attached to △*ADE* as shown. If ∠*EAD* is equal to 30° and $\overline{AE}$ is equal to $4\sqrt{3}$, then what is the area of square *ABCD* ?

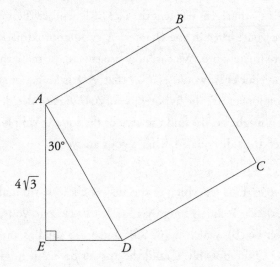

A. $8\sqrt{3}$

B. 16

C. 64

D. 72

E. $64\sqrt{2}$

Here's How to Crack It

Start with Step 1: Know the question. Underline "what is the area of square *ABCD*?" Move to Step 2 and look at the answers. We don't have any values for areas of other shapes within the figure, so there is nothing to Ballpark. But note the presence of $\sqrt{2}$ and $\sqrt{3}$ in the answers: they're an additional clue, if you haven't absorbed the info given, that either 30-60-90 and/or 45-45-90 triangles are in play.

The triangle in the figure is in fact a 30-60-90. Now move to Step 3: Break the problem into bite-sized pieces. Because angle *A* is the smallest angle, the side opposite that angle is equal to 4 and the hypotenuse is equal to 8. Now move on to Step 3a: Mark your figure with these values. Now move to Step 3b: Write down any formulas you need. The area for a square is s^2. Because that hypotenuse is also the side of the square, the area of the square must be 8 times 8, or 64. This is (C). If you forgot the ratio of the sides of a 30-60-90 triangle, go back and review it. You'll need it.

POE Pointers

If you didn't remember the ratio of the sides of a 30-60-90 triangle, could you have eliminated some answers using POE? Of course. Let's see if we can use the diagram to eliminate some answer choices.

The diagram tells us that $\overline{AE}$ has length $4\sqrt{3}$. Remember the important approximations we gave you earlier in the chapter? A good approximation for $\sqrt{3}$ is 1.7. So, $4\sqrt{3}$ = approximately 6.8. We can now use this to estimate the sides of square $ABCD$. Just using your eyes, would you say that $\overline{AD}$ is longer or shorter than $\overline{AE}$? Of course it's a bit longer; it's the hypotenuse of $\triangle ADE$. You decide and write down what you think it might be. To find the area of the square, simply square whatever value you decided the side equaled. This is your answer.

Now all you have to do is see which of the answer choices still makes sense. Could the answer be (A)? $8\sqrt{3}$ equals roughly 13.6. Is this close to your answer? No way. Could the answer be (B), which is 16? Still much too small. Could the answer be (C), which is 64? Quite possibly. Could the answer be 72? It might be. Could the correct answer be $64\sqrt{2}$? An approximation of $\sqrt{2}$ = 1.4, so $64\sqrt{2}$ equals 89.6. This seems rather large. Thus, on this problem, by using POE we could eliminate (A), (B), and (E).

FOUR-SIDED FIGURES

The interior angles of any four-sided figure (also known as a quadrilateral) add up to 360°. The most common four-sided figures on the ACT are the rectangle and the square, with the parallelogram and the trapezoid coming in a far distant third and fourth.

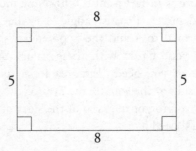

A **rectangle** is a four-sided figure whose four interior angles are each equal to 90°. The area of a rectangle is *base × height*. Therefore, the area of the rectangle on the previous page is 8 (*base*) × 5 (*height*) = 40. The perimeter of a rectangle is the sum of all four of its sides. The perimeter of the rectangle is 8 + 8 + 5 + 5 = 26.

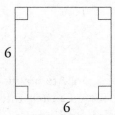

A **square** is a rectangle whose four sides are all equal in length. You can think of the area of a square, therefore, as **side squared**. The area of the above square is 6 (*base*) × 6 (*height*) = 36. The perimeter is 24, or 4*s*.

A **parallelogram** is a four-sided figure made up of two sets of parallel lines. We said earlier that when parallel lines are crossed by a third line, eight angles are formed but that in reality there are only two—the big one and the little one. In a parallelogram, 16 angles are formed, but there are still, in reality, only two.

The area of a parallelogram is also *base × height*, but because of the shape of the figure, the height of a parallelogram is not necessarily equal to one of its sides. Height is measured by a perpendicular line drawn from the base to the top of the figure. The area of the parallelogram above is 9 × 5 = 45.

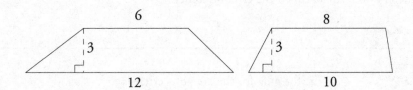

A **trapezoid** is a four-sided figure in which two sides are parallel. Both of the figures above are trapezoids. The area of a trapezoid is the *average of the two parallel sides × the height*, or $\frac{1}{2}$ (*base* 1 + *base* 2)(*height*), but on ACT problems involving

D'oh, I'm in a Square!
To help you remember the area of a four-sided figure (a square, a rectangle, or a parallelogram), imagine that Bart and Homer Simpson are stuck inside of it. To get its area, just multiply **B**art times **H**omer, (*b*)(*h*), or the base times the height.

trapezoids, there is almost always some easy way to find the area without knowing the formula (for example, by dividing the trapezoid into two triangles and a rectangle). In both trapezoids above, the area is 27.

CIRCLES

The distance from the center of a circle to any point on the circle is called the **radius**. The distance from one point on a circle through the center of the circle to another point on the circle is called the **diameter**. The diameter is always equal to twice the radius. In the circle on the left below, *AB* is called a **chord**. *CD* is called a **tangent** to the circle.

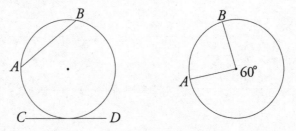

The curved portion of the right-hand circle between points *A* and *B* is called an **arc**. The angle formed by drawing lines from the center of the circle to points *A* and *B* is said to be **subtended** by the arc. There are 360° in a circle, so if the angle we just mentioned equaled 60°, it would take up $\frac{60}{360}$ or $\frac{1}{6}$ of the degrees in the entire circle. It would also take up $\frac{1}{6}$ of the area of the circle and $\frac{1}{6}$ of the outer perimeter of the circle, called the **circumference**.

The formula for the **area** of a circle is πr^2.

The formula for the **circumference** is $2\pi r$.

In the circle below, if the radius is 4, then the area is 16π, and the circumference is 8π.

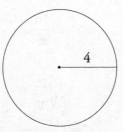

The key to circle problems on the ACT is to look for the word or phrase that tells you what to do. If you see the word *circumference*, immediately write down the formula for circumference, and plug in any numbers the problem has given you. By solving for whatever quantity is still unknown, you have probably already answered the problem. Another tip is to find the radius. The radius is the key to many circle problems.

1. If the area of a circle is 16 meters, what is its radius in meters?

A. $\dfrac{8}{\pi}$

B. 12π

C. $\dfrac{4\sqrt{\pi}}{\pi}$

D. $\dfrac{16}{\pi}$

E. $144\pi^2$

Here's How to Crack It
Step 1: Know the question. We need to solve for the radius. Step 2: Let the answers help. We don't have a figure, so there's nothing to Ballpark. But no figure? Draw your own.

Then write down any formulas you need and fill in the information you have. Set the formula for the area of a circle equal to 16, $\pi r^2 = 16$. The problem is asking for the radius, so you have to solve for r. If you divide both sides by π, you get

$$r^2 = \frac{16}{\pi}$$

$$r = \sqrt{\frac{16}{\pi}}$$

$$= \frac{4}{\sqrt{\pi}}$$

$$= \frac{4\sqrt{\pi}}{\pi}$$

The correct answer is (C).

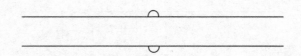

2. In the figure below, the circle with center O is inscribed inside square $ABCD$ as shown. If a side of the square measures 8 units, what is the area of the shaded region?

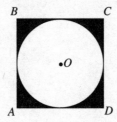

    F. $8 - 16\pi$
    G. 8π
    H. 16π
    J. $64 - 16\pi$
    K. 64π

Here's How to Crack It

Begin with Step 1 and underline "what is the area of the shaded region?" Step 2 brings us to the answers, and we see all of the answers have π in them. There is no obvious choice to Ballpark just yet, so move to Step 3. Break the problem into bite-sized pieces, but don't get hung up on "inscribed." Yes, that's an important term to know, but since we have the figure, it's irrelevant. Move to Step 3a and 3b: Mark the side of the square "8" and write down the formulas for the area of a circle and square: πr^2 and s^2.

Is there a formula for the shape made by the shaded region? Nope. We just need the basic formulas for the basic shapes. $8^2 = 64$, so we at least know the shaded region is less than 64, the area of the square. But what's the link between the square and the circle? The side of the square equals the diameter. So if the diameter is 8, then the radius must be 4. Use that in the area formula, and $4^2 \pi = 16\pi$. Subtract the area of the circle from the area of the square, and we get (J).

FUN FACTS ABOUT FIGURES

Read and review the following facts you need to know about plane geometry.

Angle Facts

- There are 90° in a right angle.
- When two straight lines intersect, angles opposite each other are equal.
- There are 180° in a straight line.
- Two lines are perpendicular when they meet at a 90° angle.
- The sign for perpendicular is ⊥ .
- *Bisect* means to cut exactly in half.
- There are 180° in a triangle.
- There are 360° in any four-sided figure.

Triangle Facts

In any triangle

- The longest side is opposite the largest angle.
- The shortest side is opposite the smallest angle.
- All angles add up to 180°.
- Area = $\dfrac{1}{2}$ (base × height) = $\dfrac{1}{2}bh$
- The height is the perpendicular distance from the base to the opposite vertex.
- *Perimeter* is the sum of the sides.
- The third side of any triangle is always less than the sum and greater than the difference of the other two sides.

In an isosceles triangle

- Two sides are equal.
- The two angles opposite the equal sides are also equal.

In an equilateral triangle

- All three sides are equal.
- All angles are each equal to 60°.

Four-Sided Figure Facts

In a quadrilateral
- All four angles add up to 360°.

In a parallelogram
- Opposite sides are parallel and equal.
- Opposite angles are equal.
- Adjacent angles are supplementary (add up to 180°).
- Area = base × height = bh
- The height is the perpendicular distance from the base to the opposite side.

In a rhombus
- Opposite sides are parallel.
- Opposite angles are equal.
- Adjacent angles are supplementary (add up to 180°).
- All 4 sides are equal.
- Area = base × height = bh
- The height is the perpendicular distance from the base to the opposite side.
- The diagonals are perpendicular.

In a rectangle
- Rectangles are special parallelograms; thus, any fact about parallelograms also applies to rectangles.
- All 4 angles are each equal to 90°.
- Area = length × width = lw
- Perimeter = 2(length) + 2(width) = $2l + 2w$
- The diagonals are equal.

In a square
- Squares are special rectangles; thus, any fact about rectangles also applies to squares.
- All 4 sides are equal.
- Area = $(side)^2 = s^2$
- Perimeter = 4(side) = $4s$
- The diagonals are perpendicular.

Circle Facts

Circle
- There are 360° in a circle.

Radius (r)
- The distance from the center to any point on the edge of the circle.
- All radii in a circle are equal.

Diameter (*d*)
- The distance of a line that connects two points on the edge of the circle, passing through the center.
- The longest line in a circle.
- Equals twice the radius.

Chord
- Any line segment connecting two points on the edge of a circle.
- The longest chord is called the diameter.

Circumference (*C*)
- The distance around the outside of the circle.
- $C = 2\pi r = \pi d$

Arc
- Any part of the circumference.
- The length of an arc is proportional to the size of the interior angle.

Area
- The amount of space within the boundaries of the circle.
- $A = \pi r^2$

Sector
- Any part of the area formed by two radii and the outside of the circle.
- The area of a sector is proportional to the size of the interior angle.

Line Facts

Line
- A line has no width and extends infinitely in both directions.
- Any line measures 180°.
- A line that contains points *A* and *B* is called $\overleftrightarrow{AB}$ (line *AB*).
- If a figure on the ACT looks like a straight line, and that line looks like it contains a point, it does.

Ray
- A ray extends infinitely in one direction but has an endpoint.
- The degree measure of a ray is 180°.
- A ray with endpoint *A* that goes through point *B* is called $\overrightarrow{AB}$. Pay attention to the arrow above the points and the order they are given; those will determine the direction the ray is pointing!

Line Segment
- A line segment is a part of a line and has two endpoints.
- The degree measure of a line segment is 180°.
- A line segment, which has endpoints of *A* and *B*, is written as $\overline{AB}$.

Tangents
- *Tangent* means intersecting at one point. For example, a line tangent to a circle intersects exactly one point on the circumference of the circle. Two circles that touch at just one point are also tangent.
- A tangent line to a circle is always perpendicular to the radius drawn to that point of intersection.
- If $\overline{AB}$ intersects a circle at point T, then you would say, "$\overline{AB}$ is tangent to the circle at point T."

PLANE GEOMETRY FORMULAS

Here's a list of all the plane geometry formulas that could show up on the ACT. Memorize the formulas for perimeter/circumference, area, and volume for basic shapes. ACT usually provides the more advanced formulas if they are needed.

Circles
- Area: $A = \pi r^2$
- Circumference: $C = 2\pi r = \pi d$

Triangles

- Area: $A = \dfrac{1}{2}bh$

- Perimeter: P = sum of the sides

- Pythagorean theorem: $a^2 + b^2 = c^2$

SOHCAHTOA
- $\sin(\theta) = \dfrac{\text{opposite}}{\text{hypotenuse}}$

- $\cos(\theta) = \dfrac{\text{adjacent}}{\text{hypotenuse}}$

- $\tan(\theta) = \dfrac{\text{opposite}}{\text{adjacent}}$

- $\csc(\theta) = \dfrac{1}{\sin}$

- $\sec(\theta) = \dfrac{1}{\cos}$

- $\cot(\theta) = \dfrac{1}{\tan}$

Quadrilaterals

Parallelograms
- Area: $A = bh$
- Perimeter: P = sum of the sides

Rhombus
- Area: $A = bh$
- Perimeter: P = sum of the sides

Trapezoids
- Area: $A = \dfrac{1}{2}h(b_1 + b_2)$
- Perimeter: P = sum of the sides

Rectangles
- Area: $A = lw$
- Perimeter: $P = 2(l + w)$

Squares
- Area: $A = s^2$
- Perimeter: $P = 4s$

Polygons
- Sum of angles in an n-sided polygon: $(n - 2)180°$

- Angle measure of each angle in a regular n-sided polygon: $\dfrac{(n - 2)180°}{n}$

3-D Figures

- Surface area of a rectangular solid: $S = 2(lw + lh + wh)$

- Surface area of a cube: $S = 6s^2$

- Surface area of a right circular cylinder: $S = 2\pi r^2 + 2\pi rh$

- Surface area of a sphere: $S = 4\pi r^2$

- Volume of a cube: $V = s^3$

- Volume of a rectangular solid: $V = lwh$

- Volume of a right circular cylinder: $V = \pi r^2 h$

- Volume of a sphere: $V = \dfrac{4\pi r^3}{3}$

GLOSSARY

Arc:	Any part of the circumference
Bisect:	To cut in half
Chord:	Any line segment connecting two points on the edge of a circle
Circumscribed:	Surrounded by a circle as small as possible
Collinear:	Lying on the same line
Congruent:	Equal in size
Diagonal (of a polygon):	A line segment connecting opposite vertices
Equilateral triangle:	All sides are equal and each angle measures 60°
Inscribed (angle in a circle):	An angle in a circle with its vertex on the circumference
Isosceles triangle:	A triangle with two equal sides
Parallel:	Two distinct lines that do not intersect
Perpendicular:	At a 90° angle
Plane:	A flat surface extending in all directions
Polygon:	A closed figure with two or more sides
Quadrilateral:	A four-sided figure
Regular polygon:	A figure with all equal sides and angles
Sector:	Any part of the area formed by two radii and the outside of the circle
Similar:	Equal angles and proportional sides
Surface area:	The sum of areas of each face of a figure
Tangent:	Intersecting at one point
Vertex/Vertices:	A corner point. For angles, it's where two rays meet. For figures, it's where two adjacent sides meet.

COORDINATE GEOMETRY

There are fewer coordinate geometry problems on the ACT Math Test than there are plane geometry problems. Most of the coordinate geometry problems are straight plug-and-chug problems. Just like in plane geometry, most questions will test the same few concepts over and over; the harder questions will just combine those same concepts in ways that are harder to identify.

Graphing Inequalities

Here's a simple inequality:

$$3x + 5 > 11$$

You solve an inequality the same way that you solve an equality. By subtracting 5 from both sides and then dividing both sides by 3, you get the expression

$$x > 2$$

This can be represented on a number line as shown below.

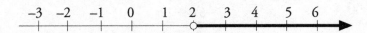

The open circle at 2 indicates that x can include every number greater than 2, but not 2 itself or anything less than 2.

If we had wanted to graph $x \geq 2$, the circle would have to be filled in, indicating that our graph includes 2 as well.

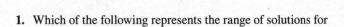

An ACT graphing problem might look like this.

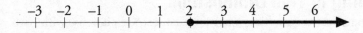

1. Which of the following represents the range of solutions for inequality $-5x - 7 < x + 5$?

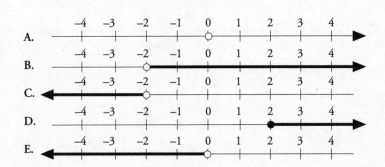

Here's How to Crack It

The ACT test writers want you first to simplify the inequality and then figure out which of the answer choices represents a graph of the solution set of the inequality. To simplify, isolate x on one side of the inequality.

$$
\begin{array}{r}
-5x - 7 < x + 5 \\
\underline{-x \qquad -x} \\
-6x - 7 < \quad 5 \\
\underline{+7 \quad +7} \\
-6x \quad < \quad 12
\end{array}
$$

Flip Flop
Remember that when you multiply or divide an inequality by a negative, the sign flips.

Now divide both sides by −6. Remember that when you multiply or divide an inequality by a negative, the sign flips over.

$$
\frac{-6x}{-6} < \frac{12}{-6}
$$
$$
x > -2
$$

Which of the choices answers the question? If you selected (B), you're right.

Graphing in Two Dimensions

More complicated graphing questions concern equations with two variables, usually designated x and y. These equations can be graphed on a Cartesian grid, which looks like this.

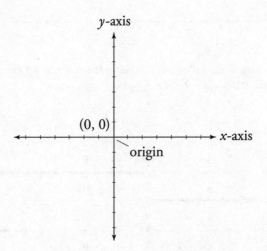

Every point (*x,y*) has a place on this grid. For example, the point *A* (3,4) can be found by counting over on the *x*-axis 3 places to the right of (0,0)—known as the **origin**—and then counting on the *y*-axis 4 places up from the origin, as shown below. Point *B* (5,–2) can be found by counting 5 places to the right on the *x*-axis and then down 2 places on the *y*-axis. Point *C* (–4,–1) can be found by counting 4 places to the left of the origin on the *x*-axis and then 1 place down on the *y*-axis.

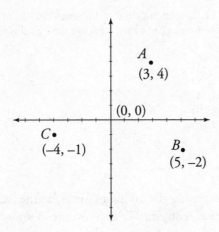

The grid is divided into four quadrants, which go counterclockwise.

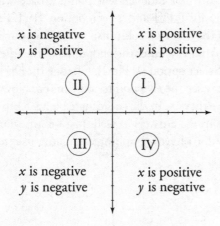

- In the first quadrant, *x* and *y* are both positive.
- In the second quadrant, *x* is negative but *y* is positive.
- In the third quadrant, *x* and *y* are both negative.
- In the fourth quadrant, *x* is positive but *y* is negative.

Note: This is when your graphing calculator (if you have one) will really get a chance to shine. Practice doing all the ACT coordinate geometry questions on your calculator now and you'll blow them away when you actually take the test.

Graphic Guesstimation

A few questions on the ACT might involve actual graphing, but it is more likely that you will be able to make use of graphing to *estimate* the answers to questions that the ACT test writers think are more complicated.

1. Point B (4,3) is the midpoint of line segment AC. If point A has coordinates (0,1), then what are the coordinates of point C?

    A. (−4,−1)
    B. (4, 1)
    C. (4, 4)
    D. (8, 5)
    E. (8, 9)

Here's How to Crack It

You may or may not remember the midpoint formula: The ACT test writers expect you to use it to solve this problem. We'll go over it in a moment, along with the other formulas you'll need to solve coordinate geometry questions. However, it is worth noting that by drawing a rough graph of this problem, you can get the correct answer without the formula.

On your TI-83, you can plot independent points to see what the graph should look like. To do this, hit $\boxed{\text{STAT}}$ and select option [1: Edit]. Enter the x- and y-coordinate points in the first two columns; use $[\text{L1}]$ for your x-coordinates and $[\text{L2}]$ for the y-coordinates. After you enter the endpoints of the line, hit $\boxed{\text{2nd}}$ $\boxed{\text{Y=}}$ to access the $\boxed{\text{STAT PLOT}}$ menu. Select option [1: Plot1]. Change the $[\text{OFF}]$ status to $\boxed{\text{ON}}$ and hit $\boxed{\text{GRAPH}}$. You should now see the two points you entered. Now you can ballpark the answers based on where they are in the coordinate plane. Keep in mind that you can also plot all the points in the answers as well. Just be sure you keep track of all the x- and y-values. If you don't have a graphing calculator, use the grid we've provided below.

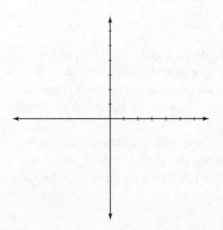

B is supposed to be the midpoint of a line segment *AC*. Draw a line through the two points you've just plotted and extend it upward until *B* is the midpoint of the line segment. It should look like this:

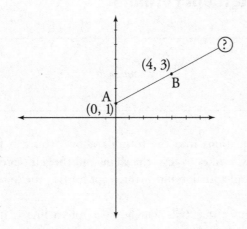

The place where you stopped drawing is the approximate location of point *C*. Now let's look at the answer choices to see if any of them are in the ballpark.

A.   (−4,−1): These coordinates are in the wrong quadrant.
B.   (4, 1):   This point is way below where it should be.
C.   (4, 4):   This point does not extend enough to the right.
D.   (8, 5):   Definitely in the ballpark. Hold on to this answer choice.
E.   (8, 9):   Possible, although the *y*-coordinate seems a little high.

Which answer choice do you want to pick? If you said (D), you are right.

───────────────────────────○───────────────────────────

THE IMPORTANT COORDINATE GEOMETRY FORMULAS

By memorizing a few formulas, you will be able to answer virtually all of the coordinate geometry questions on this test. Remember, too, that in coordinate geometry you almost *always* have a fallback—just graph it out.

And always keep your graphing calculator handy on these types of problems. Graphing calculators are great for solving line equations and giving you graphs you can use to Ballpark. Be sure you know how to solve and graph an equation for a line on your calculator before you take the ACT.

The following formulas are listed in order of importance:

The Slope-Intercept Formula

$$y = mx + b$$

To find the x-intercept

Set y equal to zero and solve for x.

By putting (x,y) equations into the formula above, you can find two pieces of information that ACT likes to test: the **slope** and the **y-intercept**. Most graphing calculators will put an equation into y-intercept form at the touch of a button.

The **slope** is a number that tells you how sharply a line is inclining, and it is equivalent to the variable m in the equation above. For example, in the equation $y = 3x + 4$, the number 3 (think of it as $\frac{3}{1}$) tells us that from any point on the line, we can find another point on the line by going up 3 and over to the right 1.

In the equation $y = -\frac{4}{5}x - 7$, the slope of $-\frac{4}{5}$ tells us that from any point on the line, we can find another point on the line by going up 4 and over 5 to the left.

The **y-intercept**, equivalent to the variable b in the equation above, is the point at which the line intercepts the y-axis. For example, in the equation $y = 3x + 4$, the line will strike the y-axis at a point 4 units above the origin. In the equation $y = 2x - 7$, the line will strike the y-axis at a point 7 units below the origin. A typical ACT $y = mx + b$ question might give you an equation in another form and ask you to find either the slope or the y-intercept. Simply put the equation into the form we've just shown you.

2. What is the slope of the line based on the equation
$5x - y = 7x + 6$?
   F. −2
   G. 0
   H. 2
   J. 6
   K. −6

Here's How to Crack It

Isolate y on the left side of the equation. You can have your graphing calculator do this for you, or you can do it by hand by subtracting $5x$ from both sides.

$$
\begin{aligned}
5x - y &= 7x + 6 \\
-5x & \quad -5x \\
\hline
-y &= 2x + 6
\end{aligned}
$$

We aren't quite done. The format we want is $y = mx + b$, not $-y = mx + b$. Let's multiply both sides by -1.

$$
(-1)(-y) = (2x + 6)(-1)
$$
$$
y = -2x - 6
$$

The slope of this line is -2, so the answer is (F).

The Slope Formula

You can find the slope of a line, even if all you have are two points on that line, by using the slope formula.

$$
\text{slope} = \frac{\text{change in } y}{\text{change in } x} \quad \text{or} \quad \frac{y_2 - y_1}{x_2 - x_1}
$$

The Slippery Slope
A line going from bottom left to upper right has a positive slope.
A line going from top left to bottom right has a negative slope.

3. What is the slope of the straight line passing through the points $(-2,5)$ and $(6,4)$?

   A. $-\dfrac{1}{16}$

   B. $-\dfrac{1}{8}$

   C. $\dfrac{1}{5}$

   D. $\dfrac{2}{9}$

   E. $\dfrac{4}{9}$

Here's How to Crack It

Find the change in y and put it over the change in x. The change in y is the first y-coordinate minus the second y-coordinate. (It doesn't matter which point is first and which is second.) The change in x is the first x minus the second x.

$$\frac{y_2 - y_1}{x_2 - x_1} = \frac{5 - 4}{-2 - 6} = \frac{1}{-8}$$

The correct answer is (B).

If you take a look at the formula for finding slope, you'll see that the part on top ("change in y") is how much the line is rising (or falling, if the line points down and has a negative slope). That change in position on the y-axis is called the *rise*. The part on the bottom ("change in x") is how far along the x-axis you move and called the *run*. So the slope of a line is sometimes referred to as "rise over run."

In the question we just did, then, the rise was 1 and the run was -8, giving us the slope $-\frac{1}{8}$. Same answer, different terminology.

Midpoint Formula

If you have the two endpoints of a line segment, you can find the midpoint of the segment by using the midpoint formula.

$$\left(x[m], y[m]\right) = \left(\frac{x_1 + x_2}{2}, \frac{y_1 + y_2}{2}\right)$$

It looks much more intimidating than it really is.

To find the midpoint of a line, just take the *average* of the two x-coordinates and the *average* of the two y-coordinates. For example, the midpoint of the line segment formed by the coordinates (3,4) and (9,2) is just

$$\frac{(3+9)}{2} = 6 \text{ and } \frac{(4+2)}{2} = 3$$
$$\text{or } (6,3)$$

Remember the first midpoint problem we did? Here it is again.

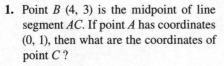

1. Point *B* (4, 3) is the midpoint of line segment *AC*. If point *A* has coordinates (0, 1), then what are the coordinates of point *C* ?

A. (−4,−1)
B. (4, 1)
C. (4, 4)
D. (8, 5)
E. (8, 9)

> **The Shortest Distance Between Two Points Is…a Calculator?**
> If you want to draw a line between two points on your TI-83, you can use the Line function. To access this, you'll want to press [2nd] [PRGM] to access the [DRAW] menu. From there, select option [2: Line]. The format of the line function is Line (X1, Y1, X2, Y2); for example, if you wanted to view the line that passes through the points (−2, 5) and (6,4), you would enter Line (−2,5,6,4). Hit [ENTER] to see your line.

Here's How to Crack It

You'll remember that it was perfectly possible to solve this problem just by drawing a quick graph of what it ought to look like. However, to find the correct answer using the midpoint formula, we first have to realize that, in this case, we already *have* the midpoint. We are asked to find one of the endpoints.

The midpoint is (4, 3). This represents the average of the two endpoints. The endpoint we know about is (0, 1). Let's do the *x*-coordinate first. The average of the *x*-coordinates of the two endpoints equals the *x*-coordinate of the midpoint. So $\frac{(0+?)}{2}=4$. What is the missing *x*-coordinate? 8. Now let's do the *y*-coordinate. $\frac{(1+?)}{2}=3$. What is the missing *y*-coordinate? 5. The answer is (D).

If you had trouble following that last explanation, just remember that you already understood this problem (and got the answer) using graphing. Never be intimidated by formulas on the ACT. There is usually another way to do the problem.

The Distance Formula

We hate the distance formula. We keep forgetting it, and even when we remember it, we feel like fools for using it because there are much easier ways to find the distance between two points. We aren't even going to tell you what the distance formula is. If you need to know the distance between two points, you can always think of that distance as being the hypotenuse of a right triangle. Here's an example.

───────────────○───────────────

4. What is the distance between points *A* (2, 2) and *B* (5, 6) ?

F. 3
G. 4
H. 5
J. 6
K. 7

Here's How to Crack It

Let's make a quick graph of what this ought to look like.

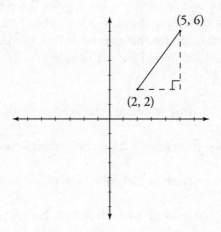

If we extend lines from the two points to form a right triangle under the line segment *AB*, we can use the Pythagorean theorem to get the distance between the two points. What is the length of the base of the triangle? It's 3. What is the length of the height of the triangle? It's 4. So what is the length of the hypotenuse? It's 5. Of course, as usual, it is one of the triples of which ACT is so fond. The answer is (H). You could also have popped the points into your calculator and had it calculate the distance for you.

───────────────○───────────────

TRIGONOMETRY

The ACT Math Test includes only four trigonometry questions. And the good news is, those questions generally cover only a few basic topics in trigonometry.

SOHCAHTOA

There are four trig questions on any given ACT Math Test, and typically two of them will ask about very basic trig concepts, covered by the acronym SOHCAHTOA. If you've had trig before, you probably know this acronym like the back of your hand. If not, here's what it means:

$$\textbf{S}\text{ine} = \frac{\textbf{O}\text{pposite}}{\textbf{H}\text{ypotenuse}} \quad \textbf{C}\text{osine} = \frac{\textbf{A}\text{djacent}}{\textbf{H}\text{ypotenuse}} \quad \textbf{T}\text{angent} = \frac{\textbf{O}\text{pposite}}{\textbf{A}\text{djacent}}$$

Sine is Opposite over Hypotenuse. Cosine is Adjacent over Hypotenuse. Tangent is Opposite over Adjacent. So in the triangle below, the sine of angle θ [*theta*, a Greek letter] would be $\frac{4}{5}$. The cosine of angle θ would be $\frac{3}{5}$. The tangent of angle θ would be $\frac{4}{3}$.

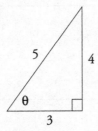

Sine, cosine, and tangent are often abbreviated as sin, cos, and tan, respectively.

The easier trig questions on this test involve the relationships between the sides of a right triangle. In the right triangle below, angle *x* can be expressed in terms of the ratios of different sides of the triangle.

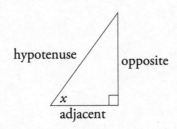

The **sine** of angle $x = \dfrac{\text{length of side opposite angle } x}{\text{length of hypotenuse}}$

The **cosine** of angle $x = \dfrac{\text{length of side adjacent angle } x}{\text{length of hypotenuse}}$

The **tangent** of angle $x = \dfrac{\text{length of side opposite angle } x}{\text{length of side adjacent angle } x}$

YOU'RE ALMOST DONE

There are three more relationships to memorize. They involve the reciprocals of the previous three.

$$\text{The cosecant} = \frac{1}{\text{sine}}$$
$$\text{The secant} = \frac{1}{\text{cosine}}$$
$$\text{The cotangent} = \frac{1}{\text{tangent}}$$

Let's try a few problems.

31. What is $\sin \theta$, if $\tan \theta = \dfrac{4}{3}$?

A. $\dfrac{3}{4}$

B. $\dfrac{4}{5}$

C. $\dfrac{5}{4}$

D. $\dfrac{5}{3}$

E. $\dfrac{7}{3}$

Helpful Trig Identities

$$\sin^2 \theta + \cos^2 \theta = 1$$

$$\frac{\sin \theta}{\cos \theta} = \tan \theta$$

Here's How to Crack It

It helps to sketch out the right triangle and fill in the information we know.

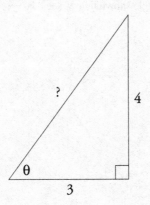

What kind of right triangle is this? That's right—a 3-4-5. Now, we need to know

the sine of angle θ: opposite over hypotenuse, or $\dfrac{4}{5}$, which is (B).

43. For all $\theta, \dfrac{\cos \theta}{\sin^2 \theta + \cos^2 \theta} = ?$

   A. $\sin \theta$
   B. $\csc \theta$
   C. $\cot \theta$
   D. $\cos \theta$
   E. $\tan \theta$

Here's How to Crack It

$\sin^2 \theta + \cos^2 \theta$ always equals 1. $\dfrac{\cos \theta}{1} = \cos \theta$. The answer is (D).

50. In a right triangle shown below, sec θ is $\dfrac{25}{7}$. What is sin θ ?

F. $\dfrac{3}{25}$

G. $\dfrac{5}{25}$

H. $\dfrac{7}{25}$

J. $\dfrac{24}{25}$

K. $\dfrac{25}{7}$

Here's How to Crack It

The secant of any angle is the reciprocal of the cosine, which is just another way of saying that the cosine of angle θ is $\dfrac{7}{25}$.

Secant $\theta = \dfrac{1}{\cos\theta}$, so $\dfrac{1}{\cos\theta} = \dfrac{25}{7}$, which means that cos θ = $\dfrac{7}{25}$. Are you done? No! Cross off (H) because you know it's not the answer.

Cosine means adjacent over hypotenuse. Let's sketch it.

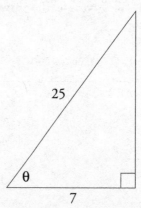

As you can see, we now have two sides of a right triangle. Can we find the third side? If you said this was one of the triples we told you about before, you are absolutely correct, although you also could have derived this by using the Pythagorean theorem. The third side must be 24. The question asks for sin θ. Sine = opposite over hypotenuse, or $\frac{24}{25}$, which is (J).

ADVANCED TRIGONOMETRY

When graphing a trig function, such as sine, there are two important **coefficients**, A and B: $A\{sin\,(B\theta)\}$.

The two coefficients A and B govern the **amplitude** of the graph (how tall it is) and the **period** of the graph (how long it takes to get through a complete cycle), respectively. If there are no coefficients, then that means A = 1 and B = 1, and the graph is the same as what you'd get when you graph it on your calculator.

- Increases in A increase the amplitude of the graph. It's a direct relationship.

That means if A = 2, then the amplitude is doubled. If $A = \frac{1}{2}$, then the amplitude is cut in half.

- Increases in B decrease the period of the graph. It's an inverse relationship.

That means if B = 2, then the period is cut in half, which is to say the graph completes a full cycle faster than usual. If $B = \frac{1}{2}$, then the period is doubled.

You can add to or subtract from the function as a whole, and also to or from the variable, but neither of those actions changes the shape of the graph, only its position and starting place.

Here's the graph of sin *x*. What are the amplitude and period?

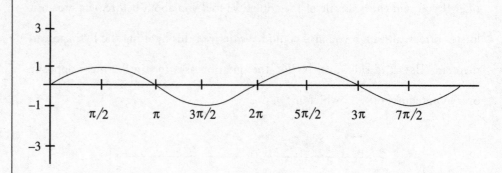

The simple function sin θ goes from −1 to 1 on the *y*-axis, so the amplitude is 1, while its period is 2π, which means that every 2π on the graph (as you go from side to side) it completes a full cycle. That's what you see in the graph above.

The graph below is also a sine function, but it's been changed. What is the function graphed here?

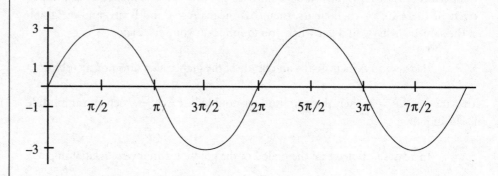

You have three things to check when looking at this graph: Is it sin or cos, has the period changed, and has the amplitude changed?

- This is a sin graph because it has a value of 0 at 0. Cos has a value of 1 at 0.
- It makes a complete cycle in 2π, so the period hasn't changed. In other words, B = 1.
- The amplitude is triple what it normally is, so A = 3. The function graphed, therefore, is 3 sin θ.

How about here?

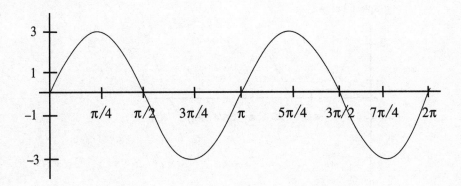

Once again, there are three things to check.

- This is a sin graph because it has a value of 0 at 0. Cos has a value of 1 at 0.
- It makes a complete cycle in π, so the period has changed—it's half of what it usually is. B has an inverse effect, which means B = 2.
- The amplitude is triple what it normally is, so A = 3. The function graphed, therefore, is 3 sin 2θ.

Let's try some practice questions.

---

49. As compared with the graph of $y = \cos x$, which of the following has the same period and three times the amplitude?

    A. $y = \cos 3x$

    B. $y = \cos \dfrac{1}{2}(x + 3)$

    C. $y = 3 \cos \dfrac{1}{2}x$

    D. $y = 1 + 3 \cos x$

    E. $y = 3 + \cos x$

Here's How to Crack It

Recall that the coefficient on the outside of the function changes the amplitude, and the one on the inside changes the period. Because the question states that the period hasn't changed, you can eliminate (A), (B), and (C). The amplitude is three times greater, you're told; because there's a direct relationship between A and amplitude, you want to have a 3 multiplying the outside of the function. That leaves only (D) as a possibility.

---

52. Which of the following equations describes the equation graphed below?

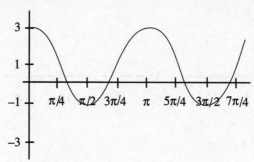

F. $2 \cos x$
G. $1 + 2 \cos x$
H. $\cos 2x$
J. $1 + \cos 2x$
K. $1 + 2 \cos 2x$

Here's How to Crack It

At first it looks like this graph has an amplitude of 3, but if you look closer, you'll see that though the top value is 3, the bottom value is –1, which means that the whole graph has been shifted up. Because (F) and (H) don't add anything to the function (which is how you move a graph up and down), they're out. The period of this graph is half of what it usually is, so B = 2, which eliminates (G). Because the amplitude has also changed, you can eliminate (J). The answer is (K).

Now try these strategies on your own. Go online to your Student Tools and answer the Chapter 11 Drills.

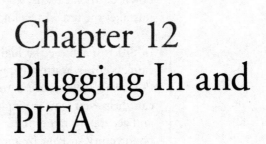

Chapter 12
Plugging In and
PITA

Chapter 11 discussed various strategies for attacking the toughest Plug and Chug questions. Once you master them, you will have the tools to attack a wide variety of ACT Math problems. This chapter will look at two more essential tools for the toughest algebra problems on the ACT: Plugging In and PITA (Plug In The Answers).

Always keep in mind that most of the ACT Math problems can be solved in multiple ways, and that the approach that seems the most familiar may not be the most efficient. Often, a strong test taker will be tempted to apply a "brute-force" method to solving problems: just start doing algebra and work through the problem until a solution presents itself. But this could take minutes, could lead you down dead-end paths, and could lead you into trap answers that are based on mistakes the test writers know you are likely to make!

In order to achieve the highest scores on the ACT, you can't afford to make any careless errors, waste any precious seconds, or fall into any traps. Plugging In and PITA will help ensure correct answers on the easy and medium questions, and can help you cut through distractions and solve difficult questions quickly and accurately, rather than wasting time taking an inefficient path. Recognize the opportunity to Plug In and use PITA, and you'll ensure high accuracy and save lots of time—time you can use to work on solving other difficult questions!

WHEN ACCURACY COUNTS, ARITHMETIC BEATS ALGEBRA

Let's take a look at a challenging algebra problem:

59. If x and y are nonzero real numbers such that $3^{x-1} = 3y$, which of the following is equivalent to 3^{x+1} in terms of y ?

    A. $\dfrac{1}{27y^3}$

    B. $\dfrac{1}{27y}$

    C. $\dfrac{1}{9y}$

    D. $9y^3$

    E. $27y$

What's your first reaction to this problem? Most likely, your inclination is to apply "brute-force" algebraic manipulations and your knowledge of exponent rules until you understand the problem and can solve for the answer. If you have excellent algebra skills, you've got a good chance of getting it right—but also a good chance of making an algebra mistake and coming up with a trap answer, or of wasting time going down dead-end paths. That's what the test writers want you to do. The problem is written in a way specifically intended to lead you into algebra errors, and the answer choices include traps for the various errors you might make. Before we attack this problem, let's talk about Plugging In.

PLUGGING IN

If you had 1 dollar and you bought 2 pieces of candy at 25 cents apiece, how much change would you have? 50 cents, of course. If you had d dollars and bought p pieces of candy at c cents apiece, how much change would you have? Your first inclination might be $d - pc$, right? But that's not the answer: it's actually $d - \dfrac{pc}{100}$, since you have to convert the cents to dollars. And the trap ($d - pc$) will be right there waiting for you in the answers.

This helps explain why some top math students do well on the "hard" questions, but make careless errors on "easy" and "medium" questions. Why does this happen? Because your mind is much better at working with concrete numbers (doing arithmetic) than it is at working with abstractions such as variables (doing algebra).

> No matter how good you are at algebra, you've been doing arithmetic a lot longer.

Numbers are a lot easier to work with than variables. Therefore, when you see variables on the ACT, you can usually make things a lot easier on yourself by using numbers instead. Whenever there are variables in the answer choices or the problem, you can use Plugging In.

- Use Plugging In when there are variables in the answer choices.
- Plugging In works on both word problems and plug-and-chug questions.
- Plugging In works on questions of any difficulty level.

Let's take another look at Question 59:

> **59.** If x and y are nonzero real numbers such that $3^{x-1} = 3y$, which of the following is equivalent to 3^{x+1} in terms of y ?
>
> **A.** $\dfrac{1}{27y^3}$
>
> **B.** $\dfrac{1}{27y}$
>
> **C.** $\dfrac{1}{9y}$
>
> **D.** $9y^3$
>
> **E.** $27y$

WHAT TO DO WHEN YOU PLUG IN

1. **Identify the opportunity.** Can you Plug In on this question?
2. **Choose a good number.** Make the math easy on yourself.
3. **Find a target answer.** Solve the question using the number you plugged in; that gives you your Target. Circle it.
4. **Test all the answer choices.** Plug the numbers you chose into the answer choices and look for the one that matches your Target. If two of them work, try new numbers until only one answer is left.

Let's try it:

Step 1: Identify the opportunity. Can you Plug In on this question? Yes: there are variables in the question and in the answer choices.

Step 2: Choose a good number. We know that x and y are "nonzero real numbers" and that $3^{x-1} = 3y$. What number might make the math more straightforward? Let's try $x = 4$. Replace x with 4 in the equation and see what happens:

$3^{4-1} = 3y$

$3^3 = 3y$

$27 = 3y$

$y = 9$

Ok, so if we Plug In $x = 4$, we find that $y = 9$. But what is the question *asking for*? We are supposed to solve for 3^{x+1}.

Step 3: Find a target answer. If $x = 4$, then $3^{x+1} = 3^{4+1} = 3^5 = 243$. So, when $x = 4$ and $y = 9$, the answer to the question is 243. Circle "243" on your paper—this is the target answer we need to match in the answer choices.

Step 4: Test all the answer choices. Since the answer choices all have y in them, replace y with 9 in each answer choice and calculate the result to find the one that matches 243.

A. $\dfrac{1}{27y^3} = \dfrac{1}{19,683}$ Not our target answer. Eliminate it. Note that calculating the actual amount is not necessary if you see that the answer will be less than 1.

B. $\dfrac{1}{27y} = \dfrac{1}{243}$ Not our target answer. Eliminate it. Note that calculating the actual amount is not necessary if you see that the answer will be less than 1.

C. $\dfrac{1}{9y} = \dfrac{1}{81}$ Not our target answer. Eliminate it. Note that calculating the actual amount is not necessary if you see that the answer will be less than 1.

D. $9y^3 = 6,561$ Not our target answer. Eliminate it.

E. $27y = 243$ ✓

Only (E) works, so it is the correct answer. How difficult was that? Not at all. How sure are we that we got the correct answer? Very sure. It's much less likely that you'll fall into an algebra trap answer when you solve the question without using any algebra!

Plugging In turns difficult problems into fairly straightforward arithmetic problems, while also greatly improving your accuracy. Could you have solved this question correctly using algebra? Sure. But more importantly, are you confident that you can solve *every* algebra question without falling into a trap and missing a couple? If you're aiming for the highest scores, you can't afford that risk. Plugging In will increase your accuracy while also saving you time that you can use to attack other difficult questions on the test.

Let's try another challenging algebra problem and see how the process works.

53. If x, y, and z are positive real numbers such that $\frac{1}{2}x = \frac{1}{3}y$ and $3y = 4z$, which of the following inequalities is true?

    A. $x < y < z$
    B. $x < z < y$
    C. $y < x < z$
    D. $y < z < x$
    E. $z < y < x$

Since the problem involves variables in the question and the answers, this looks like a great opportunity to Plug In. Try a number that looks like it will work well with the problem: since 12 is divisible by 2, 3, and 4, Plug In $x = 12$ and see what happens: $\frac{1}{2}(12) = \frac{1}{3}y$, so $6 = \frac{1}{3}y$ and $y = 18$. Now Plug In $y = 18$ to the second equation: $3(18) = 4z$, so $54 = 4z$ and $z = 13.5$. Therefore, since $x = 12$, $z = 13.5$, and $y = 18$, the correct inequality is $x < z < y$, which matches choice (B).

Compare Plugging In to the algebraic method for solving the same problem: eliminate the fractions from the first equation, by multiplying each side by 6, resulting in $3x = 2y$. But then you need to combine the two equations, so multiply the first equation again by 3 on each side, resulting in $9x = 6y$. Multiply the right equation by 2 on each side, resulting in $6y = 8z$, Then, combine the equations: $9x = 6y = 8z$. Finally, find a number that has 9, 8, and 6 as factors, such as 72, and set the equation equal to it: $9x = 6y = 8z = 72$. Therefore, $x = 8$, $y = 12$, and $z = 9$, so $x < z < y$.

Which method is more likely to result in wasted time and the risk of careless errors? Plugging In reduces those chances dramatically and saves you lots of time on the test. Sometimes, it can feel like Plugging In takes longer at first—it's a new technique, after all! But if you're diligent in practicing it and allow it to become comfortable, you may even end up moving more quickly through the test.

PLUGGING IN THE ANSWERS

As we've seen, Plugging In is a great strategy when there are variables in the question or the answers. How about when there aren't? Can we use Plugging In on questions even when they don't have variables or equations? We can.

Take a look at this difficult word problem:

51. Herman has written 75 pages of a novel, and his goal is to complete the 410-page novel over the next 12 months. He plans to write some pages next month, and then in each month thereafter, he plans to write exactly 2 more pages than he wrote in the previous month. If Herman follows this plan, what is the minimum number of pages he must write next month in order to reach his goal?

    A. 11
    B. 17
    C. 24
    D. 32
    E. 37

What's your initial reaction to this problem? First, it's time-consuming to read and it involves multiple steps. Second, it probably makes you feel like you should be writing down an algebra equation, even though it doesn't name any variables. When you get that feeling, check the answers. When you feel like writing an algebraic equation, and you see integers in the answer choices, this means you can Plug In The Answers (PITA) to solve the question.

Plug In The Answers (PITA) when:

- answer choices are numbers in ascending or descending order.
- the question asks for a specific amount. Questions will usually be "what?" or "how many?"
- you get the urge to do algebra even when there are no variables in the problem.

Okay, let's see how it works:

51. Herman has written 75 pages of a novel, and his goal is to complete the 410-page novel over the next 12 months. He plans to write some pages next month, and then in each month thereafter, he plans to write exactly 2 more pages than he wrote in the previous month. If Herman follows this plan, what is the minimum number of pages he must write next month in order to reach his goal?

    A. 11
    B. 17
    C. 24
    D. 32
    E. 37

As soon as you identify the opportunity to use PITA, go right to the end of the question to find what the problem is asking for. Here, the question asks for the *minimum* number of pages Herman must write next month to reach his goal. Label the answers as the "first month minimum."

Since the answer choices are listed in ascending order, start in the middle with (C). That way, you can save time by moving to a smaller or larger answer choice if the first one doesn't work. So, if we start with the middle choice, Herman would write 24 pages in the first month.

Now, work through the problem step by step in bite-sized pieces. What's the first calculation we can make? Herman writes 24 pages in the first month, then adds 2 pages in each month thereafter for 12 months. How many pages does he write in total? Well, we know he would write that base amount (24 pages) in each of the 12 months, so that's $24 \times 12 = 288$ pages. Also, he would write additional pages each month, starting in month 2 up to month 12: $2 + 4 + 6 + 8 + 10 + 12 + 14 + 16 + 18 + 20 + 22 = 132$ additional pages. Plus, he started with 75 pages, so his total number of pages would be $288 + 132 + 75 = 495$ pages.

Here's how your work would look on the page:

Minimum First Month	12 Months	Additional Pages	Original Pages	Total $\geq$ 410?
A. 11				
B. 17				
C. 24	288	132	75	495
D. 32				
E. 37				

Would he meet his goal of 410 pages? Yes, but the question asked for the *minimum* number of pages he must write in the first month, so let's try a smaller amount.

Try (B)—17 pages. The math is much easier once you've been through it the first time. If Herman writes 17 pages the first month, then over the 12 months he will write $17 \times 12 = 204$ pages. Also, he would write the same 2 additional pages each month, which would still add up to 132 additional pages, and he still starts with 75 pages, so his total number of pages would be $204 + 132 + 75 = 411$ pages. This would be just enough to achieve his goal of writing 410 pages. Since (A), 11 pages, would be way too low to make 410 pages, (B) is the credited response. Now here's what your work would look like:

Minimum First Month	12 Months	Additional Pages	Original Pages	Total ≥ 410?
A. 11				
B. 17	204	132	75	411 Yes! ✓
C. 24	288	132	75	495 Not min.
D. 32				
E. 37				

Since you're using PITA, once you find the correct answer, you're done—you don't need to check all five answers.

Let's look at another problem and see PITA in action:

43. After playing games of skill at the county fair, Jenny has 168 prize tickets, all of which she uses to buy prizes for herself and 10 of her friends. Small prizes cost 12 tickets, and large prizes cost 21 tickets. How many small prizes does she buy?

    A. 3
    B. 4
    C. 6
    D. 7
    E. 8

Since this word problem asks "how many" at the end, has ascending numbers in the answer choices, and may give you the urge to do algebra, it is a great opportunity to Plug In The Answers.

Start at the end of the problem with what the question is asking for: since it's asking for the number of small prizes, label the answers "small prizes." Now start with the middle answer choice, (C), and work through the problem in bite-sized pieces.

If Jenny buys 6 small prizes, they would cost $12 \times 6 = 72$ tickets. How many large prizes would she buy? Since the prizes are for *herself* and 10 of her friends, she buys a total of 11 prizes, which means she would buy 5 large prizes, which would cost $21 \times 5 = 105$ tickets, for a total cost of $72 + 105 = 177$ tickets.

Here's how your work would look on the page:

Small Prizes	Tickets	Large Prizes	Tickets	Total	= 168?
A. 3					
B. 4					
C. 6	72	5	105	177	
D. 7					
E. 8					

Since the problem states that she uses 168 tickets, eliminate (C). Since Jenny needs to spend fewer tickets, you need a larger number of small prizes, so try (D).

If Jenny buys 7 small prizes, they would cost 12 × 7 = 84 tickets. She would also buy 4 large prizes, costing 21 × 4 = 84 tickets, for a total of 84 + 84 = 168 tickets. Since this matches the amount stated in the problem, choose (D). Now here's what your work would look like:

Small Prizes	Tickets	Large Prizes	Tickets	Total	= 168?
A. 3					
B. 4					
C. 6	72	5	105	177	Too high
D. 7	84	4	84	168	Yes! ✓
E. 8					

HIDDEN PLUG INS

As you saw with Plugging In The Answers, Plugging In isn't useful only on problems with variables in the questions and answer choices. You can also Plug In on problems that ask for ratios or percentages as answer choices.

Take a look at this challenging geometry problem:

60. The two diagonals of a square divide it into four isosceles triangles of equal size. What is the ratio of the perimeter of one of the four smaller triangles to the perimeter of the original square?

F. $\dfrac{1}{4}$

G. $\dfrac{\sqrt{2}}{4}$

H. $\dfrac{1+\sqrt{2}}{4}$

J. $\dfrac{2+\sqrt{2}}{4}$

K. $\dfrac{1}{2}$

When a problem asks for the relationship between amounts, but does not provide any values for variables, you can Plug In any numbers you like, so long as you follow any rules the problem sets forth. In this case, you must follow the geometry rules for squares and triangles.

Start by drawing a square and drawing both diagonals from opposite corners. Note that this forms four 45-45-90 triangles, so you know that the hypotenuse of each triangle is equal to the sides multiplied by $\sqrt{2}$.

Pick a length for the sides of the square. Let's try 2. Therefore, each diagonal would have a length of $2\sqrt{2}$, and so each of the small triangles would have one side with a length of 2, and two smaller sides, each with a length of $\sqrt{2}$. So, the perimeter of each small triangle is $2+\sqrt{2}+\sqrt{2}=2+2\sqrt{2}$.

The perimeter of the original square is 4(s) = 4(2) = 8. Therefore, the ratio of the perimeter of one of the smaller triangles to the perimeter of the square is

$$\dfrac{2+2\sqrt{2}}{8}=\dfrac{2\left(1+\sqrt{2}\right)}{8}=\dfrac{1+\sqrt{2}}{4}\text{, which matches (H).}$$

A NOTE ON PLUGGING IN AND PITA

Plugging In and PITA are not the only ways to solve these problems, and it may feel weird using these methods instead of trying to do these problems "the real way." You may have even found that you knew how to work with the variables in Plugging In problems or how to write the appropriate equations for the PITA problems. If you can do either of those things, you're already on your way to a great Math score.

But think about it this way. We've already said that ACT doesn't give any partial credit. So, do you think doing it "the real way" gets you any extra points? It doesn't: on the ACT, a right answer is a right answer, no matter how you get it. "The real way" is great, but unfortunately, it's often a lot more complex and offers a lot more opportunities to make careless errors.

The biggest problem with doing things the real way, though, is that it essentially requires that you invent a new approach for every problem. Instead, notice what we've given you here: two strategies that will work toward getting you the right answer on any number of questions. You may have heard the saying, "Give a man a fish and you've fed him for a day, but teach a man to fish and you've fed him for a lifetime." Now, don't worry, our delusions of grandeur are not quite so extreme, but Plugging In and PITA are useful in a similar way. Rather than giving you a detailed description of how to create formulas and use them on specific questions that won't ever appear exactly the same way on an ACT again, we're giving you a strategy that will help you work through any number of similar problems on future ACTs.

Now try these strategies on your own. Go online to your
Student Tools and answer the Chapter 12 Drill.

Chapter 13
Hard Word
Problems

Sometimes strong math students will achieve high accuracy on all the "hard" questions on the ACT Math Test—particularly the plug-and-chug problems—but lose points by missing tricky word problems, even those in the "easy" and "medium" sections. Word problems can often lead you into careless error traps with tricky wording. This chapter discusses ways to see those traps in word problems and avoid falling for them by using a careful, systematic approach.

First, a review of some overall strategies:

NOW, LATER, NEVER

Hard questions generally take longer to work through than do easier questions. That's obvious, but as we've seen, the definition of an "easy" question is a tough one to pin down. That's why you'll want to be careful with ACT's Order of Difficulty on the Math Test. As we've said before, the no-brainer approach is to open the test booklet and work questions 1 through 60 in order, but you can help to lock in the higher scores by outsmarting the test. You'll have a much more successful experience by drawing your own road map for this test rather than letting ACT guide you.

Of course, a lot of the easy questions will be near the beginning, but they won't all be. So, when you arrive at each question, you'll want to first determine whether it is a Now, Later, or Never question. Do the Now questions immediately: they're the freebies, the ones you know how to do and can do quickly and accurately. Skip any questions you think might take you a bit longer, or that test unfamiliar concepts—save them for Later. First, make sure you get all the points you can on the problems you know you can do, no matter what the question number.

Once you've done all the Now questions, go back to all the ones you left for Later. For both Now and Later questions, don't rush and make careless errors. On the other hand, if you find yourself spinning your wheels on a question, circle the question number and come back to it at the end if you have time. Don't get stuck on a particular problem. In a 60-minute exam, think of how much spending 5 minutes on a single problem can cost you!

Finally, there's no problem with leaving a question or two behind in the Never category. But wait, what's a Never question for a top scorer? Sometimes a question might be on a topic that you simply didn't cover yet in school; maybe you missed the week your teacher taught matrices, or logarithms, or the unit circle. Or for whatever reason, you have no idea how to approach a problem. In that case, your time is likely better spent on other questions (and it's still possible to get the highest score on the test even if you miss a question or two).

Note, of course, that you should never leave a question blank on the ACT, since there is no penalty for guessing. If you skip any questions, fill them in with your Letter of the Day: choose one pair of letters and bubble in all blanks this way. For example, always bubble in (A) and (F) or (B) and (G). This will maximize your chance of getting some of the guesses right.

USE PROCESS OF ELIMINATION (POE)

Remember the major technique we introduced in Chapter 2: Strategy, or the Process of Elimination (POE). ACT doesn't take away points for wrong answers, so you should always guess, and POE can help you improve your chance of guessing correctly. Don't make the mistake of thinking that POE is only for medium-scoring students—it's one of the keys to protecting yourself against careless errors that could cost you that top score! And POE is not a strategy just for English, Reading, and Science. Math has its own kind of POE, one facet of which we call Ballparking.

BALLPARKING ON WORD PROBLEMS

You can frequently get rid of several answer choices in an ACT Math problem (and protect yourself against careless errors) without doing any time-consuming math. Narrow down the choices by estimating your answer. We call this Ballparking. Let's look at an example:

17. Sarah pays $2.50 per 1,000 gallons of water used at her apartment each month for any usage up to 20,000 gallons. She pays 1.5 times that rate per 1,000 gallons used in excess of 20,000 gallons. If Sarah used 30,104 gallons of water last month, what was her approximate total water bill for the month?

   A. $50.00
   B. $75.00
   C. $90.00
   D. $100.00
   E. $110.00

Here's How to Crack It

Before we do any serious math on this problem, let's see if we can get rid of some answer choices by Ballparking.

First, do some rough calculations to see what the answer should look like. Sarah pays $2.50 per 1,000 gallons, so multiply by 10 to get a price of $25 for 10,000 gallons. So 20,000 gallons would cost $50, and if she kept paying the regular rate, 30,000 gallons would cost $75. But she paid a higher rate for the extra 10,000 gallons, so the answer has to be higher than $75; eliminate (A) and (B). How much did she pay for the extra 10,000 gallons? More than $25, but less than $50, because that would be double the original rate. So, her total amount should be greater than $75 but less than $100; only (C) makes any sense.

When dealing with word problems on the ACT Math Test:

1. **Know the question.** Read the whole problem before you calculate anything, and underline the actual question.
2. **Let the answers help.** Look for clues on how to solve and ways to use POE (Process of Elimination).
3. **Break the problem into bite-sized pieces.** When you read the problem a second time, stop at each step and make the necessary calculations before moving on. Write down your calculations, and watch out for tricky phrasing.

It may feel like we somehow cheated the system by doing the problem that way, but here's what ACT doesn't want you to know: the quick, easy way and the "real" way both get you the same number of raw points. Not all problems will be as easy to Ballpark, of course, but if you think before you start frantically figuring, you can usually eliminate at least an answer choice or two, and save yourself a lot of time (and brainpower) that you can use on tougher problems later in the test!

WORD PROBLEMS

The topics tested on the ACT Math Test aren't that difficult in themselves—you learned most, if not all, of this stuff by the end of middle school. So why do you miss questions? ACT knows that one way to make any problem more difficult is to simply phrase it as a word problem. Word problems can add confusing steps to mask the simple concepts tested by the problems. Trap answers, partial answers, and weird phrasing abound in word problems. Word problems (like pretty much everything else on the ACT) are often more about reading comprehension than about the underlying knowledge itself.

Word problems take a lot of different forms and test a variety of math concepts, but if you keep these three steps in mind, you should be able to solve most word problems pretty efficiently.

Let's try a problem:

14. Zachary is organizing his movie collection. $\frac{2}{5}$ of his movies are science-fiction films. Of his movies that are not science-fiction films, $\frac{3}{10}$ are comedies. Of his movies that are not science-fiction films or comedies, $\frac{1}{6}$ are foreign films. All of his remaining movies (those that are not science-fiction films, comedies, or foreign films) are dramas. If Zachary has 300 movies, how many of them are dramas?

F. 21
G. 54
H. 105
J. 120
K. 126

Here's How to Crack It

Step 1: Know the Question There is actually a slightly tricky step on this one. First of all, the problem doesn't tell you until the very end that Zachary has 300 movies in total. Without this piece of information, the fractions don't mean much of anything. Second, the question is asking for the number of movies that are dramas, and we're going to have to figure out a bunch of other things before we figure that out.

Step 2: Let the Answers Help There aren't any crazy answers in this one, though if you noticed we're taking less than half of the movies out each time, you're probably thinking that the answer won't be one of the smaller numbers.

Step 3: Break the Problem into Bite-Sized Pieces The starting point of this word problem actually comes at the end: Zachary has 300 movies. Start with that information, then work the problem sentence by sentence, writing down the results as you go, and paying particular attention to the language of the problem.

$\frac{2}{5}$ of his movies are science-fiction films.

Zachary has 300 movies in total, and $\frac{2}{5}$ of 300 is 120, so Zachary has 120 science-fiction films.

Of his movies that are not science-fiction films, $\frac{3}{10}$ are comedies.

This looks just like the last piece, but there's a HUGE difference. This statement involves two separate calculations. The first step is to calculate the number of movies that are *not* science-fiction films. There are 300 total movies, and 120 of them are science-fiction films, so there are 180 movies that are not science-fiction films. The second step: $\frac{3}{10}$ of 180 is 54, so 54 of the movies are comedies.

Of his movies that are not science-fiction films or comedies, $\frac{1}{6}$ are foreign films.

Two steps again. First, we need to find the number of movies that are not science-fiction films or comedies. There were 180 movies left in the last step, but 54 of them are comedies, so now there are 126 movies that are not science-fiction films or comedies. The second step: $\frac{1}{6}$ of 126 is 21, so 21 of the movies are foreign films.

All of his remaining movies (those that are not science-fiction films, comedies, or foreign films) are dramas.

There were 126 movies left over in the last step, and 21 of them are foreign films, which means there are 105 movies left, and they are all dramas. Choice (H) is the correct answer. Look at those other answers, then look at the numbers you were dealing with in the problem: what a mess of partial answers!

If it seems like this took kind of a long time to do, don't worry—the strategy is actually much more efficient than it seems, and it will help you achieve that high accuracy you need to reach the top scores. The steps will come naturally after a while, and you'll have a solid base with which to begin any ACT Math problem in such a way that enables you to get to the answer as efficiently as possible.

> Now try these strategies on your own. Go online to your
> Student Tools and answer the Chapter 13 Drill.

Chapter 14
Advanced Math

The ACT Math Test often includes questions based on a few advanced math topics, such as logarithms, matrices, series, ellipses, and advanced trigonometry. While these areas of math are complex to learn, the questions on the ACT that refer to these more advanced areas of math are usually fairly straightforward. Often, the key to these questions is simply a matter of knowing the basic rules in question.

LOGARITHM RULES

A logarithm is just another way of expressing an exponent.

$$\log_b n = x \text{ means the same thing as } b^x = n$$

Since the logarithm itself represents an exponent, the $M^A D^S P^M$ rules also apply to logarithms, but in a different way:

$$\log xy = (\log x) + (\log y)$$

$$\log \left(\frac{x}{y} \right) = \log x - \log y$$

$$\log x^y = y \log x$$

MATRICES

Some (but not all) ACT Math Tests include a matrix problem. If you know the matrix rules, you should find these problems manageable. Also, if your calculator has matrix functions and you're familiar with their use, you may be able to solve matrix problems on a calculator.

On the ACT Math test, matrix problems generally test data organization, multiplication of matrices, or matrix transformations.

Data Organization

A problem on the ACT Math Test may use a matrix simply to present data in chart format. For instance, a problem might provide something like the following:

The number of employees in a corporation can be shown by the following matrix:

Managers	Supervisors	Staff
[3	6	30]

All the above matrix means is that the company has 3 managers, 6 supervisors, and 30 staff. Thus, when ACT uses the word *matrix*, sometimes the problem is simply trying to make a regular chart problem sound more difficult than it is.

Multiplication of Matrices

The size of a matrix is described as rows × columns; in order to multiply matrix A times matrix B, the number of *columns* of A must be the same as the number of *rows* of B. For instance, it would be possible to multiply a 3 × 2 matrix by a 2 × 5 matrix.

To find the product of matrix A and matrix B, each cell in the product is found by multiplying and adding the elements of the corresponding *row* of matrix A with the corresponding *column* of matrix B. For example:

$$\begin{bmatrix} a & b \\ c & d \end{bmatrix}\begin{bmatrix} w & x \\ y & z \end{bmatrix} = \begin{bmatrix} aw+by & ax+bz \\ cw+dy & cx+dz \end{bmatrix}$$

$$\begin{bmatrix} 1 & 2 \\ 3 & 4 \end{bmatrix}\begin{bmatrix} 5 & 6 \\ 7 & 8 \end{bmatrix} = \begin{bmatrix} 19 & 22 \\ 43 & 50 \end{bmatrix}$$

Matrix Transformations

The basic matrix transformation is the *identity matrix*; it is the equivalent of the number 1 for matrices. The identity matrix has 1's down the main diagonal from the top left to the bottom right, with 0 everywhere else:

$$\begin{bmatrix} 1 & 0 \\ 0 & 1 \end{bmatrix}$$

If you multiply a matrix by the identity matrix, the product is equal to the original matrix.

$$\begin{bmatrix} 1 & 2 \\ 3 & 4 \end{bmatrix}\begin{bmatrix} 1 & 0 \\ 0 & 1 \end{bmatrix} = \begin{bmatrix} 1 & 2 \\ 3 & 4 \end{bmatrix}$$

Changes to the identity matrix allow for other basic transformations:

$$\begin{bmatrix} 1 & 2 \\ 3 & 4 \end{bmatrix}\begin{bmatrix} -1 & 0 \\ 0 & -1 \end{bmatrix} = \begin{bmatrix} -1 & -2 \\ -3 & -4 \end{bmatrix}$$

SERIES

The ACT Math Test often includes a question or two about series, which include *arithmetic series* and *geometric series*. A series is simply a list of numbers that increase or decrease according to a consistent pattern.

- In an arithmetic sequence, the *difference* between consecutive terms is constant (that is, a constant amount is added or subtracted after each term).
- In a geometric sequence, the *ratio* between consecutive terms is constant (that is, each number is multiplied or divided by a constant amount to arrive at the next number).

CIRCLES, ELLIPSES, AND PARABOLAS

Very few ACT Math questions will involve using the formulas for the circle, ellipse, and parabola. As long as you are familiar with these equations, you can figure out the answer to almost any of these questions by graphing.

The standard equation for a **circle** is shown below.

$$(x-h)^2 + (y-k)^2 = r^2 \qquad \text{Center of the circle: } (h,k) \qquad \text{Radius} = r$$

You need to memorize the circle formula and be able to apply it when it comes up in questions, because it will not be provided to you. For instance, a circle with the equation $(x-2)^2 + (y+3)^2 = 25$ is a circle with a radius of 5 and a center at $(2,-3)$.

An ellipse is a circle that has been squashed into an oval shape. The standard equation for an **ellipse** is shown below.

$$\frac{(x-h)^2}{a^2} + \frac{(y-k)^2}{b^2} = 1 \qquad \text{Center of the ellipse: } (h,k)$$

$$\text{Horizontal axis} = 2a$$

$$\text{Vertical axis} = 2b$$

Unlike the circle formula, you do *not* need to memorize it for the test. Whenever a question involves an ellipse, the ellipse formula will be provided for you, and you simply need to know how to work with it. For example, an ellipse with the equation $\frac{(x-4)^2}{9} + \frac{(y+3)^2}{25} = 1$ has the center (4, −3), a horizontal axis of 6, and a vertical axis of 10.

A parabola is a U-shaped curve. The standard equation for a **parabola** is shown below.

$$y = x^2$$

Here's the equation for a parabola in a more complicated form:

$$y = a(x-h)^2 + k \quad \text{Vertex} = (h,k)$$

Parabolas with the above formula will open upward or downward. For a parabola that is "sideways" (opening to the left or the right), simply swap x and y in the equation, as shown below.

$$x = y^2 \quad x = a(y-h)^2 + k \quad \text{Vertex} = (h,k)$$

You need to know the parabola formula and recognize how to use it on the test, because it will not be provided to you. Any quadratic equation will form a parabola when graphed.

ADVANCED TRIG

Sometimes the ACT Math Test will include questions about trigonometric identities. Be sure you are familiar with the two basic identities.

$$\sin^2 \theta + \cos^2 \theta = 1$$

$$\frac{\sin \theta}{\cos \theta} = \tan \theta$$

Also, be sure you are familiar with the reciprocals of the trig functions: cosecant, secant, and cotangent.

$$\csc \theta = \frac{1}{\sin \theta} = \frac{hyp}{opp}$$

$$\sec \theta = \frac{1}{\cos \theta} = \frac{hyp}{adj}$$

$$\cot \theta = \frac{1}{\tan \theta} = \frac{adj}{opp}$$

One easy way to remember which reciprocal matches to which function is that the letters "co" appear exactly one time for each pair of reciprocals: sine and _co_secant; _co_sine and secant; and tangent and _co_tangent.

Finally, be sure you know how to use the law of sines and the law of cosines. As an added bonus, the ACT Math Test will actually give these formulas to you whenever they apply, so you only need to be familiar with their use.

Law of Sines: $\dfrac{\sin A}{a} = \dfrac{\sin B}{b} = \dfrac{\sin C}{c}$

Law of Cosines: $c^2 = a^2 + b^2 - 2ab \cos C$

Unit Circle

The *Unit Circle* is used to determine the values for trig functions.

Fill in the angle measurements in degrees and (*x,y*) coordinates for the circle below with a radius of 1.

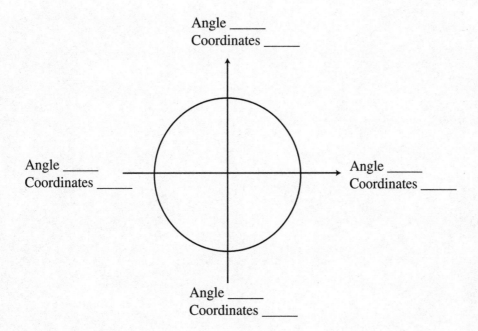

Angle _____
Coordinates _____

Angle _____
Coordinates _____

Angle _____
Coordinates _____

Angle _____
Coordinates _____

Now complete the table below, using your calculator. Make sure you are in "Degree" mode.

Angle	Sine	Cosine
90°		
180°		
270°		
0/360°		

Sine and cosine are another way of expressing *y* and *x* in the standard (*x,y*) coordinate plane.

Now try these strategies on your own. Go online to your Student Tools and answer the Chapter 14 Drill.

Chapter 15
Mathematics Test

MATHEMATICS TEST

DIRECTIONS: Solve each problem, choose the correct answer, and then darken the corresponding oval on your answer sheet.

Do not linger over problems that take too much time. Solve as many as you can; then return to the others in the time you have left for this test.

You are permitted to use a calculator on this test. You may use your calculator for any problems you choose, but some of the problems may best be done without using a calculator.

Note: Unless otherwise stated, all of the following should be assumed:

1. Illustrative figures are NOT necessarily drawn to scale.
2. Geometric figures lie in a plane.
3. The word *line* indicates a straight line.
4. The word *average* indicates arithmetic mean.

---

1. Prints Palace charges a regular fee of $1.50 per color poster for print orders up to and including 50 color posters. For each additional color poster in the order, Prints Palace charges half the regular fee. Helene orders 64 color posters from Prints Palace. What is her fee for this order?

   (Note: Amounts are before taxes are added.)
   A. $192.00
   B. $117.50
   C. $96.00
   D. $85.50
   E. $48.00

DO YOUR FIGURING HERE.

2. What value of y makes the equation $\dfrac{3(y-5)}{2} = 18$ true?

   F. 5.5
   G. 11
   H. 16.5
   J. 17
   K. 22

3. Arianna is helping her mother center a table in their dining room. As shown in the figure below, the rectangular room is 25 feet long, and the rectangular table is 4 feet wide and 7 feet long. The west edge of the table will be y feet from the west wall of the room, and the east edge of the table will be y feet from the east wall of the room. What is the value of y ?

DO YOUR FIGURING HERE.

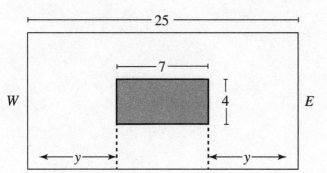

A. 7
B. 9
C. 10.5
D. 12.5
E. 18

4. What is the solution to the equation $7y - 2 = 2(y + 2)$?

F. -1

G. $\dfrac{4}{5}$

H. $\dfrac{6}{5}$

J. 1

K. 2

5. For nonzero values of a and b, which of the following expressions is equivalent to $\dfrac{-28a^5b^2}{7ab}$?

A. $-4a^2b^5$
B. $-4a^4b$
C. $-4a^6b^3$
D. $-21a^4b$
E. $-35a^4b$

6. Tessa has 7 pairs of earrings, 5 necklaces, and 6 bracelets, which can be worn in any combination. She needs to choose her jewelry to wear to a friend's wedding. How many different combinations consisting of 1 of her 7 pairs of earrings, 1 of her 5 necklaces, and 1 of her 6 bracelets are possible for Tessa to wear to the wedding?

F.   18
G.   42
H.   175
J.   210
K.   252

7. In Alpana's checking account in February, the highest available balance was $135 and the lowest available balance was −$12. This highest available balance was how many dollars greater than this lowest available balance?

A. $147
B. $133
C. $125
D. $123
E. $117

8. A new operation, @, is defined on pairs of ordered pairs of integers as follows: $(r, s) @ (t, u) = \dfrac{rs - tu}{su + rt}$. What is the value of $(1,2) @ (5,3)$?

F. $-\dfrac{13}{11}$

G. $-\dfrac{11}{13}$

H.   1

J. $\dfrac{13}{5}$

K.   13

9. The function $y = (x - 3)^2$ is graphed in the standard (x, y) coordinate plane below.

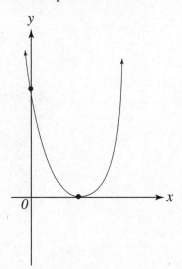

One of the following graphs in the standard (x, y) coordinate plane shows the result of shifting the function down 2 coordinate units. Which graph is it?

A.

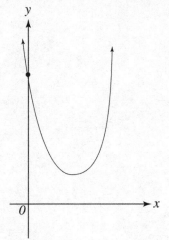

B.

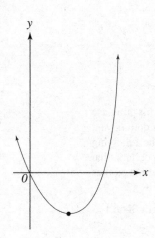

C.

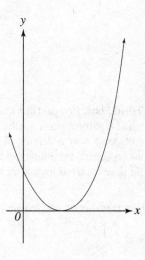

D.

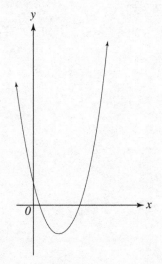

E.

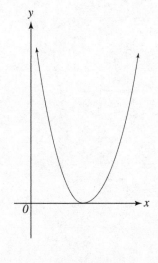

10. What is the least common denominator of the fractions $\frac{3}{10}$, $\frac{4}{9}$, and $\frac{5}{6}$?

    F.   90
    G.   120
    H.   180
    J.   324
    K.   540

11. The average of 6 numbers is 48. What is the 6th number if the first 5 numbers are 34, 43, 52, 58, and 56?

    A.   43
    B.   45
    C.   46
    D.   49
    E.   50

12. A sandbox in the shape of a right rectangular prism has a length of 24 inches and a width of 18 inches. The volume of sand in the sandbox is 5,184 cubic inches. To the nearest inch, what is the depth of sand in the sandbox?

    F.   6
    G.   12
    H.   36
    J.   42
    K.   72

13. At Nifty Thrift Shop, Ben paid less than $20 for his purchase of *n* shirts and *n* pairs of pants. Each shirt cost *s* dollars, and each pair of pants cost *p* dollars. Which of the following expressions represents the amount of money, in dollars, that Ben should have received back after he paid for his clothes with $20?

    (Note: There is no tax on purchases at Nifty Thrift Shop.)

    A. $n(p + s)$
    B. nps
    C. $20 - nps$
    D. $20 - n(p - s)$
    E. $20 - n(p + s)$

14. $\left|4(3) + 5(-7)\right| = ?$

    F.   −23
    G.   23
    H.   35
    J.   39
    K.   47

15. A circle with radius *r* inches is shown in the figure below; 4 non-overlapping squares, each with side *s* inches, are removed from the circle. The shaded region is the area of the circle remaining after 4 squares are removed. What is the area, in square inches, of the shaded region?

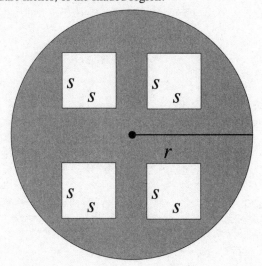

A. $\pi r^2 - 4s^2$
B. $\pi r^2 - 2s^2$
C. $\pi r^2 - s^2$
D. πr^2
E. $4s^2$

16. In the figure below, lines *q* and *r* are parallel, line *s* is a transversal, and 3 angle measures are given in degrees. What is the value of $b - a$?

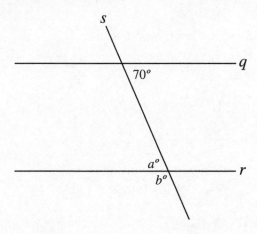

F. −20
G. 40
H. 70
J. 90
K. 110

17. Which of the following graphs shows the solution set for the inequality $2y - 1 \leq 9$?

A.
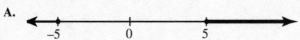

B.
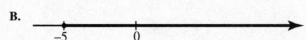

C.
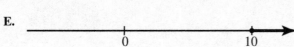

D.

E.

18. Given the function $m(n) = 2n^3 + 4$, what is $m(-2)$?

    F. 20
    G. 10
    H. −4
    J. −12
    K. −16

19. A semicircle with center X is shown below. Points A, X, and D lie on the diameter. The measure of $\angle AXC$ is 110°, the measure of $\angle BXD$ is 90°, and the measure of $\angle AXD$ is 180°. What is the measure of $\angle BXC$?

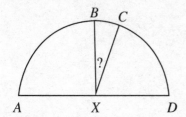

    A. 40
    B. 35
    C. 30
    D. 20
    E. 15

DO YOUR FIGURING HERE.

Use the following information to answer questions 20–22.

The table below shows the number of cups of chopped onion, carrot, and celery required to make 600 ounces of each of 3 types of soup sold at Soup-a-Palooza Restaurant. Let x represent the price of 1 cup of chopped onion, y the price of 1 cup of chopped carrot, and z the price of 1 cup of chopped celery. All prices are in dollars.

Type of Soup	Cups of Onion	Cups of Carrot	Cups of Celery
Tomato	4	5	2.5
Vegetable	3	4	6
Mulligatawny	3.5	6	7

20. How many cups of chopped onion are required to make 320 ounces of vegetable soup?

   F. 1.6
   G. 1.8
   H. 2.1
   J. 2.6
   K. 2.9

21. The restaurant has 18 cups of chopped onion, 26 cups of chopped carrot, and 28 cups of chopped celery. What is the maximum number of ounces of mulligatawny soup the restaurant can make from the ingredients in stock?

   A. 2,200
   B. 2,400
   C. 2,600
   D. 2,800
   E. 3,000

22. Which of the following expressions gives the price of the onion, carrot, and celery required to make 600 ounces of tomato soup and 600 ounces of vegetable soup?

   F. $12x + 20y + 15z$

   G. $7x + 9y + 8.5z$

   H. $4x + 5y + 2.5z$

   J. $\dfrac{12}{x} + \dfrac{20}{y} + \dfrac{15}{z}$

   K. $\dfrac{7}{x} + \dfrac{9}{y} + \dfrac{8.5}{z}$

23. In the (x,y) solution to the system of equations below, $y = ?$

$$3x = 13$$
$$2x - 4y = 3$$

DO YOUR FIGURING HERE.

A. $\dfrac{2}{3}$

B. $\dfrac{17}{26}$

C. $\dfrac{17}{12}$

D. 4

E. $\dfrac{13}{3}$

24. Pete's Artisanal Pickles sells gourmet pickles at farmer's markets. Two types of machines—sealing machines and labeling machines—are used to jar the pickles. Each sealing machine processes jars at the rate of 30 jars per minute, and each labeling machine processes jars at the rate of 2 jars per second. Pete's Artisanal Pickles is currently using 16 sealing machines. How many labeling machines should be used so that the sealing machines and the labeling machines process the same number of jars in 1 *minute*?

F. 2
G. 4
H. 8
J. 15
K. 20

25. What is the result of the subtraction problem below?

$$(\ 9y^2 \qquad + 3)$$
$$-\ (-2y^2 - 5y + 7)$$

A. $11y^2 + 5y - 4$
B. $11y^2 - 5y + 10$
C. $11y^2 - 4$
D. $7y^2 + 5y - 4$
E. $7y^2 - 5y - 4$

26. For what real number value of b is the equation $y^b = (y^3)^4(y^5)^2$ true?

F. 14
G. 19
H. 22
J. 36
K. 70

27. The number 0.07 is 1,000 times what number?

A. 0.7
B. 0.07
C. 0.007
D. 0.0007
E. 0.00007

> Use the following information to answer
> questions 28–30.

Each of the 120 people in a random sample of the 1,300 people at the grocery store today was asked which, if any, of the following types of protein he or she purchased: beef, poultry, pork, or seafood. All 120 people answered the question. The answers were tallied, and the exact percents of people who purchased the proteins are shown in the diagram below.

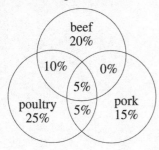 

28. Because this was a random sample, the percents in the sample are estimates for the corresponding percents among all people at the grocery store today. What estimate does this give for the number of people at the grocery store today who purchased beef but none of the other 3 types of protein?

F. 195
G. 260
H. 325
J. 520
K. 585

29. What percent of the people in the random sample purchased exactly 1 type of the 4 types of protein?

A. 45%
B. 60%
C. 75%
D. 80%
E. 95%

DO YOUR FIGURING HERE.

30. Supposed 30 additional people at random were asked the question, with the following answers: 10 purchased seafood only, 15 purchased pork and beef only, and 5 purchased pork, beef, and poultry only. Among all 150 people asked, what fraction bought seafood but none of the other 3 types of protein?

- F. $\dfrac{32}{120}$
- G. $\dfrac{32}{150}$
- H. $\dfrac{28}{120}$
- J. $\dfrac{28}{130}$
- K. $\dfrac{28}{150}$

31. Triangle $\triangle STU$ and collinear points R, S, and T are shown in the figure below. The measure of $\angle T$ is 37°, the measure of $\angle TSU$ is $(3x)°$, and the measure of $\angle RSU$ is $(9x)°$. What is the measure of $\angle U$?

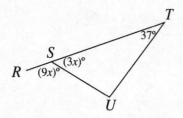

- A. 15
- B. 45
- C. 82
- D. 98
- E. 135

32. In the standard (x,y) coordinate plane, what are the coordinates of the center of the circle with equation $(x + 3)^2 + (y + \sqrt{7})^2 = 4$?

- F. $(\sqrt{7}, 3)$
- G. $(-\sqrt{7}, -3)$
- H. $(3, -\sqrt{7})$
- J. $(3, \sqrt{7})$
- K. $(-3, -\sqrt{7})$

33. Akiko wants to determine the height of a vertical water tower with antennae, shown below. She measures the angle of elevation to the top of the water tower antenna at a point 112 feet along level ground from the center of the base of the water tower. The angle of elevation is 26°. Which of the following expressions gives the best approximation of the height of the water tower, including the antennae, in feet?

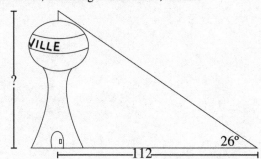

A. 112 tan 26°

B. 112 cos 26°

C. 112 sin 26°

D. $\dfrac{\tan 26°}{112}$

E. $\dfrac{\sin 26°}{112}$

34. When graphed in the standard (x, y) coordinate plane, which of the following linear equations is a line parallel to the y-axis?

F. $y = 3$
G. $y = 3x$
H. $x = 3$
J. $x = 3y$
K. $x = y$

35. Let $4x + 5y = 15$ be an equation of line f in the standard (x, y) coordinate plane. Line g has a slope that is 3 times the slope of line f and has a y-intercept that is 1 more than the y-intercept of f. Line g has which of the following equations?

A. $y = -\dfrac{2}{5}x + 1$

B. $y = -\dfrac{12}{5}x + 2$

C. $y = -\dfrac{12}{5}x + 4$

D. $y = -\dfrac{4}{5}x + \dfrac{3}{2}$

E. $y = -\dfrac{5}{4}x + \dfrac{12}{5}$

DO YOUR FIGURING HERE.

36. The graph of $y = \sec x$ is shown in the standard (x, y) coordinate plane below. What is the period of $\sec x$?

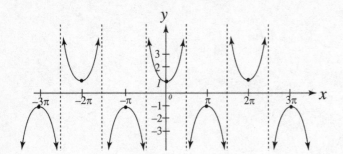

F. $\dfrac{5\pi}{2}$

G. 2π

H. $\dfrac{3\pi}{2}$

J. π

K. $\dfrac{\pi}{2}$

37. In a certain rectangle, the ratio of the lengths of 2 adjacent sides is 7 to 3. If the area of the rectangle is 84 square inches, what is the length, in inches, of the longer side?

A. 4
B. 7
C. 10
D. 14
E. 42

38. Jebediah walked 1 km from his home to the mailbox at a constant speed, then returned to his home at the same speed. A graph, with distance from his home plotted along the y-axis and elapsed time during the walk plotted along the x-axis, was constructed for the values of y from 0 km to 2 km. The shape of the graph can best be described as a:

F. line segment with a positive slope then a negative slope
G. line segment with a negative slope then a positive slope
H. vertical line segment
J. horizontal line segment
K. parabola

39. What is the area, in square inches, of the figure below?

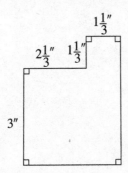

A. $10\dfrac{5}{6}$

B. $11\dfrac{5}{9}$

C. $12\dfrac{7}{9}$

D. $14\dfrac{1}{2}$

E. $15\dfrac{4}{9}$

40. In the standard (x, y) coordinate plane, $Z(-2, -4)$ is reflected over the x-axis. What are the coordinates of the image of Z?

F. $(4, -2)$

G. $(4, 2)$

H. $(2, -4)$

J. $(-2, 4)$

K. $(-4, 2)$

41. Which of the following graphs in the standard (x, y) coordinate plane shows $y \leq cx + d$ for some negative c and positive d ?

A.

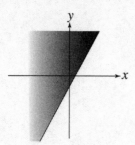

B.

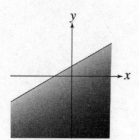

C.

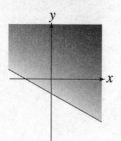

D.

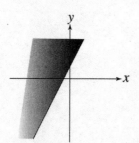

E.

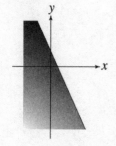

DO YOUR FIGURING HERE.

42. If $\dfrac{6a - 2b}{a + 2b} = \dfrac{3}{2}$, then $\dfrac{a}{b} = ?$

   F. $\dfrac{7}{16}$

   G. $\dfrac{2}{3}$

   H. $\dfrac{8}{11}$

   J. $\dfrac{10}{9}$

   K. $\dfrac{8}{3}$

43. Shown below are similar triangles $\triangle FGH$ and $\triangle XYZ$ with $\angle H \cong \angle Z$ and $\angle G \cong \angle Y$. The given lengths are in inches. What is the length, in inches, of $\overline{XZ}$?

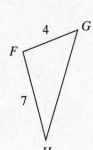 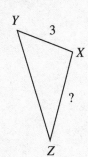

   A. $9\dfrac{1}{3}$

   B. $7\dfrac{5}{6}$

   C. 6

   D. $5\dfrac{1}{4}$

   E. 4

44. The number of hours it takes a team of workers to assemble a certain type of machine varies directly with the number of machines and inversely with the square of the number of workers on the team. If c represents the constant of variation, which of the following expressions represents the number of hours it will take n workers to assemble x machines?

F. $\dfrac{cx}{n^2}$

G. $\dfrac{cn^2}{x}$

H. $\dfrac{xn^2}{c}$

J. $\dfrac{c}{xn^2}$

K. cxn^2

45. In the circle below, radius $\overline{OP}$ is 10 inches long, $\angle LOP$ is 60°, and $\overline{OP}$ is perpendicular to chord $\overline{LN}$ at M. How many inches long is $\overline{LN}$?

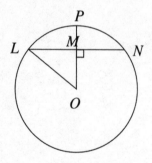

A. $10\sqrt{3}$

B. $3\sqrt{15}$

C. 10

D. $5\sqrt{3}$

E. 5

46. A prism composed of a square base, 2 congruent rectangular sides, and 2 congruent triangular sides is shown "unfolded" in the standard (x, y) coordinate plane below. Points $W(5, 14)$, $X(11, 9)$, $Y(15, 6)$ and $Z(11, 3)$ are vertices of the prism. What is the total surface area, in square coordinate units, of the prism?

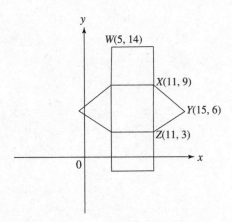

F. 120
G. 132
H. 156
J. 205
K. 360

47. The side lengths of the flat trapezoidal concrete patio in a backyard are given in the figure below. Malik will seal the entire patio with 1 coat of sealant, using sealant that costs $28 per gallon and is sold only by the full gallon. Each gallon of sealant covers an area of 80 square feet with 1 coat of sealant. What is the total cost of sealant that Malik needs to buy?

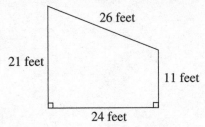

A. $28
B. $56
C. $84
D. $112
E. $140

48. In the figure below, B lies on $\overline{AD}$, and the measure of $\angle A$ is $(4z)°$. Which of the following inequalities is true?

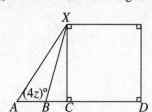

F. $120 < z < 180$
G. $60 < z < 120$
H. $30 < z < 60$
J. $15 < z < 30$
K. $0 < z < 22.5$

49. Each player of a certain game starts on the #10 space of a board with spaces numbered 1 through 150. A player flips a coin and moves forward 6 spaces for each time the coin lands on heads and moves backward 3 spaces for each time the coin lands on tails. Sven's coin landed on heads twice as many times as it landed on tails, moving him to the #100 space on the board. How many times did Sven's coin land on heads?

A. 5
B. 10
C. 15
D. 20
E. 25

50. In the standard (x, y) coordinate plane, when $f \neq 0$ and $g \neq 0$,

the graph of $h(x) = \dfrac{3x + g}{x + f}$ has a *horizontal* asymptote at:

F. $y = -\dfrac{g}{f}$

G. $y = \dfrac{g}{3}$

H. $y = -g$

J. $y = f$

K. $y = 3$

DO YOUR FIGURING HERE.

51. On the real number line, −0.578 is between $\dfrac{z}{1,000}$ and $\dfrac{z+10}{1,000}$

for some integer z. What is the value of z?

A. −5,790
B. −590
C. −580
D. −570
E. −50

52. The stem-and-leaf plot below shows the scores received on a given test by the 32 students in Mrs. Brown's algebra class. What was the median score on this algebra test?

Stem	Leaf
5	1 2 3 4 6 7
6	3 3 4 5 5 8 9
7	0 1 2 4 6 7 7 7 9
8	0 3 4 4 5 6
9	1 1 2 5

Key: 5 | 1 = 51

F. 72
G. 73
H. 74
J. 76
K. 77

53. Angle R has a measure of $\dfrac{35}{4}\pi$ radians. Angle R and angle S are coterminal. Angle S could have which of the following measures?

A. 12°
B. 36°
C. 45°
D. 90°
E. 135°

54. Which of the following complex numbers equals $(\sqrt{2} - 5i)(4 + 3i)$?

F. $4\sqrt{2} - 15i^2$
G. $(\sqrt{2} + 4) - 2i$
H. $(4\sqrt{2} + 15) + (3\sqrt{2} - 20)i$
J. $(4\sqrt{2} - 15) + (3\sqrt{2} - 20)i$
K. $(3\sqrt{2} + 15) + (4\sqrt{2} + 20)i$

55. If $y = 2$ is one solution to the equation $y^2 + cy - 8 = 0$, then the other solution is:

A. -6
B. -4
C. -2
D. 2
E. 4

DO YOUR FIGURING HERE.

56. For all x such that $\cos x \neq 0$, the expression $\dfrac{\csc x \cdot \tan x}{\cos^2 x}$ is equivalent to which of the following?

(Note: $\sec x = \dfrac{1}{\cos x}$; $\csc x = \dfrac{1}{\sin x}$; $\tan x = \dfrac{\sin x}{\cos x}$)

F. $\csc^2 x$
G. $\csc^2 x \cdot \tan x$
H. $\sec^3 x$
J. $\sin x$
K. 1

57. Which of the following categories represents quadrilaterals with diagonals that do NOT bisect each other?

A. Trapezoid (1 pair of parallel sides)
B. Parallelogram (2 pairs of parallel sides)
C. Rectangle (4 congruent angles)
D. Rhombus (4 congruent sides)
E. Square (4 congruent sides and angles)

58. Three line segments are graphed in the standard (x, y) coordinate plane below. Line segment $\overline{PQ}$ has endpoints $P(0, -1)$ and $Q(0, -5)$, $\overline{P'Q'}$ is the image of $\overline{PQ}$ after a rotation counterclockwise by 150° about the origin, and $\overline{P''Q''}$ is $\overline{P'Q'}$ projected onto the x-axis. What is the length, in coordinate units, of $\overline{P''Q''}$?

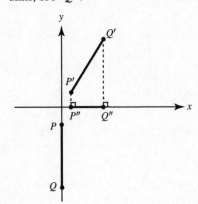

F. $\dfrac{4}{\sqrt{3}}$

G. $\dfrac{4}{\sqrt{2}}$

H. $2\sqrt{3}$

J. $2\sqrt{2}$

K. 2

59. Consecutive terms of a certain geometric sequence have a constant integer ratio between adjacent terms. The product of the first three terms of the sequence is 1,728. Which of the following values CANNOT be the first term of the arithmetic sequence?

A. 7
B. 6
C. 4
D. 3
E. 2

DO YOUR FIGURING HERE.

60. Given $p(x) = \sqrt[3]{x - 4}$, which of the following expressions is equal to $p^{-1}(x)$ for all real numbers x?

F. $\sqrt[3]{x} - 4$

G. $-\sqrt[3]{x - 4}$

H. $\sqrt[3]{x + 4}$

J. $(x - 4)^3$

K. $x^3 + 4$

Chapter 16
Mathematics
Test: Answers and
Explanations

ANSWER KEY

1.	D	31.	D
2.	J	32.	K
3.	B	33.	A
4.	H	34.	H
5.	B	35.	C
6.	J	36.	G
7.	A	37.	D
8.	F	38.	F
9.	D	39.	C
10.	F	40.	J
11.	B	41.	E
12.	G	42.	J
13.	E	43.	D
14.	G	44.	F
15.	A	45.	A
16.	G	46.	F
17.	C	47.	E
18.	J	48.	K
19.	D	49.	D
20.	F	50.	K
21.	B	51.	C
22.	G	52.	G
23.	C	53.	E
24.	G	54.	H
25.	A	55.	B
26.	H	56.	H
27.	E	57.	A
28.	G	58.	K
29.	C	59.	A
30.	K	60.	K

MATH TEST EXPLANATIONS

1. **D** Helene's first 50 posters will cost $1.50 each. The cost for these is 50 × $1.50 = $75.00. Helene orders 64 posters, so she needs 14 more. These will cost half the regular fee, or $0.75 each. The additional cost is 14 × $0.75 = $10.50. Add the two amounts together to get $75.00 + $10.50 = $85.50. Choice (D) is the credited response.

2. **J** When asked for a specific value and given numbers in the answer choices, Plug In The Answers. Start with (H) and plug in 16.5 for y. The equation becomes $\frac{3(16.5-5)}{2} = \frac{3(11.5)}{2} = \frac{34.5}{2} =$ 17.25. This is not equal to 18, so (H) can be eliminated. The value is too small, so (F) and (G) can also be eliminated. Try plugging in the value in (J) next, since the previous result was only a bit too small. The equation becomes $\frac{3(17-5)}{2} = \frac{3(12)}{2} = \frac{36}{2} = 18$, so (J) is the credited response.

3. **B** When asked for a specific value and given numbers in the answer choices, Plug In The Answers. The length of the room equals y + the length of the table + y. Start with the value in (C), and Plug In 10.5 for y in the equation. If $y = 10.5$, the length of the room is 10.5 + 7 + 10.5 = 28. The question states that the room is 25 feet long, so this value of 28 is too big. Choice (C) can be eliminated, and (D) and (E) are too big as well. Try the value in (B) next. If $y = 9$, the length of the room is 9 + 7 + 9 = 25. This is the correct length, so (B) is the credited response.

4. **H** When asked for a specific value and given numbers in the answer choices, Plug In The Answers. Start with the value in (H) and plug in $\frac{6}{5}$ for y in the equation. The equation becomes $7(\frac{6}{5}) - 2 =$ $2(\frac{6}{5} + 2)$. Simplify the left side of the equation first to get $\frac{42}{5} - 2$. Now, find a common denominator to subtract the two numbers. 2 is equal to $\frac{10}{5}$, so the left side equals $\frac{42}{5} - \frac{10}{5} = \frac{32}{5}$. Now work on the right side, getting a common denominator so it becomes $2(\frac{6}{5} + \frac{10}{5}) = 2(\frac{16}{5}) = \frac{32}{5}$. The two sides are equal, so (H) is the credited response.

5. **B** With questions that have multiple variables to different powers, it is best to concentrate on one piece at a time. Starting with the coefficients in this expression, $-\frac{28}{7} = -4$. Choices (D) and (E) do not start with −4, so they can be eliminated. To divide values when the bases are the same, subtract the exponents. The values for a are $\frac{a^5}{a} = a^{(5-1)} = a^4$. Choices (A) and (C) can be eliminated because they have different exponents for a. Choice (B) is the only remaining answer choice and is the credited response.

6. **J** For questions asking for the number of possible combinations, draw a line on the paper for each category in the question and label them.

_____ _____ _____

earrings   necklaces   bracelets

Fill in each blank with the number of possible options in that category.

___7___   ___5___   ___6___

earrings   necklaces   bracelets

Multiply the numbers together to get the total number of combinations. $7 \times 5 \times 6 = 210$, so (J) is the credited response.

7. **A** The questions asks how much greater the value of $135 is than the value of −$12, which is the difference between the two numbers. When the smaller value is subtracted from the larger value, the result is $135 − (−$12) = $135 + $12 = 147$. Choice (A) is the credited response.

8. **F** This is a Plugging In question for which the values to plug in have been provided. Plug the value given for each variable into the equation, being careful to put each value in the correct spot. The equation becomes $\frac{(1)(2) - (5)(3)}{(2)(3) + (1)(5)} = \frac{2 - 15}{6 + 5} = \frac{-13}{11}$. Therefore, (F) is the credited response.

9. **D** Use Process Of Elimination to get rid of answers that contain graphs that do not reflect a movement of two units down from the original graph. The graph in (A) is shifted up from the original, not down, so it can be eliminated. The graphs shown in (C) and (E) are both still touching the x-axis, so they have not moved down and can be eliminated. The graphs in (B) and (D) have both been shifted down 2 units. However, the graph in (B) is much wider than the original graph, while (D) retains the original shape. Therefore, (B) can be eliminated, and (D) is the credited response.

10. **F** Rather than trying to find the least common denominator manually, use the answer choices to determine if each one is divisible by 10, 9, and 6. When Plugging In The Answers on a question that asks for the "least" value that works, start with the smallest answer choice. Using the value in (F), $90 \div 10 = 9$, $90 \div 9 = 10$, and $90 \div 6 = 15$. Therefore, (F) contains the least common denominator for the fractions and is the credited response.

11. **B** Total = Average × Number of Things, so here the total = 48 × 6 = 288. The total of the first 5 numbers = 34 + 43 + 52 + 58 + 56 = 243. The difference between the total of all 6 numbers and the total of the first 5 numbers = 288 − 243 = 45, so the 6th number is 45. Choice (B) is the credited response.

12. **G** When asked for a specific value and given numbers in the answer choices, Plug In The Answers. Start with the value in (H), and plug in 36 for the depth of the sand. Volume = Length × Width × Depth, so multiply 24 × 18 × 36 to get 15,552. This value is much larger than the stated volume of 5,184, so (H) can be eliminated. Choices (J) and (K) are also too large and can be eliminated. Plug in the value in (G) to get Volume = 24 × 18 × 12 = 5,184. This matches the stated volume, so (G) is the credited response.

13. **E** When given variables in the answer choices, Plug In. Say shirts at Nifty Thrift Shop cost $1 and pants cost $2, and Ben buys 3 of each. So, $s = 1$, $p = 2$, and $n = 3$. The 3 shirts would cost Ben $3, and the 3 pants would cost him $6, for a total purchase cost of $9. If Ben pays with $20, his change will be $11. This is the target answer. Now, plug the values for n, s, and p into the answer choices to see which one equals $11. Choice (A) is $3(2 + 1) = 3(3) = 9$. This is not $11, so (A) can be eliminated. Choice (B) is $3 × 2 × 1 = 6$, so (B) can also be eliminated. Choice (C) is $20 − (3 × 2 × 1) = 20 − 6 = 14$, so (C) can be eliminated. Choice (D) is $20 − 3(2 − 1) = 20 − 3(1) = 20 − 3 = 17$. This is not $11, so (D) can be eliminated as well. Choice (E) is $20 − 3(2 + 1) = 20 − 3(3) = 20 − 9 = 11$. This is the target answer, so (E) is the credited response.

14. **G** Absolute values are always positive, so (F) can be eliminated immediately. With absolute-value questions involving negative values, do one step of math at a time and calculate carefully. The equation becomes $|4(3) + 5(−7)| = |12 + 5(−7)| = |12 + (−35)| = |−23| = 23$. Choice (G) is the credited response.

15. **A** The shaded region has some missing pieces. Therefore, the credited response must include subtraction, so (D) and (E) can be eliminated. When solving geometry questions, write out any necessary formulas. The formula for the area of a circle is $A = \pi r^2$, and all the remaining answer choices contain that element. The formula for the area of a square is $A = s^2$, and there are 4 squares, so the total area for the squares is $4s^2$. The area of the shaded region is the difference between the area of the circle and the area of the squares, which is $\pi r^2 − 4s^2$, so (A) is the credited response.

16. **G** When parallel lines are crossed by a transversal, two kinds of angles are created—big and small. Any big angle equals any other big angle, and any small angle equals any other small angle. The angle labeled 70° and the angle labeled $a°$ are both small angles, so $a = 70°$. The angle that is $a°$ and the angle that is $b°$ add up to 180°, so $b = 110°$. Therefore, $b − a = 110 − 70 = 40$, so (G) is the credited response.

17. **C**   Solving inequalities is just like solving equations, except that the inequality sign must be flipped whenever multiplying or dividing by a negative number. To solve this inequality, start by adding 1 to each side. The inequality becomes $2y \leq 10$. Now divide both sides by 2 to get $y \leq 5$. When graphing this inequality, the dot must be on the number 5. Choices (B), (D), and (E) can be eliminated, since the endpoints for those are on different numbers. The inequality sign opens toward the 5, which means that y is smaller than or equal to 5. The graph in (C) includes all numbers less than or equal to 5, so (C) is the credited response.

18. **J**   This is a Plugging In question for which the value to plug in has been provided. Plug the value given for n into the equation, being careful with the negative signs. The equation becomes $2(-2)^3 + 4 = 2(-8) + 4 = -16 + 4 = -12$. Therefore, (J) is the credited response.

19. **D**   Start by labeling the given angle measurements on the figure. $\angle AXD = \angle AXC + \angle CXD$, so if $\angle AXD = 180°$ and $\angle AXC$ is 110°, then $\angle CXD = 70°$. $\angle BXD$ is 90° and is equal to $\angle BXC + \angle CXD$, so $\angle BXC = 20°$. Therefore, (D) is the credited response.

20. **F**   The chart indicates that 3 cups of onion are needed to make 600 ounces of vegetable soup. To make 320 ounces of soup, or about half a batch, the cook will need about half as much onion, or close to 1.5 cups. Since 320 is slightly more than half a batch, the cook needs slightly more than 1.5 cups. Therefore, by using Ballparking, it seems like (F) is the correct answer. To actually calculate how many cups of onion are needed, set up a proportion, with cups of onion over ounces of soup on each side.

$$\frac{3}{600} = \frac{x}{320}$$

Now cross-multiply to get $3(320) = 600(x)$ or $960 = 600x$. Divide both sides by 600 to get $x = 1.6$. Choice (F) is the credited response.

21. **B**   According to the chart, mulligatawny soup requires 3.5 cups of chopped onion, 6 cups of chopped carrot, and 7 cups of chopped celery. With the onion in stock, the restaurant can make a bit more than 5 batches of soup. The carrot stock is enough for just over 4 batches of soup, and the celery stock is enough for exactly 4 batches of soup. Therefore, the restaurant can only make 4 batches of soup. Each batch makes 600 ounces of soup, so 4 batches make 4(600) or 2,400 ounces of soup. Choice (B) is the credited response.

22. **G**   Look at the chart to determine the amounts of onion, carrot, and celery needed for both tomato and vegetable soup. Starting with onion, the amount needed is 4 cups for tomato soup and 3 cups for vegetable soup, for a total of 7 cups. The price of onion is x, so any answer choice that does not associate 7 with x can be eliminated. Therefore, (F), (H), and (J) can be eliminated, leaving only (G) and (K). If the onion costs x per cup, the number of cups will be multiplied by x to get the total. Therefore, (G) is the credited response. Plugging In values for x, y, and z would also work here, but it may be a bit time consuming to check all five answer choices.

23. **C** When given a system of equations, solving for one variable and substituting the value into the other equation is an option. Usually, though, it is easier to stack the equations one above the other and add or subtract them. The goal is to make one of the variables disappear, and in this case, the question asks for the value of y, so the x terms need to go. First, line the x terms up, so the equations look like this:

$$3x \quad = 13$$
$$2x - 4y = 3$$

If the equations were added together, both variables would still appear in the result. Therefore, they need to be manipulated a bit first to get a common coefficient on the x terms. Multiply the top equation by 2 and the bottom equation by –3, like so:

$$2(3x \quad = 13)$$
$$-3(2x - 4y = 3)$$

Multiply the equations and add them together, as shown below:

$$6x \quad = 26$$
$$\underline{-6x + 12y = -9}$$
$$12y = 17$$

Now divide both sides by 12 to get $y = \dfrac{17}{12}$, making (C) the credited response.

24. **G** Start by calculating how many jars are currently processed per minute by the sealing machines. If there are 16 machines working at a rate of 30 jars per minute, together they seal 16×30 or 480 jars in 1 minute. A labeling machine will process 2 jars per second, and there are 60 seconds in a minute, so it will process 2×60 or 120 jars in 1 minute. This rate is $\dfrac{1}{4}$ the rate of the sealing machines, because $\dfrac{120}{480} = \dfrac{1}{4}$, so there must be 4 labeling machines to keep up with the rate of the sealing machines. Choice (G) is the credited response.

25. **A** Before any subtraction is done, it is necessary to distribute the negative sign to each term in the bottom equation. If the negative sign remains outside the parenthesis, the chances for a sign error are very high. When the negative is distributed, the subtraction problem becomes:

$$9y^2 \qquad + 3$$
$$\underline{+2y^2 + 5y - 7}$$

Now it is an addition problem and much more straightforward. Start by adding the terms that contain y^2. This results in $9y^2 + 2y^2 = 11y^2$. Choices (D) and (E) do not contain this term, so they can be eliminated. The credited response must contain $+5y$, so (B) and (C) can be eliminated. Finally, $3 - 7 = -4$, so (A) is the credited response.

26. **H** The acronym to remember for exponent problems is $M^AD^SP^M$, which stands for Multiply Add Divide Subtract Power Multiply. The order of operations must also be followed, so parentheses and exponents must come before multiplication. The right side of the equation becomes $y^{(3\times4)}y^{(5\times2)}$, which equals $y^{12}y^{10}$. Then, to multiply these terms, add the exponents, to get $y^{(12+10)}$ or y^{22}. Now the equation is $y^b = y^{22}$, so $b = 22$, and (H) is the credited response.

27. **E** When asked for a specific number, Plug In The Answers. Start with the value in (C) and multiply it by 1,000. If the result equals 0.07, the target number, then that is the credited response. $0.007 \times 1,000 = 7$, so the value in (C) is too large. Therefore, (C) can be eliminated, as can the larger values in (A) and (B). Try plugging in the value in (E). $0.00007 \times 1,000 = 0.07$, which is the target number, so (E) is the credited response.

28. **G** According to the diagram, the percent of people who purchased only beef, with no overlap to any of the other circles, was 20%. To find the estimate for the number of people who bought only beef, multiply this percent by the total number of people in the grocery store. $\frac{20}{100} (1,300) = 260$, so (G) is the credited response.

29. **C** For this question, find the percents in each circle that do not represent any overlap with another circle. This is 20% for beef, 25% for poultry, 15% for pork, and 15% for seafood. Add these numbers to get the total. $20\% + 25\% + 15\% + 15\% = 75\%$, so (C) is the credited response.

30. **K** The question says to find the fraction of people "among all 150 asked" who purchased only seafood. The fractions in the answers have not been reduced, so the credited response must have 150 in the denominator. Therefore, (F), (H), and (J) can be eliminated. To find the actual number of people who purchased only seafood, start by finding the number in the original sample that fit this requirement. According to the diagram, 15% of the 120 people asked purchased only seafood. $\frac{15}{100} (120) = 18$ people. The questions states that an additional 10 people purchased seafood from the 30 additional people asked the question. (The rest of the information is just there as a distraction.) The 18 people who originally purchased only seafood plus the 10 in the additional group yields a total of 28 people who purchased only seafood. Therefore, the fraction of people who purchased seafood only is $\frac{28}{150}$, and (K) is the credited response.

31. **D**   Try Ballparking first. $\angle U$ looks like it is about 90°. Choice (A) is too small and (E) is too large, so these can be eliminated. Choices (C) and (D) are the closest to 90°, so one of these would make a good guess. To actually solve this problem, use the applicable geometry facts for straight lines and triangles. R, S, and T are collinear, and there are 180° in a straight line. Therefore, $\angle TSU$ and $\angle RSU$ add up to 180°, and $3x + 9x = 180$. This becomes $12x = 180$, so $x = 15$. $\angle TSU$ equals $(3x)°$, so the measure of that angle is 45°. There are 180° in a triangle, so $45 + 37 + \angle U = 180$. This becomes $82 + \angle U = 180$, so $\angle U = 98$. Choice (D) is the credited response.

32. **K**   If the center of a circle is at (h, k), the formula for the equation for that circle is $(x - h)^2 + (y - k)^2 = r^2$. The x-coordinate of the circle is in parentheses with the x, and the y-coordinate is in parentheses with the y. Therefore, (F) and (G) can be eliminated, because they switch the x- and y-coordinates. The signs in the circle equation in the question are both positive, so they should still match in the credited response. Choice (H) can now be eliminated, since the numbers in that answer have opposite signs. Finally, the equation of a circle has x <u>minus</u> the x-coordinate of the center. The equation in the question has addition, which means there must have been subtraction of a negative x-coordinate. The two negatives cancel each other out to become a positive. The correct answer should have two negative values as a result, not two positive values—so (K) is the credited response.

33. **A**   The answer choices indicate that this is a trigonometry question. Write SOHCAHTOA down and then determine which trig function to use. The question asks for the height of the water tower, so label that h on the diagram. For this triangle, the height of the water tower (h) is opposite the given angle of 26°. The distance along the ground from the center of the base (112 feet) is the adjacent side. This means the tangent function will be used to find the height, because the "TOA" part of SOHCAHTOA indicates that tangent = $\dfrac{opposite}{adjacent}$. As a result, (B), (C), and (E) can be eliminated, since they don't involve the tangent function. Now plug the given values into the tangent expression to get $\tan 26° = \dfrac{h}{112}$. To solve this for the height, multiply both sides of the equation by 112 to get $h = 112 \tan 26°$. Choice (A) is the credited response.

34.   H   Draw the standard (x, y) coordinate plane and sketch the lines in the answer choices. Most of these equations are easy to sketch, but (J) is a little more difficult. Start with the other four equations, labeling each one carefully. It should look like this:

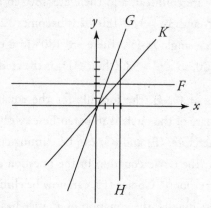

The line for the equation in (H) is parallel to the y-axis, so sketching (J) is unnecessary. Choice (H) is the credited response.

35.   C   The first step is to put the equation for line f, which is $4x + 5y = 15$, into $y = mx + b$ form. Subtract $4x$ from both sides to get $5y = -4x + 15$. Now divide both sides of the equation by 5, so the equation becomes $y = -\dfrac{4}{5}x + 3$. Slope is the m in the $y = mx + b$ form, so the slope of line f is $-\dfrac{4}{5}$. The slope of line g is 3 times that, so it is $(-\dfrac{4}{5})(3)$ or $-\dfrac{12}{5}$. At this point, (A), (D), and (E) can be eliminated, as those do not have the correct slope. The y-intercept is the b in $y = mx + b$, so the y-intercept of line f is 3. For line g, the y-intercept is one more than that, or 4, so (C) is the credited response.

36.   G   Period is defined as the distance required for a function to make one full cycle, or how long before it starts to repeat itself. Start at the origin and look at the function to the right of the y-axis. First, the graph slopes up, like the right side of a parabola, between $x = 0$ and the asymptote, or dashed line, at $x = \dfrac{\pi}{2}$. Between the asymptotes at $x = \dfrac{\pi}{2}$ and $x = \dfrac{3\pi}{2}$, it looks like an upside-down parabola. Between $x = \dfrac{3\pi}{2}$ and $x = 2\pi$, the graph looks like the left side of a parabola. At $x = 2\pi$, it starts sloping up again like the right side of a parabola. Since this is the point where it starts to repeat itself, the period is 2π. Choice (G) is the credited response.

37.   D   When asked for a specific value and given numbers in the answer choices, Plug In the Answers. Start by labeling the answers "longer side," and then make column headings for "shorter side" and "ratio." Starting with (C), assume the longer side is 10. To figure out the shorter side, use the easier piece of information, which is that the area is 84. The area of a rectangle = length × width, so 84 = 10 × (shorter side), making the shorter side 8.4. Now use the more complicated information about ratios to check these values. If these are the correct dimensions, the ratio of the longer side to the shorter one will be 7 to 3, which can also be written as $\frac{7}{3}$. Because $\frac{10}{8.4} \neq \frac{7}{3}$, (C) can be eliminated. For (C), the lengths of the longer side and shorter side were very close together, so the correct values need to be farther apart. Choices (A) and (B) won't do that, and the values are too small for the "longer" side, so try the value in (D). Again, use the area information to determine the other side length. 84 = 14 × (shorter side), so the shorter side is 6. The ratio of $\frac{14}{6} = \frac{7}{3}$, so (D) is the credited response.

38.   F   Draw an (x, y) coordinate plane and label the axes. Take the information in the problem one step at a time and sketch out the graph. Jebediah starts at his home, so the initial distance from his home is 0 km. Then he starts walking away from his home, so the distance from his home will increase with time. This will yield a line with a positive slope. Therefore, (G), (H), and (J) can definitely be eliminated. Choice (F) is most likely the answer, but plot out the rest of the information to be sure. Once Jebediah reaches the mailbox, he turns around and goes home. For the second half of his trip, his distance from his home will be steadily decreasing. The graph of this part will be a line segment with a negative slope, so (F) is the credited response.

39.   C   There is no formula for the area of a shape like this, so carve up the figure into common shapes such as rectangles or squares. One way to do it is like this:

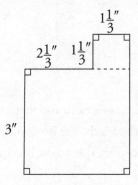

Since all the labeled angles are right angles, the figure now consists of one square on top of one rectangle. The sides of the square are $1\frac{1}{3}$, and the area of a square equals s^2. Mixed fractions are difficult to multiply, so turn the value for s into an improper fraction. $1\frac{1}{3} = 1 + \frac{1}{3} = \frac{3}{3} + \frac{1}{3} = \frac{4}{3}$.

Plug this value into the area formula to get $A = (\frac{4}{3})^2 = \frac{16}{9}$ or $1\frac{7}{9}$. The area of the rectangle equals length times width or base times height. The height is given as 3, but the base is not labeled. However, because all the angles are right angles, the base will be equal to the sum of the other two horizontal lines, the segment labeled $2\frac{1}{3}$ and the top of the square labeled $1\frac{1}{3}$. This can be written as $2\frac{1}{3} + 1\frac{1}{3} = 3\frac{2}{3}$. Again, turn this mixed fraction into an improper fraction for easier multiplication: $3\frac{2}{3} = 3 + \frac{2}{3} = \frac{9}{3} + \frac{2}{3} = \frac{11}{3}$. Plug this value into the area formula for a rectangle to get $A = (\frac{11}{3})(3) = 11$. Add the two areas together to get $1\frac{7}{9} + 11 = 12\frac{7}{9}$ for the entire area of the figure. Therefore, (C) is the credited response.

40. **J** Draw the standard (x, y) coordinate plane and plot point Z at an x-coordinate of -2 and a y-coordinate of -4. It will look like this:

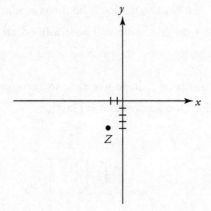

A reflection of a point over an axis means to use that axis as a sort of mirror line, or line of reflection. If the line of reflection is the x-axis, the image of Z will be above the x-axis. It will still be 2 units from the y-axis and 4 units from the x-axis, like the original point, as shown:

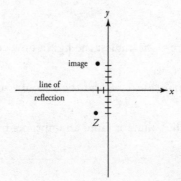

The *x*-coordinate of the image point is still –2, and the *y*-coordinate is now 4, so (J) is the credited response.

41. **E** When given variables in the question, Plug In values to get an actual equation. Try $c = -2$ and $d = 3$, which makes the equation $y \leq -2x + 3$. The slope is negative, so (A), (B), and (D) can be eliminated. The *y*-intercept is positive, so (C) can be eliminated and (E) is the credited response. Another way to determine which answer choice contains the graph of the equation is to plug in a point such as (0, 0). With this point, the equation $y \leq -2x + 3$ becomes $0 \leq -2(0) + 3$, or $0 \leq 3$. This is true, so the correct graph will have this point included in the shaded area. Therefore, (C) and (D) can be eliminated. Now try (0, 10), which makes the equation $10 \leq -2(0) + 3$, or $10 \leq 3$. This is not true, so (A) can be eliminated, since it includes this point in the shaded area. For the point (10, 0), the equation is $0 \leq -2(10) + 3$ or $0 \leq -17$. This is not true, so (B) can be eliminated, and (E) is the credited response.

42. **J** When two fractions are set equal to each other, the numerator on the left equals the one on the right. The same is true for the denominators on both sides. Use this to create two separate equations, $6a - 2b = 3$ and $a + 2b = 2$, which can then be stacked one above the other and added together. This will make the *b* terms disappear. The result is $7a = 5$, so $a = \dfrac{5}{7}$. Use this in one of the equations to solve for *b*. The second equation is the simplest: $\dfrac{5}{7} + 2b = 2$, so $2b = 2 - \dfrac{5}{7} = \dfrac{9}{7}$. Divide both sides by 2 to find that $b = \dfrac{9}{14}$. Now find the value of $\dfrac{a}{b}$: $\dfrac{\frac{5}{7}}{\frac{9}{14}} = \dfrac{\frac{10}{14}}{\frac{9}{14}}$, which simplifies to $\dfrac{10}{9}$, so (J) is the credited response. If the opportunity to Stack-and-Add is not immediately obvious in this problem, don't worry! Cross-multiplying and manipulating the equation until one side equals $\dfrac{a}{b}$ will also work.

43. **D** Similar triangles have the same angles and proportional sides. The proportion can be written two different ways: $\dfrac{\overline{FG}}{\overline{FH}} = \dfrac{\overline{XY}}{\overline{XZ}}$ or $\dfrac{\overline{FG}}{\overline{XY}} = \dfrac{\overline{FH}}{\overline{XZ}}$. Pick one way and Plug In the given values. For the second proportion, this becomes $\dfrac{4}{3} = \dfrac{7}{\overline{XZ}}$. Cross-multiply to get $4(\overline{XZ}) = 3(7)$, or $4(\overline{XZ}) = 21$. Divide both sides of the equation by 4 to get $\overline{XZ} = 5.25$ or $5\dfrac{1}{4}$. Choice (D) is the credited response.

44. **F** When two things vary directly, as one variable increases the other also increases. Plug In values for the different variables, then change the value for the number of machines to determine if it varies directly with the number of hours. Try $c = 2$, $n = 3$, and $x = 4$. For (F), the number of hours with these values is $\dfrac{2 \times 4}{3^2} = \dfrac{8}{9}$. If the number of machines (x) is increased to 5, the new value is $\dfrac{2 \times 5}{3^2} = \dfrac{10}{9}$. This value increased, so (F) could be the credited response. Now try (G) using the same values. The first set of values gives $\dfrac{2(3)^2}{4} = \dfrac{18}{4}$, and the second set gives $\dfrac{2(3)^2}{5} = \dfrac{18}{5}$. This is smaller than the first value, so (G) can be eliminated. The values for (H) are $\dfrac{4(3)^2}{2} = \dfrac{36}{2}$ and then $\dfrac{5(3)^2}{2} = \dfrac{45}{2}$, so (H) could be the credited response. The values for (J) are $\dfrac{2}{4(3)^2} = \dfrac{2}{36}$ and then $\dfrac{2}{5(3)^2} = \dfrac{2}{45}$, so (J) can be eliminated. The values for (K) are $(2)(4)(3^2) = 72$ and then $(2)(5)(3^2) = 90$, so (K) could be the credited response. Now check the remaining answer choices by varying the value for n. If the number of hours varies inversely with the square of n, the number of hours will decrease with an increasing n. For the initial values of $c = 2$, $n = 3$, and $x = 4$, (F) was equal to $\dfrac{8}{9}$. If $n = 5$, (F) becomes $\dfrac{2 \times 4}{5^2}$ or $\dfrac{8}{25}$. The value for (F) got smaller, so (F) is the credited response. Choices (H) and (K) both get larger when the value of n is increased.

45. **A** Start by labeling the length of $\overline{OP}$ and the measurement of $\angle LOP$ on the figure. $\overline{LO}$ is another radius of the circle, so label that with a length of 10 inches as well. $\triangle LMO$ is a 30:60:90 triangle, with $\angle MLO$ equal to 30°. $\overline{LO}$ is opposite the 90° angle, so $\overline{LO}$ is the $2x$ side. If $2x = 10$, then $x = 5$. $\overline{MO}$ is opposite the 30° angle, so $\overline{MO}$ is the x side and is equal to 5. $\overline{LM}$ is opposite the 60° angle, so it is the $x\sqrt{3}$ side and is equal to $5\sqrt{3}$. This is part of the length of $\overline{LN}$, but the length of $\overline{MN}$ still needs to be found. Draw in the radius connecting points N and O to create another triangle. Because $\overline{LO}$ and $\overline{NO}$ are the same length and $\overline{LN}$ is perdendicular to $\overline{OP}$, the new triangle is congruent to $\triangle LMO$. Therefore, $\overline{MN}$ is equal to $\overline{LM}$, and $\overline{LN}$ equals $5\sqrt{3} + 5\sqrt{3}$ or $10\sqrt{3}$. Choice (A) is the credited response.

46. **F** To find the surface area of this prism, the lengths of the sides of each shape need to be determined. Then their individual areas can be calculated and added together. $\overline{XZ}$ is one of the sides of the square base. The difference in the y-coordinates of the two endpoints will give the length of the side of the square, so $\overline{XZ}$ is $(9 - 3)$ or 6 units long. The area of a square = s^2, so the area of the base

is 6^2 or 36. The base of the top rectangle is also the side of the square, so the base is 6. The difference in the y-coordinates of points W and X will give the height of the top rectangle, so the height is $(14 - 9)$ or 5. The area of a rectangle = bh, so the area of the top rectangle is $(6)(5)$ or 30. The bottom rectangle is also 30, since the two rectangles are congruent. Now, the area of each triangle, defined as $\frac{1}{2} bh$, needs to be calculated. $\overline{XZ}$ can be used as the base of the triangle on the right, and the height is the difference in the x-coordinates of point Y and the line containing $\overline{XZ}$. The height is $(15 - 11)$ or 4, so the area of the triangle on the right is $\frac{1}{2} (6)(4)$ or 12. The triangles are congruent, so the triangle on the left also has an area of 12. Now add all the areas of all the shapes to get the total surface area of the prism. $36 + 30 + 30 + 12 + 12 = 120$, so (F) is the credited response.

47.   E   Start by finding the area of the patio. Rather than trying to remember the formula for the area of a trapezoid, draw a horizontal line to divide the shape into a triangle sitting on top of a rectangle. The dimensions of the rectangle are 24 feet by 11 feet, so the area of the rectangle is 24(11) or 264 square feet. The height of the triangle is 10 feet, since the whole left side is 21 feet and the rectangle portion is 11 of those. Plug the base, which is 24 feet, and the height into the formula for the area of a triangle, $A = \frac{1}{2} bh$, to get $A = \frac{1}{2} (24)(10) = 120$. Therefore, the total area of the patio is $264 + 120$ or 384 square feet. Each gallon of sealant will cover 80 square feet, so Malik needs $\frac{384}{80}$ or 4.8 gallons of sealant. He has to buy full gallons, so he needs 5 gallons at $28 each. His total cost is 5($28) or $140, so (E) is the credited response.

48.   K   To figure out the measures of the angles within $\triangle ACX$, use the information provided in the rest of the figure. $\angle DCX$ is 90°, so $\angle ACX$ is also 90°. There are 180° in a triangle, so $\angle A + \angle AXC + 90 = 180$. Subtract 90 from each side to get $\angle A + \angle AXC = 90°$. No information is given about the measure of $\angle AXC$, but it has to have some value, so $\angle A$ is less than 90°. $\angle A = 4z$, so $4z < 90$. Divide both sides by 4 to find that $z < 22.5$. Therefore, (K) is the credited response.

49.   D   When asked for a specific amount and given numbers in the answer choices, Plug In The Answers. Start with (C) and assume that Sven's coin landed on heads 15 times. This would mean that his coin landed on tails half as many times as that, or 7.5 times. It is not possible to flip a coin 7.5 times, so (C) cannot be the credited response. It is now clear that an even number is needed, so (A) and (E) can also be eliminated. Try the value in (D) and assume Sven's coin landed on heads 20 times and tails 10 times. He moved forward 6 spaces for each coin toss that resulted in heads, so he moved forward 20(6) or 120 spaces. He started on the #10 space, so that would move him to the (10 + 120) or #130 space. He moved backward 3 spaces for each coin toss that resulted in tails, so he moved back 10(3) or 30 spaces. From the #130 space, this would move him back to the (130 − 30) or #100 space. The question states that Sven did end up on the #100 space, so (D) is the credited response.

50. **K** An asymptote is a line that a graph approaches but does not (usually) reach. A horizontal asymptote can occasionally be crossed, but a graph of an equation will usually reveal the line that is the boundary of the *y*-value. To graph this function on a calculator, however, values need to be set for *f* and *g*. Given these variables in the question and answer choices, Plug In numbers for *f* and *g*, following the restriction that 0 is not used. Try *f* = 1 and *g* = 2. Now the function is $h(x) = \dfrac{3x + 2}{x + 1}$ or *y* = (3*x* + 2) / (*x* + 1). Graphed on a calculator with a window of 10 units in all directions from the origin, the resulting image looks like this:

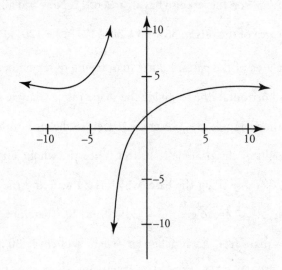

The graph gets close to, but does not seem to reach the horizontal line at *y* = 3. Choice (K) looks like the credited response, but check the other answers to make sure that none of them also equals 3. Choice (F) is $y = -\dfrac{2}{1}$ or –2, (G) is $y = \dfrac{2}{3}$, (H) is *y* = –2, and (J) is *y* = 1. None of these are *y* = 3, so they can be eliminated, and (K) is the credited response.

51. **C** When asked for a specific value and given numbers in the answer choices, Plug In The Answers. Start with (C) and assume that *z* = –580. The value for $\dfrac{z}{1{,}000}$ is $\dfrac{-580}{1{,}000}$ or –0.58. The value for $\dfrac{z + 10}{1{,}000}$ is $\dfrac{-580 + 10}{1{,}000}$, which equals $\dfrac{-570}{1{,}000}$ or –0.57. The given value of –0.578 is between these two numbers on the number line, so (C) is the credited response.

52. **G** Each of the numbers on the stem-and-leaf plot under the "leaf" heading represents one score on the test. To find the median of this list of scores, the middle number needs to be determined. Start by crossing off 4 scores from the top row of the list and 4 scores from the bottom of the list, like this:

```
Stem | Leaf
   5 | 1̶ 2̶ 3̶ 4̶ 6 7
   6 | 3 3 4 5 5 8 9
   7 | 0 1 2 4 6 7 7 7 9
   8 | 0 3 4 4 5 6
   9 | 1̶ 1̶ 2̶ 5̶
```

Continue in this manner, crossing off the same numbers of scores from the front and back ends of the list, until the middle of the list is reached.

```
Stem | Leaf
   5 | 1̶ 2̶ 3̶ 4̶ 6̶ 7̶
   6 | 3̶ 3̶ 4̶ 5̶ 5̶ 8̶ 9̶
   7 | 0̶ 1̶ 2 4 6̶ 7̶ 7̶ 7̶ 9̶
   8 | 0̶ 3̶ 4̶ 4̶ 5̶ 6̶
   9 | 1̶ 1̶ 2̶ 5̶
```

If there were an odd number of scores on the list, the single score in the middle would be the median. With an even number of scores, the median is the average of the middle two scores. In this case, the middle two numbers are 72 and 74. The average of these two numbers is 73, so (G) is the credited response.

53.　E　The question gives the measure of angle R in radians, but the answers contain degree measures. Start by converting $\frac{35}{4}\pi$ radians into degrees. The unit circle is 2π radians and a circle has $360°$, so $2\pi = 360°$ and $\pi = 180°$. Therefore, $\frac{35}{4}\pi$ radians $= \frac{35}{4}(180°) = 1{,}575°$. "Coterminal," or having the same terminal angle, means that the angle measures are equivalent on the unit circle. From a measure of $1{,}575°$, it is necessary to go down to the much smaller measures in the answer choices. So, subtract $360°$ from $1{,}575°$ as many times as is needed to hit one of the answer choices. $1{,}575° - 360° = 1{,}215° - 360° = 855° - 360° = 495° - 360° = 135°$. Therefore, $1{,}575°$ and $135°$ are coterminal, so (E) is the credited response.

54.　H　This looks ugly, but there are pairs of numbers in parentheses. That indicates that it is possible to use FOIL (First, Outer, Inner, Last) to multiply the binomials together. The result is $4\sqrt{2} + 3\sqrt{2}\,i - 20i - 15i^2$. The middle two terms can be combined to get $4\sqrt{2} + (3\sqrt{2} - 20)i - 15i^2$. At this point, (G) and (J) can be eliminated because they do not contain $4\sqrt{2}$. Choice (F) does not contain $(3\sqrt{2} - 20)i$, so it can be eliminated as well. Neither (H) nor (J) match the equation exactly, but now there is a fifty-fifty chance of choosing the right answer. To get the exact answer, however, it is necessary to know that i^2 is equal to –1, so $15i^2$ equals –15. Most calculators also include a button for i, so calculating i^2 on a calculator can help if this rule doesn't come to mind. This changes the equation into $4\sqrt{2} + (3\sqrt{2} - 20)i - (-15)$ or $4\sqrt{2} + (3\sqrt{2} - 20)i + 15$, which makes (H) the credited response.

55. **B** If $y = 2$ is a solution to the equation, that means to Plug In 2 for y to solve the equation for c. The equation becomes $2^2 + c(2) - 8 = 0$, which simplifies to $4 + 2c - 8 = 0$ or $2c - 4 = 0$. Add 4 to both sides of the equation to get $2c = 4$, so $c = 2$. Plug this value for c into the original equation to get $y^2 + 2y - 8 = 0$. Now use FOIL to determine the two factors of this equation. The factors are $(y - 2)$ and $(y + 4)$. To find the solutions for a quadratic, set each factor equal to zero and solve. The question already stated that $y = 2$ was a solution, so focus on $(y + 4) = 0$. Subtract 4 from each side to get $y = -4$. (B) is the credited response.

56. **H** One way to solve a tricky trig question like this would be to get everything into terms of sine and cosine before trying to simplify it. A better approach on most tricky trig problems is to Plug In a value for x and to rely on the calculator to do the hard work. Pick a value like $x = 20°$ and Plug In, making sure the calculator is in degrees, not radians. Taking it in bite-sized pieces to avoid errors, calculate that $\csc 20° = \dfrac{1}{\sin 20°} = 2.924$ (approximately), $\tan 20° = 0.364$, and $\cos^2 20° = (0.940)^2$ $= 0.884$. Therefore, $\dfrac{\csc x \cdot \tan x}{\cos^2 x} = \dfrac{(2.924)(0.364)}{(0.884)} = 1.204$. Now Plug in $x = 20$ on each of the answer choices to see which one equals approximately 1.204. Choice (K) definitely does not, so it can be eliminated. For (F), $\csc 20° = 2.924$, so $\csc^2 20° = (2.924)^2 = 8.550$. This is not 1.204, so (F) can be eliminated. Choice (G) can be rewritten as $\left(\dfrac{1}{\sin^2 20°}\right)(\tan 20°) = \left(\dfrac{1}{(0.342)^2}\right)(\tan 20°)$ $= (8.55)(0.364) = 3.112$, so (G) can also be eliminated. Choice (H) equals $\dfrac{1}{\cos^3 x} = \dfrac{1}{(0.939)^3} =$ 1.204, so (H) seems to be the credited response. Check (J) just to be certain; $\sin 20° = 0.342$, which is not 1.204, so (J) can be eliminated, and (H) is the credited response.

57. **A** Draw examples of each of these types of quadrilateral, including the diagonals. If the diagonals bisect each other, or divide each other in two equal parts, eliminate them. Choice (A) will look like this:

Trapezoid

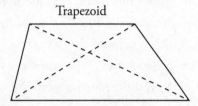

The diagonals do not bisect each other, so (A) seems to be the credited response. Check the other answer choices, just to be certain. They will look like this:

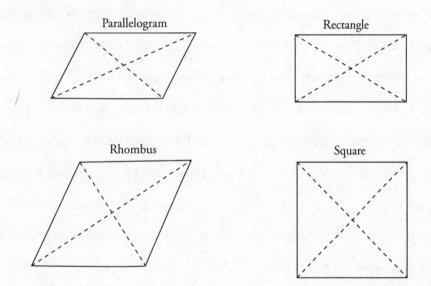

Parallelogram

Rectangle

Rhombus

Square

The diagonals in all these categories do bisect each other, so (A) is the credited response.

58. **K** Start by determining the length of $\overline{PQ}$. Since it spans the *y*-coordinate values from −1 to −5, it is 4 units in length. This means that $\overline{P'Q'}$ is also 4 units in length, since it is just a rotation of $\overline{PQ}$. Now make $\overline{P'Q'}$ the hypotenuse of a right triangle by drawing a line from point P' out to the right and a line from point Q' down so that they meet in a right angle, like this:

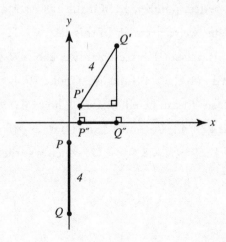

As $\overline{PQ}$ rotated counterclockwise, the first 90° it rotated brought it up to the positive x-axis. The rest of the rotation brought it to its current position, so it rotated an additional 60° into the first quadrant, because 150° − 90° = 60°. This means that the angle between $\overline{P'Q'}$ and the base of the right triangle is 60°, and the other angle is 30°. $\overline{P'Q'}$ is the hypotenuse, so it is the $2x$ side of this 30:60:90 triangle. The base, which is opposite the 30°, is the x side, so it is 2 units in length. This base is the same length as the projection of $\overline{P'Q'}$ onto the x-axis, also known as $\overline{P''Q''}$. Therefore, $\overline{P''Q''}$ is 2 units in length, and (K) is the credited response.

59. **A**   A geometric sequence is a series of numbers in which each term after the first is obtained by multiplying by the same number, which could be positive, negative, or fractional. For example, 3, 6, 12 is a geometric sequence because each term is multiplied by 2 to get the next term. Similarly, the ratio between adjacent terms is the same because $\dfrac{12}{6} = \dfrac{6}{3} = 2$. To check if each of the answer choices could be the first term of the given geometric sequence, Plug In The Answers. The constant must be positive because the product of the 3 terms is positive. For (A), assume 7 is the first term and multiply it by a small, positive integer, such as 2. The sequence in this case would be 7, 14, 28, and the product would be 2,744. This is too big, but there can't be a sequence with a ratio of 1, so there is no way to make it smaller. Therefore, (A) contains the number that cannot be the first term. Choice (B) works if the sequence is 6, 12, 24, (C) works with 4, 12, 36, (D) works with 3, 12, 48, and (E) works with 2, 12, 72.

60. **K**   When there are variables in the answer choices, Plug In. The $p^{-1}(x)$ notation means the inverse of the $p(x)$ function, or the function that undoes what $p(x)$ does to a number. To Plug In on these, plug a number into the first function, get a value out, and plug that value into the second function. If the second function is the inverse of the first, the original number will be the result. Start with the function in the question and try to pick a value of x that will make the math simple, but don't worry about finding the perfect number. Even if the answer is a weird decimal, only one answer choice should have the same weird decimal. In this case, $x = 12$ will work nicely, because $p(12) = \sqrt[3]{12-4} = \sqrt[3]{8} = 2$. Plug this value of 2 into each answer choice to see which function equals 12, the number originally plugged into the $p(x)$ function. Choice (F) becomes $\sqrt[3]{2} - 4 = 1.26 - 4 = -2.74$, which is not equal to 12, so (F) can be eliminated. Choice (G) will also be negative, so it can be eliminated. Choice (H) is $\sqrt[3]{2+4} = \sqrt[3]{6} = 1.817$, and (J) is $(2 - 4)^3 = (-2)^3 = -8$, so both answers can be eliminated. Choice (K) is $2^3 + 4 = 8 + 4 = 12$, which was the original value of x, so (K) is the credited response.

Part IV
ACT Reading

Chapter 17
Introduction to the ACT Reading Test

To pursue a perfect or near-perfect score on the Reading Test, you have to employ superior critical-thinking and time-management skills. To go from good to great, you have to be flexible, willing to try a variety of approaches and find the best strategy for you. The passages change on every ACT, so you have to be willing to adapt to variations and switch up strategies mid-test and even mid-passage when one isn't working.

We'll teach you how to evaluate the order you work the passages. We'll also review strategies for working the passages and distinguishing among close answers, all to help you pursue perfection on the Reading Test.

WHAT'S ON THE READING TEST

On the Reading Test, you have 35 minutes to work though four passages and a total of 40 questions. The category, or genre, of the passages always appears in the same order: Prose Fiction, Social Science, Humanities, and Natural Science. The passages are roughly the same length, 800–850 words, and each is followed by 10 questions.

Passage Content

Within the four categories, ACT selects excerpts from books and articles to create one long passage or two shorter passages. For each test, they choose four new passages, but the topics are always chosen from the same content areas of study.

Prose Fiction (aka Literary Narrative)

The passages can be excerpts from novels or short stories, or even short stories in their entirety. While there are occasional uses of historical fiction, most passages are contemporary, emphasize diversity, and often center on family relationships.

Social Science

Topics are drawn from the fields of anthropology, archaeology, biography, business, economics, education, geography, history, political science, psychology, and sociology.

Humanities

These passages are nonfiction, but they are usually memoirs or personal essays that can read much like fiction. Topics include architecture, art, dance, ethics, film, language, literary criticism, music, philosophy, radio, television, and theater.

Natural Science

Content areas include anatomy, astronomy, biology, botany, chemistry, ecology, geology, medicine, meteorology, microbiology, natural history, physiology, physics, technology, and zoology.

The passages feature authors and topics that the ACT writers judge typical of the type of reading required in first-year college courses. And your goal, according to ACT, is to read the passages and answer questions that prove you understood both what was "directly stated" as well as what were the "implied meanings."

HOW TO CRACK THE READING TEST

If you are pursuing a perfect or near-perfect score, you likely are already doing a very good job of reading the passages and finding both the directly stated and implied meanings. To go from good to great, evaluate your current approach and determine whether (and how) it can be improved.

Pick the Best Order of the Passages for You

You can work the passages in the order ACT presents, *if you like that order*. But there is no rule that says you have to do them in ACT's order, and we recommend working the passages in an order that works best for you and makes best use of the time constraints.

Now, Later

We recommend working first the passages you like best and/or typically perform best on. A tough passage can easily steal too much time from the others, and if you rush through the rest (or even run out of time), you're giving up points you otherwise could have banked.

If you have already taken a fair number of practice tests, then you're ready to analyze your performance:

- Regardless of where it is in your order, do you consistently do the best on social science and natural science? If so, then consider starting with those two.
- Do you usually prefer the prose fiction and humanities to the social science and natural science? Do you consistently earn more points on those passages? If so, consider completing both before tackling the other two.
- Do you rarely read fiction outside of school? If so, then the prose fiction is unlikely to be a smart choice to do first.

Here is some additional information about the four categories to help you reflect on your own Personal Order of Difficulty (POOD).

Prose Fiction

Facts may matter less than do the setting, the atmosphere, and the relationships between characters. The plot and dialogue may even be secondary to the characters' thoughts and emotions, not all of which will be directly stated. In fact, the questions are more likely to involve identifying the implied meanings than what was directly stated.

If you like to read fiction for school assignments or for pleasure, you may find the prose fiction one of the easier passages. If you don't like to read fiction, you may find the passages unclear and confusing.

Social Science

Social science passages should remind you of the papers you write for school. The organization will flow logically with clear topic sentences and well-chosen transitions to develop the main idea. The author may have a point of view on the subject or may simply deliver informative facts in a neutral tone.

Humanities

Humanities passages are nonfiction, but if they are memoirs or personal essays, they may feel similar to the fiction passages. The narrative may use a more organic development instead of a linear one, and the tone will be more personal and perhaps more emotional than the more objective tones found in social and natural science. In other cases, the Humanities passage has the same objective tone and organization as the science passages, differing only in featuring a topic related to the arts.

Natural Science

Natural science passages feature a lot of details and sometimes very technical descriptions. Similar to the passages on social science, natural science features a linear organization with clear topic sentences and transitions to develop the main idea. The author may or may not have an opinion on the topic.

The next time you take a practice Reading Test, incorporate this analysis and adjust your order and analyze the results. With enough practice and self-analysis, you will be able to determine your Personal Order of Difficulty (POOD).

Subscores

On your official score report, ACT groups your performance on prose fiction and humanities under an Arts/Literature subscore, and your performance on social science and natural science under a Social Studies/Science subscore. The subscores don't connect mathematically to the Reading score or the composite, but the groupings may help you think about your own order.

When Good POOD Goes Bad

Each ACT features all new passages, and certain characteristics may vary enough to affect the difficulty of a passage. Pay attention to the particulars of each test and be willing to adapt your order for that day's test.

> - **Paragraphs:** smaller and many are better than big and few
> - **Questions:** the more line references, the better
> - **Answers:** short are better than long

Danger Signs

The passages all run roughly the same number of words (800–850), and each features 10 questions followed by four answer choices. But the way the passages, questions, and answers *look* can provide valuable clues that you should use to determine that day's order.

Paragraphs

Which passage would you rather work, one with eight to ten medium-sized paragraphs or one with three huge paragraphs? The overall length is the same, but the size and number of the paragraphs influences how easily you can navigate the passage and retrieve answers as you work the questions.

Some fiction passages can feature too many paragraphs, with each paragraph an individual line of dialogue. Too many paragraphs can make it just as difficult to locate the right part of the passage to find answers.

Ideally, a passage should feature eight to ten paragraphs, with each paragraph made up of five to fifteen lines.

Questions

The questions on the Reading Test don't follow a chronological order of the passage, and not every question comes with a line reference. Line references (and paragraph references) are maps, pointing to the precise part of the passage to find the answer. You waste no time getting lost, hunting through the passage to find where to read. Therefore, a passage with only one or two line- or paragraph-reference questions will be more challenging than one that features four, five, six, or more (eight is the most we've ever seen).

Answers

Long answers usually answer harder questions, and short answers usually answer easier questions. A passage with lots of questions with short answers is a good sign of an easier passage.

Need More Practice?
1,460 ACT Practice Questions provides 6 tests' worth of Reading passages. That's 24 passages and 240 questions.

Need Even More Practice?
The Princeton Review's *English and Reading Workout* has 4 more full-length Reading Tests.

Use Your Eye, Not Your Brain

There's no guarantee that the four passages will be uniform in number or length of paragraphs, or that there will be an equal number of line-referencing or short-answer questions. Especially as an Elite scorer, you'll need to be prepared to tackle any passage, especially if you find that the presence or absence of these features increases the overall difficulty.

Look at the passages to evaluate the paragraphs, line references, and answer choices. Don't thoughtfully ponder and consider each element, and don't read through the questions.

Use your eye to scan the paragraphs, look for numbers amidst the questions, and the length of answer choices. If you see lots of warning signs on what is typically your first passage, leave it for Later. If you see manageable paragraphs, line references, and lots of short answers on the passage you typically do Later, consider bumping it up to second, maybe first. This should take no more than two seconds.

The Questions

In Chapter 18, we'll teach you the basic approach of how to attack the passage and the questions, and go into more depth about how to order the questions.

The only order you need to know now is the one we recommend avoiding: ACT's. The questions aren't in chronological order, nor are they in any order of difficulty from easiest to hardest. You shouldn't work the questions in the order given *just because ACT numbered them in order.*

Now Questions

Work the questions in an order that makes sense for you.

> Do Now questions are easy to answer or easy to *find* the answer to.

Easy to Answer

A question that is easy to answer often simply asks what the passage says, or as ACT puts it, what is directly stated. ACT in fact calls these "Referring questions," requiring the use of your "referral skills" (ACT's words, not ours) to find the right part of the passage. Referring questions don't require much reasoning; the answer will be right there in the passage, waiting in black and white, and the correct answer will be barely paraphrased, if at all. Most answers are also relatively short: That's why many questions with short answers reliably predict an easier passage.

Easy to *Find* the Answer

A question with a line or a paragraph reference comes with a map, showing you where in the passage to find the answer. Some of these questions may be tough to answer, but as long as they come with line or paragraph references, they direct you where to read.

Questions that come with a great lead word can also make finding the answer easy. Lead words are the nouns, phrases, and sometimes verbs that are specific to the passage. They're not the boilerplate language like "main idea" or "the passage characterizes."

Look at the following questions. All the lead words have been underlined.

> **11.** Mark Twain probably would have said that lawyers:
>
> **12.** The author states that maritime law is unique in that:
>
> **13.** According to the passage, the primary danger steamboats posed were:
>
> **35.** Which of the following statements most accurately summarizes how the passage characterizes opiates and benzodiazepines?

Lead words are words and phrases that can be found in the passage.

Great lead words are proper nouns, unusual words, and dates.

Your eye can spot great lead words in the passage just by looking and without reading. They leap off the page. In Chapter 18, we'll teach you how to use lead words as part of the basic approach.

Later Questions

Later questions are both difficult to answer and difficult to find the answer to, like Question 35 in the last set of examples. Most questions that are difficult to answer require reasoning skills to "show your understanding of statements with implied meaning."

Reasoning Questions

Reasoning questions require more thought than do Referring questions, so they do not qualify as "easy to answer." However, they should be tackled Later only if they don't come with a line or paragraph reference, which makes the answer easy to find.

In its description of the Reading Test, ACT lists the various tasks that reasoning skills must be applied to.

- determine main ideas
- locate and interpret significant details
- understand sequences of events
- make comparisons
- comprehend cause-effect relationships
- determine the meaning of context-dependent words, phrases, and statements
- draw generalizations
- analyze the author's or narrator's voice and method

Any insight into the test writers' purpose and intent always benefits your preparation. However, you don't need to name the specific task when you come across it in a question. During the actual exam, identify questions as Now or Later, and don't forget that questions with line or paragraph references are Now, regardless of the task assigned in the question.

Pace Yourself

It would be logical to assume that you should divide the 35 minutes evenly across four passages, spending precisely eight minutes and 45 seconds on each passage. In reality, you will likely spend more time on one or two of the passages and less time on the others. To earn a perfect or near-perfect Reading score, you can neither rush and risk misreading, nor can you belabor one or two questions when more are waiting, perhaps an entire passage.

> Focus on the number of raw points you need, and don't get stuck on one or two tough questions.

Don't spend more than 10 minutes on one passage, and try to leave *at least* six minutes for the last passage. In later chapters, we'll teach you different strategies to improve your time-management skills.

Be Flexible and Aggressive

Flexibility is key to your ACT success, particularly on the Reading Test.

Get out of a passage on which you've already spent too much time, cutting yourself off at 10 minutes on any given passage. Force yourself to guess on the question you've been rereading for minutes, make smart and swift guesses on any questions still left, and move on.

We're not saying this is easy. In fact, changing your own instinctual behavior is the hardest part of cracking the Reading Test. Everyone has made the mistake of ignoring that voice that's screaming inside your head to move on, and we've all answered back "But I know I'm almost there and if I take just a little more time, I know I can get it."

You may in fact get that question. But that one right answer likely cost you two to three others. And even worse, you had probably already narrowed it down to two answer choices. You were down to a 50-50 chance of getting it right, and instead you wasted more time to prove the one right answer.

In Chapters 18 and 20, we'll show you how to use that time more effectively to begin with and what to do when you're down to two choices. But both skills depend on the process of elimination, or POE.

POE

POE is a powerful tool on a multiple-choice, standardized test. On the Reading Test, you may find several Now questions easy to answer and be able to spot the right answer right away among the four choices. There will be plenty of tough Reasoning questions, however, whose answers aren't obvious, either in your own words or among the four choices. You can easily fall into the trap of rereading and rereading to figure out the answer. Wrong answers, however, can be more obvious to identify. They are there, after all, to hide the right answer. In fact, if you can cross off all the wrong ones, the right answer will be waiting there for you. Even if you cross off only one or two, the right answer frequently becomes more obvious.

We'll spend more time with POE in the following chapters. You don't get extra points for knowing the answer before you look at the answer choices. You get a point for a correct answer, and you need to get to as many questions as possible in order to answer them. Use POE to escape the death-spiral questions that will hold you back.

Process of Elimination
Each time you eliminate a wrong answer, you increase your chance of choosing the correct answer.

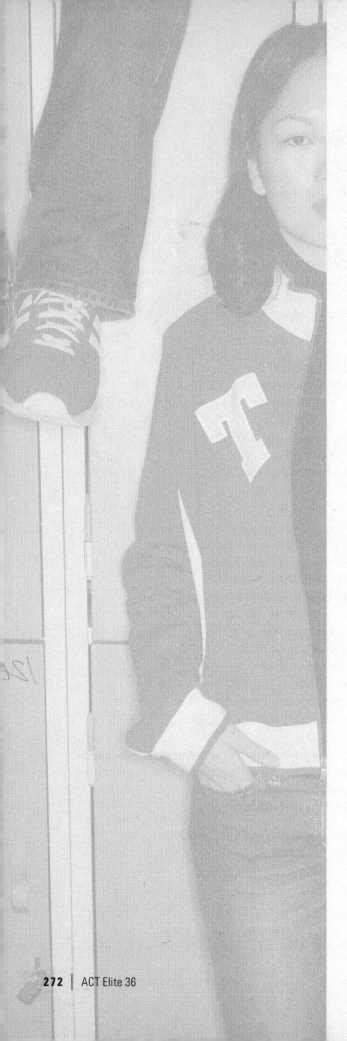

Summary

- There are always four passages and 40 questions on the Reading Test.

- The passages are always in the same order: Prose Fiction, Social Science, Humanities, Natural Science.

- Each passage has 10 questions.

- The passages are all roughly the same length, between 800–850 words.

- Follow your POOD to pick your own order of the passages.

- Look for passages to do Now whose categories and topics you like best or find easier.

- Be aware of danger signs that could indicate a harder passage: longer, fewer paragraphs; few line-reference questions; many or all questions with long answers.

- Pace yourself. Don't let one tough passage or question derail you.

- Be Flexible. Be ready to adapt your order, leave a tough passage, or guess on a tough question.

- Use Process of Elimination to cross off wrong answers and save time.

Chapter 18
The 4-Step Basic Approach

To earn a perfect or near-perfect score on the Reading Test, you need an efficient strategy. In this chapter, we'll teach you our 4-Step Basic Approach to working the passages, questions, and answers.

THE 4-STEP BASIC APPROACH

You may have already developed a strategy that works well for you, but you want to find a way to answer the handful of questions that are keeping your Reading score down. We urge you to read through this chapter and try our 4-Step Basic Approach. You may find that you like the entire strategy better than your own, or you may pick and choose certain elements to incorporate and enhance your current approach.

Step 1: **Preview.** Check the blurb and map the questions.

Step 2: **Work the Passage.** Spend 2–3 minutes reading the passage.

Step 3: **Work the Questions.** Use your POOD to find Now and Later questions.

Step 4: **Work the Answers.** Use POE.

Step 1: Preview

The first step involves two parts. First, check the blurb at the beginning of the passage to see whether it offers any additional information. Ninety-nine percent of the time, all it will offer will be the title, author, copyright date, and publisher. There is also no guarantee that the title will convey the topic. But occasionally, the blurb will define an unfamiliar term, place a setting, or identify a character.

True to form, this offers only the basic information.

The real value in Step 1 comes in the work you do with the questions.

Map the Questions

Take no more than 30 seconds to *scan* the questions. Underline the lead words. Star any line or paragraph reference. Do not *read* the questions and try to ponder their meaning: Let your eyes run through the questions to identify the line/paragraph references and lead words.

Second Time Around
You'll check the blurb twice. Once when you're confirming your order and now as part of Step 1.

Scan, Skim, Read
There are important distinctions among these different skills. We'll explain the differences on the following pages.

Lead Words

We introduced the idea of lead words in the Introduction. These are the specific words and phrases that you will find in the passage. They are not the boilerplate language like "main idea" or "author's purpose." They are usually nouns, phrases, or verbs.

Map the following questions that accompany the prose fiction passage. If a line/ paragraph reference features a direct quote, do not worry about underlining the quote, but you can underline any lead words outside of the direct quotation.

1. The narrator states that she had NOT thought that:

2. It can most reasonably be inferred from the passage that the narrator interprets Gretchen's "I'll go get you a Band-Aid" (line 73) to mean which of the following?

3. When the narrator mentions "a natural rhythm of domesticity" (line 34), she's most nearly referring to:

4. The narrator speculates that one reason for Gretchen's comfort with her might have been that:

5. The passage reveals that when Gretchen's mother announces that they had to move, Gretchen asks the narrator if she and her mother can move in. The narrator indicates that she views this request as:

6. As it is used in line 59, the word *minefield* most nearly means:

7. The narrator claims that since her children had moved away, her living situation has been marked by:

8. As the narrator reflects on the past year spent with Gretchen, the narrator realizes that she:

9. The references to *calm* and *explosions* in lines 59–60 are most likely intended to suggest that at the time, the narrator felt:

10. In the context of the passage, the concluding two sentences (line 73–74) are most likely meant to suggest:

The Benefits of Previewing

Your mapped questions should look like this.

1. The narrator states that she had NOT thought that:

☆ 2. It can most reasonably be inferred from the passage that the narrator interprets <u>Gretchen's</u> "I'll go get you a Band-Aid" (line 73) to mean which of the following?

☆ 3. When the narrator mentions "a natural rhythm of domesticity" (line 34), she's most nearly referring to:

4. The narrator speculates that one reason for <u>Gretchen's comfort</u> with her might have been that:

5. The passage reveals that when <u>Gretchen's mother</u> announces that they <u>had to move,</u> <u>Gretchen asks the narrator if she and her mother can move in</u>. The narrator indicates that she views this request as:

☆ 6. As it is used in line 59, the word *minefield* most nearly means:

7. The narrator claims that since her <u>children had moved away,</u> <u>her living situation</u> has been marked by:

8. As the narrator reflects on the <u>past year spent with Gretchen,</u> the narrator realizes that she:

☆ 9. The references to *calm* and *explosions* in lines 59–60 are most likely intended to suggest that at the time, the narrator felt:

☆ 10. In the context of the passage, the concluding two sentences (lines 73–74) are most likely meant to suggest:

Mapping the questions provides two key benefits. First, you've just identified with stars five questions with easy-to-find answers. With the lead words, you have three or four more questions whose answers will be easy to find. Second, you have the main idea of the passage *before* you've read it.

Reading Actively

Look again at all the words you've underlined. They tell you what the passage will be about: a narrator whose children have moved away and who has a friend named Gretchen, who has asked to move in along with her mother. You will read the passage better because you know going in what to look for.

Reading actively means knowing in advance what you're going to read, and that's exactly what mapping the questions has provided. You have the important details to look for, and you won't waste time on details that never appear in a question. Reading passively means walking into a dark cave, wandering in the dark trying to see what dangers or treasures await. Reading actively means walking into the cave with a flashlight and a map, looking for what you know is in there.

Skimming, Scanning, and Reading

Reading needs your brain on full power. You're reading words, and your brain is processing what they mean and drawing conclusions. Reading is watching the road, searching for directional signs, and glancing at the scenery, all for the purpose of trying to figure out where the road is leading.

Skimming means reading only a few words, maybe just the first sentence of each paragraph. Skimming is reading only the directional signs and ignoring the scenery.

Scanning needs very little of your brain. Use your eyes. Look, don't think, and don't try to process for understanding. Scanning is looking for Volkswagen Beetles in a game of Slug Bug.

Step 2: Work the Passage

You can *read* the whole passage, or you can *skim* the passage, or you can just *scan* it for the lead words.

You may have been skimming or reading the passages up until now. For the following passage, you can try a new approach or you can use your typical method to work the passage. In either case, add the following three rules.

Rule 1: Look for and underline any lead words.

You'll have more questions whose answers are easy to find.

Rule 2: Finish in 2–3 minutes.

If you don't think you can *read* the passage in two or three minutes, then try to *skim* or *scan* for lead words. In later chapters, we'll discuss in greater detail how to manage your time, including what to do if you're a slow reader.

Potholes

If you're driving and you
hit a pothole, do you back
up and drive over it again?
Rereading text you didn't
understand is the literary
equivalent of
repeatedly driving over
the same pothole.

Rule 3: Do not read anything more than once.

If you read text you do not understand, just move on. You should only come back to it again *if* there is a question about this text. Why waste time trying to understand something that you might not even be asked about?

Your Mapped Questions

Here are the 10 mapped questions for easy reference when you work the passage on the facing page. On a real test, you'll have the passage on the left side, and the questions facing you on the right page. We'll repeat the passage, with the lead words underlined, on the following page, along with the 10 mapped questions and their answers.

1. The narrator states that she had NOT thought that:

☆ **2.** It can most reasonably be inferred from the passage that the narrator interprets <u>Gretchen's</u> "I'll go get you a Band-Aid" (line 73) to mean which of the following?

☆ **3.** When the narrator mentions "a natural rhythm of domesticity" (line 34), she's most nearly referring to:

4. The narrator speculates that one reason for <u>Gretchen's comfort</u> with her might have been that:

5. The passage reveals that when <u>Gretchen's mother</u> announces that they <u>had to move</u>, <u>Gretchen asks the narrator if she and her mother can move in</u>. The narrator indicates that she views this request as:

☆ **6.** As it is used in line 59, the word *minefield* most nearly means:

7. The narrator claims that since her <u>children had moved away</u>, <u>her living situation</u> has been marked by:

8. As the narrator reflects on the <u>past year spent with Gretchen</u>, the narrator realizes that she:

☆ **9.** The references to *calm* and *explosions* in lines 59–60 are most likely intended to suggest that at the time, the narrator felt:

☆ **10.** In the context of the passage, the concluding two sentences (lines 73–74) are most likely meant to suggest:

PROSE FICTION: This passage is adapted from the short story "Goodbye Gretchen" by Katherine Craig (© 2003 by Northeast Review).

I remember very clearly the first time I saw Gretchen. It was early fall, just after Labor Day when the weather still felt like summer, but school was in session and the evenings were getting darker. She was inside the house, peeking out at me
5 from behind the ancient lace curtains as I watered my tomatoes. Over the next several weeks, she got slowly braver: I saw her standing inside the screen door watching me, then peering over the fence. I never related very well to children; my own had long ago moved away, and we spoke on the phone only a few
10 times a year, rarely saw each other. Because of my general discomfort, I didn't try to speak to her. Looking back, I realize that probably made her feel more comfortable around me.

Eventually, Gretchen worked up the courage to venture over to my yard, and I put her to work. It wasn't so much because I
15 needed the help as I didn't know what else to do, and she did make my chores easier. She was watchful and deliberate, a quick learner. I came to rely on her to do most of the weeding, since bending down was easier on her young back than on mine. She was careful to pull the roots all the way out, not just pull
20 the tops off the plants and leave the roots in the soil to grow again. Her small hands could easily reach between the wires of the tomato cages to retrieve the ripe fruits growing in close to the stalk, and she followed me around the yard as I watered, making sure the hose wasn't kinked and keeping it carefully
25 out of the garden beds.

As the autumn progressed and the evenings got darker, Gretchen began helping me inside the house also. It was a natural progression, from picking cucumbers and tomatoes to canning pickles and stewing tomatoes into sauce.

30 Gretchen's clothes were ill-fitting, and sometimes in need of mending, so once gardening season was over, I started giving her sewing lessons. We hemmed her pants and sewed on buttons. I taught her to embroider flowers to make the patches look prettier. We fell into a natural rhythm of domesticity.

35 I hadn't thought that I minded living alone, but during that year I looked forward to the time when Gretchen got home from school. Gretchen was mostly quiet as we went about our work, but sometimes she would tell me about school. She described her teacher, Ms. Kanaley, as "amiable." The girls in
40 her class who teased her about her second-hand clothes were "spiteful," and the ones who were nice to her were "gracious." I was always struck, when she did talk, by how well-spoken she was. Her vocabulary was better than mine, but her speech wasn't affected. Everything that came out of her mouth was
45 spoken with a solemnity that made me listen carefully to her.

As the winter wore on, Gretchen and I began making a quilt together. It was to be for the bed in what used to be my daughter's bedroom. Gretchen picked out the pattern and the colors for the quilt, and we started to refer to the room as hers,
50 since her quilt was going to go on the bed. I never thought, though, that she would take all our talk so seriously.

Gretchen and her mother had moved in next door so Gretchen could attend school in a better district. In the spring, her mother told her that they had to move—she had tried,
55 but just couldn't make ends meet living there. It might have been wonderful to have Gretchen move in with me. But when she asked me, I could only think of the years when my own children were teenagers, which had been like walking through a minefield: sometimes it was calm and beautiful, but I never
60 knew when the next explosions were coming. Gretchen wasn't far from that age, and even just imagining a teenager living with me again made me long for the solitude I hadn't even lost.

"It would be easier on you if Mom and I lived here," Gretchen said, "you're always saying there's too much space for just you.
65 We'll help you with the housework. If we lived here, you could teach me to cook for you." We were sitting in the living room, each of us on one side of the quilting frame. I quickly glanced up at her pale, serious face. She was twirling a lock of her thin, brown hair nervously around her index finger. I didn't know how
70 to respond to this plea, so I looked back down and just cleared my throat instead. But I wasn't really looking at the quilt, and I stabbed my thumb with the needle hard enough that it drew blood. "I'll go get you a Band-Aid," Gretchen said in a small, deflated voice. "You don't want to get blood on your quilt."

Steps 3 and 4: Work the Questions and Answers

Since you've spent two or three minutes working the passage, try to work the questions and answers in no more than seven or eight minutes. Make smart choices about which questions to do Now, and which questions to do Later. Use POE to work the answers. Your goal should be to get at least nine out of the ten questions correct.

Passage I

PROSE FICTION: This passage is adapted from the short story "Goodbye Gretchen" by Katherine Craig (© 2003 by Northeast Review).

I remember very clearly the first time I saw Gretchen. It was early fall, just after Labor Day when the weather still felt like summer, but school was in session and the evenings were getting darker. She was inside the house, peeking out at me
5 from behind the ancient lace curtains as I watered my tomatoes. Over the next several weeks, she got slowly braver: I saw her standing inside the screen door watching me, then peering over the fence. I never related very well to children; my own had long ago moved away, and we spoke on the phone only a few
10 times a year, rarely saw each other. Because of my general discomfort, I didn't try to speak to her. Looking back, I realize that probably made her feel more comfortable around me.

Eventually, Gretchen worked up the courage to venture over to my yard, and I put her to work. It wasn't so much because I
15 needed the help as I didn't know what else to do, and she did make my chores easier. She was watchful and deliberate, a quick learner. I came to rely on her to do most of the weeding, since bending down was easier on her young back than on mine. She was careful to pull the roots all the way out, not just pull
20 the tops off the plants and leave the roots in the soil to grow again. Her small hands could easily reach between the wires of the tomato cages to retrieve the ripe fruits growing in close to the stalk, and she followed me around the yard as I watered, making sure the hose wasn't kinked and keeping it carefully
25 out of the garden beds.

As the autumn progressed and the evenings got darker, Gretchen began helping me inside the house also. It was a natural progression, from picking cucumbers and tomatoes to canning pickles and stewing tomatoes into sauce.

30 Gretchen's clothes were ill-fitting, and sometimes in need of mending, so once gardening season was over, I started giving her sewing lessons. We hemmed her pants and sewed on buttons. I taught her to embroider flowers to make the patches look prettier. We fell into a natural rhythm of domesticity.

35 I hadn't thought that I minded living alone, but during that year I looked forward to the time when Gretchen got home from school. Gretchen was mostly quiet as we went about our work, but sometimes she would tell me about school. She described her teacher, Ms. Kanaley, as "amiable." The girls in
40 her class who teased her about her second-hand clothes were "spiteful," and the ones who were nice to her were "gracious." I was always struck, when she did talk, by how well-spoken she was. Her vocabulary was better than mine, but her speech wasn't affected. Everything that came out of her mouth was
45 spoken with a solemnity that made me listen carefully to her.

As the winter wore on, Gretchen and I began making a quilt together. It was to be for the bed in what used to be my daughter's bedroom. Gretchen picked out the pattern and the colors for the quilt, and we started to refer to the room as hers,
50 since her quilt was going to go on the bed. I never thought, though, that she would take all our talk so seriously.

Gretchen and her mother had moved in next door so Gretchen could attend school in a better district. In the spring, her mother told her that they had to move—she had tried, but
55 just couldn't make ends meet living there. It might have been wonderful to have Gretchen move in with me. But when she asked me, I could only think of the years when my own children were teenagers, which had been like walking through a minefield: sometimes it was calm and beautiful, but I never
60 knew when the next explosions were coming. Gretchen wasn't far from that age, and even just imagining a teenager living with me again made me long for the solitude I hadn't even lost.

"It would be easier on you if Mom and I lived here," Gretchen said, "you're always saying there's too much space for just you.
65 We'll help you with the housework. If we lived here, you could teach me to cook for you." We were sitting in the living room, each of us on one side of the quilting frame. I quickly glanced up at her pale, serious face. She was twirling a lock of her thin, brown hair nervously around her index finger. I didn't know how
70 to respond to this plea, so I looked back down and just cleared my throat instead. But I wasn't really looking at the quilt, and I stabbed my thumb with the needle hard enough that it drew blood. "I'll go get you a Band-Aid," Gretchen said in a small, deflated voice. "You don't want to get blood on your quilt."

1. The narrator states that she had NOT thought that:

   A. she needed help with the chores.
   B. Gretchen was very well-spoken.
   C. she minded living alone.
   D. she wished she had more company.

2. It can most reasonably be inferred from the passage that the narrator interprets Gretchen's "I'll go get you a Band-Aid" (line 73) to mean which of the following?

   F. "I care more about the quilt than you do."
   G. "You don't want us to move in."
   H. "I'm glad I asked you."
   J. "You're grateful for the offer."

3. When the narrator mentions "a natural rhythm of domesticity" (line 34), she's most nearly referring to:

   A. unusual acts of spite made by young children against perceived outsiders.
   B. seasonal cycles of planting, harvesting, and canning foods.
   C. renting rooms to friends who have fallen on hard times.
   D. regular chores typically coordinated with a partner.

4. The narrator speculates that one reason for Gretchen's comfort with her might have been that:

   F. the narrator didn't try to speak to Gretchen because of the narrator's own discomfort.
   G. the girls at Gretchen's school had told Gretchen the narrator could be trusted.
   H. Gretchen and the narrator's children had been friends, which made the narrator a maternal figure for Gretchen.
   J. the narrator knew how to communicate with Gretchen because of the narrator's positive experience with her own children.

5. The passage reveals that when Gretchen's mother announces that they had to move, Gretchen asks the narrator if she and her mother can move in. The narrator indicates that she views this request as:

   A. possibly sarcastic, which left the narrator feeling hurt.
   B. somewhat impulsive, which explains the narrator's uncertainty.
   C. completely welcome, which left the narrator speechless.
   D. somewhat surprising, which explains the narrator's struggle to respond.

6. As it is used in line 59, the word *minefield* most nearly means:

   F. war zone.
   G. tense situation.
   H. pressure cooker.
   J. booby trap.

7. The narrator claims that since her children had moved away, her living situation has been marked by:

   A. comfortable solitude.
   B. lonely isolation.
   C. overwhelming chores.
   D. social obligations.

8. As the narrator reflects on the past year spent with Gretchen, the narrator realizes that she:

   F. resented the time Gretchen's company took up and kept her away from her household chores.
   G. criticized Gretchen too much, and now regrets driving her away.
   H. appreciated it at the time, but now is grateful that she has her privacy back.
   J. enjoyed it, but was unaware that Gretchen thought seriously about moving in.

9. The references to *calm* and *explosions* in lines 59–60 are most likely intended to suggest that at the time, the narrator felt:

   A. guilty that she preferred Gretchen's company to that of her own children.
   B. appreciative that Gretchen and her mother would make her feel less lonely.
   C. worried about the conflicts and challenges a teenager in the house would bring.
   D. suspicious that Gretchen was trying to take advantage of her.

10. In the context of the passage, the concluding two sentences (lines 73–74) are most likely meant to suggest:

    F. a mutual benefit for two people has been acknowledged.
    G. an earnest offer of help has been eagerly accepted.
    H. a painful rejection is being handled with grace.
    J. a longtime rift has been healed.

SELF-ANALYSIS

The answers to the questions are 1. (C), 2. (G), 3. (D), 4. (F), 5. (D), 6. (G), 7. (A), 8. (J), 9. (C), 10. (H). How did you do? Again, your goal was to get nine or ten correct in a total of seven to ten minutes spent on all four steps. If you missed more than one question or you answered all of them correctly but spent more than ten minutes, analyze what you did on this passage and consider what changes you can make the next time.

- Did one question take up more time than the rest?
- Did you do the questions in the order given?
- Did you answer the questions from memory?
- Did you find yourself rereading selections of text to identify a correct answer?
- Did you find yourself torn between two answers, yours and the correct one?

In the following lessons, we'll address in greater depth both critical-reading and time-management skills. After all, success on the Reading Test requires polishing both sets of skills. But applying the 4-Step Basic Approach can help you right away.

Step 3: Work the Questions

Don't work the questions in the order given. Work the Now questions first: these are the questions that are easy to answer and have easy-to-find answers. Question 1 is neither: it has no star and nothing underlined. Even worse, it's a NOT question, which makes it particularly tricky to answer.

You also can't answer questions from memory, at least not without confirming your answer is right. You may get *most* of the questions right, but does that matter when you need to get *all* of the questions right? You will inevitably face answer choices that all seem right, or you will fall right into an ACT trap, choosing an answer choice that sounds right with some familiar words, but which in reality doesn't match what the passage said.

> Work the Questions
> - Pick your order of questions. Do Now questions that are easy to answer, easy to find the answer, or best of all, both.
> - Read the question to understand what it's asking.
> - If you think you know the answer, confirm it by finding its exact place in the passage.
> - If you don't know the answer, read a window of 5–10 lines to find the answer.

Questions 2, 3, 6, 9, and 10 all have line references. They are all smart choices to do Now. Even if you predicted the answer, you can easily check the line references to confirm your answer. These questions are also all Reasoning questions, which means it's important to be careful with the question, the window of text, and the answer choices.

Reasoning Questions

Reasoning questions require you to read between the lines. Instead of being directly stated, the correct answer is implied or suggested. In other words, look for the larger point that the author is making.

If Reasoning questions come with a line or paragraph reference or a great lead word, they should be done Now. Reasoning questions aren't *that* much harder than Referral questions, but they should be read and answered carefully. Reasoning questions also work best with POE, which brings us to Step 4, Work the Answers.

Step 4: Work the Answers

> Work the Answers
> - If you can clearly identify the answer in the passage, look for its match among the answers.
> - If you aren't sure if an answer is right or wrong, leave it. You'll either find one that's better or three that are worse.
> - Cross off any choice that describes something not found in your window.
> - If you're down to two, focus on key words in the answer choices and determine whether you can find support for those key words in the window of text.

> How to Spot Reasoning Questions
> - Questions that use *infer*, *means*, *suggests*, or *implies*
> - Questions that ask about the purpose or function of part or all of the passage
> - Questions that ask what the author or a character in the passage would agree or disagree with
> - Questions that ask you to characterize or describe all or part of the passage
> - Questions with long answers

Here's How to Crack Questions 2, 3, 9, and 10

If you missed any of these, go back and reread the window of text to find the line(s) that supports the correct answer. The answer for Question 2 is supported by *small, deflated voice* (lines 73–74). The answer for Question 3 is supported by the tasks mentioned in the prior paragraphs, from line 21 through line 34. The answer to Question 9 is supported by lines 56–62. The answer to Question 10 is supported in the answers to Questions 2 and 9 as well as the last two paragraphs. If you missed any of these questions, examine your choices. Do they feature trap language? Do they overstate the emotions and actions described?

Steps 3 and 4: Repeat

Continue to work the questions in an order that makes sense, choosing to do Now all questions that are easy to answer or whose answers are easy to find.

Vocabulary in Context

In some Referral questions, you'll have to determine the meaning of a word or phrase as it's used in context. The level of the vocabulary can vary, but most of these questions use relatively common words, but their meaning in the passage can be figurative more than literal.

You don't need to read a full window of five to ten lines for Vocabulary in Context questions, but you do need to read at least the full sentence to determine the meaning in its context. Cross off the word or phrase and try to substitute your own word. Then move to the answers and use POE to eliminate choices that don't match your word. The correct answer has to be the literal definition of the meaning. Don't choose a word that could be used figuratively to convey the meaning.

Here's How to Crack Question 6

The meaning of *minefield* is provided immediately following the colon on lines 59–60 and is described well by *tense situation* in (G). The rest of the answers provide options that would possibly convey the same figurative sense as *minefield* but do not provide a literal translation.

How to Spot Referral Questions
- Questions that begin with *According to the passage*
- Questions that ask what the passage or author states
- Questions with short answers

Referral Questions

Referral questions are easy to answer because they ask what was directly stated in the passage. Read the question carefully to identify what it's asking. The passage directly states something about what? Once you find your window to read, read to find the answer. The correct answers to Referral questions are barely paraphrased and will typically match the text very closely.

Here's How to Crack Questions 4 and 7

Questions 4, 7, and 8 are Referral questions. Notice that each asks what is stated in the passage. The lead words in the questions are underlined in the passage. For Question 4, *Gretchen's comfort* doesn't appear exactly, but those lead words in the question should make you underline *her feel more comfortable* on line 12. For Question 7, the narrator's *children* appear in lines 8 and again in lines 57–58, but the answer to Question 7 is in lines 52–62. Question 8 does not have a great lead word, however. *Past year* never appears in the passage. Leave it for Later.

Later Questions

Do Later questions that are difficult to answer and whose answers are hard to find. These include any questions that have neither a star nor any underlining, as well as questions whose lead words are difficult to find. The later you do such questions, the easier they become. Working the Now questions, you'll either stumble across the hard-to-find lead word or gain a deeper sense of the main idea.

Here's How to Crack Question 8

Question 8 is a Referral question, but its lead words *past year* do not appear in the passage. *That year* does, on lines 35–36; however, none of the answers are supported by the lines around 35–36. Use the references to months and seasons that are in the passage: *Labor Day* (line 2) *autumn* (line 26), and *winter* (line 46). At the end of that paragraph, the narrator expresses her realization that Gretchen had hopes of moving in (lines 50–51).

The Pencil Trick
When you have to look harder for a lead word, use your pencil to sweep over each and every line from beginning to end. By keeping your pencil moving, you will keep your brain from actually reading and will let your eyes look for the word.

Here's How to Crack Question 5

Question 5 is a Reasoning question, but its lead words make finding Gretchen's request to move in relatively easy to find in lines 53–57. The answers to Questions 2, 10, and even 9 help identify (D), but the proof in the text spans several paragraphs, from lines 50–51 through the end of the passage.

Here's How to Crack Question 1

Question 1 is a Referral question, but it doesn't have any lead words, and it's a negative question. It can be easy to miss the NOT or get confused. The work on all of the prior questions helps, as do the lead words in the answers. Choice (B) is wrong because the narrator did think Gretchen was well-spoken (line 42). Choices (A) and (D) are never stated, but in lines 35–37, the narrator admits that she had NOT thought she'd minded living alone.

Summary

- Use the 4-Step Basic Approach.
  - **Step 1: Preview.** Check the blurb and map the questions. Star line and paragraph references and underline lead words.
  - **Step 2: Work the Passage.** Finish in 2–3 minutes. Look for and underline lead words.
  - **Step 3: Work the Questions.** Do Now questions that are easy to answer or whose answers are easy to find. Read what you need in a window of 5–10 lines to find your answer. Save for Later questions that are both hard to find and hard to answer.
  - **Step 4: Work the Answers.** Use POE to find your answer, particularly on Reasoning questions.

- Skim and scan when you work the passage.

- Read windows of text when you work the questions.

Chapter 19
Critical-Reading Skills

In this lesson, we'll help you hone your critical-reading skills to crack the most challenging of difficult text. We'll also build on your mastery of the 4-Step Basic Approach by teaching you advanced POE (Process of Elimination) strategies.

CRITICAL READING

By now, your use of the 4-Step Basic Approach and your personal order of difficulty (POOD) of both passages and questions should make you feel more confident on the Reading Test. But you also may still be struggling with time and feel that you just can't work fast enough to get to enough questions.

Critical-reading skills and time-management skills are entwined on the ACT, and it's likely that when you struggle with time, it's less because you don't *read* fast enough and more that you can't *read and understand* fast enough. You probably waste a lot of time when you read and reread a window of text, or even an entire passage, trying to figure out what it's saying. When you're stuck on a question, you likely reread the window of text several times. You may have even eliminated two answers, but when you're still not sure what the correct answer is, what do you do? You read the window yet again, desperate to figure out the meaning and correct answer.

We've all been there. Part of what makes standardized tests so evil is how they encourage us to listen to our worst instincts. You can't treat the Reading Test as you would a school assignment, and you can't fall prey to your own panicked responses. You have to develop both strategies and skills specific to *this* test.

Critical Thinking

The key to developing better reading skills is to learn to *think* better, which means to think critically. Getting lost in even a small window of text that makes no sense is like getting lost on unfamiliar roads. You wouldn't stare down at the yellow line, would you? Instead you'd look around, looking for landmarks and road signs, trying to figure out where you are and where the road is going.

When you're lost in a tough section of text, use topic sentences and transitions as your landmarks and road signs. Use the topic sentences to identify what the main point of the paragraph is. Look for transitions to see whether points are on the same or different sides from each other. Transition words are like great road signs. They show you the route, direct you to a detour, and get you back on the path of the main idea.

Topic Sentences and Main Points

Think of how you write papers for school. A good topic sentence clarifies the main subject of the paragraph, and it may even provide the author's main point on the subject. The rest of the paragraph will be details or examples that support that

---

Passage, Interrupted

This lesson uses a natural science passage and questions, but the passage will not be presented in its entirety nor chronologically. The blurb contains some useful additional information.

Passage IV

NATURAL SCIENCE: This passage is adapted from the article "Who's Domesticating Whom?" by Rachel Hunter (© 2002 by Wilson's Quarterly).

Hunter is reviewing the book *The Botany of Desire: A Plant's-Eye View of the World* by Michael Pollan.

point, and it may also include a more explicit statement of the main point. If you don't understand the details, focus on the main point. Examples and details usually come right before or right after the main point. But, if you don't understand the main point, read the sentence before or after to see if the details explain it for you.

Let's see how this works. Read the following topic sentence.

> Most people define domesticated species from a typically anthropocentric context.

What's going to come next in the paragraph? The author could provide examples of *domesticated species* under this definition, and thereby make clearer what she means by *typically anthropocentric context*. The author could explain why people use such a definition, or the author could state that *most people* are in fact wrong and there is a better definition to be had. You would be safe anticipating any of those outcomes, but the anticipation is the key. Don't sit back and wait to see where the road is going. Lean forward and look for the fork in the road or the detour sign telling you to turn around. In other words, look for transitions.

Transitions

The first word or phrase after the topic sentence can tell you what direction you're heading.

Let's look at some choices for our domesticated-species sentence.

If the next words were *For example*, what does that tell you is coming next? You'd expect to see examples of the species and how they've been defined.

If the next words were *In other words*, what does that tell you is coming next? You'd expect to see a restatement, most likely a clearer version of the author's point.

If the next word were *However*, what does that tell you is coming next? You'd expect to see a contradiction to this belief, possibly one the author herself agrees with.

Transitions play a key role in critical thinking. Look for transitions to announce additional points, contradictory points, cause-and-effect relationships, examples, or conclusions. Here are just a few common transitions.

Additional Points	Cause-and-Effect Relationships
And	Because
Also	Since
As well	So
In addition	
Furthermore	**Examples**
Moreover	For example
	For instance
Contradictory Points	In particular
Although	Such as
But	
Even though	**Conclusions**
However	Consequently
Nevertheless	In other words
On the other hand	That is
Rather	Therefore
Yet	Thus

Consider the two versions of the same sentence below, and note how changing the transition word affects the meaning.

> Pollan has a deep grasp of and appreciation for the principles of evolution and botany, **yet** he tells his stories in an entertaining and easily understandable manner.

> Pollan has a deep grasp of and appreciation for the principles of evolution and botany, **and** he tells his stories in an entertaining and easily understandable manner.

In the first version, the use of *yet* implies that there is a difference between *principles of evolution and botany* and writing in an *entertaining and easily understandable manner*. *Yet* implies that the author would not necessarily expect a book on evolution and botany to be either entertaining or easily understandable.

In the second version, the author supplies two facts about Pollan's writing. There is nothing to infer about expectations of how the topic may be addressed. But even in the second version, there is something to infer. Note the modifiers *deep, entertaining*, and *easily understandable*. What do you know about the passage author? She approves of Pollan's intellect and writing style.

Modifiers

Modifiers are the key to reading critically. Facts in a sentence provide information, but authors use modifiers to make a point with the facts.

Nouns and verbs reliably give you the facts in a statement, but they don't necessarily provide the author's point.

Look at the adverbs in the previous sentence and see how they helped shape the point: *Reliably* means you can infer that nouns and verbs *almost always* give facts. *Necessarily* modifies the verb phrase *don't provide*. Without it, you could infer that nouns and verbs never give you the point. Adjectives and adverbs are just as useful as transitions, conveying the author's opinion on what would otherwise be a statement of fact.

Consider the first topic sentence again.

> Most people define domesticated species from a typically anthropocentric context.

How does the adverb *typically* affect *anthropocentric context*? The author implies that this should be expected. What does the choice of using *most people* imply? At the very least, some other people think differently, and it's fair to presume the author is one of them. After all, if she agreed with this definition, wouldn't she have just written a sentence providing this fact?

> Domesticated species are defined from an anthropocentric context.

Without the modifiers, this sentence is a neutral statement of facts. The author's deliberate choices of *most people* and *typically* allow us to infer her opinion on this stance and anticipate her own viewpoint to come.

Pronouns

Transitions and modifiers do not have a monopoly on conveying meaning and connections. Certain pronouns, used alone or as a modifier when paired with a noun or other modifiers, provide clear maps from one idea to another. Consider the following topic sentence.

> This problem of monoculture is not unique to the potato; a similar situation is described in the case of the apple.

This problem of monoculture directly identifies the topic of the prior paragraph, and the author characterizes the topic as a *problem*. Moreover, the phrase *this problem of monoculture* applies to the *similar situation* of the apple. The topic sentence allows us to infer that the rest of the paragraph will discuss how this problem of monoculture applies to the apple. Furthermore, the use of the pronoun *this* in front of the noun makes clear that monoculture was discussed and perhaps defined in the preceding paragraph.

The pronouns *another, it, this, that*, and *such* can be very useful road signs. These pronouns indicate that the subject has been discussed previously. Consider the following examples and what you can infer.

> *Such a technique has its advantages.*

What's the technique? It must have been explained in the preceding sentence. The following sentences will show its benefits.

> *It's tempting, but it's wrong.*

It was explained in the preceding sentence, likely in a very positive manner (it's "tempting"). But, the next sentence will explain why *it* is wrong.

Translation

When you're struggling to make sense of a window of confusing text, look for transitions and modifiers to help you determine the main point. You may be in the thick of a body paragraph with the topic sentence in the rearview mirror, or the topic sentence fails to illuminate the main point of the paragraph. Instead of focusing on every single word, use the transitions, modifiers, and pronouns to get the general direction of points and the connections between them.

Let's look at a tough paragraph and see how this works.

Pollan is not a botanist; he is a journalist who has written extensively on food and food production, tracing the human relationship with food from farm and garden to table and plate. Pollan himself is a gardener, and in his latest book on his favorite
5 subject, he describes an afternoon in his garden planting potatoes. He realizes that both he and the bees that are busily pollinating an apple tree nearby are performing essentially the same evolutionary role. That is, the bees promote certain varieties of apples based on useful features. Many people would find such
10 a notion absurd, but we have no trouble believing that humans cultivated certain varieties of potatoes based on their desirable traits. Pollan makes a convincing case that we are more like the bees than we have been accustomed to think: in his case, the potato adapted to its particular size and flavor so that humans
15 would plant it and disseminate its genes. In the case of the bees, the apple trees developed perfectly symmetrical blossoms and sweet scents to entice the bees to pollinate it.

Here's How to Crack It

You may have struggled to understand the middle part of the paragraph and even opted to reread the whole paragraph, but a second time through probably still failed to clarify the author's meaning

Focus on key modifiers, transitions, and pronouns. *Same* indicates a comparison between humans and bees, while the adverb *essentially* softens the similarity a bit. The transition *that is* leads into a restatement of the point. *Such* a notion about bees that we would find *absurd* is the claim that they promoted certain apples trees. The transition *but* leads into our having *no trouble* having the same notion about humans. The similarity between bees and humans is reinforced in the next sentence, *we are more like the bees*. Moreover, this sentence includes the author's blessing: she calls Pollan's case *convincing*. The parallel structure of *in his case* and *in the case of the bees* reasserts the similarity and in fact introduces specific examples of that *same evolutionary role*. The potato used humans. The apple trees used bees.

ACT BOOK CLUB

Critical thinking also extends to knowing more about the test writers themselves. You may find the passages dry and boring, but the folks at ACT would not agree with you. They have gone out of their way to select passages whose topics they find interesting and worthy of being read. They choose authors whose work they respect.

Thus, when it comes time to writing questions and correct answers, the ACT test writers will not make these chosen authors look bad by putting rude, silly, or offensive words in their mouths. The topics may include some challenging facts and ideas, but they are unlikely to be divisive or controversial. In the nonfiction passages, the authors may be critical or supportive of their subject, but they will state their opinions professionally and respectfully. Correct answers, therefore, must use the same level of diplomacy and respect to paraphrase the authors' ideas.

> - Topics are interesting and worthy.
> - Authors are professional and respectful.
> - Correct answers are not rude, silly, or offensive.

Use this knowledge to eliminate at least one wrong answer below. If you've retained the brief information we've gleaned so far about the passage and what the author thinks of Michael Pollan, you may be able to eliminate one more or identify the correct answer. If not, stay tuned to the end of the lesson when the answer will be provided.

31. Which of the following best describes how the passage's author describes Pollan?

 A. A well-intentioned environmentalist willing to challenge the accepted practices of industrial food production.
 B. A trained botanist attempting to replace the practice of monoculture with genetically modified foods.
 C. A knowledgeable journalist able to use his story-selling skills to promote the importance of biodiversity.
 D. A cynical author willing to shock readers in efforts to promote his book.

Here's How to Crack It

Choice (D) is out. It's offensive both to Michael Pollan and the passage's author if it's not true. On the extreme likelihood that the passage actually did discuss such an author, the correct answer would paraphrase it in a more tactful way. Choice (B) is also out. The paragraph cited for the Translation exercise stated the opposite. See the last section of this lesson for confirmation of the correct answer.

ADVANCED POE SKILLS

In an ideal situation, you would read a question, read the window of text looking for your answer, and then work through the answer choices to find the best match, using POE to get rid of those that don't.

But situations are seldom ideal on the Reading Test. When you don't quite understand the window and therefore have no clue about the answer, go straight to working the answers. You can reread your window to spot transitions and modifiers; do this in conjunction with working the answers.

The Art of Wrong Answers

If you worked for ACT, you'd have to sit in a cubicle all day writing test questions. The easy part of the job is writing the correct answer (in respectful language, of course). You may even know the correct answer before you write the question. The harder part is coming up with three wrong answers. If you didn't write great wrong answers, everyone would get a 36. So you have to come up with temptingly wrong answers.

Let's take a look at some ways to make wrong answers.

Read the following question, correct answer, and text. We don't care about the right answer in this exercise, so you can read it before you read the window.

35. The main point of the fourth paragraph (lines 1–45) is that:

    A. some species may play a role in their domestication by developing traits that make them useful to humans.

        In the introduction to his new book, *The Botany of Desire,* Michael Pollan points out that today there are fifty million dogs in the United States alone and only ten thousand wolves. Pollan uses this fact to question the standard understanding of domes-
5 tication. He argues that dogs have the evolutionary advantage over wolves because they have developed a survival strategy that involves making humans desire their company. The idea that domestication is something for which humans are unilaterally responsible and that we impose on other species he calls a
10 "failure of imagination."

Our goal here is to examine *why* the three wrong answers are wrong.

    B. humans developed an evolutionary strategy by making themselves desirable to dogs.

Look carefully at lines 6–7. Choice (B) took tempting words out of the passage and garbled them. The passage does not support this answer.

    C. the evolutionary strategy of dogs has been more successful than that of wolves.

Lines 2–3 indicate that there are many more dogs than wolves, so you could infer that the dogs have developed a more successful strategy. But (C) is incorrect because the example of dogs is used to support the main point but is not itself the main point of the paragraph.

    D. bees developed an evolutionary strategy dependent on the desirable traits of apples trees.

Bees and apple trees are not mentioned in this window and have instead been taken from a different window. Any choice that references facts or points from different windows is wrong.

Answers can be wrong because they don't match what the passage says, because they answer the wrong question, or because they're not even found in the right window. But no matter how tempting or obvious wrong answers are, they are all easier to understand than five to ten lines of text from the passage, simply because they're shorter. So when you're stuck on tough questions that reference tough windows, rely on the answers and POE.

Work the Answers

Instead of rereading the window to try to understand it, read the answer choices for their meaning. Then see if you can match that meaning back to part of the passage.

> - Look for lead words or phrases in the answer choices.
> - Determine whether the words or meaning match words or meaning in the window.
> - Use POE to cross off choices that don't match what's in the window.

Let's see how this works. Read the following question and window.

> Even before he gets to the era of humans and domestication of plants in the grand scheme of biological history, Pollan maintains that, without angiosperms—plants that produce fruit, thereby inducing animals to do the work of spreading their
> 5 seeds—mammals would not have evolved as they have, and the reptiles that had no need of delicious plants and fruits would likely still rule Earth. Thus, the co-evolutionary relationship between plants and mammals began hundreds of millions of years ago. There is no reason to think that the human relationship to plants
> 10 is appreciably different than that of a squirrel burying acorns or a bee pollinating an apple tree.

37. It can reasonably be inferred that the author provides the example of angiosperms (line 3) in order to:

Take the answer choices one at a time. In each choice, we've identified a lead word or phrase in the answer by making it bold. Can you match these words, or a paraphrased meaning of them, in the window of text?

A. argue that **mammals developed traits more useful to plants than to reptiles**.

The paragraph suggests that mammals were more useful to plants than were most reptiles, but it does not mention specific traits developed by mammals, and it does not discuss the relationship between mammals and reptiles at all.

B. reveal what traits made reptiles **lose their dominance to mammals**.

Likely still rule Earth is a good paraphrase of *lose their dominance* and *that had no need of delicious plants and fruits* could be the trait, or lack thereof, that disadvantaged reptiles. But this doesn't give us a reason for including the example of angiosperms.

      C.   explain why **dinosaurs became extinct**.

The passage never mentions dinosaurs, so (C) can't be right.

      D.   illustrate that the evolution of mammals **depended on useful traits developed by plants**.

The ability of angiosperms to produce fruit and get mammals to spread their seeds is a *useful trait*. Moreover, *depended on* is a good paraphrase of *co-evolutionary relationship between plants and mammals*. Choice (D) is the correct answer.

Try the next two examples. Choose your own words or phrases out of each answer to work backwards with. Does the answer match the passage?

This problem of monoculture is not unique to the potato; a similar situation is described in the case of the apple. The first grafted apple trees to arrive in America did not fare well. But thanks to the efforts of John Chapman (aka Johnny Appleseed),
5   who is the main focus of Pollan's apple chapter, many thousands of apple trees were planted from seeds, allowing genetic variation to provide species that would thrive in the new environment. But with modern industrial-scale food production and marketing, fewer and fewer varieties of apples are grown today, and genetic
10   variation is quickly dwindling. In the end, Pollan urges us to pay attention to our co-evolutionary role in agriculture and strive to preserve biodiversity, rather than rely on the idea that human (and chemical) ingenuity will always come to the rescue.

32. How does the passage's author characterize the genetic variation of apples within the context of modern food production?

F. Threatened, to the point that several new varieties of apples planted today fail to thrive.
G. Declining, to the point that relatively few varieties are planted.
H. Declining, in that varieties derived from genetically modified seeds will replace the varieties descended from the seeds sown by Johnny Appleseed.
J. Threatened, in that several varieties of apples could soon be extinct.

33. Based on the passage, Pollan would most likely say that relying on human ingenuity is more a matter of:

A. being practical than of being naïve.
B. dismissing scientific facts than of learning from evolutionary history.
C. hoping for a solution to a problem than addressing the causes.
D. accepting hysteria than of remaining optimistic.

Here's How to Crack Questions 32 and 33

For Question 32, the four answer choices all begin with a word that is a good paraphrase of *dwindling. Fail to thrive* in (F) misuses *thrive*, used to describe the trees grown from Johnny Appleseed. *Few varieties planted* in (G) is accurately placed in the paragraph and confirms (G) as the correct answer. *Genetically modified seeds* in (H) is not mentioned in the paragraph. *Extinct* in (J) cannot be supported by the passage.

For Question 33, *practical* and *naïve* in (A) may be possibilities, but they are in the wrong order. *Human ingenuity* is what Pollan discourages; thus *naïve* can't match what he is encouraging. *Evolutionary history* in (B) could refer to *our co-evolutionary role in agriculture* but *dismissing scientific facts* is almost opposite to *(chemical) ingenuity*. *Hoping for a solution* in (C) matches well with *come to the rescue*, and (C) is the correct answer. In (D), *remaining optimistic* is in the wrong place, a better paraphrase of what Pollan discourages rather than what he encourages.

PULL IT ALL TOGETHER

Try using all of your critical-reading skills on the next question.

Many pet dogs would stand no chance of survival in the wild. Though pugs and poodles are descended ultimately from wolves, they bear little resemblance to their wild cousins. Archaeological remains indicate that somewhere between 15,000 and 30,000
5 years ago, wolves began to be domesticated; that is, they began to live with and become dependent on humans. As this relationship became more common, people chose those animals with the most desirable traits to breed, and the obedient and loyal *Canis lupus familiaris* (domestic dog) was born.

36. The main purpose of the first paragraph is to:

    F. provide an example to introduce a concept that the rest of the passage will examine.

    G. list the desirable traits that made humans domesticate dogs.

    H. pose a theory that the rest of the passage will disprove.

    J. explain how the process of domestication benefits biodiversity.

Here's How to Crack It

The correct answer is (F). Dogs and wolves are an example of the concept of domestication, which is examined in the rest of the passage. Choice (G) is incorrect because the paragraph does not *list the desirable traits*. Choice (H) is tempting because the rest of the passage discusses Pollan's point that dogs played some role in their domestication (see Question 35), but *disprove* is too strong. Choice (J) is incorrect because the paragraph does not *explain* anything, much less address *biodiversity*.

Agreement

Question 36 above was easier to answer because of the knowledge gained from working the prior questions. No matter how well you may read a passage, you learn the main points better as you work the questions. The questions, after all, all come from the same passage and it only makes sense that they should agree with one another.

Take another look at Question 31, now paired with another question.

---

31. Which of the following best describes how the passage's author describes Pollan?

   A. A well-intentioned environmentalist willing to challenge the accepted practices of industrial food production.

   B. A trained botanist attempting to replace the practice of monoculture with genetically modified foods.

   C. A knowledgeable journalist able to use his story-selling skills to promote the importance of biodiversity.

   D. A cynical author willing to shock readers in efforts to promote his book.

39. As a piece of writing, Pollan's book is judged by the author to be:

   A. inscrutable to all but trained experts in the field of botany.

   B. revolutionary in its challenge of traditional understandings of domestication.

   C. simplistic in an effort to attract gardeners and casual readers.

   D. accessible and enjoyable in its mixture of anecdote and history.

Here's How to Crack Questions 31 and 39

From several questions and selections of text, we have proof that the author approves of Pollan. One selection of text explicitly gave praise to his writing skills.

> Pollan has a deep grasp of and appreciation for the principles of evolution and botany, **yet** he tells his stories in an entertaining and easily understandable manner.

This is the proof for (C) in Question 31 and (D) in Question 39. If you chose (A) for Question 31, the selection of (D) for Question 39 should make you change your answer. Keep your radar up as you make your way through the questions. Make sure your answers agree, and look for the Golden Thread.

The Golden Thread

Place yourself again in the cubicle of an ACT test-writer. When you determine which details to test in a question, you would likely choose the important ones, those that support the main point. Thus, the main idea runs throughout the correct answers of at least a few of the specific questions, like a golden thread that ties the questions together.

34. It can reasonably be inferred from the passage that by titling his book *Botany of Desire,* Pollan was trying to suggest that plants:

    F. have the same feelings as mammals.
    G. **played some role in their own domestication.**
    H. have been cultivated as part of natural selection.
    J. are dependent on humans for their evolution.

Here's How to Crack It

Look at the answers to Questions 35 and 37. These answers identify (G) as the correct answer for Question 34. The paragraph we used in the translation exercise provides the proof from the passage for (G), but so too do the answers to the other questions, and in a more concise fashion.

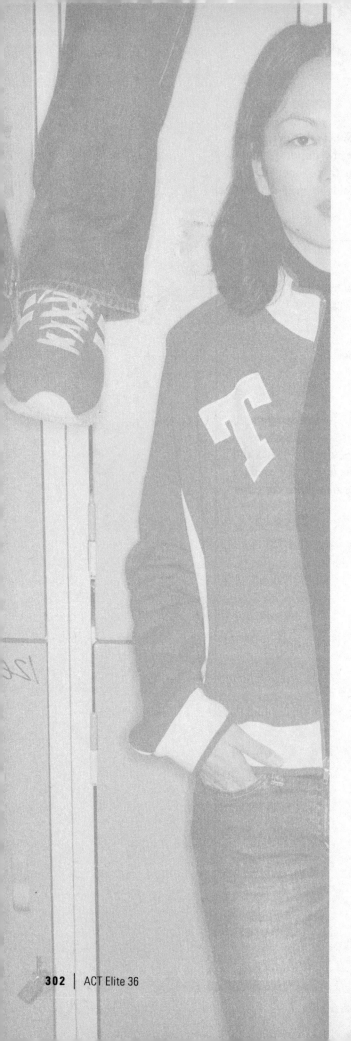

Summary

- Use critical-reading skills to crack difficult passages and windows of passages.

- Use topic sentences, transitions, modifiers, and pronouns to help translate confusing windows of text.

- Eliminate answer choices that are rude, silly, or offensive.

- Work backwards with answer choices. Try to match the answer to the passage instead of the passage to the answer.

- Correct answers should agree with one another.

- Look for the Golden Thread of the main idea as it appears in correct answers to at least a few of the specific questions.

Chapter 20
Time-Management Skills

The ACT Reading Test offers 35 minutes to answer 40 questions on four passages. To earn a perfect or near-perfect score, you have to use your time efficiently, pacing yourself to go slowly enough to avoid careless errors and quickly enough to get to all questions. You also need strategies to use when pacing doesn't go as planned.

READING WITHOUT TIME LIMITS

For school, most of your reading is done with no time limits, at least theoretically. You have assignments of chapters, essays, and articles that you read, reread, highlight, and notate out of class. You may even make flash cards. In class, group discussions and even lectures from the teacher help you grasp the significance, meaning, and context of what you have read. You may need to "show your understanding" in a quiz, test, in-class essay, or paper, but you have usually had plenty of time to work with the text to develop a thorough understanding.

Outside of school, serious readers take time to process what they've read and form an opinion. As a college student, you'll be asked not only to read but also to think about what you've read and offer an opinion. Any professor will tell you that understanding takes thought, and thought usually takes time, more than 35 minutes.

This Isn't School

In school, you have been rewarded for your ability to develop a thorough, thoughtful grasp of the meaning and significance of the text. But in school, you have the benefit of time, not to mention the aid of your teachers' lectures, class discussions, and various tools to help you not only understand but also remember what you've read. On the ACT, there is a time limit, which means you have none of those tools available. And on the Reading Test, it's dangerous to approach the passages as if you do.

You don't earn points from reading the passage. You earn points from answering the questions correctly. Even strong readers can take too much time reading the passage, and everyone has made the mistake of wasting time by rereading confusing, dense text.

Practice, Practice, Practice

1,460 ACT Practice Questions provides 6 tests' worth of Reading passages. That's 24 passages and 240 questions.

PACING

To work four passages in 35 minutes, you can divide the time in several different ways. It might seem logical to spend eight minutes and 45 seconds on each passage, but reality on the Reading Test is seldom that neat.

There is no single pacing strategy that works best for all students. Some do best by investing the most amount of time on the two passages on which they typically earn the most points, regardless of topic. Others can tackle their strongest passages in less time and give more time to the passages that they usually find more challenging. And on any given test, the topic or features such as the size and number of paragraphs and the number of line-reference questions can vary widely and have a significant impact on your pacing. The best way to determine *your* best pacing plan is to try various approaches and see which one helps you earn the most points most consistently.

Sample Pacing Strategies

These are general guidelines. Every time you do a practice Reading Test, analyze your performance, tracking how much time you spent on each passage and where you lost points—and why. Find the pacing strategy that works best for you.

Strategy 1

First passage:	*9–10 minutes*
Second passage:	*9–10 minutes*
Third passage:	*7–8 minutes*
Fourth passage:	*7–8 minutes*

Strategy 2

First passage:	*6–7 minutes*
Second passage:	*7–8 minutes*
Third passage:	*10 minutes*
Fourth passage:	*11 minutes*

Be Flexible

Our best advice is to be flexible. Just as you develop a typical order of the passages, you need to develop a typical pacing strategy. But be prepared to adapt both on each Reading Test if you have to.

THE 4-STEP BASIC APPROACH

Let's look at how to incorporate pacing into the 4-Step Basic Approach. Remember, each step is designed to help you use your time effectively.

Step 1: **Preview**. Check the blurb and map the questions.

Step 2: **Work the Passage**. Spend 2–3 minutes reading or skimming the passage.

Step 3: **Work the Questions**. Use your POOD to find Now and Later Questions.

Step 4: **Work the Answers**. Use POE.

When you preview the questions, you learn the main idea of the passage and know what to look for. Whether you read or skim the passage, you will do both better and in less time, and will avoid wasting time on unimportant details. Apply the critical-reading skills we cover in Chapter 19 to work the questions and answers. Read what you need to confirm or find an answer. Work backwards with the answers when you are confronted with difficult, dense text.

Pacing the Basic Approach

If you invest eight to nine minutes on a given passage, do so wisely. This is how we suggest using the time.

Step 1: **Preview**. *15–30 seconds*

Step 2: **Work the Passage**. *2–3 minutes*

Steps 3 and 4: **Work the Questions and Answers**. *6 minutes*

When you struggle with time, there are several places that could be eating up the minutes.

Step 1: Preview

To move at the fastest speed when you preview, you can't read the questions. Let your eye *look* for lead words and numbers. Don't let your brain *read*. Or, in other words, *scan*. Ignore common question words like "main idea," "in order to," or "author suggests." Those words won't show up in the passage, so just let your eye move right past them.

Time yourself to see if you can preview the following blurb and questions in 15–30 seconds.

SOCIAL SCIENCE: This passage is adapted from the article "Turning Trees Green Again" by Liza Clement (©2012 by Sustainability Quarterly).

11. It can most reasonably be inferred that the author's reason for including a variety of concerns surrounding the harvesting and processing of trees is to:

12. The passage's description of the Forest Stewardship Council reveals that the project lists one of its successes as the:

13. The main idea of the eighth paragraph (lines 73–86) is that:

14. The passage indicates that the impact of illegal logging on wildlife and biodiversity may result in:

15. The passage states that certification programs have positively impacted all of the following EXCEPT:

16. The passage indicates that compared to products made from reclaimed lumber, conventionally made wood products are somewhat more:

17. The passage notes that companies engage in illegal logging despite the fact that:

18. The passage refers to *patina* as a product of:

19. The passage indicates that Detroit offers programs that train workers to reclaim lumber because in that city:

20. The last paragraph leaves the reader with the clear impression that awareness of environmental and social impacts has:

Step 2: Work the Passage

This step should take no more than three minutes, and you should not be trying to read the passage thoroughly. Your only goal is to find as many of your lead words as you can and underline them.

If you struggle to work the passage in three minutes, there are ways to adapt the Basic Approach. You can incorporate these adaptations as a regular strategy, or you can use them when your pacing strategy goes awry on a particular test.

BASIC APPROACH ADAPTATIONS

Your approach does not need to be uniform for all four passages on every test. The key to flexibility is having a few different strategies in your toolbox and knowing when to use them.

Read the Topic Sentences

Read only the first sentence of each paragraph. You may find fewer lead words, but you will give yourself more time to spend on working the questions and answers and can find lead words then. Below, the first version of the passage removes the temptation to read the whole passage. On page 310, you'll have the same passage in its entirety along with the 10 questions and their answer choices. For now, apply the critical-reading skills you honed in Chapter 19 and let the topic sentences and transitions help you anticipate the content and organization of the passage.

Products made of wood surround us in our daily lives. Blah blah blah blah blah Blah blah blah blah blah Blah blah blah blah blah Blah blah blah blah blah Blah blah blah blah blah Blah blah blah blah Blah blah blah blah blah Blah blah blah blah blah Blah blah blah blah blah Blah blah blah blah blah Blah blah blah blah.

There has been a growing interest in recent years in organic food, and the "farm to table" and locavore movements that focus on getting to know the people and places that produce the food we eat, but many people don't realize that they can be making similar efforts when it comes to wood. Blah blah blah blah blah Blah blah blah blah blah Blah blah blah blah blah Blah blah blah blah blah blah blah blah Blah blah blah blah blah blah Blah blah blah blah blah Blah blah blah blah Blah blah blah blah blah Blah blah blah blah blah.

In response to such concerns, several organizations and governments have established policies and certification processes for sustainably harvested wood and wood products. Blah blah blah blah blah Blah blah blah blah blah Blah blah blah blah blah Blah blah blah blah blah blah blah blah Blah blah blah blah blah blah Blah blah blah blah blah Blah blah blah blah Blah blah blah blah blah Blah blah blah blah blah.

The FSC has ten principles about growing and harvesting lumber designed to protect both ecosystems and communities. blah blah blah blah blah Blah blah blah blah blah blah blah Blah blah blah blah blah blah blah blah blah blah blah blah blah Blah blah blah blah blah blah blah blah blah blah Blah blah blah blah blah blah blah blah blah blah Blah blah blah blah blah blah blah Blah blah blah blah blah blah blah blah.

Through its certification program for cooperatives, the FSC is helping to make real change in national policy on forest management and logging. blah blah blah blah Blah blah blah blah blah blah Blah blah blah blah blah Blah blah blah blah blah Blah blah blah blah blah Blah blah blah blah blah.

"Despite initial skepticism in many quarters that certification could bring about genuine benefits for people and forests," says Andre Giacini de Freitas, executive director of FSC, "FSC has grown and matured with exceptional success." blah blah blah blah Blah blah blah blah blah blah Blah blah blah blah blah Blah blah blah blah blah Blah blah blah blah blah Blah blah blah blah blah.

Consumers of furniture and building products have an even more conservation-minded option than certified wood: recycled lumber is increasingly used for flooring, paneling, furniture, and cabinetry. Blah blah blah blah Blah blah blah blah blah blah Blah blah blah blah blah Blah blah blah blah blah blah Blah blah blah blah blah Blah blah blah blah blah.

Reclaimed lumber is labor-intensive on the demolition end: workers pry boards out of buildings one at a time and remove screws and nails from them. blah blah blah blah Blah blah blah blah blah Blah blah blah blah blah Blah blah blah blah blah Blah blah blah blah blah Blah blah blah blah blah.

As our awareness of the long-term environmental and social impacts of everyday products grows, so too do the efforts to make those products more sustainable.

Steps 3 and 4: Work the Questions and Answers

You should have spent no more than four minutes *total* on Steps 1 and 2. Spend no more than six additional minutes to Work the Questions and Answers on page 311. Remember to do the questions in an order that makes sense to you.

SOCIAL SCIENCE: This passage is adapted from the article "Turning Trees Green Again" by Liza Clement (©2012 by Sustainability Quarterly).

Products made of wood surround us in our daily lives. Our houses and furniture are made of it; the paper that surrounds us in the form of books and magazines, junk mail and flyers, and tissues and toilet paper are all made from wood. Although
5 worldwide consumption of wood and paper products is on the rise, consumption in the United States is more than three times that in other developed countries. American consumption of paper products alone averages 886 pounds per person annually.

There has been a growing interest in recent years in organic
10 food, and the "farm to table" and locavore movements that focus on getting to know the people and places that produce the food we eat, but many people don't realize that they can be making similar efforts when it comes to wood. Although trees take longer to reach harvestable maturity than corn or toma-
15 toes do, their harvest and processing brings up many concerns similar to those related to industrial farming. Illegal logging is hazardous to the environment because it destroys wildlife habitats and biodiversity, contributes to global warming, and threatens food and water supply. Companies that engage in such
20 practices are not taking into account the long-term effects of their actions: by haphazardly cutting down old-growth trees in sensitive ecosystems, they are destroying the future possibility of harvesting more lumber from the same areas.

In response to such concerns, several organizations and gov-
25 ernments have established policies and certification processes for sustainably harvested wood and wood products. One of the best-known of these organizations is the Forest Stewardship Council (FSC), which was started in 1993 after the previous year's Earth Summit failed to establish international policies to
30 halt deforestation. The FSC provides both forest management certification, for those who harvest trees, and chain-of-custody certification, for companies that process and sell lumber and wood products.

The FSC has ten principles about growing and harvesting
35 lumber designed to protect both ecosystems and communities. Participating forests and logging operations that abide by the principles earn FSC certification. Currently, about 10 percent of forests worldwide are certified by FSC or another sustain-ability program, and participation in the programs is growing
40 quickly. A large international packaging company is increasing the percentage of FSC-certified fiber it uses every year, with the end goal of using exclusively FSC-certified fibers. "It's in our best interest," says a spokesperson for the company, "to help ensure the long-term viability of the raw materials our
45 business depends on."

Through its certification program for cooperatives, the FSC is helping to make real change in national policy on forest management and logging. For example, a growers' cooperative in Indonesia composed of individuals who provide sustainable
50 teak for outdoor furniture was started in 2005 with 196 individual members. Today, that cooperative has grown to 744 members. Its success has led the Indonesian government to assign the co-op to the management of state-owned teak plantations. Now local growers of other crops in high international demand,
55 such as cocoa and cashew nuts, are also seeking similar kinds of certification based on the success of the teak cooperative.

"Despite initial skepticism in many quarters that certifica-tion could bring about genuine benefits for people and forests," says Andre Giacini de Freitas, executive director of FSC, "FSC
60 has grown and matured with exceptional success." Though critics say that certification has little meaning, a study of the effects of certification programs on U.S. forests found that organizations seeking certification made on average 14 significant changes to their social, environmental, and/or economic practices.

65 Consumers of furniture and building products have an even more conservation-minded option than certified wood: recycled lumber is increasingly used for flooring, paneling, furniture, and cabinetry. Recycled wood has the patina that only age and wear can provide, keeps useable materials out of landfills, and
70 also provides a story. Consumers are willing to pay a little bit more for flooring that came from the old high-school gym, or beautifully weathered paneling from an old barn.

Reclaimed lumber is labor-intensive on the demolition end: workers pry boards out of buildings one at a time and
75 remove screws and nails from them. But this is seen as a win-win situation for many. In communities such as Detroit, which has a large stock of abandoned buildings to demolish, a program trains people to deconstruct buildings and make new products from the reclaimed wood. This program benefits the
80 community by providing jobs and job training, by removing urban blight, and by promoting the city of Detroit to consumers who purchase products made from the recycled wood. Every piece of reclaimed lumber is stamped with the address of the building from which it was taken. To consumers who want to
85 know the social and environmental effects of their purchases, the extra cost of such products is worthwhile.

As our awareness of the long-term environmental and social impacts of everyday products grows, so too do the efforts to make those products more sustainable.

11. It can most reasonably be inferred that the author's reason for including a variety of concerns surrounding the harvesting and processing of trees is to:

   A. urge readers not to buy teak furniture.
   B. present to readers the need for the sustainability efforts discussed in the passage.
   C. prompt readers to contemplate investing in recycled wood production.
   D. inspire readers to invent new solutions to the problems of wood production.

12. The passage's description of the Forest Stewardship Council reveals that the project lists one of its successes as the:

   F. improved practices in harvesting and processing wood.
   G. reduced consumption of paper products.
   H. establishment of international policies on deforestation.
   J. improved quality of recycled wood products.

☆ 13. The main idea of the eighth paragraph (lines 73–86) is that:

   A. products made from reclaimed lumber are becoming increasingly expensive to purchase.
   B. the process of reclaiming lumber illustrates the benefits of logging old-growth trees.
   C. the process of reclaiming lumber poses great dangers to workers.
   D. the process of reclaiming lumber can offer social and economic benefits.

14. The passage indicates that the impact of illegal logging on wildlife and biodiversity may result in:

   F. old-growth trees losing their patina.
   G. food and water supplies being threatened.
   H. much of the lumber being wasted.
   J. trees reaching maturity at later ages.

15. The passage states that certification programs have positively impacted all of the following EXCEPT:

   A. growers' cooperatives for teak, cocoa, and cashew nuts.
   B. ecosystems and communities of some U.S. forests.
   C. an international packaging company.
   D. workers in Detroit.

16. The passage indicates that compared to products made from reclaimed lumber, conventionally made wood products are somewhat more:

   F. difficult to recycle.
   G. labor-intensive to demolish.
   H. dangerous to workers.
   J. affordable to purchase.

17. The passage notes that companies engage in illegal logging despite the fact that:

   A. overharvesting may limit the availability of future growth in the same areas.
   B. most paper products are made from trees harvested legally.
   C. sensitive ecosystems are being destroyed.
   D. international policies permit deforestation.

18. The passage refers to *patina* as a product of:

   F. teak furniture.
   G. old-growth trees.
   H. age and wear.
   J. certified wood.

19. The passage indicates that Detroit offers programs that train workers to reclaim lumber because in that city:

   A. landfills are filled with old wood products.
   B. many abandoned buildings are being demolished.
   C. trained carpenters are in short supply.
   D. reclaiming lumber is less labor-intensive.

☆ 20. The last paragraph leaves the reader with the clear impression that awareness of environmental and social impacts has:

   F. increased over time.
   G. struggled to grow.
   H. decreased substantially.
   J. remained flat.

Score and Analyze Your Performance

The answers are 11. (B), 12. (F), 13. (D), 14. (G), 15. (D), 16. (J), 17. (A), 18. (H), 19. (B), 20. (F). How did you do with regard to accuracy and time? If you were unable to get all of the questions right using only six additional minutes, analyze where you spent your time and consider what changes you can make next time.

Do Now Questions 13 and 20 because both have line references. Question 19 is a Referral question and has a great lead word (*Detroit*), which you should have found in the eighth paragraph when you answered Question 13. The same paragraph features the lead words in Question 16. Question 12 also has great lead words, and while it may require a window spanning a few paragraphs to answer it (lines 24–56), that work allows you to answer Question 15 immediately afterward, even though it's a negative question.

Do Later questions that are neither easy to answer nor whose answers are easy to find.

Questions 14 and 17 are Referral questions that have the same lead words (*illegal logging*) and can be answered from the same window found in the last third of the second paragraph (lines 16–23).

The Pencil Trick

When you have to look harder for a lead word, use your pencil to sweep each and every line from beginning to end. This will keep your brain from reading and let your eye look for the word.

Question 18 has a lead word that is unusual, but it still may be difficult to find. Since you haven't run into it answering any of the prior questions, look first in the paragraphs you haven't read, and you'll find it in the seventh paragraph (lines 65–72). Do Question 11 last.

As You Go

As You Go is another adaptation to working the passage. It's a slight adjustment of the 4-Step Basic Approach. This strategy works well for many students, and it can be a good option for all students when a passage has five line/paragraph references or more.

Step 1: **Preview.** Check the blurb. Underline lead words. Mark the passage with the questions with line references.

Step 2: **Work the Passage and Questions.** Read the passage and work the questions as you go.

Step 3: **Work the Answers.** Use POE.

Step 1: Preview

When you map the questions, just underline the lead words in those questions. For the questions with line or paragraph references, map the passage. Write the question number in the margin next to the appropriate lines on the passage.

Step 2: Work the Passage and Questions

Read the passage, but answer the questions you marked in the margin as you go. Resume reading until the next question marked in the margin. As you read, keep an eye out for the lead words you underlined in the questions. When you spot a question's lead words, stop and do the question.

Step 3: Work the Answers

Whether you work the passage up front and the questions later or work the passage and questions as you go, good use of POE will save you time and help you get every question right.

HUMANITIES: This passage is adapted from the memoir *Under the Jujube Trees: Growing up in India* by Amrita Mehra (© 2002 by Amrita Mehra).

My days as a schoolgirl in Jaipur had a distinct rhythm to them. My mother would wake my sisters and me early and guide us to the bathroom for our morning beauty routine. We would splash on our faces the fresh milk that was delivered
5 directly from the barn to us, inhaling its grassy, sweet aroma and rubbing the yellowish blobs of fat into our skin.

After completing the beauty routine and then brushing our teeth, we would dress in our matching starched blue pinafores, then report to the dining room for breakfast.

10 In the winter, we would bundle ourselves in our matching tweed coats, and my mother would carefully inspect us, making sure the black bows of our braids were perfectly symmetrical, and our shiny, stiff leather shoes tightly double-knotted. I imagined us as a chain of identical paper dolls standing side by
15 side, our hands and the edges of our coats touching. She would also inspect my father, brushing imaginary pieces of lint from his 3-piece suit and straightening his tie. On these days I felt more like a British schoolgirl from one of the stories we read at school than like a Hindu girl in northern India.

20 My father would leave to walk to the textile factory where he was the manager as my sisters and I piled into the back seat of the car that would take us to our Catholic school. My mother stood in the doorway waving, resplendent in her perfectly pressed sari, elegant wool shawls draped around her instead
25 of the Western-style overcoats the rest of us wore.

For holidays, our family would return to Delhi, to my grandfather's house where my many aunts and uncles and cousins lived. The house was outside the city gates, in an orchard. Here, among my extended family, I felt freed from the
30 constraints of life in Jaipur. This was not only because of the long days at school—there were many rules to be followed, and the nuns were very strict—but also because of the starched blue uniforms and the tight braids we wore every day. Everything in Jaipur seemed regimented and confining.

35 By contrast, grandfather's house, which we called by its address, Number 12, was relaxed and free. Here I didn't have to wear braids, and I could wear boys' shorts and spend my afternoons climbing trees in the orchard with my many cousins. The transition to life in Delhi made me feel the way I
40 imagined a caged tiger would feel upon being set free to once again prowl the forest.

Although there were many more people around Number 12 than at our house in Jaipur, there was far less supervision. All of us children were largely left to roam about on our own.
45 This was especially true on the hot afternoons, when the adults would retreat inside the house for naps.

Some days, we would venture down to the Yamuna River, which ran along the edge of my grandfather's property, to fish and swim. Other days, we would raid the guavas. The older
50 cousins would climb the small trees, pick the hard, unripe fruits, and quarter them with pocket knives. They would hand wedges of guava down to the younger children, and we would eat them greedily after dipping them in salt mixed with cumin and red chilies. The tartness of the guava was highlighted by the
55 contrast with the spicy salt, leaving fireworks on our tongues.

Perhaps my favorite time at my grandfather's house was when there was a family wedding. Several days before the festivities began, scores more relatives would arrive, along with the caterers. The women would be in a flurry of preparing
60 clothing and flower garlands. The caterers, meanwhile, would be bustling about in their tent, a myriad of magical aromas wafting out to give us a hint of the feasts to come.

Amidst all the chaos, the children would run back and forth from indoors to outdoors, keeping tabs on the progress
65 of the different groups. Sometimes my mother would assign me a task: "Go and tell the gardener we need more jasmine." Outside, if we were lucky, the caterers would allow us a taste of spicy lamb meatballs or tart tamarind chutney.

Most of the marriages were arranged, and the bride and
70 groom had often not met each other before the wedding. The bride always looked beautiful in her richly embroidered, bright red *lehenga*, her face covered by a veil. I always found myself holding my breath at the moment at which the veil was lifted. Once, the veil had revealed a cousin in tears, making no effort
75 to hide her disappointment in her new husband. More often, the veil revealed a face as radiant as the ornaments the bride wore.

The double life I lived as a child, in Jaipur and in Delhi, has fundamentally shaped me as the person I am today. I keep different parts of my life compartmentalized in my mind: work
80 goes in one area, family in another, and so on. The thought of those places that feel free and unconstrained the way my grandfather's house did help me cope with the parts that are more burdensome.

21. The point of view from which the passage is told is best described as that of:

A. an adult recounting various experiences of her childhood.
B. an adult relating in third person the thoughts and events of her childhood.
C. a young girl discussing being a servant in Number 12.
D. a young girl explaining how she uses fantasy and daydreaming to escape her regimented daily life.

22. In the passage, which of the following activities is NOT mentioned as one where the author's mother was present?

F. Getting ready for a wedding
G. Spending holidays at Number 12
H. Standing for inspection before school
J. Raiding orchards for guava

23. In the passage, the author compares herself to:

I. a caged tiger.
II. a British schoolgirl.
III. a boy.

A. I and II only
B. I and III only
C. II and III only
D. I, II, and III

24. The author most likely describes her clothes as *starched* and her braids as *tight* in line 33 to suggest:

F. she felt relaxed and free to spend time unsupervised in Delhi.
G. she was proud to attend school looking her best.
H. she felt constrained by following strict rules in Jaipur.
J. she felt feminine at school because she wore boys' shorts on holidays.

25. In the fifth and sixth paragraphs (lines 26–41), the author draws a contrast primarily between the:

A. regimented life she led in Jaipur and the relaxed freedom of holidays spent at Number 12.
B. relationship she had with her sisters and the one she had with her cousins.
C. preparation adults made for a wedding and the relaxation enjoyed by children.
D. the academic challenge of school in Jaipur and the unsupervised playtime in Delhi.

26. As it used in line 9, the phrase "report to the dining room" most nearly means:

F. the author and her sisters rush through their morning beauty routine in order to make it to breakfast on time.
G. the author's mother pays careful attention to the appearance of her husband and daughters.
H. the author's father leaves for work without his daughters if they are late.
J. the author and her sisters dress in a manner of their choosing rather than in one chosen by their mother.

27. The statement "I always found myself holding my breath at the moment at which the veil was lifted" (line 72–73) most strongly suggests that the author was:

A. disappointed in the appearance of the bride.
B. concerned about the bride's reaction.
C. imagining her own wedding.
D. radiant with happiness.

28. The details the author recounts of her childhood adventures with her cousins are based most often on which physical sense?

F. Taste
G. Sight
H. Sound
J. Touch

29. When the author writes that she "imagined us as a chain of identical paper dolls" (line 14), she is most likely making the point that:

A. she felt constrained by the formality of her school uniform.
B. she and her sisters dressed precisely and similarly.
C. she and her sisters disappointed their mother with their appearance.
D. she wished she wore a sari instead of a Catholic school uniform.

30. In the context of the passage, the phrase *compartmentalized in my mind* (line 79) can most nearly be paraphrased as:

F. divided in loyalties between work and family.
G. kept work and family concerns separate.
H. sorted a list of priorities.
J. suffered mental confusion.

Score and Analyze Your Performance

The answers are 21. (A), 22. (J), 23. (A), 24. (H), 25. (A), 26. (G), 27. (B), 28. (F), 29. (B), 30. (G). How did you do in accuracy and time? If you were unable to get all of the questions right or used more than 10–11 minutes, analyze where you spent your time and consider what changes you can make next time. Here is some general advice that may help you pinpoint where you can save time.

Stop and do Now Questions 26 and then 29. Resume reading until you get to the several questions in the 5th and 6th paragraphs, Questions 24 and 25. In your search for the lead words in the Roman numerals, spot both *British schoolgirl* and *caged tiger* after working the first four questions, and try Question 23. Eliminate (B) and (C). If you spotted *boys' shorts* and knew that the phrase failed to live up to a comparison to *a boy*, you have the correct answer. If not, return to this question after you've finished the passage and find no comparison to a boy.

Continue reading and stop and do Question 28 when you spot another mention of *cousins* with a more specific description of *adventures*. Finish the passage and do question 30. Do Questions 21 and 22 last.

DUAL READING PASSAGES

You may also see a "Dual Passage" on the Reading Test. Like the "Fighting Scientist" sections found later on in the Science Test (see Chapter 26, Hard Passages and Questions), this section features multiple viewpoints, with questions asked about each passage individually and then together. Because you'll be comparing in addition to analyzing, these passages require a bit more reading, but they are also susceptible to more strategic thinking.

Here's the strategy we'll be using in this section:

1. **Preview.** Read the blurb and map the questions as you would in a typical passage. Do a quick count of how many questions are asked about each passage.

2. **Work the Popular Passage.** If one passage has more questions than the other, work that one first. Take the questions that ask only about that passage and reorder them chronologically, reading through the passage as you do the questions.

3. **Work the Other Passage.** Before you jump to the questions that deal with both passages, work the other the same way you worked the first. Reorder the questions chronologically and read through the passage as you answer the questions in the new chronological order.

4. **Work the Questions that Deal with Both Passages.** By this point, you've hopefully got a good sense of what unites the passages. Answer the questions that deal with both passages, and make sure that these answers agree with the others regarding each individual passage!

A Note on the Golden Thread

As you may have noticed, correct answers seem to repeat in a lot of ACT passages. You may find that if you get one answer, you can get three more with the same information. We call this phenomenon "The Golden Thread," named for some main idea or topic that threads through many of the answer choices.

On Dual Passages, it's more important than ever to find the Golden Thread. If you think about it, the questions that ask about both passages are really just variations on the theme, "What do these two passages have to do with each other?"

As you read through the two passages separately, try to answer this question, even if only in a vague way. Any answers you can generate for this "Golden Thread" question will help you throughout parts of the rest of the passage.

Here is what one of the passages will look like. Note how kindly ACT has separated the questions for you.

HUMANITIES: Passage A is adapted from the essay "From West Orange to Paris and Back" by Ashley C. Throckmorton. Passage B is adapted from the essay "Train Robberies and Magic" by Abigal Colorado Tintype.

Passage A

While it may be impossible to know when the history of the cinema properly begins, there is no question that it had its first real flowering in the late-nineteenth and early-twentieth centuries. The history of photography goes back much further—
5 to the 1830s at least—, but the history of cinema properly began when the technological advancements caught up with the theoretical advancements in photography. English photographer Eadweard Muybridge was the first to figure out how to take photographs in rapid enough succession as to produce the illusion
10 of movement. First created in 1877, his series of photographs of "animal locomotion" (a running horse in Muybridge's case) look like early film strips, as they seem to capture the horse's movement in minute intervals.

Around this same time, Thomas Edison invented one of
15 the most popular technologies of the century: the phonograph. In 1888, Edison wanted a visual component to add to the now near-universal phonograph, and he commissioned one of his lab assistants, William Dickson, to do so. Dickson incorporated the work of Muybridge and others into a series of mechanisms
20 that could both record motion pictures and then "play" them back. The tangible result of this process was the Kinetoscope, which would, with internal battery power, "play" the pictures in rapid enough succession that they produced the illusion of continuous movement. Edison established a Kinetograph studio
25 in West Orange, NJ, where he and his assistants made short pieces for the Kinetoscope, usually portraying simple actions like kisses or individual dances. As the phonograph had before it, the Kinetoscope took the world by storm.

Inspired by Edison's invention, two French brothers, Au-
30 guste and Louis Lumière, sought to make it more available for public consumption. To that end, they invented the first com-mercially viable projector, the *cinématographe*, which made the single-viewer mechanism of the Kinetoscope available to many viewers at once. Where the Kinetoscope could weigh
35 more than 1,000 pounds, the *cinématographe* weighed only 20. As a result, the Lumières were able to shoot much larger scenes and did not require the stability of a particular studio as Edison had. Their most famous film, "The Arrival of a Train at La Ciotat Train Station," was just that, and while it may be
40 dull by contemporary standards, this simple 50-second film thrilled and amazed audiences.

Here, from the hands of nearly a half-century of inventors, was the birth of the cinema. We have them to thank when we go to the movies or even, one could argue, watch videos on
45 our computers and video-chat on our phones. Indeed, if we are

able to suspend our disbelief for just a moment, we can put ourselves back in that early cinema moment. Watch the Lumière film of the arriving train in just the right mood, and it can fill you with the same wonder that overtook the original audiences.

Passage B

50 While the history of the cinema is inconceivable without the efforts of Thomas Edison and the Lumière brothers, they in fact contributed little more than the invention of a technology. After all, when we think of the cultural force that the cinema has become, we do not refer to the miniature documentary curiosi-
55 ties of the Kinetoscope. Without this mechanism, the cinema would have been impossible, but Edison and the Lumières are no more responsible for the history of the cinema than a dairy farmer is responsible for a delicious milkshake.

The real birth of the cinema began in the early years of
60 the twentieth century. With the technology that had been given to him, a French magician named Georges Méliès started to experiment. As a magician, Méliès saw the new film cameras as working in his professional favor: he saw the cinema as producing illusions along the lines of those he created on the
65 stage. In the nearly 500 films he produced between 1896 and 1913, Méliès not only showed the artistic capabilities of "trick" cinema. He also created some of the first and most complex narrative films ever to be seen on screen: *A Trip to the Moon* (1902) was 14 minutes long and had 30 scenes.

70 Around this same time, a former Edison employee, the American Edwin S. Porter, was creating some narrative films of his own. Porter worked as a projectionist for the Edison company, where he would arrange fifteen-minute programs from a series of short films. This assembly no doubt inspired
75 Porter to think of how a narrative film could be assembled, and Porter was the first to see that scenes could be portrayed from multiple perspectives at once. Inspired by but departing from Méliès's theatrically staged narrative films, Porter found a new way, one that was only available in the cinema. In *The*
80 *Great Train Robbery* (1903), Porter used a technique that has since been dubbed "parallel editing," which enabled him to tell the story of both the train robbers and the train passengers, themselves in different places for much of the film's action, at what seemed to be the same time.

85 Therefore, while the contributions of Edison and the Lu-mières are indispensable, the cinema as we know it today began a few years later with Porter and Méliès. Indeed, the cinema has its cultural power today because of its *artistic* achievements, not merely its technological ones. Edison and the Lumières may
90 have provided the canvas, but Porter and Méliès were the first to use that canvas to create real art.

21. According to information in the second paragraph (lines 14–28), the early film camera was related to the phonograph in that the camera was

    A. conceived as a technology to accompany the sounds produced by the phonograph.
    B. designed to replace the phonograph within fifteen to twenty years.
    C. inspired by the work of Eadweard Muybridge, the inventor of the phonograph.
    D. limited by its weight and size in the same way that the phonograph was.

22. According to Throckmorton, the primary advantage of the *cinématographe* over the Kinetoscope was that the *cinématographe* was

    F. invented in France, where inventors could take proper credit for their inventions.
    G. mobile in a way that the Kinetoscope was not and could therefore capture new subjects on film.
    H. able to shoot films that were as much as fifty seconds longer than Kinetoscope films.
    J. intimate for the viewer in a way that the Kinetoscope's large projections could not be.

23. The word "play" (line 20) is set off in quotation marks in order to signify that the

    A. Kinetoscope was invented before movies were considered fun to watch.
    B. *cinématographe* was the first film technology to use electricity.
    C. films produced by the Kinetoscope were intended mainly for children.
    D. technology used still photographs to produce the illusion of motion.

24. According to Throckmorton, why do contemporary viewers have Edison and the Lumières "to thank" (line 43)?

    F. Edison and the Lumières created some of the first and most thrilling narrative films of the nineteenth century.
    G. Edison and the Lumières popularized the inventions of William Dickson and Eadweard Muybridge.
    H. Edison and the Lumières contributed to the invention of a technology that is now almost universally accessible.
    J. Edison and the Lumières contributed major parts to the invention of the computer and smartphone.

25. When Tintype states that Edison and the Lumières "provided the canvas" but that Méliès and Porter were the first "to create real art," (lines 90–91) she most nearly means that

    A. the narrative innovations of Porter and Méliès would have been possible without the work of Edison and the Lumières.
    B. the narrative innovations of Porter and Méliès were less significant in the history of science than the work of Edison and the Lumières.
    C. the technological innovations of Edison and the Lumières were not supposed to be used to create narrative films.
    D. the technological innovations of Edison and the Lumières enabled the early cinematic achievements of Porter and Méliès.

26. According to Tintype, Porter and Méliès are the true inventors of the cinema because they

    F. made the first blockbuster films that made significant amounts of money.
    G. proposed that films should be longer than a few seconds.
    H. introduced the artistic elements that made cinema a cultural force.
    J. predicted that films would one day be universally accessible.

27. Tintype compares Edison and the Lumières to "a dairy farmer" (lines 57–58) in order to suggest that

    A. those who produce the raw material do not necessarily deserve credit for what is done with that raw material.
    B. people who cannot invent significant technologies should consider work in industries where they will be more useful.
    C. scientific innovators maximize their use of resources in order to produce things that people find interesting or necessary.
    D. some of the most interesting technological innovations come from those who work in the field of agriculture.

28. The accounts of Throckmorton and Tintype are similar in that they believe

    F. Porter and Méliès were the true inventors of the medium of film as a storytelling medium.

    G. cinema's greatest achievements would not have been possible without the work of Edison and the Lumières.

    H. the history of film would have been much different if the Lumières had perfected their camera before Edison perfected his.

    J. Méliès's background in magic suited him especially well for work in the illusionistic medium of cinema.

29. What is the main component of Tintype's essay that is not addressed in Throckmorton's essay?

    A. Technological innovation

    B. Particular films

    C. Camera size

    D. Narrative storytelling

30. Throckmorton would most likely see *A Trip to the Moon* as

    F. a copy of a Lumière film produced ten years earlier.

    G. superior to Porter's *The Great Train Robbery*.

    H. an extension of earlier technological innovations.

    J. the subpar work of an amateur magician.

How to Work Through a Dual-Passage Reading Section

Step 1: Preview
As the blurb indicates, these passages are adapted from a couple of essays. It doesn't tell much more than that. Lead words include *early film camera, phonograph, cinématographe, Kinetoscope, Edison, Lumière, Méliès, Porter,* and *A Trip to the Moon.*

A quick count will show that there are more questions about Passage A than there are about Passage B. Let's do Passage A first!

Step 2: Work the Popular Passage
Before you start reading, rearrange the questions in the order of their appearance in the passage. When there aren't line references, use lead words to determine the order in which to work the questions. In this case, it looks like the questions will appear in the passage in roughly this order: 23, 21, 22, 24.

Read through the passage and stop as you come to the lines in each question. Now that you've ordered the questions, you don't have to worry about missing anything.

Use the techniques you've learned throughout these reading chapters! POE still applies like crazy, and bad answers are just as bad here as they are in any other passage.

Step 3: Work the Other Passage
Rinse and repeat! These questions will fall roughly into this order chronologically: 27, 25, 26. Work through these questions, always looking to eliminate bad answers.

Step 4: Work the Questions that Deal With Both Passages
By this point, you have hopefully noticed what unites these passages. Before you get to the questions that deal with both passages, make sure to jot down a sentence or two about what you see as the "Golden Thread" that unites the two passages. Try it for these passages we've just read:

You probably came up with something like this:

Passage A (Throckmorton) sees Edison and the Lumières as the inventors of the cinema because they invented the cameras. Passage B (Tintype) sees Edison and the Lumières as important but sees Méliès and Porter as the inventors because they made it a narrative form.

Now let's look again at those questions that deal with both passages. Use the Golden Thread whenever possible!

28. The accounts of Throckmorton and Tintype are similar in that they believe:

  F. Porter and Méliès were the true inventors of the medium of film as a storytelling medium.
  G. cinema's greatest achievements would not have been possible without the work of Edison and the Lumières.
  H. the history of film would have been much different if the Lumières had perfected their camera before Edison perfected his.
  J. Méliès's background in magic suited him especially well for work in the illusionistic medium of cinema.

Here's How to Crack It

Remember, we want something that both authors talk about. Porter and Méliès were only mentioned in the second passage, so (F) and (J) can be eliminated. Then, (H) can be eliminated because it doesn't take into account that Passage B is about something other than Edison and the Lumières. We need an answer that encapsulates both passages, and only (G) does so.

29. What is the main component of Tintype's essay that is not addressed by Throckmorton?

  A. Technological innovation
  B. Particular films
  C. Camera size
  D. Narrative storytelling

Here's How to Crack It

Throckmorton is all about the technology aspect of the cinema. Tintype is all about the narrative and artistic aspects of the cinema. As a result, Throckmorton is way more interested in (A) and (C) than Tintype is, so those can be removed. Then, because a quick glance at the italics will show that both authors mention particular films, you can also eliminate (B). But you may have arrived at the answer already using the Golden Thread: the best answer is (D), because only Tintype is interested in the narrative and artistic aspects of the cinema.

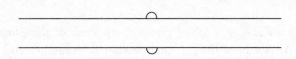

30. Throckmorton would most likely see *A Trip to the Moon* as:

    F. a copy of a Lumière film produced ten years earlier.
    G. superior to Porter's *The Great Train Robbery*.
    H. an extension of earlier technological innovations.
    J. the subpar work of an amateur magician.

Here's How to Crack It

Keep that Golden Thread in mind! Throckmorton is all about the technology. Tintype is all about the art. Therefore, even though Throckmorton doesn't talk about *A Trip to the Moon*, she would almost certainly be interested in something *technological* about it, not anything about its artistic merits, thus eliminating (G) and (J). Even (F) doesn't quite address the technological aspects of the film, so that can also be eliminated. After all, Throckmorton says that the work of Edison and the Lumières was foundational: she doesn't say that other people copied their particular films. As a result, only (H) can work.

Score And Analyze Your Performance

We've already discussed the trickier questions that combine elements of both Passage A and Passage B, but don't forget that the questions about each individual passage are worth just as many points. Go back and check your work: 21. (A), 22. (G), 23. (D), 24. (H), 25. (D), 26. (H), 27. (A). If you're getting these questions wrong, you might want to review Chapter 18, "The 4-Step Basic Approach."

BE FLEXIBLE

We started this chapter with the exhortation to be flexible and we'll repeat it here. The techniques and strategies we've outlined are designed to give you options of how to replace or adapt your own strategy. When you are answering almost every question correctly, it can be difficult to change what's working for you so well. But to achieve a perfect or near-perfect score on the Reading Test, you have to both tweak a few things and be ready to switch gears when your typical approach isn't working on a particular test.

When you take a Reading Test for practice, try some of the different strategies we've covered. Always be willing to analyze your performance and evaluate what you can change. The more you practice different techniques, the easier it will be to adapt when the particulars of a challenging test demand a change.

We're not saying this is easy. In fact, changing your own instinctual behavior is the hardest part of cracking the Reading Test. Everyone has made the mistake of ignoring that voice that's screaming inside your head to move on, and we've all answered back "But I know I'm almost there and if I take just a little more time, I know l can get it." Know your strengths, know your weaknesses, know when to adapt, and know when to just guess and move on.

In closing, here are a few guidelines to help you think about your specific challenges with time management and pacing yourself.

SPEND TIME WISELY

To use your time most effectively, know where to invest time and where to save it. Rushing in crucial places is just as damaging as wasting time.

The Passage

Most students waste the bulk of their time reading (and rereading) the passage, disconnected from working the questions. Some students can read the whole passage, and process the points, moving to the questions with a good prediction of the answers and the location in mind of where to confirm an answer, if needed. If that's not you, spend no more than two to three minutes reading or skimming the passage. Do not reread any sentence or paragraph. Let topic sentences and transitions help to confirm the important points. Save your time to spend on a question that references difficult text, not on your initial read of the passage.

The Questions

When you Preview, *look* for lead words to underline and line/paragraph references to star, but don't spend time *reading* the questions. However, when you work the questions, slow down and read the questions carefully. Don't rush and then answer incorrectly because you misread the question. If you struggle with a window of text, use topic sentences, transitions, modifiers, and pronouns to decipher the point and predict the answer.

Work questions in an order that makes sense, doing Now questions that are easy to answer or whose answers are easy to find. Do questions that are difficult to answer and whose answers are difficult to find Later.

If you struggle to find lead words on some Later questions, it's important to *look* for and find them before you lock into reading for comprehension. Do not read the passage again to try to find them. Work on the paragraphs you haven't read, and use the pencil trick.

The Answers

Do not rush reading through the answers. You can choose a wrong answer because you missed that it was only half right. But half right is all wrong. Work backwards with the answers when you struggle with the window of text needed to answer a question.

Adapt

When your pacing strategy goes awry, read just the topic sentences in Step 2. When it goes really off base and you have five minutes for your last passage, skip Step 2 entirely. Go straight to Step 3 and Work the Now questions. Look for the Golden Thread on the most general questions saved for last.

If a passage has five or more line/paragraph references, try As You Go.

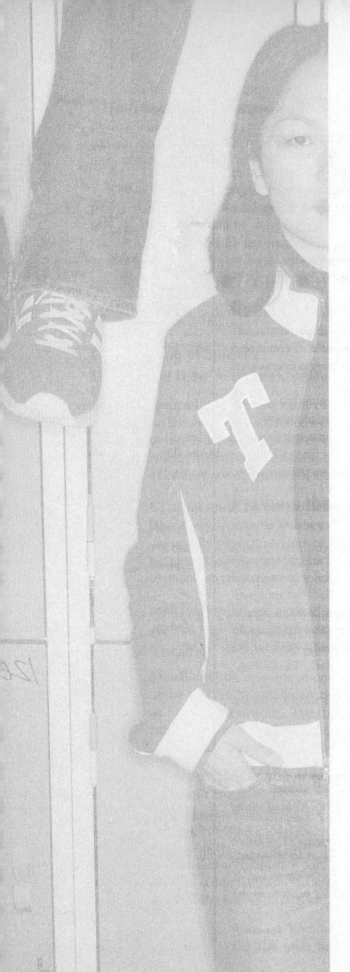

Summary

- Use the 4-Step Basic Approach to save time.
  - **Step 1: Preview.** Check the blurb and map the questions. Star line and paragraph references and underline lead words.
  - **Step 2: Work the Passage.** Finish in two to three minutes. Look for and underline lead words.
  - **Step 3: Work the Questions.** Do Now questions that are easy to answer or whose answers are easy to find. Read what you need in a window of five to 10 lines to find your answer. Save Later questions to the end that are both hard to find and hard to answer.
  - **Step 4: Work the Answers.** Use POE to find your answer, particularly on Reasoning questions. Work backwards on challenging questions.

- Skim and scan when you work the passage.

- Read windows of text when you work the questions.

- Do not reread the passage in Step 2.

- Do not reread a window of text in Step 3 without working backwards with the answers.

- Use As You Go when a passage has five or more line/paragraph references.

- Break up Dual Passages into their component parts.

- Be ready and willing to adapt when your strategy is not working.

Chapter 21
Reading Test

READING TEST

DIRECTIONS: There are four passages in this test. Each passage is followed by several questions. After reading a passage, choose the best answer to each question and fill in the corresponding oval on your answer document. You may refer to the passages as often as necessary.

Passage I

PROSE FICTION: This passage is adapted from the novel *Prima Ballerina* by Laurie Sigel (© 2008 by Laurie Sigel).

Alicia Alonso (born 1921) is a Cuban ballet dancer.

After the revolution, her life had become different in many ways, but the ballet was the thing that stood out in vivid color among her faded black-and-white memories of early childhood.
5 Going to school was strange enough. Her older sister hadn't gone, because girls didn't, and her brother didn't, because they couldn't afford the fees. Under the new regime, however, not just poor children, but even poor girls went to school.

Nevertheless, school was at least something she had
10 known about. That cold, bright day in January of 1967, when she boarded a rusty, sputtering bus for a class field trip to the *Palace of the Galician Centre* to see Alicia Alonso dance *Giselle,* felt like a rebirth to her, as if she were emerging from her cocoon into a new and bigger world. She couldn't believe
15 she was going to actually walk into such a stately building, and was half-afraid that the marble statues keeping watch over the entrance would come to life and forbid her to enter. Enter she did though, and the grandness of the interior forced her into a hush, as if she were in the Cathedral, not a theater. She tried to
20 walk quietly, but her hard-soled school shoes insisted on asserting their presence on the shiny floor and the immense marble staircase that curved insistently upward, seemingly to heaven.

Years later, Isabel Moreno would go to that theater many times, confidently clicking her high-heeled shoes on the same
25 staircase, but that day as a schoolgirl, she hadn't known such places existed. She sat gingerly on the edge of her seat, afraid to lean back into the luxurious plush red upholstery. Then, when the music started and the dancers appeared, she couldn't lean back because she was so mesmerized by what was happening
30 on stage. The elegance of the ballerinas in their pointe shoes was unlike anything she had seen; the dancers' movements, impeccably controlled and flawlessly in time with the music,

transported Isabel to the joyful and yearning world of peasant girls celebrating the bountiful harvest and young love. She knew
35 those feelings, but had never been able to imagine or express them as perfectly as the dancers did.

After that performance, Isabel had begged her mother to let her try out for the ballet school—she felt as though her life
40 would never have meaning unless she could be one of those dancers on stage. She wasn't accepted, and wept for weeks afterwards. Even as an adult, every time she went to the ballet she felt that overwhelming sadness again that became so powerful it felt strangely joyful. The *pas de deux* of Siegfried and
45 Odette in Act 2 of *Swan Lake* seemed to her a more truthful presentation of the awakening of love than anything she would experience in real life. When Cinderella had to leave the ball at the end of Act 2 for fear of being discovered as her dress turned back to rags, Isabel felt keenly the anxiety of living a
50 relatively comfortable life, so far removed from the poverty of her childhood.

Isabel's son, Alejandro, had been trying to get her to come visit Miami for years, but she had never accepted, claiming that the paperwork was too complicated, that she couldn't take
55 the time off from the hospital. Alejandro had tried to entice his mother with visits to the Miami Ballet, but Isabel wasn't interested. The dancers in Miami weren't as good as the Cuban dancers, she'd say. Eventually, Alejandro realized he had to tempt her with something she couldn't see in Havana. When
60 he called Isabel to say he had purchased tickets to see Mikhail Baryshnikov in Miami, it was as if she were the mechanical doll Coppélia suddenly brought to life. She needed to see the legendary Russian dancer who had defected from the Soviet Union and abandoned classical ballet for modern dance with
65 a fierceness that overcame her hesitations about paperwork and vacation time.

The program started with a short solo dance by Baryshnikov, and he was a marvel of unassuming, fluid grace. Isabel had often thought that male dancers were too assertively athletic,
70 that the ballerinas were the real stars of the show. But that

evening, in that short, simple dance, Isabel understood that the classical Cuban ballet she so loved was only one small part of the expressive possibility of dance. She was transported back to that first day at the ballet when she was a schoolgirl, and
75 she felt that same sense of wonder that she hadn't known about this heartbreakingly beautiful art form before. When the first dance ended, she was too stunned to clap. Alejandro touched her arm lightly, worried that Isabel hadn't liked it. After a moment, Isabel turned to her son, tears now leaking out of the
80 corners of her eyes, and embraced him warmly. "*Gracias, mi hijo*," she whispered, "thank you, my son."

1. The point of view from which the passage is told is best described as that of:

   A. a son who understands his mother's thoughts.
   B. a narrator who relates events from the perspective of Alejandro.
   C. a school girl seeing classical ballet for the first time.
   D. an impartial narrator who understands what the characters are thinking.

2. The passage establishes all of the following about Isabel EXCEPT that she:

   F. had wanted to be a dancer when she was a child.
   G. could identify with some of the issues that Cinderella faced.
   H. felt that *Swan Lake* accurately portrayed the process of falling in love.
   J. enjoyed performing.

3. Which of the following statements best characterizes Alejandro's relationship with his mother, as it is presented in the passage?

   A. He feels isolated from her.
   B. He hopes to become a dancer to please her.
   C. He would like his mother to visit him.
   D. He is hesitant to spend time with her.

4. In the passage, lines 10–14 primarily serve to:

   F. suggest that the theater building was more important to Isabel than the ballet performance.
   G. describe the experience of going to the Cathedral.
   H. imply that the fear Isabel felt prevented her from enjoying the ballet.
   J. provide details that show how new and strange an experience it was.

5. Isabel's reaction to the *Giselle* performance is most clearly reflected in the way Isabel:

   A. "tried to walk quietly" (lines 19–20).
   B. "couldn't lean back" (lines 28–29).
   C. "wept for weeks afterwards" (lines 40–41).
   D. "embraced him warmly" (line 79).

6. The passage indicates that Alejandro ultimately decided to buy the tickets to see Baryshnikov because Alejandro:

   F. decided to take a chance on an obscure dancer.
   G. thought his mother loved Baryshnikov.
   H. was unable to get tickets to the Miami Ballet.
   J. realized that Baryshnikov was unlikely to perform in Cuba.

7. The phrase *insistently upward* (line 22) is most likely included in the passage to suggest that Isabel:

   A. was awed by the grandeur of the theater.
   B. believed the staircase led to heaven.
   C. became tired climbing the stairs.
   D. was afraid of heights.

8. The statement in lines (41–43) most nearly means that Isabel:

   F. was ashamed of the poverty of her childhood.
   G. thought her feelings could only be expressed through ballet.
   H. believed she would never experience love.
   J. was deeply moved by ballet performances.

9. The statement "she hadn't known such places existed" (lines 25–26) most directly refers to the fact that Isabel:

   A. was unaware that there was anything like the *Palace of the Galician Center* in Cuba.
   B. had never travelled to the country to celebrate the bounty of the harvest.
   C. wore only shoes with no heels before she became an adult and started shopping at fancier shoe stores.
   D. had heard stories about what the interior of the Cathedral looked like but had never visited it herself.

10. According to the passage, the event that made Isabel feel "as if she was the mechanical doll Coppélia suddenly brought to life" (lines 60–61) was:

    F. the time her son called to say he had tickets to see Baryshnikov.
    G. traveling to Miami to see Baryshnikov dance.
    H. going to the see Alicia Alonso perform when she was a school girl.
    J. attending the Miami Ballet's performance of *Giselle*.

Passage II

SOCIAL SCIENCE: This passage is adapted from the article "Conservationist and Diplomat: The Grey Areas of Panda Conservation" by Ellen N. Simons (© 2014 by The Washington Gazette).

Dr. Dajun Wang has learned to walk a fine line between advocating for wildlife habitat conservation and advocating for zoos. Wang has spent hours in the mountains of western China, tracking the giant panda, one of the most endangered,
5 elusive, and beloved creatures in the world. As a conservation biologist, his ultimate goal is to preserve species in the wild, and animal-rights activists say that confining animals in zoos runs counter to this philosophy. In recent years, critics have attacked zoos for spending huge sums of money on breeding
10 endangered species such as giant pandas in captivity while little is being done to stem the tide of habitat destruction in the wild.

At the National Zoo in Washington, D.C., the latest product of these breeding efforts, a 4-month-old giant panda named Bao Bao, is now on view to the public, and her fuzzy baby antics
15 are attracting so many visitors that the zoo has extended its weekend hours to accommodate them all. The pandas at the National Zoo are easy for visitors to see, thanks to the 2006 opening of a 12,000 square foot, state-of-the-art habitat. Wang sees this new habitat as part of a positive trend in zoo design,
20 with new elements that are making a difference in conservation.

As the National Zoo was preparing to build its new panda habitat, landscape designers consulted with researchers, including Wang, to learn what the animals need to stay comfortable, happy, and engaged. The new exhibit closely mimics the pandas'
25 natural habitat, and is more interactive for visitors than was the small, spare one originally built in the 70s for the zoo's first pair of pandas, Hsing Hsing and Ling Ling. Visitors to the new exhibit can try out some of the same features the pandas enjoy, such as a cooling rock that has cold water piped through it to
30 keep the bears comfortable during hot weather, a panda grotto, and a fog grove.

What Wang likes best about the exhibit, however, are the Decision Stations that teach visitors about habitat loss and conservation efforts. His research has shown that human
35 development, which has shrunk the pandas' natural habitat and broken it up into small parcels, is the main threat to the bears' survival in the wild. The Decision Stations give visitors a taste of what it's like to weigh economic decisions against the need to preserve panda habitats, and Wang says this experience helps
40 them understand that the problem is a wider socio-economic one that biologists can't solve on their own.

Wang is concerned about all the animals affected by habitat loss, not just giant pandas, and he understands the argument of the growing number of critics who say that the focus on
45 pandas means that too much money is being spent on a single species. However, he's also quick to point out the importance of animals such as pandas that can serve as ambassadors for conservation. The giant panda is an example of what scientists call "charismatic megafauna." Because of its universal appeal,
50 it was chosen as the icon for the World Wildlife Federation, and has become a symbol for endangered species worldwide.

"In Chinese culture, pandas have long been symbols of peace and diplomacy," says Wang. He sees their role within the animal kingdom in the same way. Just as gifts of pandas
55 have helped China negotiate diplomatic relations in years past, so too the bears now bring attention to conservation issues, and the money and research that they generate benefit other species as well. Panda conservation funds have made possible the construction of "corridors" of wild land that connect iso-
60 lated remaining parcels of habitat, providing the pandas with better access to land, as well as to each other. In recent years, the wild panda population has begun to increase, indicating that the corridors are working. The corridors have also helped the snow leopard, another endangered species that shares the
65 panda's habitat. Wang characterizes the corridors as rivers, where water can easily flow, instead of isolated ponds that are constantly in danger of drying out.

The panda's black-and-white fur is understood in China to be a physical manifestation of the idea of yin and yang, the
70 balance of positive and negative energy in the world. Wang sees this idea as also integral to the future success of conservation efforts. He stresses the need to find balance between spending money on breeding cute baby pandas and addressing the underlying human behaviors that have endangered the panda
75 in the first place.

Even Wang is not immune, though, to the charms of the giant pandas he studies. He is best known among the general public for a YouTube video in which he plays with a panda cub whose mother he had been tracking. The mother panda got so
80 accustomed to Wang following her that on one occasion she left him in charge of her cub while she went to feed. One of Wang's colleagues captured the remarkable event on video. Though babysitting panda cubs isn't the focus of Wang's research, he doesn't mind the attention he's received from the video. "That
85 was the best time in my life," he says.

11. The main purpose of the passage is to:

   A. discuss the panda exhibit at the National Zoo, and Wang's role in helping to design it.
   B. explain the job of a conservation biologist through the example of Wang.
   C. describe Wang's work and his position on the role of zoos in conservation efforts.
   D. give an overview of the history of panda conservation, with emphasis on the importance of Wang's research.

12. The passage indicates that the new panda exhibit at the National Zoo includes all of the following EXCEPT:

   F. a cooling rock.
   G. Decision Stations.
   H. wildlife corridors.
   J. a panda grotto.

13. The phrase in quotation marks in line 49 most nearly means that pandas:

   A. symbolize peace and diplomacy in Chinese culture.
   B. should continue to be bred in captivity to ensure their survival.
   C. are the only important endangered species in China.
   D. attract attention to conservation issues because of their widespread popularity.

14. The fourth paragraph (lines 32–41) primarily does which of the following regarding Wang's work and the panda exhibit at the National Zoo?

   F. Indicates how new features of the panda exhibit are relevant to his work
   G. Describes how zoo visitors respond to his work
   H. Shows how the zoo has revealed problems with his work
   J. Lists specific influences his work had on the new exhibit

15. The main purpose of the fourth paragraph (lines 32–41) is to:

   A. explain the importance of pandas in Chinese culture.
   B. describe the benefits of wildlife corridors.
   C. compare the importance of pandas in wildlife conservation to water flowing down a river.
   D. illustrate the positive effect attention on pandas has had on wider conservation efforts.

16. Based on the passage, the critics' claim that zoos spend too much money on breeding pandas in captivity is best described as:

   F. valid; money spent on pandas would be better spent on snow leopards.
   G. valid; habitat destruction is the biggest threat to pandas' survival in the wild.
   H. invalid; pandas have no hope of surviving without the help of captive breeding programs.
   J. invalid; captive-bred pandas are required for Chinese political diplomacy.

17. In the passage, Wang says that public interest in pandas is:

   A. misguided and narrow.
   B. beneficial to zoos.
   C. good for wildlife conservation in general.
   D. growing because of Bao Bao.

18. Wang is said to have reacted to a mother panda leaving him to watch over her cub with:

   F. concern.
   G. joy.
   H. diplomacy.
   J. surprise.

19. The characterization of which of the following is used in the passage to illustrate the effect of the construction of wildlife corridors?

   A. Rivers
   B. Mountains
   C. Fog groves
   D. Ponds

20. The passage implies that the design of the new panda exhibit at the National Zoo was intended to:

   F. warn visitors about the dangers of panda extinction.
   G. provide a place for visitors to keep cool during hot weather.
   H. give visitors a chance to experience some elements of panda habitat.
   J. reproduce the size and style of the original panda exhibit.

Passage III

HUMANITIES: Passage A is adapted from the essay "Leaving the Ivory Tower" by Elizabeth Dempsey (©1986 by Elizabeth Dempsey). Passage B is adapted from *The Dolphin and the Anchor* (©1978 by Elizabeth Dempsey).

Passage A by Elizabeth Dempsey

In a former life, I spent hours in the State Archives in Venice, researching the influence of the Venetian book printer Aldo Manuzio on the intellectual development of Early Modern Europe. Even then, I was a story-teller, but I found the constant
5   worry about whether I had missed a document that might disprove my hypotheses exhausting.

Archival research can be tedious, and I spent many precious research hours in the archives distracted by the mundane details of correspondence and municipal documents that did
10 little to further my projects.

I would make up elaborate scenarios that led a citizen to submit a complaint to the senate, ponder the long-term ins and outs of the relationship between the people on either side of the dispute.

15 At a certain point, I stopped worrying about finding historical proof for those larger cultural claims. Writing historical fiction allowed me to run away with the characters whose lives I so enjoyed imagining. It is important to stay true to the time period and major historical events, but the mental shift from
20 "I am a historian" to "I write historical fiction" opened the floodgates of my writing. Where once I would agonize over whether there was enough documentary evidence to back up my ideas, now I simply write.

The stories themselves, and the relationships between
25 characters, have been alive in my mind since my first trip to Italy.

I write not by typing my stories on a computer late at night, but with pen on paper, by the morning light in my east-facing office. It helps me think like I live in the sixteenth century.

When writing about a time period so far removed from
30 our own, every detail of the character's life must be historically accurate. I have developed a ritual that helps me travel back in time five hundred years.

My office is filled with pictures of Venice: gondolas, gothic palaces lining the Grand Canal, the sun glinting off the mosaics
35 on the façade of San Marco. I listen to madrigals while drinking my coffee and imagine the gentle lapping of the water against the sides of the canals.

I also imagine the smell of human waste dumped straight into the canals on a hot summer day, and what it would be like
40 to drink wine in the morning instead of coffee.

I am fortunate that I mostly write about a city that has been well-barricaded against the hurricane of the automobile. My own experiences of navigating the narrow alleyways and steep bridges of Venice on foot are not substantially different
45 from the way my characters get around the city.

Passage B by Elizabeth Dempsey

Glancing out the window on his way down the hall, Bastian noted the gentle mist rising off the canal in the early morning gloom. There was a slight chill in the air that signaled the beginning of autumn, and he hoped for relief from the
50 oppressive heat of the past week and the foul stench of the canals that came with the heat.

Bastian slipped into Signore Vendramin's study, opened the drapes, and surveyed the remnants of the previous evening. There were two wine goblets on the table, and a small stack
55 of books. He must have had a visit from Signore Manuzio, the printer. He came to see Signore Vendramin regularly, and he never arrived without a new book to present to the wealthy merchant.

As he set about cleaning the room, Bastian was drawn to
60 the books on the table. Reasoning with himself that he had to move the books to dust the table, he ventured to look inside the one on the top of the stack. Even though he couldn't read, he had always been fascinated by the inky, leathery smell of the books Signore Manuzio brought, and the crisp patterns of
65 the newly printed black letters against the clean white pages.

To his surprise, the book was filled not just with words, but also with pictures that were a far cry from the paintings he was used to looking at in church. The first rays of morning sun shone through the window, illuminating Bastian's discovery.

70 He slowly turned the pages, taking in the strange images. He was particularly mesmerized by a picture that spanned the width of two pages, of a procession. A young woman holding a swan in her lap sat on an ornate cart that was pulled by the oddest-looking little horses with large, floppy ears and long,
75 thin noses that curled up at the ends. A musician sat atop each horse, and in the background was a swarm of men holding ornate banners and staffs.

"Do you want to be able to read it?"

Bastian nearly jumped out of his skin as the voice of
80 PierAntonio, Signore Vendramin's manservant, pierced his reverie.

"I- I'm sorry, I won't do it again!" he exclaimed, ducking his head and closing the book.

"I asked if you want to be able to read it."

85   Bastian ventured a glance up at the young man, and found that he was smiling. He didn't know what to say.

"I mean it. I know how, I can teach you."

In spite of his surprise at getting caught and his fear of what would happen if their master found out, Bastian smiled 90 back and slowly nodded.

Questions 21–25 ask about Passage A.

---

21. When Dempsey claims, "The stories themselves, and the relationships between characters, have been alive in my mind since my first trip to Italy" (lines 24–25), she's most nearly referring to:

  A. the deep and lasting friendships she created with people she met in Venice while doing archival research.

  B. the documented historical facts about a person that lead her to write a story about his life.

  C. the scenarios she would make up for herself about the people she read about at the archives.

  D. gossip she read in the newspapers about Italian celebrities the first time she visited Venice.

22. Passage A indicates that Dempsey believes archival research:

  F. is not always fascinating.

  G. should always be the first step in writing historical fiction.

  H. can never disprove a hypothesis.

  J. does not help those who want to be story-tellers.

23. Dempsey's statement "I write not by typing my stories on a computer late at night, but with pen on paper, by the morning light in my east-facing office" (lines 26–28) most strongly suggests that during her writing sessions, Dempsey:

  A. tries to imagine living in the time period about which she is writing.

  B. rejects the conveniences of modern technology so that she doesn't get distracted from writing.

  C. enjoys the warmth of the sunlight shining on her desk.

  D. daydreams about riding through the canals of Venice in a gondola.

24. In the eighth and ninth paragraphs of Passage A (lines 33–40), Dempsey explains her habit, when preparing to write a story, of:

  F. imagining what it was like to live in Venice five hundred years ago.

  G. traveling to Venice so she can write from the place her characters live.

  H. drinking wine and listening to the water lapping against the sides of the canals.

  J. looking through old photo albums from her trips to Venice over the years.

25. Passage A explains that when researching Aldo Manuzio, Dempsey had:

  A. gone through an important stage of intellectual development.

  B. worried that she might have missed an important document.

  C. stayed focused at all times and never thought about undocumented details.

  D. exhausted the possibilities of archival research.

Questions 26 and 27 ask about Passage B.

---

26. In the fifth paragraph of Passage B (lines 70–77), the narrator describes a picture in the book in a manner that:

  F. suggests that Bastian had seen many pictures just like it in church.

  G. confuses the reader, because horses do not have noses that curl up at the end.

  H. conveys Bastian's limited knowledge of animals and lack of imagination.

  J. emphasizes how strange Bastian found it because it was like nothing he had seen before.

27. Within Passage B, the image in lines 68–69 functions figuratively to suggest that:

  A. the sunlight shining on the book helped Bastian see the pictures more clearly.

  B. Bastian's understanding of what pictures could be like was expanded by looking at the book.

  C. cleaning the room gave it the feeling of a fresh start, like the beginning of a new day.

  D. the pictures helped Bastian to understand what the words in the book said.

> **Questions 28–30 ask about both passages.**

28. Both Passage A and Passage B highlight Dempsey's use of:

   F. historical detail to evoke a setting many years ago.
   G. metaphor to draw unexpected comparisons.
   H. personification to present well-rounded characters.
   J. multiple viewpoints to present all sides of a story.

29. Based on Dempsey's description in Passage A of her writing process, which of the following methods hypothetically depicts a way Dempsey might have begun to write the story in Passage B?

   A. Searching through the State Archives for documents proving a connection between Signore Vendramin and Signore Manuzio
   B. Finding a letter in the State Archives from a merchant to a publisher, wondering whether they were friends, then imagining what the details of their friendship might have been like
   C. Forming the characters of the servants in her imagination, then looking for documents to support her ideas
   D. Writing a story about modern-day characters in Venice, then revising it to take place in the sixteenth century

30. Elsewhere in the essay from which Passage A is adapted, Dempsey writes:

> The printer Aldo Manuzio and the merchant Luca Vendramin were both high-profile men in early sixteenth-century Venice. There is an inventory that indicates that Vendramin owned many of the books from Manuzio's press. Beyond that, little is known about any relationship between the two.

How does this statement apply to both the information about Dempsey's approach as a writer of historical fiction provided in Passage A and the story of Manuzio and Vendramin provided in Passage B?

   F. It indicates that Dempsey's stories are based only on documented historical facts.
   G. It casts doubt on Dempsey's accuracy as a historical researcher.
   H. It reveals how Dempsey gets caught up in details and has trouble finishing stories.
   J. It shows how Dempsey imaginatively fills in the details of relationships that might have existed between historical figures.

THIS PAGE IS INTENTIONALLY LEFT BLANK.

Passage IV

NATURAL SCIENCE: This passage is adapted from the article "The Microbial World Within" by Janet Fisher (© 2013 by Science Monthly).

"I'm not your typical new dad," says biologist Rob Knight. "When the baby's diaper needs changing, I'm always excited to do it." Knight runs a lab that is part of the American Gut project, through which thousands of people have paid to send
5   in samples of their feces to be analyzed, and his sixteen-month-old daughter's diapers play an important role in his research.

"I know it sounds a bit crazy that people pay to send us their poop, but we're using a crowd-funding model to both help pay for the research and get a wide variety of samples," explains
10 Knight. As for his daughter's diapers, he's been studying the way her microbiome, the make-up of bacteria and other microbes in her digestive tract, has been changing since she was born.

Humans have around 100 trillion microbes living on and in them, typically of several hundred different species. They
15 are not visible to the naked eye, but all together they account for about three pounds of a person's weight. Recent research indicates that they have a huge influence on our health.

What Knight and his colleagues do with the feces samples they receive from around the country is analyze the genetic
20 material present to establish what kinds of microbes live in the donors' guts. They combine the genetic information with data from a survey that donors fill out and enter all the information in a giant database. Their goal is to have enough samples to be able to start to decode the influence of lifestyle on the char-
25 acteristics of a microbiome. The survey asks donors questions about their diets, where they live, whether they have pets, and even how frequently they wash their hands, all of which can affect the numbers and kinds of bacteria present in a person's digestive tract.

30 Microbes were first discovered in the seventeenth century, but not extensively studied until Louis Pasteur began formulating his germ theory in the nineteenth century. Even then, the focus of microbial research mainly had to do with pathogens, the microbes that make us sick.

35 The technique used by Knight for analyzing the genetic makeup of microbes wasn't widely used until the 1980s. This genetic analysis allows scientists to see all the different strains of microbes that are present in a microbiome, the vast majority of which are beneficial. The understanding of just how many
40 there are is leading to new research in treatments for chronic health problems such as obesity, cardiovascular disease, and even cancer.

For example, several studies have found that obese mice that are given transplants of intestinal colonies from lean mice
45 lose weight. There is growing evidence to suggest that inflam-
mation may be behind cardiovascular disease, diabetes, and other such conditions. Patrice Cani at the Université Catholique de Louvain in Brussels has been studying the role of microbes in maintaining a healthy epithelium, the lining of our diges-
50 tive system that is supposed to allow nutrients through to the bloodstream, but keep toxins out.

Cani's research has shown that mice fed a high-fat diet have lower numbers of the microbes that help keep the epithelium healthy, which means that more toxins are able to make their
55 way into the bloodstream. In turn, the toxins lead to general inflammation, which eventually leads to metabolic syndrome, the precursor to diseases such as diabetes.

Microbes may also play a role in our mental health: the bacteria in our guts produce neurochemicals, including sero-
60 tonin, which helps to regulate mood, sleep, and appetite and can affect memory and learning. For this reason, our digestive tract is sometimes referred to as our "second brain."

A study conducted by Dr. Premysl Bercik at McMaster University studied the effect of changing the composition of
65 shy mice's gut bacteria by feeding them a specially designed mix of antibiotics. "Their behavior completely changed," Bercik says. "They became bold and adventurous."

The question of how to regulate the microbes in our guts for optimal health is one that can't be answered until scientists
70 have a better picture of what constitutes a healthy microbiome. This is part of the goal of the American Gut Project, and other scientists are going even further. María Gloria Dominguez-Bello, a microbiologist at New York University, travels to remote areas of the world to collect samples from peoples who have
75 had very little contact with the Western world.

Dominguez-Bello has found that the microbiomes of people who have never had antibiotics or processed food are far more diverse than the typical Western microbiome, and the people they come from have a very low rate of allergies, asthma, and
80 chronic conditions such as diabetes and cardiovascular disease.

It's too early for microbiologists to promise that regulation of a patient's microbiome will be able to cure chronic health conditions, but the research is quickly gaining traction, and some patients with gastro-intestinal disorders are already being
85 treated with "fecal transplants" from healthy donors.

Though there is still much to be learned about the relationship between our bodies and the teeming colonies of unseen organisms living within them, scientists are optimistic about the paths such research is leading them down.

31. The main idea of the passage is that:

  A. a healthy microbiome can help a person maintain a healthy weight.

  B. scientists are just beginning to understand how important our intestinal microbes are to our overall health.

  C. taking a specially designed mix of antibiotics can affect serotonin levels, which will improve mental health.

  D. new understandings of beneficial microbes have led scientists to believe that old notions of germ theory are incorrect.

32. The passage's mention of scientists' efforts to "decode the influence of lifestyle on the characteristics of a microbiome" (lines 24–25) most nearly refers to their efforts to:

  F. determine how important pets are in maintaining a healthy microbiome.

  G. track how a baby's microbiome develops over time.

  H. analyze the genetic material of the beneficial microbes in a feces sample.

  J. understand how choices in diet and living conditions affect intestinal microbes.

33. Which of the following is NOT mentioned in the passage as something that scientists believe is influenced by intestinal microbes?

  A. Mental health

  B. Lifestyle

  C. Metabolic syndrome

  D. Diabetes

34. Rob Knight's statement in line 1 is based mainly on the assumption that most people:

  F. understand the importance of studying a baby's microbiome.

  G. believe changing diapers is an important skill.

  H. don't think the contents of a baby's diaper are worthy of study.

  J. enjoy hearing stories about the experiences of new fathers.

35. Within the passage, the eleventh and twelfth paragraphs (lines 68–80) primarily serve to:

  A. prove a connection between a Western lifestyle and chronic cardiovascular disease.

  B. indicate the importance of introducing antibiotics to remote areas of the world.

  C. explain one way in which scientists are trying to establish what a healthy intestinal microbiome looks like.

  D. resolve a disagreement among scientists about which strains of bacteria should be present in a healthy microbiome.

36. The passage indicates that all of the following contribute to intestinal microbes' influence on metabolic syndrome EXCEPT:

  F. a high-fat diet.

  G. diabetes.

  H. an unhealthy epithelium.

  J. toxins that lead to inflammation.

37. According to the passage, how do intestinal microbes affect mental health?

  A. Intestinal microbes produce neurochemicals that can regulate moods.

  B. Serotonin affects the brain function of intestinal microbes.

  C. The second brain is regulated by the neurochemicals that also regulate intestinal microbes.

  D. Antibiotics can change the serotonin levels produced by the microbes in an adventurous person's intestines.

38. According to the passage, research in intestinal microbiomes is:

  F. promising; fecal transplants have already helped some patients.

  G. promising; scientists have found a cure for metabolic syndrome.

  H. unpromising; scientists don't have enough information to make such research useful.

  J. unpromising; the effects of lifestyle choices on microbiomes is unclear.

39. The passage indicates that the diversity of bacteria living in a person's gut is directly related to:

  A. the person's age.

  B. the health of the person's epithelium.

  C. how many pets the person has.

  D. whether the person has ever taken antibiotics.

40. According to the passage, which of the following was the focus of early microbe studies?

  F. Babies

  G. Pathogens

  H. Obesity

  J. Genetics

Chapter 22
Reading Test:
Answers and
Explanations

ANSWER KEY

Passage I	Passage II	Passage III	Passage IV
1. D	11. C	21. C	31. B
2. J	12. H	22. F	32. J
3. C	13. D	23. A	33. B
4. J	14. F	24. F	34. H
5. B	15. D	25. B	35. C
6. J	16. G	26. J	36. G
7. A	17. C	27. B	37. A
8. J	18. G	28. F	38. F
9. A	19. A	29. B	39. D
10. F	20. H	30. J	40. G

READING TEST EXPLANATIONS

1. **D** Choice (D) is correct because the passage is written in the third person, and is mostly about Isabel. Choices (A) and (C) are incorrect because the story is told about Isabel and Alejandro, but is in the third person. It is not told by either of them in the first person. Choice (B) is incorrect because the narrator treats Alejandro and Isabel the same way.

2. **J** This is an EXCEPT question, so the answer choice that does not appear in the passage is correct. Choice (J) is correct because the story does not mention Isabel ever performing. Choice (F) is incorrect because the passage describes how *Isabel had begged her mother to let her try out for the ballet school.* Choice (G) is incorrect because the passage states that *When Cinderella had to leave the ball… Isabel felt keenly the anxiety of living a relatively comfortable life, so far removed from the povery of her childhood.* Choice (H) is incorrect because the passage says that *…the pas de deux…seemed to her a more truthful representation of the awakening of love….*

3. **C** Choice (C) is correct because the passage states that *Isabel's son, Alejandro, had been trying to get her to come to Miami for years.* Although the fact that Isabel didn't go visit her son might lead the reader to believe that Alejandro feels isolated from her, there is no direct support for (A) in the passage. Choice (B) is incorrect because there is no mention of whether Alejandro is—or hopes to become—a dancer. Choice (D) is incorrect because the passage says that Alejandro wanted Isabel to come visit him, and there is no indication that he was hesitant about wanting to spend time with her.

4. **J** At the beginning of these lines, the experience of going to the theater is described as feeling to Isabel *as if she were emerging from her cocoon into a new and bigger world.* The rest of the excerpt describes her first impressions of going into the theater, and thus best supports (J), the correct answer. Choices (F) and (H) are incorrect because Isabel did enjoy the ballet, and there is no indication that the building was more important. Choice (G) is incorrect because the Cathedral is used as a simile; it is not the building described.

5. **B** Isabel's experience at the performance of *Giselle* is described in the second and third paragraphs, which means that the correct answer must come from that part of the passage. Choice (B) is the correct answer because it most directly refers to her reaction to the performance. Choice (A) is incorrect because it describes Isabel's experience walking into the theater, but not her reaction to the performance. Choice (C) is incorrect because it describes Isabel's reaction to not getting into ballet school, and (D) is incorrect because it describes her reaction to seeing Baryshnikov dance.

6. **J** Choice (J) is the correct answer because the passage states that Alejandro bought tickets to see Baryshnikov when he *realized he had to tempt her with something she couldn't see in Havana.* Choice (F) is incorrect because the passage refers to Baryshnikov as *the legendary Russian dancer,* so he is not unknown. Choice (G) is plausible, but there is no direct support for it in the passage. Choice (H) is incorrect because the passage states that *Alejandro had tried to entice his mother with visits to the Miami Ballet.*

7. **A** Choice (A) is the correct answer because the phrase in question appears in a part of the passage that describes how *stately* and *grand* Isabel thought the theater was. Choice (B) is incorrect because it is too literal a reading of the phrase *seemingly to heaven*. There is no evidence in the passage to support (C) or (D).

8. **J** The phrase in question describes an *overwhelming sadness* Isabel felt that *became so powerful it felt strangely joyful*. The descriptions of strong emotions give support to (J), the correct answer. Choice (F) is incorrect both because it refers to a sentence later in the same paragraph and because there is no evidence that Isabel was ashamed. Choice (G) is incorrect because it takes an idea from an earlier sentence from the same paragraph, *she felt as though her life would never have meaning unless she could be one of those dancers*, and mixes it up with the idea of emotions in the sentence in question. Choice (H) may sound as though it might be a good choice, but the passage says that Isabel felt a dance was *a more truthful presentation of the awakening of love than anything she would experience in real life*, not that she would *never experience love*, so it is incorrect.

9. **A** The words *such places* in the phrase in question most directly refer back to *that theater*, or the *Palace of the Galician Center*, which lends support to (A), the correct answer. Choice (B) is incorrect because, while *peasant girls celebrating the bountiful harvest* are mentioned, they are characters in the ballet; Isabel did not actually travel to the country. Choice (C) is incorrect because, while the passage describes Isabel *confidently clicking her high-heeled shoes*, there is no mention of any shoe stores. Choice (D) is incorrect because the Cathedral is used in the previous paragraph as a simile, but the passage does not address whether she had ever visited it.

10. **F** Isabel felt like Coppélia when Alejandro *called Isabel to say he had purchased tickets to see Mikhail Baryshnikov in Miami*, so (F) is the correct answer. Choices (G) and (H) are both things that happened to Isabel, but not in connection with the phrase in question. Choice (J) is incorrect because Isabel never attended a performance of *Giselle* at the Miami Ballet.

11. **C** Choice (C) is the correct answer because the passage is primarily about Wang and his views on wildlife conservation. Choice (A) is incorrect because it is only a small part of what the passage is about, not the main purpose. Choice (B) is incorrect because the passage only discusses one conservation biologist, Wang, and it does not discuss anything that any other conservation biologists do. Choice (D) is incorrect because it only addresses current efforts in panda conservation, not the history of the issue.

12. **H** On EXCEPT questions, eliminate answers that *are* in the passage. Choice (H) is the correct answer because construction of wildlife corridors is described as an effort that is being made in the wild in China to help preserve pandas, not an element at the zoo. Choices (F) and (J) are incorrect because the cooling rock and panda grotto are described in the third paragraph as elements of the new panda exhibit, and (G) is incorrect because Decisions Stations are described in the fourth paragraph.

13. **D**   The phrase in quotations, *charismatic megafauna*, is used to describe the giant panda. In the following sentence, the passage states that the panda has *universal appeal*, and that it *has become a symbol for endangered species worldwide*. These phrases support (D), the correct answer. Choice (A) is stated in the following paragraph, but is not related to the discussion of *charismatic megafauna*, so it is not the correct answer to this question. Choices (B) and (C) are both incorrect because there is no support for them in the passage.

14. **F**   The fourth paragraph mentions that Wang's research *has shown that human development, which has shrunk pandas' natural habitat and broken it up into small parcels, is the main threat to the bears' survival in the wild*. The paragraph also describes the Decision Stations at the zoo, which *teach visitors about habitat loss*. Thus, (F) is the correct answer. Choice (G) is incorrect because there is no description of *how zoo visitors respond*. Choice (H) is incorrect because there is no mention of flaws in Wang's work. Choice (J) may seem tempting, but the passage does not say that Wang's work influenced this part of the exhibit, so (J) is incorrect.

15. **D**   The sixth paragraph describes the corridors of wild land that are being built to help pandas, and how the corridors have helped other species as well. Choice (D) is correct because it best describes these ideas. Choices (A), (B), and (C) are all incorrect because they each refer to only a small part of the sixth paragraph.

16. **G**   The first paragraph states that Wang *has learned to walk a fine line* between critics and zoos. The fifth paragraph states that Wang *understands the argument of the growing number of critics who say that… too much money is being spent on a single species*. Therefore, the critics have a valid point. Choice (G) is correct because it refers to Wang's research as described in the sixth paragraph. Choice (F) is incorrect because there is no evidence that money should be spent on another species instead of on pandas. Choice (H) is incorrect because it is too strongly worded: there is no indication in the passage that pandas have *no hope of surviving without the help of captive breeding programs*. Choice (J) is incorrect because, while pandas are mentioned as tools of diplomacy, there is no indication that they are *required*.

17. **C**   The sixth paragraph states that Wang believes pandas *bring attention to conservation issues, and the money and research that they generate benefit other species*, which supports (C), the correct answer. Choice (A) is incorrect because Wang never criticizes public interest in pandas. Choices (B) and (D) are incorrect because they fail to mention the wider conservation issues that help other species.

18. **G**   In response to being left in charge of the panda cub, Wang said, *"That was the best time in my life,"* which best fits with (G), the correct answer. Choices (F) and (H) are both words that appear elsewhere in the passage, but are incorrect because they have nothing to do with Wang's response to the cub. Choice (J) seems plausible, but is incorrect because there is no support for it in the passage.

19. **A** Choice (A) is correct because the sixth paragraph states *Wang characterizes the corridors as rivers.* Choices (B) and (C) are incorrect because they are mentioned elsewhere in the passage, but in relation to other things. Choice (D) is incorrect because a pond is what Wang uses to describe an isolated piece of habitat, not the corridors.

20. **H** Choice (H) is correct because the third paragraph states that the new exhibit is *interactive for visitors*, and that *visitors can try out some of the same features the pandas enjoy.* Choice (F) is incorrect because the fourth paragraph states that the exhibit *teach[es] visitors about habitat loss and conservation efforts*, which is related to efforts to save the giant panda from extinction, but the wording used in the answer choice is much stronger than that in the passage. Choice (G) is incorrect because it uses words from the passage, but does not have the same meaning. Choice (J) is incorrect because the passage states that the new exhibit is different from the original one, not similar to it.

21. **C** Choice (C) is correct because after discussing how tedious research can be, the author explains that she would "make up elaborate scenarios" (line 11). In the following paragraph, she discusses how she could finally "run away with the characters whose lives [she] enjoyed imagining" (lines 17–18). Choice (A) is incorrect because there's no mention of the author making friends and (D) is incorrect because the passage doesn't mention gossip or celebrities. Choice (B) states the opposite of what the passage discusses: in lines 15–18, the author states that she stopped worrying about finding proof to use as the basis of her stories.

22. **F** Choice (F) is correct because the author describes archival research as a "worry" (line 5), "tedious" (line 7), and full of "mundane details" (lines 8–9). This supports the idea that this research is "not always fascinating." The extreme language of (G), "always be the first step," and (H), "never disprove," are not supported by the passage. In the latter, the author actually states her concern that her research might disprove her theories (lines 5–6). Choice (J) is the opposite of what the passage discusses: in the first paragraph, she is researching Venice, the topic of her writing. (Also note the extreme language, "does not help.")

23. **A** The author states in lines 26–28 that writing with a pen and paper helps her think as if she were alive in the sixteenth century. This is further supported by her statement in line 31 that she has a "ritual that helps" her imagine the earlier time period. These lines suggest that (A) is correct. Choice (B), on the other hand, is too extreme—"rejects"—and (D) is not supported by the passage, which mention nothing about daydreaming about a gondola ride. Choice (C) paraphrases from lines 26–28, but fails to answer the question asked, which is what this suggests Dempsey does.

24. **F** These paragraphs discuss the different strategies Dempsey uses in order to imagine the time period: using pen and paper (line 27), looking at pictures (lines 33–35), listening to madrigals (line 35), and other examples. Choice (F) best summarizes these. In (G), it's true that she went to Venice "In a former life" (line 1), but there's no indication that she does this before every story she writes. Likewise, while (H) correctly recycles words from the passage, lines 39–40 state that she imagines the comparison between drinking wine as opposed to coffee. Finally, (J) is not supported by the

passage, for while her office does have many pictures of Venice, there's no mention of where they came from or whether they are from photo albums.

25. **B** The first paragraph mentions that the author found the constant worry that she was missing a document that would disprove her to be exhausting (lines 5–6), which makes (B) correct. Choice (A) is incorrect because the passage doesn't suggest any "intellectual development," so it's not a strong enough answer. Choice (C) presents the opposite of what happens in the passage, for the author specifically states that the documents were so boring that she would often daydream (lines 11–14). Finally, while (D) reuses words from the passage, it's not supported by it: "exhausted the possibilities" means that she had explored all of the ways in which archival research could be used.

26. **J** The passage states that the pictures in the book were "a far cry" from those the protagonist was exposed to at church (lines 67–68). This means that there's a difference between what Bastian had seen before and what he sees now, which means (J) is correct. Choice (F) is the opposite of what the passage says. There's no evidence for (G), as Bastian doesn't appear confused by the pictures, and the author doesn't seem to be intentionally trying to confuse the reader. Choice (H) is wrong because it's too extreme. Just because the images were new to Bastian does not mean that he "lacked imagination."

27. **B** According to the passage, Bastian is surprised (line 66) and "mesmerized" (line 71) by the pictures in the book, which suggests that they were "expanding" Bastian's understanding, (B). Choice (A) addresses the rays of sunshine from lines 68–69, but in a literal sense, not the figurative one the question asks for. Choice (C) talks about cleaning the room, which is what Bastian was doing before seeing the book, and is therefore wrong. There is evidence against (D) back on line 62, where it is revealed that Bastian does not know how to read.

28. **F** Both passages either mention the way in which Dempsey uses historical details to write (Passage A, lines 38–40) or demonstrate those details in action (Passage B, lines 48–51). That makes (F) correct. Choices (G) and (H) are incorrect because neither the use of metaphor nor personification are supported by the passages. Choice (J) is too extreme: Dempsey is not trying to present "all sides of a story" even if she uses multiple sources.

29. **B** Passage A suggests that Dempsey would read "mundane details" (lines 8–9) and then spend hours making up "elaborate scenarios" for those details (lines 11–14). This is in line with (B), which implies that the story of friendship in Passage B was inspired by a historic detail she'd read earlier. Choice (A) is incorrect because while Dempsey used archival research to find important details, lines 15–16 note that she "stopped worrying about finding historical proof for those larger cultural claims." Choice (C) is the opposite of what Dempsey does, as she researches before writing. Choice (D) is also incorrect, as Passage A explicitly states that Dempsey imagines herself in the earlier time before beginning to write.

30. **J** Choice (J) is correct because Passage A mentions several times how Dempsey uses her imagination as a writer (lines 11, 18, 25, and 38). Passage B uses Manuzio and Vendramin as characters with added details about a servant named Bastian (lines 52–58). The use of "only" makes (F) too strongly worded; it's also stated that Dempsey uses her imagination to fill in the gaps (lines 11–14). Choice (G) is also too extreme ("casts doubts"), for while it's true that Dempsey stopped worrying about being entirely accurate, it's also stated that she believed that "every detail of a character's life must be historically accurate" (lines 30–31). Choice (H) can also be eliminated because it's the opposite of what happens in Passage A; it's only after Dempsey stopped worrying about the details that she was able to write (lines 18–23).

31. **B** Choice (B) is the correct answer because it most accurately represents the passage as a whole, which describes a promising new field of scientific research. Choice (A) is incorrect because it is only one small detail in the passage. Choice (C) is incorrect because, while the passage mentions both *serotonin* and *antibiotics*, it never directly states that individuals would benefit by taking antibiotics to increase serotonin levels; even if it did, it does not address the main idea of the passage. Choice (D) is incorrect because, while the fifth paragraph mentions *germ theory*, there is no indication in the passage that *old notions of germ theory are incorrect*.

32. **J** The fourth paragraph describes how the scientists are combining genetic information with answers from a survey into one large database, which best supports (J), the correct answer. Choices (F) and (H) are incorrect because they refer only to small parts of the project described in the fourth paragraph. Choice (G) is incorrect because it refers to the wrong part of the passage.

33. **B** When answering a NOT question, remember that answer choices that appear in the passage are incorrect. Choice (B) is the correct answer because lifestyle is mentioned in the fourth paragraph as something that can affect intestinal microbes, not the other way around. Choice (A) is incorrect because it is described in the ninth and tenth paragraphs. Choices (C) and (D) are incorrect because they are described in the seventh and eighth paragraphs.

34. **H** The first paragraph states that Knight's *daughter's diapers play an important role in his research*, which gives support to (H), the correct answer. While (F) is related to the subject of the first two paragraphs, it is not relevant to how Knight is *not your typical new dad*. Choices (G) and (J) are incorrect because there is no support for either one in the passage.

35. **C** The beginning of the eleventh paragraph states that *the question of how to regulate the microbes in our guts for optimal health is one that can't be answered until scientists have a better picture of what constitutes a healthy microbiome*, then goes on to describe research related to that idea. Therefore, (C) is the correct answer. Choice (D) is incorrect because there is no indication of a conflict. Choice (A) is incorrect because, while the passage mentions that *the microbiomes of people who have never had antibiotics or processed food are far more diverse than the typical Western microbiome* and that these same people *have a very low rate of…chronic conditions such as diabetes and cardiovascular*

disease, there is no indication of *proof* that a *Western lifestyle* causes cardiovascular disease. Choice (B) is incorrect because the passage never indicates that antibiotics should be introduced to remote areas of the world.

36. **G** When answering an EXCEPT question, remember that answer choices that appear in the passage are incorrect. Choice (G) is the correct answer because diabetes is a result of metabolic syndrome, not something that influences it. Choices (F), (H), and (J) are all incorrect because they are described in the eighth paragraph as factors that contribute to metabolic syndrome.

37. **A** The ninth paragraph states *the bacteria in our guts produce neurochemicals, including serotonin, which helps to regulate mood*, which makes (A) the correct answer. Choice (B) is incorrect because, according to the passage, intestinal microbes *produce serotonin*, but there is no indication that the microbes have brain functions that are affected by the serotonin. Choice (C) is incorrect because, while the passage mentions *the second brain* and *neurochemicals*, the neurochemicals *regulate mood, sleep, and appetite*, not intestinal microbes. Choice (D) is incorrect because, while the passage mentions behavior changing after taking antibiotics, it is the behavior of *shy mice* that changes, not an *adventurous person*.

38. **F** The last paragraph states that *scientists are optimistic* about research in intestinal microbiomes. Choice (F) is correct because it accurately reflects this optimism, and because paragraph thirteen uses the example of fecal transplants as a positive development in the research. Choice (G) is incorrect because there is no evidence of a *cure for metabolic syndrome*. Choices (H) and (J) are incorrect because there is no evidence that the research is *unpromising*.

39. **D** Diversity of microbiomes is discussed in the twelfth paragraph, which states that *the microbiomes of people who have never had antibiotics or processed food are far more diverse than the typical Western microbiome*. Choice (D) is therefore the correct answer. Choices (A), (B), and (C) are all incorrect because none of those factors are discussed in relation to *diversity of bacteria*.

40. **G** The fifth paragraph states that when microbes were *first discovered*, they were *extensively studied* and mentions that *the focus of microbial research mainly had to do with pathogens, the microbes that make us sick*. Choice (G) is therefore the correct answer. Choices (F), (H), and (J) are all incorrect because they are not discussed in the relevant part of the passage.

Part V
ACT Science

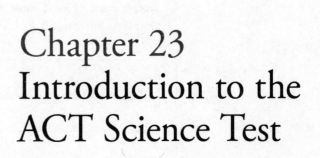

Chapter 23
Introduction to the
ACT Science Test

HOW TO CRACK THE SCIENCE TEST

The Science Test on the ACT is, initially, one of the most intimidating things you will see on a standardized test. After all the standardized-test basics of English grammar, math, and reading comprehension, science seems to require something else entirely. It can test subjects ranging from biology to chemistry to ecology, from classes you've had and classes you haven't, and it does so with a specificity that none of the other parts of the ACT demand.

But we're here to tell you that, with a little shift in perception, you will find that ACT Science is one of the easiest sections on the test and one in which you can receive some of your most significant improvements. It all comes down to one simple, counterintuitive idea:

> Don't try to understand the science. Just get the points.

This may seem like an oversimplification, but follow along in the next few chapters, and you'll see exactly what we mean.

Believe it or not, you actually apply this strategy in reading all the time, whether you've been using our techniques or not. Let's say, for example, that you get a passage on the Reading Test about bear-baiting in the 1500s and 1600s. If you had to work only with your outside knowledge of this subject, you'd probably be in pretty bad shape. A question like this would be pretty impossible:

1. Which of the following does the passage include to demonstrate the popularity of bear-baiting in the 1600s?

   A. Biological records of the evolutionary history of bears
   B. Evidence that both commoners and royalty enjoyed the sport
   C. Parliamentary legislation that freed bear-baiters from significant restrictions
   D. Indications that the sport eventually became popular in France as well

Even if you're an expert on the subject (and why would you be?), this question is nearly impossible to answer without the passage. And you know that, on the Reading Test, everything you need *must* be in the passage. Here's the relevant section:

Someone walking the streets of London from about 1550 to 1700 would have seen any number of bear-gardens, arenas designed for exactly this purpose of bear-baiting. The main bear-garden in London was the Paris Garden, which stood until 1670. A pole would be set at the edge of a pit, and a bear would be tormented (or baited) by dogs and humans alike until it was exhausted or killed. While the sport may seem wildly inhumane to us today, the English of this era had no such qualms about animal cruelty. Not only were the seats around the pit always full of spectators, Henry VIII had a pit constructed in Whitehall, and Elizabeth I overruled an attempt by Parliament to outlaw the sport on Sundays.

1. Which of the following does the passage include to demonstrate the popularity of bear-baiting in the 1600s?

   A. Biological records of the evolutionary history of bears
   B. Evidence that both commoners and royalty enjoyed the sport
   C. Parliamentary legislation that freed bear-baiters from significant restrictions
   D. Indications that the sport eventually became popular in France as well

Now we know that the answer is (C), for which evidence is given in the last sentence of the paragraph.

It may seem like we just completed a fairly obvious exercise, because of course that's how Reading works on the ACT. The topic of a Reading passage is almost irrelevant because everything we need to know about it will be contained within the passage itself. We don't need to understand or retain any of what we've read—we just have to get the points and move on.

So what's different about questions like these?

2. According to the data in Experiment 1, as the number of molecules increases, the concentration of the compound:

   F. increases only.
   G. decreases only.
   H. remains constant.
   J. varies, but with no general trend.

3. Suppose the experimenters discovered a new compound, Compound E, which contains 700 million molecules. Which of the following would most likely be the concentration of that compound, in mass percent?

   A. 22
   B. 36
   C. 75
   D. 90

As with the previous question, you likely have no idea how to answer these. But remember how we approached the example from Reading. Even though we had no previous knowledge of bear-baiting in the 1600s, we could answer the question easily because the information was given in the passage. *The same is true in Science.* For more than 90% of the questions, all the information that you need will be given in the passage itself.

Let's look at those questions again, this time with the aid of Table 1 from Experiment 1.

Compound	# of molecules (millions)	Concentration (mass %)
A	500	26
B	800	40
C	1200	60
D	2000	81

Table 1

2. According to the data in Experiment 1, as the number of molecules increases, the concentration of the compound:

   F. increases only.
   G. decreases only.
   H. remains constant.
   J. varies, but with no general trend.

3. Suppose the experimenters discovered a new compound, Compound E, which contains 700 million molecules. Which of the following would most likely be the concentration of that compound, in mass percent?

   A. 22
   B. 36
   C. 75
   D. 90

Here's How to Crack It

Now, the relationships are much clearer. We can see from the chart that as "# of molecules" increases, so too does "concentration," meaning that the correct answer to Question 2 is (F).

We can use the same relationship in Question 3. We know that as "# of molecules" increases, so too does "concentration." Therefore, if Compound E contains 700 million molecules, its concentration will fall between that of Compound A (with 500 million molecules) and Compound B (with 800 million molecules). In other words, the concentration will need to fall between 26 and 40, as only (B) does.

Let's pause for a moment to realize how little traditional "science" we've just done. Not only did we simply pull the information from the table, the concepts being tested were essentially irrelevant to the points we earned. Table 1 features "# of molecules" and "concentration," but we didn't use this information at all except to match what's in the question with what's in the introduction. If this table had said "# of froyo toppings" and "units of deliciousness," we wouldn't have treated the information any differently.

This no-science approach usually works on the most seemingly scientific of questions, like this one:

———————————————○———————————————

4. Based on the information in the passage, which of the following is a possible chemical formula for an ethanolamine?

   F. $HO—(CH_2)_2—NH_3$
   G. $HO—(CH_2CF_2)_2—CH_3$
   H. $H3C—(CH_2)_4—NH_3$
   J. $H3N—(CH_2CHCl)_2—NH_3$

Here's How to Crack It

In the passage from which this is taken, there is no indication of how chemical compounds are formed and nothing that lists ethanolamine's chemical formula. However, the first line of the passage reads as follows:

> Ethanolamines *are compounds that contain both alcohol (—OH or HO—) and amine (—NH₂, —RNH₂, —R₂NH, or —R₃N) subgroups.*

It may seem that we still haven't illuminated much about this question, because you may not know the names of the molecules listed. But whatever the molecules are called, we know that the answer will need at least one from the first group and one from the second group.

With this information alone, we can eliminate (H) and (J), which do not contain either an OH or an HO. Then we can see that (F) must be correct because it contains NH_3, which is listed as one of the amines.

If there was any "science" at all in how we tackled Question 4, it was the science of Process of Elimination (POE), which is the cornerstone of approaching the Science Test on the ACT.

———————————————○———————————————

POE AND LEARNING THE PASSAGE FROM THE QUESTIONS

Because there is so little actual science on the ACT, we'll need to employ one of our cornerstone techniques frequently on the Science Test: POE. Even if we cannot pluck the data directly from the charts or tables, we can get to the correct answer almost every time with POE.

Above all, ACT Science is about your ability to recognize patterns and make logical deductions about them. Even when you're not working with numbers or trends specifically, the things you'll need to see in each chart or table are based on the numbers or trends within those charts.

Let's look at an example.

Passage III

Osmotic pressure (Π) is the amount of pressure, in atm, required to maintain equilibrium of a solvent across a semipermeable membrane. At a constant temperature, osmotic pressure is dependent only on a solute's ability to dissociate or ionize in the solvent (*van 't Hoff factor, i*) and the concentration of solute particles. The osmotic pressure is determined by the equation:

$$\Pi = iMRT$$

M represents the concentration (in molarity, *M*), *R* is the ideal gas constant (0.0821 L atm mol^{-1} K^{-1}), and *T* (300 K) is the temperature in Kelvin (K). The value of *R* is assumed to be a constant for all osmotic pressure calculations.

The dissociation of a solute depends on its unique chemical properties. The van 't Hoff factors for some common substances are displayed in Table 1. Higher van 't Hoff factors correlate with greater dissociation or ionization. The effect of the van 't Hoff factor on the osmotic pressure may be seen in Figure 1.

Table 1	
Substance	van 't Hoff factor *
sucrose	1.0
NaCl	1.9
MgCl$_2$	2.7
FeCl$_3$	3.4
*Values at 300 K	

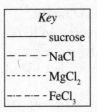

Key
——— sucrose
— — — NaCl
-------- MgCl$_2$
—·—·— FeCl$_3$

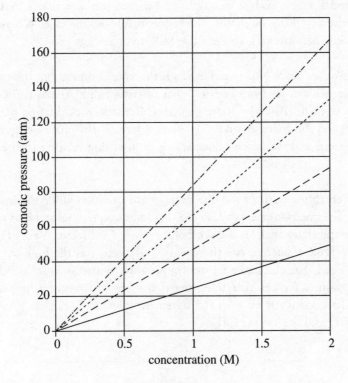

Figure 1

17. A scientist recently discovered a compound that ionizes
readily in solution ($i = 3.8$) and results in low osmotic pressure. Are the findings of this scientist consistent with
Figure 1?

    A. Yes, because FeCl$_3$ causes higher osmotic pressure than
does sucrose.

    B. Yes, because sucrose causes higher osmotic pressure than
does FeCl$_3$.

    C. No, because FeCl$_3$ causes lower osmotic pressure than
does sucrose.

    D. No, because sucrose causes lower osmotic pressure than
does FeCl$_3$.

Here's How to Crack It

There's a lot going on in this question, not only because we may be unsure from the passage what i refers to, but also because, as we will soon find, the question refers to Figure 1 but actually requires Table 1 as well.

That said, let's start with Process of Elimination. The answers each feature a "Yes" or "No" and a reason. While we might be inclined to think that a "Yes" or "No" answer is the first thing we should determine, this is not the case. Whenever ACT gives multiple-part answers, you can use POE to attack any part.

In this case, the "Yes"/"No" question is a little more complex, but the reasons are very simple. We can see from Figure 1 that the reasons in (A) and (D) are correct, and the reasons in (B) and (C) are incorrect. Regardless of the first part of each answer, we can eliminate (B) and (C). We now have a 50% chance of guessing the correct answer, and we haven't done much of anything relating to the question itself.

With the remaining parts of the question, let the question guide the information you need. The question refers to i, so use that italicized symbol as a lead word. The first paragraph states that i is the symbol for van 't Hoff factor. Van 't Hoff factor appears in Table 1: sucrose has the lowest, and $FeCl_3$ has the highest. Then, on Figure 1, $FeCl_3$ has the highest osmotic pressure, where sucrose has the lowest osmotic pressure. We can therefore infer that a higher i means a higher osmotic pressure. This doesn't agree with the statement made in Question 17, so we can choose "No," and the answer is (D).

Let's pause for a moment to go over what we've just done. This is a relatively difficult question, and you may suspect that this explanation made it seem easier than it actually was. All we've done, though, is apply a few basic principles that we will always apply throughout the Science Test:

- Don't try to understand the science.
    - In answering Question 17, do we have a clearer sense of why concentration should increase osmostic pressure? Or why i should influence osmotic pressure?
    - Do we know what "osmotic pressure" refers to?
    - Do we even know how to pronounce "van 't Hoff factor"?
    - No to all of the above! But we got the point anyway.
- Use POE.
    - More parts in a question mean more opportunities for POE.
    - If you can't answer the question directly, use POE to attack the reasons.
- Let the questions teach you about the passage.
    - You may not have initially seen the relationship between Table 1 and Figure 1.
    - You may not have known what i referred to, but you didn't have to until Question 17 required it.

- o   In general, it's easier to find specific information than general information, so let the questions focus your attention for you.
  - •   What's an easier question to answer with this figure?
    - o   What does *i* refer to?
    - o   What is "van 't Hoff factor" and how does it work?

Let's try another passage in which we will apply these three basic principles. This is one of the more difficult passages we've seen.

Passage IV

The *Citric cycle* is an essential process used to transform carbohydrates, lipids, and proteins into energy in aerobic organisms. If yeast is unable to produce *succinate*, it cannot survive. The Citric cycle steps leading to the creation of succinate in yeast are shown in Figure 1. Each step in this cycle is catalyzed by an enzyme, which is essential to overcome the energy barrier between reactant and product. In the first step, Enzyme 1 is the enzyme, citrate is the reactant, and isocitrate is the product.

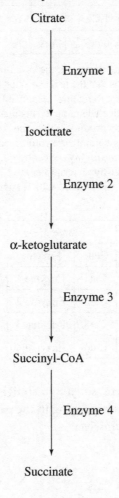

Citrate

Enzyme 1

Isocitrate

Enzyme 2

α-ketoglutarate

Enzyme 3

Succinyl-CoA

Enzyme 4

Succinate

Figure 1

Experiment

A scientist grew four strains of yeast on several different growth media. Each strain was unable to produce succinate because it lacked one of the enzymes required for the reaction pathway shown in Figure 1. Table 1 shows the results of the scientist's experiment: "Yes" indicates that the strain was able to grow in the basic nutrition solution (BNS) + the particular chemical. An undamaged strain of yeast would be able to grow in the basic nutrition solution without any additional chemical. If a strain was able to grow in a given growth medium, then it was able to produce succinate from the additional chemical added to the basic nutrition solution.

Table 1				
Growth Medium	Yeast Strain			
	W	X	Y	Z
BNS				
BNS + Isocitrate	Yes			
BNS + α-ketoglutarate	Yes	Yes		
BNS + Succinyl-CoA	Yes	Yes	Yes	
BNS + Succinate	Yes	Yes	Yes	Yes

If certain genes are damaged, the essential enzymes cannot be produced, which means that the reactions that the enzyme catalyzes cannot go. Table 2 lists the genes responsible for the enzymes in the steps of the Citric cycle leading to succinate production in yeast. If an enzyme cannot be produced, then the product of the reaction that enzyme catalyzes cannot be synthesized and the reactant in that reaction will become highly concentrated. If a gene is damaged, then it is notated with a superscript negative sign, as in Cat3$^-$; if a gene is not damaged it is notated with a superscript positive sign, as in Cat3$^+$.

Table 2	
Gene	Enzyme
Cat1	Enzyme 1
Cat2	Enzyme 2
Cat3	Enzyme 3
Cat4	Enzyme 4

There are no obvious trends here, so let's go straight to the questions. There's no use trying to understand what's happening in the passage because we'll learn what we need from the questions themselves.

17. Based on the information presented, the highest concentration of isocitrate would most likely be found in which of the following yeasts?

  A. Yeast that cannot produce Enzyme 1
  B. Yeast that cannot produce Enzyme 2
  C. Yeast that cannot produce Enzyme 3
  D. Yeast that cannot produce Enzyme 4

Here's How to Crack It

Typically, when we see words like "highest," we're looking to the figures and tables. No clear relationship exists in the tables here, however, so let's pay attention to the other key words: *isocitrate*, *yeast*, and *Enzyme* (from the answer choices).

Enzymes 1–4 appear with *isocitrate* in Figure 1. The meaning of this figure is not entirely clear, but we can make a few simple inferences from it. Enzyme 1 is above isocitrate, and Enzyme 2 is below it, so one of these is likely to be the answer, thus eliminating (C) and (D). Then, use the arrows. Enzyme 1 seems to lead to isocitrate, but if Enzyme 2 were not there, the flow would be broken, and the arrows would stop at isocitrate. We can infer, then, that this would create a large amount of isocitrate, or a high concentration, making (B) the correct answer.

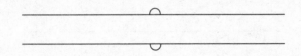

18. According to the information in the passage and Table 2, a strain of yeast that is $Cat1^+$ $Cat2^-$ $Cat3^-$ $Cat4^+$ CANNOT produce:

  F. Enzyme 1 and Enzyme 4.
  G. Enzyme 3 and Enzyme 4.
  H. Enzyme 2 and Enzyme 3.
  J. Enzyme 1 and Enzyme 2.

Here's How to Crack It

The "Cat"s appear in Table 2, so that's a purrfect place to start right meow. Each Cat seems to match up with an Enzyme of the same number.

Start by using POE. Cat1 and Cat4 have a +, and Cat2 and Cat3 have a –. Therefore, the pair of answers will have to refer to one or another of these pairs, eliminating (F), (G), and (J). The only remaining is (H), the correct answer. The last line of the passage tells us what the pluses and minuses refer to, but who cares?

19. Which of the following statements best describes the relationships between citrate, isocitrate, and α-ketogluterate as shown in Figure 1?

    A. Isocitrate is a product of a reaction of -ketoglutarate, and α-ketoglutarate is a product of a reaction of citrate.

    B. α-ketoglutarate is a product of a reaction of isocitrate, and isocitrate is a product of a reaction of citrate.

    C. α-ketoglutarate is a product of a reaction of citrate, and citrate is a product of a reaction of isocitrate.

    D. Citrate is a product of a reaction of isocitrate, and isocitrate is a product of a reaction of α-ketoglutarate.

Here's How to Crack It

The question refers to Figure 1 and uses a chemistry term ("product"), which you probably know, but which you don't actually need to know to answer the question.

Use POE and follow the arrows. α-ketoglutarate and citrate don't come into contact at all, so eliminate any answer that puts them into contact: (A) and (C). Then, follow the arrows: citrate first, then isocitrate, then α-ketoglutarate, as (B) indicates.

20. Strain X was most likely unable to synthesize:

    F. isocitrate from citrate.

    G. α-ketoglutarate from isocitrate.

    H. succinyl-CoA from α-ketoglutarate.

    J. succinate from succinyl-CoA.

Here's How to Crack It

"Strain X" appears in Table 1, and while it seems like we might need to read the passage to see what's going on here, we don't. Look for patterns within the table. The most obvious one here is the downward staircase of the word "Yes." That's all.

Let the POE begin. "Citrate" doesn't appear on this figure at all, so (F) can be eliminated. Then, the pattern of "Yes" in column X breaks off between "BNS + Isocitrate" and "BNS + α-ketoglutarate," so this must be where Strain X is "unable" to do something and should get us close to the answer. Choice (H) doesn't mention isocitrate, and (J) doesn't mention isocitrate or α-ketoglutarate, which means that both of these answers can be eliminated, and (G) is therefore the correct answer.

21. One of the growth media shown in Table 1 was a control that the scientist used to demonstrate that all four strains of yeast had genetic damage that prevented the reactions shown in Figure 1, the reactions that are responsible for the synthesis of succinate. Which growth media was used as a control?

A. BNS
B. BNS + Succinate
C. BNS + Isocitrate
D. BNS + Succinyl-CoA

Here's How to Crack It

The word "control" is among those very few science terms that you should know for ACT Science. A control is something that is held constant in an experiment and something against which the results of the experiment can be tested. In this case, the control is pretty clear, in that "BNS" is common to every growth medium. So, BNS must be the control, as (A) suggests.

22. For each of the four strains of yeast, W–Z, shown in Table 1, if a given strain was able to grow in BNS + succinyl-CoA, then it was also able to grow in:

F. BNS.
G. BNS + isocitrate.
H. BNS + α-ketoglutarate.
J. BNS + succinate.

Here's How to Crack It

As with Question 20, it might seem that we need to read the passage in order to be able to answer the question. But again, we need to do no such thing. Whereas in Question 20 we were looking for a difference, we are now looking for a similarly ("also able to grow in"). Let's use the "Yes" columns again, and look for the row that is most similar to Succinyl-CoA. Keep it simple! "BNS + Succinyl-CoA" has three "Yes" columns. The only other one that does is "BNS + Succinate," which has four. On this information alone, (J) must be correct.

We have just completed a very difficult ACT Science passage by doing almost no science at all. But that's what the Science Test is all about: not science, points.

You may be thinking...

Didn't I buy the Elite book? If I stopped thinking in my honors classes at school, I'd get terrible grades. Why are these people telling me I shouldn't use science on a science test? If I only used the figures on my AP bio test, I'd get a 1, if that!

The answer is simple: this is not your science class at school, and it's not an AP science test. Science on the ACT is a unique entity, and we've developed a strategy that can help to maximize your ACT Science score.

And don't forget: willingness to change your method of test-taking is the only way to get a big score improvement. ACT knows how the average student takes this test because the test writers know what is taught in schools. What we're showing you how to do, though, is to think like those who write the test rather than those who take it.

The best test takers are those who can CHOOSE how they will take the test. If you learn the tricks specific to the ACT, you'll be miles ahead of those who take the test the way they think they're supposed to.

OUTSIDE KNOWLEDGE

Now that we have convinced you of science's unimportance, we should admit that ACT does test some very basic outside knowledge. We realize that, if you've purchased this book, you're looking to get a very high score, and you need to correctly answer most or all of the questions in order to do so. You'll probably encounter one or two outside-knowledge questions per test, and in fact, you should be able to get most of the way through these with POE.

The cornerstone of the outside knowledge you need on ACT Science is The Scientific Method. The Scientific Method may not even seem like outside knowledge because it is something we use from our very first interactions with science in any form.

Think about the following scenario:

> *One day, you wear a new sweater, use a new skin lotion, and eat strawberries. The next day, you wake up with a skin rash. How do you figure out what gave you the rash?*

If you answered something like, "Go one day with the new sweater but no lotion and no strawberries. Then go one day with the lotion but no sweater and no strawberries," and so on, then you know how to use The Scientific Method.

The basic principle as it applies to the ACT is that if you want to test something, you need to keep everything else constant and make sure nothing is skewing your results. We have already seen how ACT asks about the "control," which they will sometimes give a different name like "standard of comparison," but ACT will also ask about what is being tested and experimental procedures.

Here are a few examples of each:

Experiment 3

The procedure for Experiment 1 was repeated with the wooden object, varying the temperature of the polymer ramp. Results for 5 temperatures were recorded in Table 3.

Table 3	
Temperature (°C)	θ (degrees)
0	18.5
25	22.0
50	25.4
75	29.0
100	32.5

6. The main purpose of Experiment 3 was to determine the effects of temperature on which of the following variables?

F. Coefficient of static friction between wood and wood
G. Coefficient of static friction between wood and polymer
H. Mass of the wooden object
J. Total frictional force of the polymer on all objects placed on the ramp

Here's How to Crack It

We don't have a ton of information here, but we can still answer this question by falling back on The Scientific Method. The things being tested are the things changing. Choice (H) refers to mass, which does not appear on the chart, and (J) refers to force, which does not appear on the chart, so both can be eliminated. Then, the blurb mentions a *polymer ramp*, suggesting that polymer is a relevant variable, thus making (G) the correct answer.

---

7. Which of the following statements is most likely the reason that the students used identical springs in Trials 1–3?

    A. To ensure that the springs stretched similarly when a weight was attached

    B. To ensure that the springs did not share the weight evenly

    C. To compensate for the effects of oscillation on the results of the experiment

    D. To compensate for the weight of the board exerted on each of the springs

Here's How to Crack It

If a science experiment uses three identical things, the scientists must be trying to prevent some particular effect from influencing the results. In this case, there are three "identical springs," so we can assume the scientists are trying to make it so the springs act identically on all the trials. Using this logic, (B) is fairly preposterous, and (C) and (D) aren't about the springs at all. Choice (A) is the only one that could work.

As for other outside knowledge, ACT is unfortunately very inconsistent. Outside-knowledge questions are not typically repeated, and there can be questions from biology, chemistry, and physics. But if you're unsure how to answer an outside-knowledge question, you can still use POE aggressively and get close.

Here are a few basic ideas it may help to understand.

There are three phases of matter: gas, liquid, and solid.
    -When a *solid* gets too hot, it becomes a *liquid*.
    -When a *liquid* gets too hot, it becomes a *gas*.

These operations also work in reverse, which means that the moments of transition are the same. Think about water.
    -At 0°C, *ice* becomes *water*, and *water* becomes *ice*.
        -In other words, this temperature represents both the *freezing* and the *melting* point of water.
    -At 100°C, *water* becomes *vapor*, and *vapor* becomes *water*.
        -In other words, this temperature is both the *boiling* and the *condensation* point of water.

Because ACT is so fond of relationships, remember that when…

Heat increases
    …there is no change in *mass*.
    …the *volume* is increased
        …because the *space between the molecules* increases
        …and the *density* decreases
    …the *speed of the molecules' movement* is increased.

The *speed* of an object increases
    …the *momentum* of that object increases.
    …the *kinetic energy* of that object increases.
    …at a set time, the *distance* increases
    …at a set distance, the *time* decreases

And some odds and ends:

pH is the measure of the *acidity* of a solution. The magic number with pH is 7.
    -At 7, a substance has neutral acidity.
    -Below 7, a substance is called "acidic."
    -Above 7, a substance is called "alkaline."

Chromosomes
    -Most humans have 46 chromosomes, or 23 pairs.
    -A male has both an X and Y chromosome.
    -A female has two X chromosomes.
    -On the reproductive level, the male sperm and female egg are called *gametes*.
        -They combine to form the *zygote*, the basic cell from which all the other cells in a unique organism are generated.

The Order of the Planets
    -Remember: *My Very Excellent Mother Just Sent Us Nachos*
    -Mercury, Venus, Earth, Mars, Jupiter, Saturn, Uranus, and Neptune.

Here are a few outside-knowledge questions with relevant details.

Table 1	
Group	Conditions
1	These areas had significantly decreased populations of marine mammals consumed by polar bears.
2	These areas had significantly increased populations of seaweed commonly consumed by marine mammals.
3	These areas had been subject to excess thawing of Arctic sea ice.

8. Which of the following is most likely an organism that the researchers identified as exhibiting a significantly decreased population when defining Group 1?

   F. Snowy owl
   G. Seal
   H. Salmon
   J. Polar bear

Here's How to Crack It

The answer must be (G) because *snowy owls* and *salmon* are not marine mammals, and *polar bears* are not (we hope!) *consumed by polar bears*.

Question 9 comes from a passage that begins with the following:

Bats of the family *Vespertilionidae* (Vesper bats) are commonly found in North America.

9. Which of the following best describes the family *Vespertilionidae*?

   A. Mammals
   B. Protists
   C. Lampreys
   D. Birds

Here's How to Crack It

Not sure what "protists" or "lampreys" are? You're not alone, but you probably know that bats are *mammals*, making (A) the correct answer. Don't sweat the others!

10. As the object is dropped from the rooftop, a transformation of energy takes place involving the object's heat (Q), its potential energy due to Earth's gravity (GPE_o), and its kinetic energy (KE_o). Which of the following best describes the relationship between these three variables?

   F. Energy is conserved as GPE_o and Q are converted into KE_o.
   G. Energy is lost as KE_o and Q are converted into GPE_o.
   H. Energy is conserved as GPE_o is converted to KE_o and Q.
   J. Energy is lost as Q is converted to GPE_o and KE_o.

Here's How to Crack It

We haven't provided any part of the passage for this question because no part of the passage can help us. This one is purely based on outside knowledge. The correct answer is (H). Energy is always conserved: even energy that is "lost" technically becomes something else, so no energy is ever lost, which eliminates (G) and (J). Then, *kinetic energy* is the energy of movement, so that must be on the other side of the conversion. The same is true for *heat*, because an object will not heat up when it's sitting at rest.

NO SCIENCE DRILL

In this passage, we have removed all the "science" from the passage. All the variables have been renamed with silly names, and all the text has been removed. You only have the charts and five questions. Good luck! No thinking!

Passage I

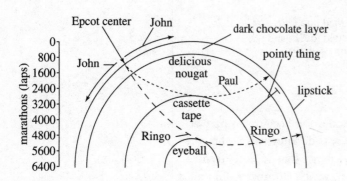

Figure 1

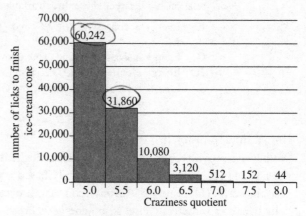

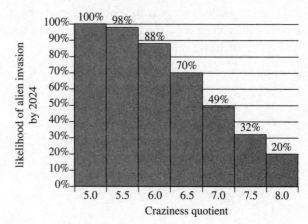

Figure 2

Table 1		
Beatle	Marathon lap range (laps)	Lipstick brightness (omg)
John	0–10	2.0–4.5
Paul	0–2921	3.0–4.0
Ringo	0–5180	5.0–7.0

1. Figure 1 defines the pointy thing as a region of the Smiley Face that overlaps with which of the following savory appetizers?

   I. Cassette tape
   II. Delicious nougat
   III. Dark chocolate layer

   A. II only
   B. I and II only
   C. II and III only
   D. I, II, and III

2. A Beatle was fawned over in a green room. The average lipstick brightness of this Beatle was 3 omgs, and his maximum marathon laps occurred in the delicious nougat. Based on Figure 1 and Table 1, the Beatle observed was most likely:

   F. John.
   G. Paul.
   H. George.
   J. Ringo.

3. Given the data in Figure 2, the likelihood of an alien invasion by 2024 decreases by more than half when comparing which of the following two Craziness quotients?

   A. 5.0 and 6.0
   B. 6.0 and 6.5
   C. 6.5 and 7.5
   D. 7.5 and 8.0

4. According to Figure 2, the likelihood of an alien invasion by 2024 is lowest for which of the following ranges of Craziness quotient?

   F. 5.5 to 6.0
   G. 6.0 to 6.5
   H. 6.5 to 7.0
   J. 7.0 to 7.5

5. Based on Figure 2, the ratio of Craziness quotient 5.5 ice-cream-cone licks to Craziness quotient 5.0 ice-cream-cone licks can be expressed approximately by which of the following fractions?

   A. $\dfrac{1}{3}$

   B. $\dfrac{1}{2}$

   C. $\dfrac{2}{3}$

   D. $\dfrac{3}{2}$

NO SCIENCE DRILL ANSWERS AND EXPLANATIONS

1. **C**   Find the pointy thing on the figure. The solid line representing the pointy thing covers only the delicious nougat and the dark chocolate layer, but does not cover the cassette tape. The correct answer will therefore include II and III, but not I. Choice (C) is the only possible answer.

2. **G**   The Beatles with lipstick brightness ranges that include 3.0 omgs are John and Paul. This eliminates (J), because Ringo's lipstick brightness range doesn't not include 3.0, and George does not appear anywhere on any of the tables. Then, follow the lines on Figure 1. John does not move past the lipstick, but Paul's arrow goes into the delicious nougat, as the question requires, making (G) the correct answer.

3. **C**   Choice (A) shows a decrease from 100% to 88%, which is not half. Choice (B) shows a decrease 88% to 70%, which is also not half. Choice (C) shows a decrease of 70% to 32%, which is just over half. Choice (D) shows a decrease from 32% to 20%, which is not half. Only (C) gets close, so it must be the correct answer.

4. **J**   According to the second graph in Figure 2, the likelihood of an alien invasion by 2024 decreases as the Craziness quotient increases. Therefore, the lowest likelihood must occur at the highest Craziness quotient, so (J), which gives the highest Craziness quotient, must be correct.

5. **B**   According to the first graph in Figure 2, the number of ice-cream-cone licks at Craziness quotient 5.5 is 31,860. The number of ice-cream-cone licks at Craziness quotient 5.0 is 60,242. This creates a ratio of approximately 30,000:60,000, or 1/2, as (B) indicates.

Chapter 24
Basic Approach

THE BASIC APPROACH AND "NOW" PASSAGES

The introduction to this Science section sought to make a very simple point. By the end of the previous chapter, you should have been able to work a passage from which the real science had been removed entirely. This is all part of our big strategy for the Science Test—from which everyone, from low scorers to high scorers, can benefit:

Don't try to understand the science. Just get the points.

We will continue to deepen this point as we go along, and you've already seen how Process of Elimination (POE) and the Scientific Method can help with passages that might otherwise seem hopelessly arcane.

In this chapter, we're going to talk about the basics of how to take the Science Test. We will particularly focus on POOD, or Personal Order of Difficulty, as a means to guide us through the Science Test in the most efficient way possible.

THE NUTS AND BOLTS OF ACT SCIENCE

The Science Test will always be the last of the multiple-choice sections on the ACT. Like the other three tests, the Science Test is scored from 1 to 36 and is factored into the composite score. Like the Reading Test, the Science Test takes 35 minutes and is made up of 40 questions.

The Science Test consists of six or seven passages. ACT breaks them down into three categories: Data Representations, Research Summaries, and Conflicting Viewpoints. The last one, which we've fondly renamed "Fighting Scientists," is the only one you really need to be on the lookout for. See Chapter 26 for more on the strange animal known as "Fighting Scientists."

We break sections down in a more useful way. As this chapter will discuss in detail, we break the passages down according to their difficulty rather than to the fairly arbitrary category names that ACT gives them. Who cares if we're dealing with a "Data Representations" passage or a "Research Summaries" passage if we're going to approach them both the same way?

Pacing

We have discussed pacing in previous chapters, and pacing is no less important on the Science Test than it is elsewhere on the ACT.

That said, there are 40 questions on the Science Test and 36 scaled points. That practically amounts to a one-to-one ratio, so if you're looking for a score in the 30s, you will have to do most or all of the questions.

Here is the higher end of a scale from a recent ACT exam.

Scaled Score	Raw Score
36	40
35	39
34	38
33	—
32	37
31	36
30	—
29	35
28	33–34

On this scale, you can see that each question is essentially worth one scaled point, and if you want anything greater than a 28, you'll need to complete all of the passages.

Because there is so much weight on each passage, you must work as efficiently as possible. As such, the emphasis on the Science Test is much more on your POOD than on pacing. Even though you will need to attempt all the questions, that's not the end of the story by a long shot.

POOD

When we break down a Science Test, we're not overly concerned with the "type" of passage we're dealing with. We've got our own rubric: Now, Later, and Last passages. ACT will give you the six or seven passages in a random order of difficulty. It's up to you to put the passages in an order than makes sense.

The order you select will ultimately be about what *you* find easiest, but here are a few guidelines as to which ACT passages we've found our students have the easiest time with.

Note: You may be asking, "If I have to do all the passages anyway, what difference does it make what order I do them in?"

- The answer is simple: even if you have to do all the passages, the Now passages still provide your best chance to maximize your score. It makes sense to focus the most attention on the passages that will generate the most points. The question that takes five seconds is worth the same amount as the question that takes five minutes!
- There is also value in warming up on the Science Test. It really is a unique section on the ACT (and there's nothing like it on the SAT or PSAT), so if you can warm up on some easy stuff, your brain will be primed for the harder stuff.

Let's think about what makes easy and hard passages. Because we're talking about POOD here, remember that this is all about what *you* find easiest, but even for the most idiosyncratic test taker, we've got one big piece of advice about reordering the passages:

Go with your gut. If a passage or question looks easy, it probably is.

As we've said above, we like to divide passages into Now, Later, and Last. This is an inexact science (surprise on the ACT!), but here are a few basic guidelines:

Now Passages

Now passages are the ones on which you can usually get the most points in the least time. Here's what you want to look for in Now passages:

- **Easy-to-read tables and graphs**
- **Numbers in the figures**
  You'll see some figures that have words or symbols—those are much more challenging to evaluate. It's a lot easier to spot trends and patterns when you have numbers in the figures.
- **Easy-to-spot, consistent trends**
- **Numbers and number words in the questions**
  Just as figures with numbers are easy to read, questions with numbers are typically easier to answer. Also be on the lookout for what we call "number words": words like "greater," "less," "increase," and "decrease."
- **Shortness and white space**
  Short passages and short questions are typically easier for the simple reason that they contain less information. The passages with the most blank space are typically the easier ones.

Let's look at an example. Below are seven figures from seven different passages within a single test. Which would be the Now figures among them?

I.

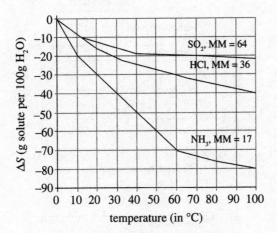

Figure I

II.

Scientist	Model			
1	Z	W	X	Y
2	W	Z	X	Y
3	ZY	W	X	
4	Y	W	ZX	

Figure II

III.

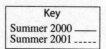

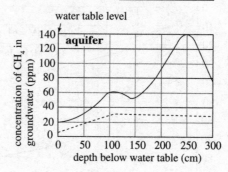

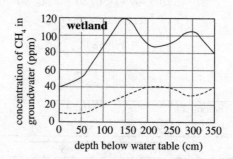

Figure III

IV.

Volcanic eruption models		Percent composition of gas			
		1	2	3	4
Study 1 (low H$_2$ atmosphere)	H$_2$	3	2	1	0
	H$_2$O vapor	85	80	75	70
	CO$_2$	10	10	10	15
	H$_2$S	2	5	7	8
	N$_2$	0.5	1	2	2
	CH$_4$	0.3	0.3	0.3	0.3
	CO	0.05	0.05	0.05	0.05
Study 2 (high H$_2$ atmosphere)	H$_2$	45	40	35	30
	H$_2$O vapor	40	40	35	35
	CO$_2$	10	10	10	15
	H$_2$S	2	5	7	8
	N$_2$	0.5	1	2	2
	CH$_4$	0.3	0.3	0.3	0.3
	CO	0.05	0.05	0.05	0.05

Table 1

Figure IV

V.

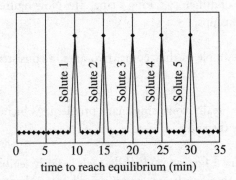

Figure V

VI.

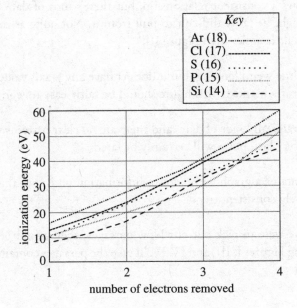

Figure VI

VII.

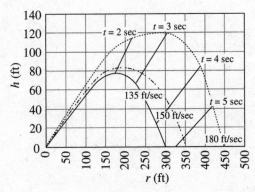

Figure VII

With no context at all, and with only one figure from each passage, you can likely already see an order of difficulty taking shape. The Now figures are those with the most obvious relationships:

Figure I is about as simple as they come: two axes, a consistent relationship, and three variables.

Figure II looks like a really confusing math problem. Whichever passage this belongs to will go near the end.

Figure III contains two figures, and while each is fairly legible, the relationships in them are not all that consistent, so we would certainly save this one for after Figure I.

Figure IV shows a consistent relationship, but there's tons of data on it, and the data points might be fairly difficult to pull from it. Not quite as easy as Figure I, but probably a little easier than Figure III.

Figure V is a little weird looking, but it doesn't have any y-axis values, and each of the peaks is clearly marked. This figure should be fairly easy to work with.

Figure VI contains all kinds of data, and there are no clear patterns within it. This might not be very last, but it will certainly be later.

Figure VII contains a graph with a lot of information on it, but that information shows a relatively consistent trend.

Therefore, if we were to pick out our Now passages, they would probably be the ones containing Figures I, III, and IV. We'll save the passages containing Figures II and VI for last.

THE BASIC APPROACH

Now that we've reviewed the overall layout of the Science Test and how to spot the easier passages within it, let's dive into the Basic Approach.

Our Basic Approach is informed by the three main tenets we established in Chapter 23:

- Don't try to understand the science.
- Use POE.
- Let the questions teach you what you need to know about the passage.

Our Basic Approach is just that: basic. It consists of three steps:

1. **Work the Figures**
   Look for variables and trends.

2. **Work the Questions**
   Work from easy to hard, from short to long.

3. **Work the Answers**
   Use POE.

You may note that there's nothing in this approach that says "Read the Passage." That's intentional. You will rarely need to refer to the text in an ACT Science passage. Most of the information you need will be contained within the figures. Don't read unless something in the question requires you to do so.

With all of this in mind, let's work the Now passage we selected in the previous section.

Passage I

When introduced into H_2O, many solid substances are able to dissolve, or disperse evenly throughout the solvent. Salts have been found to dissolve easily when introduced into H_2O, since they readily dissociate to yield ions that may interact directly with H_2O. Molecular compounds, on the other hand, do not dissolve as easily, since their interactions with water typically do not permit *ionization*, the physical process of converting an atom or molecule into an ion by adding or removing charged particles such as electrons or other ions. Two experiments were conducted to better understand the solubility of salts and molecules in water at various temperatures. The *solubility*, *S*, was measured as follows:

$$S = (m_{sub}) / (m_{H_2O})$$

where m_{sub} was the mass of the substance dissolved in water and m_{H_2O} was the mass of the water itself. ΔS, or the change in solubility (from 0°C), was calculated in the experiments for three salts and three molecules with increasing temperature. The mass of water was held constant at 100g for each of these experiments.

Figure 1 shows the results of comparing the solubilities of three salts with increasing temperature, while Figure 2 shows the results of comparing the solubilities of three molecules with increasing temperature. Molecular masses (MM) are shown for each substance.

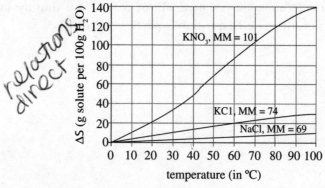

Figure 1

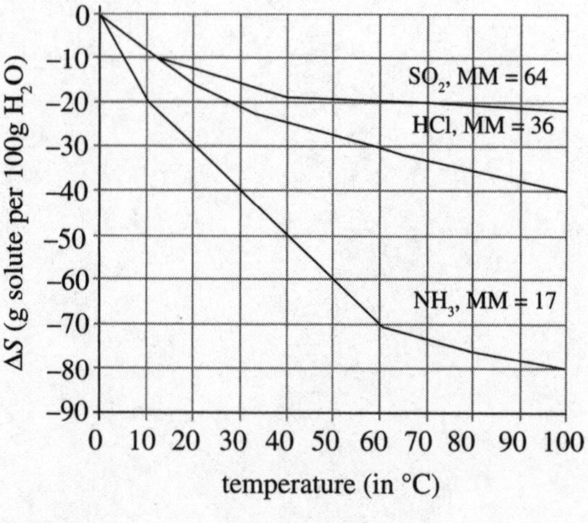

Figure 2

Let's start by Working the Figures. On your practice passages and the actual test, make sure to mark these figures with arrows. Ignore the text until you need it!

Figure 1

The variables are ΔS (g solute per 100g H_2O), temperature (°C), and MM.

The relationships are direct:
- As temperature increases, ΔS also increases.
- As ΔS increases, MM also increases.

Figure 2

The variables are the same as those in Figure 1: ΔS (g solute per 100g H_2O), temperature (°C), and MM.

The relationships have changed a bit:
- As temperature increases, ΔS decreases.
- As ΔS increases, MM also increases.

That's it! Let's move on to the questions.

1. Based on Figure 1, at 40°C as the molecular masses of the salts increase, the ΔS:

   A. decreases, because a greater mass of substance dissolves in the same mass of water.
   B. decreases, because a smaller mass of substance dissolves in the same mass of water.
   C. increases, because a greater mass of substance dissolves in the same mass of water.
   D. increases, because a smaller mass of substance dissolves in the same mass of water.

2. Consider the trials represented in Figure 1 that occurred at 60°C. As the molecular mass of the substance decreased, the observed ΔS:

   F. increased only.
   G. increased, then decreased.
   H. decreased only.
   J. decreased, then increased.

3. If an additional trial had been done in which KCl dissolved in H_2O at 102°C, while it was still in aqueous form, the ΔS most likely would have been:

   A. less than 25.
   B. between 25 and 35.
   C. between 35 and 45.
   D. greater than 45.

4. According to Figure 2, when NH_3 was added to water at 20°C, the solubility of the resulting solution:

    F. increased, because ΔS was positive.
    G. increased, because ΔS was negative.
    H. decreased, because ΔS was positive.
    J. decreased, because ΔS was negative.

5. Based on Figures 1 and 2, which of the following combinations of solute and temperature at a known m_{H_2O} would produce the greatest increase in solubility?

    A. CH_4 (molecular compound, MM = 16) at 40°C
    B. NaF (salt, MM = 42) at 40°C
    C. CH_4 (molecular compound, MM = 16) at 80°C
    D. NaF (salt, MM = 42) at 80°C

Working the Questions is largely a matter of selection. The first step is to choose the easiest available question. Use the same criteria here that you used in selecting a passage: look for numbers, number words, shortness, and simplicity.

Question 2 looks simple: a short question and answers filled with number words.

---

2. Consider the trials represented in Figure 1 that occurred at 60°C. As the molecular mass of the substance decreased, the observed ΔS:

    F. increased only.
    G. increased, then decreased.
    H. decreased only.
    J. decreased, then increased.

Here's How to Crack It

This question will draw upon the relationships we established as we Worked the Figures. We already know, for example, that the relationships were all consistent in that they were pure increases or decreases, no fluctuation. This eliminates (G) and (J).

Now work from the data given in the question. Identify 60°C on Figure 1. Any relevant data will occur along this gridline. Then, given that the only other variable in this question is "MM," this must be the "molecular mass" referred to in the question. If you can't go on without knowing for sure, check the blurb quickly, but common sense will help here: why would ACT ask about a variable that's not on any of the charts? On Figure 1, as we saw when Working the Figures, "As ΔS increases, MM also increases." Therefore, if the molecular mass *decreased*, ΔS would do the same, as (H) indicates.

Question 3 looks like an easy one, too: numbers and another relationship.

———————————○———————————

3. If an additional trial had been done in which KCl dissolved in H_2O at 102°C, while it was still in aqueous form, the ΔS most likely would have been:

   A. less than 25.
   B. between 25 and 35.
   C. between 35 and 45.
   D. greater than 45.

Here's How to Crack It

Again, let's pull this information directly from the chart. KCl appears on Figure 1, so we will use that relationship: "As temperature increases, ΔS also increases."

The relationship is useful here because the question asks for a value not shown on the chart. Still, if we know the basic relationship, we will have an easy time figuring out what happens later. At 100°C, KCl has a ΔS of approximately 35. At 102°C, the ΔS must be about the same or a little higher, or between 35 and 45, as (C) indicates. Although (D) also shows an increase, the line for KCl seems to flatten out a bit at the end, and 102°C is not a significant enough temperature difference to increase the ΔS-value by 10.

———————————○———————————

Question 4 looks similarly short and numerical. Let's try that next.

———————————○———————————

4. According to Figure 2, when NH_3 was added to water at 20°C, the solubility of the resulting solution was:

   F. increased, because ΔS was positive.
   G. increased, because ΔS was negative.
   H. decreased, because ΔS was positive.
   J. decreased, because ΔS was negative.

Here's How to Crack It

These answer choices have two parts, so let's take them one at a time. ΔS appears on the figures, so let's start there. On Figure 2, all ΔS-values are negative, so (F) and (H) can be eliminated. Then, as we saw when we worked the figures, ΔS decreased throughout the whole figure, so the answer must be (J).

Notice on this question that we avoided the issue of figuring out the relationship between "solubility" and ΔS. That relationship is stated in the too-long introduction, but if we work the questions in a smart, efficient way, we can continue to avoid that introduction.

Question 1 is the best one remaining: it has number words and deals with the relationships we've already established.

1. Based on Figure 1, at 40°C as the molecular masses of the salts increase, the ΔS:

   A. decreases, because a greater mass of substance dissolves in the same mass of water.
   B. decreases, because a smaller mass of substance dissolves in the same mass of water.
   C. increases, because a greater mass of substance dissolves in the same mass of water.
   D. increases, because a smaller mass of substance dissolves in the same mass of water.

Here's How to Crack It

As above, these answer choices have two parts, so let's take them one at a time. The "increases"/"decreases" part is easier to handle, so we'll start there.

We've already seen that all the relationships in Figure 1 are direct: temperature, MM, and ΔS all increase. We can eliminate (A) and (B), then, because as the molecular masses of the salts increase, the ΔS will increase. Then, the second part of each answer choice might seem like outside knowledge, but let's simply match it with our first answer. In other words, choose (C) because the "greater mass" makes more sense with "increases."

Again, we could go back to the introduction for this information, but we don't need to.

On Question 5, however, we will have to use some of the introduction. This contains some chemical symbols and variables that we have not seen before. Question 5 is therefore a good question to save for last.

———————————◯———————————

5. Based on Figures 1 and 2, which of the following combinations of solute and temperature at a known m_{H_2O} would produce the greatest increase in solubility?

A. CH_4 (molecular compound, MM = 16) at 40°C
B. NaF (salt, MM = 42) at 40°C
C. CH_4 (molecular compound, MM = 16) at 80°C
D. NaF (salt, MM = 42) at 80°C

Here's How to Crack It

Start with what you know. The "increases" appear in Figure 1, and in this figure, higher temperatures mean higher ΔS values. Whatever chemical thing we end up selecting, we will certainly want the higher temperature, thus eliminating (A) and (B).

Now, because these combinations do not appear on the graphs themselves, and because MMs are similarly scattered through Figures 1 and 2, let's look at the introduction to see the relevance of "molecular compound" and "salt." The passage states the following:

Figure 1 shows the results of comparing the solubilities of three salts with increasing temperature, while Figure 2 shows the results of comparing the solubilities of three molecules with increasing temperature.

In other words, Figure 1 (which shows more significant *increases*) shows the "salts," while Figure 2 shows the "molecular compounds." This question is looking for an increase, so we must need a salt, and (D) is correct.

———————————◯———————————

Passage I offers a simple application of the steps that we will use in most of the Science passages. The questions here are fairly simple, but the steps we used to answer them are the same steps that will help us to answer the most difficult questions.

Now let's look at something a bit more difficult. Remember the Basic Approach.

1. **Work the Figures**
   Look for variables and trends.

2. **Work the Questions**
   Work from easy to hard, from short to long.

3. **Work the Answers**
   Use POE.

For this passage, as we delve into each question, we'll also provide you with tips on how to handle some of the more complex things ACT can throw at you.

Passage V

Simple diffusion (SD) is the process by which an uncharged solute in water migrates directly across an uncharged membrane, while *facilitated diffusion* (FD) is the process by which a charged or polar solute travels through a channel or transporter that crosses the membrane. Figure 1 illustrates how two solutes can diffuse, one by SD and one by FD.

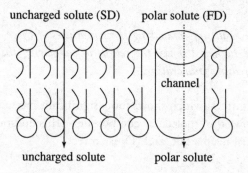

Figure 1

Solutes that cross a membrane by SD or by FD show different rates of flow across a membrane, also known as *flux*. As a solute crosses a membrane by SD, the flux follows a linear pattern over time, with smaller solutes having the greatest increase in flux over time. As a solute crosses a membrane by FD, the flux follows a logarithmic pattern, leveling off at a maximum flux since there are only a limited number of channels or transporters through which the solute can travel.

Experiment 1

One scientist introduced five different solutes of the same concentration to similar membranes at a constant temperature. The molecular masses of these solutes are shown in Table 1.

Table 1	
Solute	Molecular mass (amu)
1	160
2	800
3	2,000
4	10,000
5	40,000

This scientist then measured the time it took for the solute to reach *equilibrium*, which is a state of equal concentration of the solute on both sides of the membrane. The results are shown in Figure 2.

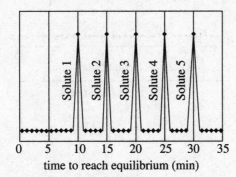

time to reach equilibrium (min)

Figure 2

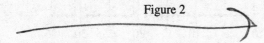

Experiment 2

Mixtures of solutes are subsequently introduced near three different membranes with different properties. The results of these three trials are presented in Figure 3.

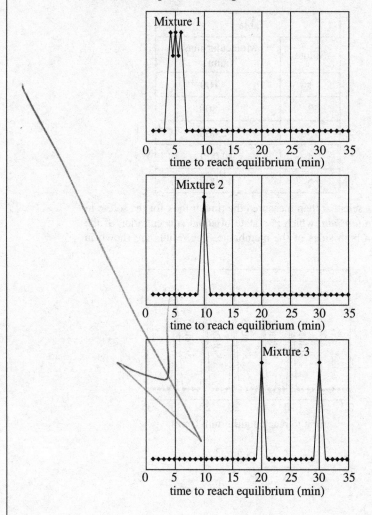

Figure 3

There is a good deal of text in this passage, and Figure 1 doesn't have anything that's obviously helpful, so let's ignore the text and Figure 1 until we need to pay attention to them.

Table 1

The variables are "solute" and "molecular mass (amu)".
The trends are consistent:

    -As the solute number gets higher, the molecular mass increases.

Figure 2

The variables are "time to reach equilibrium (min)" and the different solutes.
The trends are consistent:

-As the solute number gets higher, the time to reach equilibrium is greater.

Figure 3

The variables are "time to reach equilibrium (min)" and different mixtures.
The general trends are consistent:

-As the mixture number gets higher, the time to reach equilibrium is greater.

It will probably be relevant that, in Figure 3, the mixtures have different shapes and peaks on the graph—but there's no reason to worry about this until a question tells us to!

Since there are no real numerical values in the answer choices, let's work through the questions in order. Anything we don't know now, we can figure out when a question tells us to.

---

23. Based on the results of Experiments 1 and 2, Mixture 3 is likely to consist of which solutes from Experiment 1?

    A. Solute 1 only
    B. Solutes 1 and 3 only
    C. Solutes 3 and 5 only
    D. Solutes 2, 4, and 5 only

Here's How to Crack It

Let's go to what we know first: Mixture 3. On Figure 3, Mixture 3 has peaks at 20 min and 30 min. Given that the "Solute" graph in Figure 2 has the same *x*-axis, let's try to match these values with those on Figure 2. It may seem obvious to point out, but we're using a mini-strategy here, one that we could phrase as:

Shapes matter. Match the pictures to one another.

Solute 3 peaks at 20 min, and Solute 5 peaks at 30 min. Therefore, we can say that Mixture 3 likely consists of these two Solutes, as in (C).

No science necessary! Even for all the talk of "equilibrium" and "solutes," we just looked at the graphs and matched the pictures to one another.

24. In Experiment 1, which solute spends the least amount of time flowing across the membrane before reaching equilibrium?

F. Solute 1
G. Solute 2
H. Solute 3
J. Solute 4

Here's How to Crack It

This question asks about the "least" of something, so the answer must be one of the extremes, eliminating (G) and (H). According to Figure 2, Solute 1 peaks around 10 min, and Solute 4 peaks around 25 min, so the "least amount of time" belongs to Solute 1, (F).

In general, when ACT is asking for a "least" or a "greatest," the answer will need to be one of the extremes.

Pay close attention to extremes on ACT Science. ACT loves consistency!

25. Based on the results of Experiments 1 and 2, which of the following ranks Solute 3, Solute 4, and Mixture 2 in order of smallest to largest average molecular mass?

A. Solute 3, Solute 4, Mixture 2
B. Solute 4, Mixture 2, Solute 3
C. Mixture 2, Solute 3, Solute 4
D. Mixture 2, Solute 4, Solute 3

Here's How to Crack It

We've only been dealing with time and equilibrium peaks so far, so we'll have to look elsewhere for molecular mass. This variable appears in Table 1, which shows that as Solutes increase in number, their molecular masses increase as well. With this information, we know that Solute 3 has a smaller molecular mass than Solute 4, which already eliminates (B) and (D), as they reverse the order of those two solutes.

Now, though, we've got to figure out the molecular mass of Mixture 2, which is not listed in Table 1.

When you're stuck like this, it can be useful to ask this question:

What's the link between the different figures and tables within the passage?

We've already seen that Figure 2 and Figure 3 have a common *x*-axis, so we can read data points relative to one another.

There is a link between Table 1 and Figure 2 also: Solutes. As we determined when we initially Worked the Figures, as the solute number gets higher, so do the molecular masses. And as the solute number gets higher, so too do the times of peaks on Figure 2. We can draw a further conclusion, then, that as molecular masses increase, so too do the times of peaks on the equilibrium graph.

This new relationship makes Question 25 a simple matter of figuring out where Mixture 2's peak is relative to the peaks of Solute 3 and Solute 4. Mixture 2 peaks at 10 min, Solute 3 peaks at 20 min, and Solute 4 peaks at 25 min. We can therefore infer that Mixture 2 must have a smaller molecular mass than the Solutes, making (C) the correct answer.

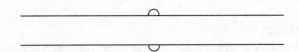

26. In Experiment 1, on average, did molecules of Solute 3 or molecules of Solute 4 more easily diffuse across the membrane?

F. Solute 3, because it has a larger molecular mass.
G. Solute 3, because it has a smaller molecular mass.
H. Solute 4, because it has a larger molecular mass.
J. Solute 4, because it has a smaller molecular mass.

Here's How to Crack It

This is the first we've heard of ease of diffusion, so we'll have to do some additional digging to answer this question. Before we do, however, we should remember that these answers have two parts, which are great POE opportunities. Though we may not know which solute is the correct choice, we definitely know that Solute 4 has a larger molecular mass than Solute 3, and this eliminates (F) and (J) right off the bat for saying the opposite.

Then, this question is asking about a relationship—but about a variable that is not shown on the graph. A good rule of thumb is this:

If a question asks about a variable that is not in a table or graph, there's a good chance that variable actually *is* on the table or graph. Use the relationships you know.

Question 26 is no exception to this rule. Diffusion across a membrane certainly has something to do with equilibrium, but "more easily" should point us back to the graph. If something is easy to do (whether it's an ACT question, learning a song on the guitar, or memorizing the first ten numbers in a foreign language), it doesn't take as long as something that's harder to do (like a really tough ACT question, learning any Yes song on the guitar, or memorizing the first 1,000 numbers in a foreign language).

As a result, we can say that Solute 3 has an easier time because it reaches its peak earlier than Solute 4, and given that we've already eliminated some of the answer choices in this question, we know that the answer will be (G).

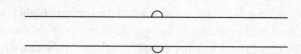

27. In which mixture is the molecular mass most likely less than 160 amu?

    A. Mixture 1
    B. Mixture 2
    C. Mixture 3
    D. Neither Mixture 1, 2, or 3

Here's How to Crack It

We actually already did the work for this question when we figured out that higher Solute numbers and higher Mixture numbers mean higher molecular masses. Again, it may seem like an obvious point, but don't forget:

Correct answers must agree with each other. Use answers from questions you've already completed to help with those you haven't.

According to Table 1, Solute 1 has a molecular mass of 160 amu, and according to Figure 2, it peaks at 10 min. If something is to have a smaller molecular mass than Solute 1, it will have to peak earlier than 10 min. Mixture 1 has a series of peaks that all occur earlier than 10 min, so it is reasonable to infer that Mixture 1 has a molecular mass less than 160 amu, as (A) suggests.

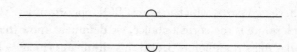

28. How does the number of molecules in 1 gram of Solute 1 compare with the number of molecules in 1 gram of Solute 5? The number of molecules in 1 gram of Solute 1 is:

    F. less, because Solute 1 has a larger molecular mass than Solute 5.
    G. less, because Solute 1 has a smaller molecular mass than Solute 5.
    H. more, because Solute 1 has a larger molecular mass than Solute 5.
    J. more, because Solute 1 has a smaller molecular mass than Solute 5.

Here's How to Crack It

We have two-part answer choices here, so let's use POE to eliminate what we can. We may not be sure whether the answer is "less" or "more," but we know from Table 1 that Solute 5 has a larger molecular mass than Solute 1, which eliminates (F) and (H).

Then, there's nothing in the passage that can help us to answer this question. And because we don't know what the Solutes are, we can't exactly draw on any outside science knowledge. Here, we're going to have to draw on one of the skills we all bring to the Science Test: common sense. If you can think of easy examples, do that, or if things make a kind of logical sense to you, go with the logical choice. In short:

When in doubt, use common sense. Take a leap of faith, pick an answer, and move on.

On this question, we know that Solute 1 has a smaller molecular mass than Solute 5, but we're dealing with 1 gram of each of them.

Common sense to the rescue! Let's say we have one ton of bowling balls, and one ton of ping-pong balls. The bowling balls have a greater individual mass than the ping-pong balls, but we're going to need WAY more ping-pong balls to get to that ton than we will need bowling balls. In other words, in a given weight, there will be *more* of a lighter object than of a heavier object.

In this question, that translates to the idea that there will be more of Solute 1 (the lighter of the two) than of Solute 5 (the heavier of the two). We've already done some POE, so let's finish it off and pick (J).

CONCLUSION

In these two passages, we've shown you all the basic skills you'll need on the Science Test. Our strategy is driven by three main ideas:

- Don't try to understand the science.
- Use POE.
- Let the questions teach you what you need to know about the passage.

We'll talk more about the third idea in the next chapter, but we've already applied all of these ideas in the above passages. Notice how much easier the Science Test becomes when we remove all that distracting "science" from it!

These three main ideas have encouraged us to keep our Basic Approach simple and applicable to all Science Test passages. The Basic Approach consists of three steps:

1. **Work the Figures**
   Look for variables and trends.

2. **Work the Questions**
   Work from easy to hard, from short to long.

3. **Work the Answers**
   Use POE.

This approach will work on any Science passage, though some steps will be easier or harder depending on the type of passage. As we saw in this chapter as we worked through Passage V, there are a few basic trends and tricks for attacking ACT Science questions. Bear these in mind if you get stuck on a particular question:

1. **Pretty pictures.**
   Shapes matter. Match the pictures to one another.

2. **Extreme consistency.**
   Pay close attention to extremes on ACT Science. ACT loves consistency!

3. **Hidden in plain sight.**
   If a question asks about a variable that is not in a table or graph, there's a good chance that variable actually *is* on the table or graph. Use the relationships you know.

4. **Right now, right again.**
   Correct answers must agree with each other. Use answers from questions you've already completed to help with those you haven't.

5. **Common sense.**
   When in doubt, use common sense. Take a leap of faith, pick an answer, and move on.

Now try these strategies on your own. Go online to your
Student Tools and answer the Chapter 24 Drill.

Chapter 25
Trends and Patterns

"LATER" AND "LAST" PASSAGES: THE QUESTIONS HOLD THE ANSWERS

In this chapter, we will look at some more difficult Science passages and some of the ways that the answer choices can teach us what we need to know about challenging passages. Our Basic Approach remains the same:

1. **Work the Figures**
   Look for variables and trends.

2. **Work the Questions**
   Work from easy to hard, from short to long.

3. **Work the Answers**
   Use POE.

Believe it or not, as the passages become more complex, it is equally important to remember: *Don't try to understand the science.* In this chapter, we will particularly focus on effective ways to use POE and to let the questions teach us about the passage.

Passage VII is a bit of a monster, but if we use the questions, we can find everything we need to know and select answer choices confidently.

Passage VII

Engineers studied the trajectories of a cannonball launched from a cannon under various conditions.

Study 1

On a level surface during a mild day, engineers launched a cannonball from a cannon as shown in Figure 1.

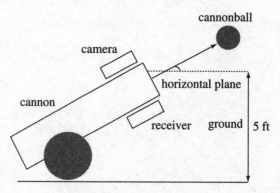

Figure 1

A camera was fixed atop the cannon so that it would point in the direction of the cannonball's launch. A receiver was also fixed to the cannon to record the cannonball's position as recorded by the camera.

As the cannonball traveled through the air, angle θ, which is defined in Figure 1, consistently changed. The change in θ was captured by the camera every 0.25 second after launch until the cannonball landed. For each recorded image, θ was measured (Figure 2).

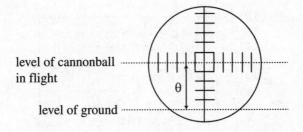

level of cannonball in flight

θ

level of ground

Figure 2

Furthermore, every 0.25 sec after launch, the receiver sent out a radar pulse, part of which was reflected by the cannonball to the receiver. The roundtrip travel time of each pulse was recorded to determine the distance, d, between the receiver and the ball at any given time (see Figure 3).

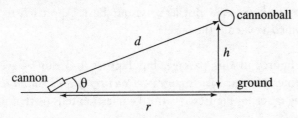

cannonball

d

h

cannon

θ

ground

r

Figure 3

Using d and θ, the engineers determined the ball's height, h, and distance, r, at the end of each 0.25 sec interval. A curve plotting h versus r was constructed.

This procedure was followed using cannonball launch starting speeds of 135 ft/sec, 150 ft/sec, and 180 ft/sec. For each launch speed, the ball was launched at θ = 30°. The curves representing h and r for each of the launch speeds were connected by lines for time, $t = 2$ sec, 3 sec, 4 sec, and 5 sec after launch (see Figure 4).

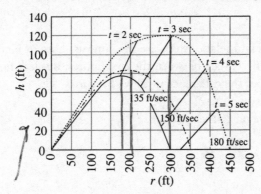

Figure 4

Study 2

Using an algorithm, the engineers calculated h and r at 0.25 sec intervals for the same cannonball launched in a vacuum in otherwise similar conditions to those in Study 1. The results are plotted in Figure 5.

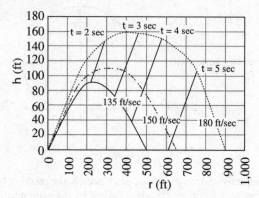

Figure 5

There is a lot of content in this passage, which already makes it a bit more difficult than the others we have seen. But let's use our Basic Approach to see if we can simplify it as much as we did the others.

There are five figures in this passage, but Figures 1–3 don't have any obvious trends. If we remember our basic mantra—*Don't try to understand the science*—we should feel okay ignoring Figures 1–3 until a question tells us that we need them.

Figure 4

The variables are r (ft), h (ft), t (sec), and some unspecified values in ft/sec.

There are a few basic relationships in this figure as well:
- As r increases, h increases then decreases.
- As r increases, t increases.
- As r increases, the ft/sec values increase.

Figure 5

All of the variables and relationships are the same as those in Figure 4. A question might ask us to differentiate between the two figures, but let's not waste our time trying to understand the difference until we have to.

That's it! Let's move on to the questions.

35. Suppose the cannonball were launched at 30 ft/sec in a vacuum from a height of 5 ft. Based on Figure 5, the cannonball would land approximately how many feet farther from the cannon if it were launched at 150 ft/sec than if it were launched at 135 ft/sec?

   A. 50 ft
   B. 150 ft
   C. 500 ft
   D. 650 ft

36. While the cannonball was in flight, how often did the camera record the position of the ball?

   F. Once per second
   G. Twice per second
   H. Three times per second
   J. Four times per second

37. The cannon was an instrumental weapon used during the Ottoman invasion of the city of Constantinople in 1453. Assume that cannonballs identical to those used in Study 1 were launched on a windless day with a starting height of 5 ft above the ground and an angle of $\theta = 30°$. If the launch speed of each cannonball were 180 ft/sec, how close would the cannon have needed to be to the 40-foot-tall wall surrounding Constantinople in order to travel over it?

   A. 425 ft
   B. 575 ft
   C. 700 ft
   D. 850 ft

38. Based on Figure 4, as the initial speed of the launched cannonball was increased, how did the values of h and r change at $t = 4$ sec?

	h	r
F.	decreased	decreased
G.	decreased	increased
H.	increased	decreased
J.	increased	increased

39. Based on Figure 5, if the ball were launched in a vacuum from a height of 5 ft at 135 ft/sec and $\theta = 30°$, how long would the cannonball most likely be in flight from launch to landing?

   A. Between 4 sec and 5 sec
   B. Between 5 sec and 6 sec
   C. Between 6 sec and 7 sec
   D. Between 7 sec and 8 sec

40. Based on Figure 3, if c represents the speed of light, which of the following represents the time taken by each radar pulse to make the roundtrip between the receiver and the ball?

   F. $2c/d$
   G. $2d/c$
   H. c/r
   J. r/c

As in the previous chapter, a large part of Working the Questions consists of answering the questions in a good order. Look for numbers, number words, and relationships.

Question 38 seems like a good place to start because the question is relatively short, and the answers are entirely composed of number words.

———————○———————

38. Based on Figure 4, as the initial speed of the launched cannonball was increased, how did the values of h and r change at $t = 4$ sec?

	h	r
F.	decreased	decreased
G.	decreased	increased
H.	increased	decreased
J.	increased	increased

Here's How to Crack It

Recall the initial relationships we determined. There was one, in ft/sec, that we didn't have a name for. This question has given it to us: "initial speed."

The question asks us to synthesize information about four different variables. Start with the most specific: $t = 4$ sec. This value represents the diagonal line toward the right edge of the graph. Then, move to the next specific piece of information, "as the initial speed of the launched cannonball was increased." Each of the curves represents a different speed, and it seems that as the speeds go from 135 to 150 to 180, they move further along the x-axis, or their r-values increase. Already, we can eliminate (F) and (H), which both say that the r-value decreases.

Finally, let's simply pull the rest of the information from the graph. At $t = 4$, the curve for the 135 ft/sec initial speed has an h-value of approximately 30 ft. At $t = 4$, the curve for the 150 ft/sec initial speed has an h-value of approximately 80 ft. The h-value is increasing, so only (J) can work as the correct answer.

This is a difficult first question, but notice how much assistance it provided us in clarifying how all these variables relate to one another. We now know what all the variables are called, and we can see some of the basic ways that those variables interact.

———————○———————

The remaining questions are all either long or unfamiliar, so let's do them in order. We'll start with Question 35.

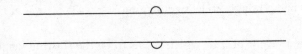

35. Suppose the cannonball were launched at 30 ft/sec in a vacuum from a height of 5 ft. Based on Figure 5, the cannonball would land approximately how many feet farther from the cannon if it were launched at 150 ft/sec than if it were launched at 135 ft/sec?

   A. 50 ft
   B. 150 ft
   C. 500 ft
   D. 650 ft

Here's How to Crack It

Start with the information you know. Figure 5 shows 135 ft/sec and 150 ft/sec, and we can see the arcs that each of those initial speeds create. The 150 ft/sec seems to go a bit farther along both axes, but we need to figure out which one we're dealing with.

We can use the units in the answer choices as a guide: "ft" will likely go with either h or r. We'll need to figure out which one it is, so *now* we'll use the weird figures we ignored before. Think of how much more intelligible Figure 3 becomes when you approach it with a specific question! We now see that there's a cannon that creates a right triangle: h is its vertical height from the ground, and r is the horizontal distance from the cannon itself. The cannonball, then, must be launched more or less on this path from various initial speeds. In this case, as in many others, the question has elucidated a new part of the passage.

This question asks "how many feet farther from the cannon" will a cannonball launched from one initial speed be from a cannonball launched at another initial speed. Distance from the cannon, we've just learned, is r. In Figure 5, the cannonball with an initial speed of 135 ft/sec maxes out around 500 ft/sec, and the cannonball with an initial speed of 150 ft/sec maxes out around 650 ft/sec. The faster ball, therefore, goes about 150 feet further, as (B) indicates.

36. While the cannonball was in flight, how often did the camera record the position of the ball?

   F. Once per second
   G. Twice per second
   H. Three times per second
   J. Four times per second

Here's How to Crack It

The only *t*-values we have seen are in increments of one second, but the curves seem to be more precise than that. Let's use the introduction but read it selectively. We're looking for the lead words "camera," "record," "position," or anything relating to time.

The relevant piece of information shows up above Figure 3: ...*every 0.25 sec after launch, the receiver sent out a radar pulse, part of which was reflected by the cannonball to the receiver.* It's not quite "camera," but this would seem to be what we're looking for, and if the pulse is captured every 0.25 second, that makes 4 times per second, (J).

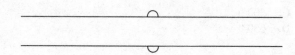

37. The cannon was an instrumental weapon used during the Ottoman invasion of the city of Constantinople in 1453. Assume that cannonballs were launched on a windless day with a starting height of 5 ft above the ground and an angle of θ = 30°. If the launched speed of each cannonball were 180 ft/sec, how close would the cannon have needed to be to the 40-foot-tall wall surrounding Constantinople in order to travel over it?

   A. 425 ft
   B. 575 ft
   C. 700 ft
   D. 850 ft

Here's How to Crack It

As riveting as all the military history in this question is, let's ignore it and go straight to the data. We've got a few data points: a starting height of 5 ft, an angle of θ = 30°, an initial speed of 180 ft/sec, and a 40-foot-tall wall (or a value of $h = 40$ ft.)

Since we already know what to do with initial speeds and *h*-values, let's figure out what's going on with these other two figures, which also showed up in Question 35, but in that case we knew to go to Figure 5, so we ignored them. We have no such guidance here, though, so let's go digging.

Figure 1 shows a height of 5 ft, which seems to be the starting height of the cannonball. Then, Study 1 mentions an angle of θ = 30°. Typically, if certain values that don't show up anywhere on the graphs or tables are mentioned frequently, those values are the constants for the entire experiment. Remember the basic Scientific Method: change what you are measuring and keep everything else constant. Any experiment will contain a number of variables that are held constant, and for this experiment, the starting height and the angle are fixed values.

Next, we need to figure out whether to draw information from Figure 4 or Figure 5. What's the difference? It seems that Figure 4 represents the actual trials of the experiment, and Figure 5 is done *using an algorithm* for a *cannonball launched in a vacuum*. In other words, Figure 4 shows how the cannon works when it is actually fired, while Figure 5 shows how the cannon *should* work under ideal mathematical conditions.

This question is asking about a historical moment (i.e., one *not* taking place in a laboratory or a series of equations), so we will need to draw on Figure 4. Let's recall the two bits of information we haven't used yet: 180 ft/sec initial speed, and $h = 40$ ft. We see the 180 ft/sec curve on the graph, and it seems to intersect $h = 40$ ft at two different points, once around $r = 60$ ft and once around $r = 425$ ft. We won't have to choose, fortunately, because the only one that appears in our answer choices is 425, (A).

We should now have more than enough information to answer the remainder of the questions.

39. Based on Figure 5, if the ball were launched in a vacuum from a height of 5 ft at 135 ft/sec and $\theta = 30°$, how long would the cannonball most likely be in flight from launch to landing?

   A. Between 4 sec and 5 sec
   B. Between 5 sec and 6 sec
   C. Between 6 sec and 7 sec
   D. Between 7 sec and 8 sec

Here's How to Crack It
We've already seen that we can ignore the 5 ft and $\theta = 30°$ values, and we know that *vacuum* refers to Figure 5 (note that the question tells us this as well). Let's go to the curve for 135 ft/sec.

This cannonball travels approximately 500 feet, and it reaches its endpoint between $t = 4$ sec and $t = 5$ sec. Only (A) works. Alternatively, once we understood how this question worked, we could have immediately eliminated (B), (C), and (D) because those values don't show up anywhere on the table.

40. Based on Figure 3, if c represents the speed of light, which of the following represents the time taken by each radar pulse to make the roundtrip between the receiver and the ball?

F. $2c/d$

G. $2d/c$

H. c/r

J. r/c

Here's How to Crack It

This question asks us to draw upon some very basic outside knowledge: distance = rate × time. The question is asking about time, and it tells us that the "rate" will be represented as c. In other words, $d = ct$. Rearrange this equation to solve for time, $t = d/c$. We know that c has to be in the denominator, which eliminates (F) and (H). Finally, the question asks about a "roundtrip," which means whichever distance we are dealing with will need to be doubled, so only (G), which contains a 2, can be the correct answer.

Let's try another passage bearing what we've learned in mind.

Passage VI

The term "evolution" is often used in the context of biological changes in organism populations over time, but it can also be applied to the change in the chemical composition of the Earth's atmosphere. The hypotheses of two studies claim that this *chemical evolution* has altered the types of chemicals found in the atmosphere between the early stages of Earth's existence and the present day.

Study 1

Based on the hypothesis that volcanic eruptions were the source of gases in the early Earth's atmosphere, scientists recreated four model volcanic eruptions in closed chambers, each containing different percentages of the same volcanic particulate matter. They then observed the gases in the air above this model over time. The percent composition of this air after 1 day, when the air achieved a *steady state* of constant gas concentrations, is represented in Table 1.

Since the experiment provided only a suggestion of the gas levels in the early Earth's atmosphere, the scientists then analyzed the amount of trapped gases in sediment layers, which indicate the changing atmospheric levels of gases over billions of years. The data collected on O_2 and H_2O vapor are presented in Figure 1.

Study 2

A separate study used the same volcanic models as in Study 1, but hypothesized that the scientists in Study 1 underestimated the amount of H_2 in the early Earth atmosphere. They proposed a different composition of gases, highlighting an increased H_2 level in the atmosphere, also represented in Table 1. Based on this new data, the scientists proposed an alternative graph for the changing atmospheric levels of O_2 and H_2O vapor, also shown in Figure 1.

Table 1					
		Percent composition of gas			
Volcanic eruption models		1	2	3	4
Study 1 (low H_2 atmosphere)	H_2	3	2	1	0
	H_2O vapor	85	80	75	70
	CO_2	10	10	10	15
	H_2S	2	5	7	8
	N_2	0.5	1	2	2
	CH_4	0.3	0.3	0.3	0.3
	CO	0.05	0.05	0.05	0.05
Study 2 (high H_2 atmosphere)	H_2	45	40	35	30
	H_2O vapor	40	40	35	35
	CO_2	10	10	10	15
	H_2S	2	5	7	8
	N_2	0.5	1	2	2
	CH_4	0.3	0.3	0.3	0.3
	CO	0.05	0.05	0.05	0.05

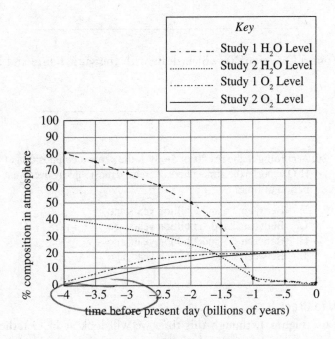

Key

- – . – . – Study 1 H_2O Level
- .... Study 2 H_2O Level
- –..–..– Study 1 O_2 Level
- ——— Study 2 O_2 Level

Figure 1

When we Work the Figures in this passage, we come up with almost nothing. Table 1 has no consistent trends, and Figure 1 has two contrary trends. The one thing we can see from Figure 1 is that the H_2O levels go down as the O_2 levels go up. Since there's not much we can do with the figures, let's see if the questions can help to elucidate the passage.

Question 29 is clearly the place to start because it is short and has number words in the answer choices.

29. According to the results of Study 2, between 4 and 3 billion years before the present day, the percent composition of O_2 in the atmosphere:
   A. increased only.
   B. increased, then decreased.
   C. decreased only.
   D. decreased, then increased.

Here's How to Crack It

This question is about as easy as they come. Let's go back to Figure 1 and look between 4 and 3 billion years before the present day. The question asks about the O_2 level, which increases during this period. The best answer in (A).

Let's move on to Question 30, which deals with the same figure and is similarly short.

30. According to the results of Study 1, the percent composition of H_2O vapor in the atmosphere decreased most rapidly over what period of time?
   F. Between 2.5 and 2 billion years ago
   G. Between 2 and 1.5 billion years ago
   H. Between 1.5 and 1 billion years ago
   J. Between 1 and 0.5 billion years ago

Here's How to Crack It

Again, let's use Figure 1, though this time we will look at H_2O rather than O_2. Because it's hard to know exactly which range showed the most rapid decrease, let's use the answer choices and POE.

Between 2.5 and 2 billion years ago, the percent composition decreased by about 10. Between 2 and 1.5 billion years ago, it decreased by about 15. Between 1.5 and 1 billion years ago, it decreased by about 30. Between 1 and 0.5 billion years ago, it decreased very little. The greatest decrease occurred between 1.5 and 1 billion years ago, as (H) suggests.

———————◯———————

Question 31 asks about Table 1, which we have not yet used because we found no consistent trends. This question will help us to see how the table works.

———————◯———————

31. Suppose that the actual early Earth atmosphere had a high H_2 composition of 42%. Based on Study 2, is it likely that the corresponding H_2S and N_2 compositions of this atmosphere were each 3%?

	3% H_2S	3% N_2
A.	Yes	Yes
B.	Yes	No
C.	No	Yes
D.	No	No

Here's How to Crack It

This question asks us to determine a relationship where we could not find one before. Let's look back at the chart now that we know what we're looking for: an H_2 composition of 42%.

In Study 2 on Table 1, H_2 values decrease from left to right. The other relevant values for this question, H_2S and N_2, increase as H_2 values decrease. With this pattern in place, we can begin to make some predictions. An H_2 composition of 42% would fall between volcanic eruption models 1 and 2. As a result, the H_2S and N_2 will need to be between the model 1 and 2 values as well. That puts H_2S between 2% and 5% and N_2 between 0.5% and 1%. With these ranges, we can answer the question: H_2S could be 3%, but N_2 could not, as (B) indicates.

———————◯———————

Question 32 asks a very similar question, one that begins with the word "Suppose."

———○———

32. Suppose that in a new trial in Study 2, the percent composition of H_2 in the atmosphere was set at 33% and the percent composition of N_2 was found to be 2%. The percent composition of H_2O vapor in this trial would most likely be:

   F. greater than 40%.
   G. greater than 35% and less than 40%.
   H. exactly 35%.
   J. greater than 30% and less than 35%.

Here's How to Crack It

We saw in the last question that there are more relationships in Table 1 than initially meets the eye. H_2, for example, decreases, making predictions about H_2 levels possible.

If the H_2 level in this question is 33%, that would put the value right between volcanic eruption models 3 and 4. Further, the N_2 value in both models 3 and 4 is 2%, which matches what is given in our question. Finally, we look at H_2O vapor, which is 35% in both trials, at H_2 compositions of both 30% and 35%. We have no good reason to think that the H_2O vapor levels will change, so we can infer that the value will be exactly 35%, as it was in the other two models. Choice (H) is the only answer that can work.

———○———

Question 33 is much wordier than the others we've seen, but hopefully by this point, you're able to see all the POE opportunities in the answer choices before you've even read the question.

———○———

33. Consider an early Earth environment that featured microorganisms. Based on the results of Study 2, is it more likely that *aerobic organisms* (those that require O_2 to survive) or *anaerobic organisms* (those that do not require O_2 to survive) would have existed on Earth 4 billion years ago?

   A. Aerobic organisms, because of the high H_2O level 4 billion years ago
   B. Aerobic organisms, because of the low O_2 level 4 billion years ago
   C. Anaerobic organisms, because of the high H_2O level 4 billion years ago
   D. Anaerobic organisms, because of the low O_2 level 4 billion years ago

Here's How to Crack It

Right off the bat, we can eliminate (A) and (C), which address the H_2O levels in a question that is exclusively concerned with O_2 levels. Then, because all that remains are options that refer to "the low O_2 level 4 billion years ago," the organisms *must* be anaerobic, given that anaerobic organisms "do not require O_2 to survive." Only (D) can work, and we didn't need the figures at all! All you need is POE.

———————○———————

Question 34 seems to ask for a synthesis of all the information in the passage, but let's see.

———————○———————

34. According to Study 2, how long did it take the H_2O vapor level to decrease to 75% of its composition 4 billion years before the present day?

   F.   500 million years
   G.   1 billion years
   H.   1.5 billion years
   J.   2 billion years

Here's How to Crack It

We're back to the graph. Don't overthink this one! In Study 2, 4 billion years ago, the H_2O vapor level was 40%. 75% of that would be an H_2O vapor level of 30%. In Study 2, the H_2O vapor level is 30% approximately 2.5 billion years ago. From 4 billion to 2.5 billion is 1.5 billion, or (H).

———————○———————

In conclusion, we entrusted our knowledge of this passage to the questions, and as we've now seen, we need to know *very* little about the passage itself beyond the figures. The questions helped us to see the relationships in the figure that we would not have otherwise seen, and they guided us through a series of figures we had an almost impossible time trying to "work" in the first step.

CONFUSING FIGURES AND THE QUESTIONS WHO LOVE THEM

In this exercise, you will be given a confusing figure and a question associated with it. Note how the question tells you what you need to know about the figure. Answers and explanations will be at the end of the exercise.

Table 1			
% shells with the following scute pattern:			
Age of shells (years)	M-m-M-M-m	M-M-m-m-M	M-m-M-m-M
120,000	46	44	10
90,000	42	54	4
87,000	30	67	3
85,000	21	72	7
80,000	20	66	14
50,000	76	21	3
27,000	100	0	0
15,000	100	0	0
8,000	100	0	0
4,000	100	0	0
1,000	68	28	4
300	74	20	6
0	86	2	12

1. Suppose, in Study 1, the scientists had found another seabed layer with fossilized shells that were radiocarbon dated and found to be 86,000 years old. Based on the results of Study 1, the scute pattern percents for the group of shells would most likely have been closest to which of the following?

	M-m-M-M-m	M-M-m-m-M	M-m-M-m-M
A.	100%	0%	0%
B.	50%	25%	25%
C.	36%	61%	4%
D.	26%	69%	5%

Table 1					
	Relative abundance (%)			Altitude above cloud tops where most abundant (km)		
Gas	Jupiter	Neptune	Saturn	Jupiter	Neptune	Saturn
H	86.1	79.0	96.1	−1,000 to −70,000	−10,000 to −23,000	−1,000 to −60,000
He	13.6	18.0	3.3	−500 to −1,000	−500 to −10,000	−500 to −900
CH_3	0.2	3.0	0.4	0 to 300	−100 to 0	0 to 200
NH_3	0.0045	0	0.0035	0 to −100	−	−50 to −200
H_2O vapor	0.0055	0	0.0065	−50 to −100	−	−200 to −300

2. Considering only the gases listed in Table 1, which gas is more abundant in the atmosphere of Jupiter than in the atmosphere of either Neptune or Saturn?

F. H
G. CH_3
H. NH_3
J. He

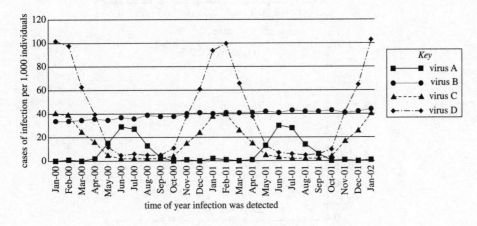

Figure 1

3. According to Figure 1, the incidence of *at least 3* of the viruses is most alike during which of the following months?

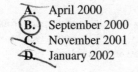

A. April 2000
B. September 2000
C. November 2001
D. January 2002

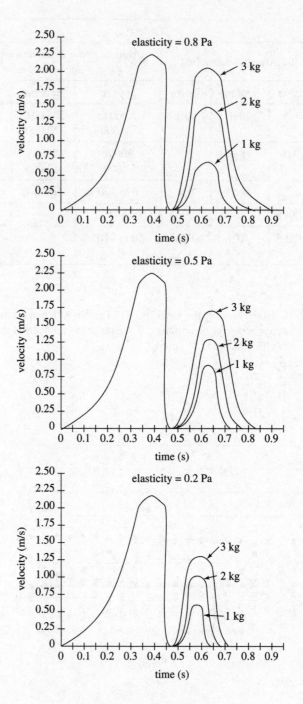

Figure 2

4. Based on the information in Figure 2, a ball being dropped from a 1 meter height with an elasticity of 0.2 Pa and a weight of 0.5 kg would have a maximum post-impact velocity of:

F. less than 0.50 m/s.
G. 0.75 m/s.
H. 1.0 m/s.
J. greater than 1.25 m/s.

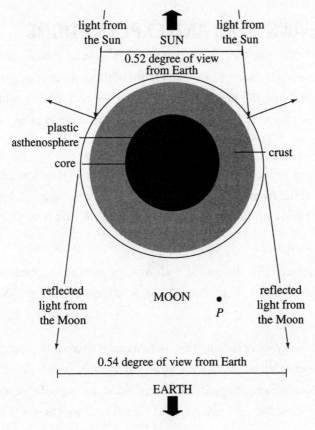

light from
the Sun

light from
the Sun

SUN

0.52 degree of view
from Earth

plastic
asthenosphere

core

crust

reflected
light from
the Moon

MOON

•
P

reflected
light from
the Moon

0.54 degree of view from Earth

EARTH

Figure 1

5. Figure 1 shows that a lunar orbiter at point *P* would be able to
view which of the following?

A. The Moon only
B. The Sun only
C. The Moon and the Earth only
D. The Moon, the Sun, and the Earth

CONFUSING FIGURES DRILL ANSWERS AND EXPLANATIONS

1. **D**   There are no obvious trends in the table other than the fact that "Age of shells" decreases from the top of the table to the bottom. This allows us to situate 86,000 years between two values on the table: 87,000 and 85,000. Because the new value is between the two known values, we can assume that the other values will be as well. Choice (D) gives three values that fit between the others in the table.

2. **H**   While we may not know what any of the terms mean or how they relate to the three planets listed, we can pull this information directly from the chart. The answer must be choice (F), because NH_3 has a relative abundance of 0.0045% on Jupiter but of 0% on Neptune and 0.0035% on Saturn. POE got us there!

3. **B**   Find three overlapping dots. Choices (A), (B), and (D) all refer to months in which the dots are fairly spread out. Only (B) gives a month, September 2000, in which three of the dots are very close to one another.

4. **F**   Work with the specific information given in the question. 0.2 Pa leads to the third graph in Figure 2, and the weight of 0.5 kg will lead to the second hump within that graph, which shows 3 kg, 2 kg, and 1 kg. Because those three curves seem to go in increasing order, we can infer that 0.5 kg will be somewhere below 1 kg. 1 kg maxes out at a velocity of 0.50 m/s, so a weight of 0.5 kg will max out at a velocity less than that, as (F) indicates.

5. **C**   Find point P on the figure (which, by the way, looks like a big eyeball). Point P, it seems, is between the eyeball (the Moon) and the Earth, so someone standing at point P would be able to see both. This eliminates (A) and (B), which don't contain both elements. As for the Sun, it looks like the eyeball is blocking point P from a good view of it, so (D) can be eliminated as well. Choice (C) contains the correct elements.

Now try these strategies on your own. Go online to your
Student Tools and answer the Chapter 25 Drill.

Chapter 26
Hard Passages and Questions

FIGHTING SCIENTISTS

The last two chapters have discussed how to work just about any science passage on the ACT, particularly giving some tips and tricks for how to deal with even the most difficult questions. In particular, we've shown how to work with any type of figure—whether working that figure early on or using the questions to understand the figures.

But there's one type of ACT Science passage that sometimes has no figures at all. In fact, this kind of passage is frequently all words, and the questions are long with no numbers or number words. If you come across one of these passages, don't worry. You're probably looking at ACT Science's anomaly: "Conflicting Viewpoints," or as we like to call it, "Fighting Scientists."

We've given these passages their own chapter because they require a different approach. Whereas the other passages are built around working with figures, Fighting Scientists passages don't give us that luxury. Sometimes they'll have figures, sometimes they won't. Sometimes the paragraphs are short, sometimes they're really long. Sometimes there will be two scientists duking it out, sometimes there will be more.

We do know a few things for sure, though:

- There will always be one Fighting Scientists passage on the Science Test.
- That passage will have 7 questions.
- That passage will have more text than many of the others in the section.

This isn't much info, but from this alone, we can see also that Fighting Scientists is last in many people's POODs. Think about all the things that are made for "Now" passages (numbers, number words, trends, charts, graphs, shortness). None of that is necessarily in the Fighting Scientists passage.

If you love to read, however, or if you're scoring 32 or above on the Reading Test, then Fighting Scientists might draw on some of your most refined skills. For you, the Fighting Scientists might be the first section because it will give you the natural transition in from the Reading Test.

Whatever your skill set may be, we've got a Basic Approach for Fighting Scientists that will help you on this part of the test whether you're doing it first or last.

Fighting Scientists Basic Approach

- **Read the Introduction**
  - Look in particular for what the substance of the disagreement is. In other words, try to answer the question: *What are these scientists fighting about?*
  - Note: The longer the introduction, the more the questions will ask about it.

- **Preview the Questions**
  - As we saw in the last chapter, the questions can often help to elucidate difficult passages.
  - In Fighting Scientists, preview the questions to see where most of them focus—the Introduction? Scientist 1? Scientist 2?

- **Do One Hypothesis at a Time**
  - Fighting Scientists is long: don't take it all in one gulp!
  - Pick the more popular Scientist from the previous step, and read his or her theory first.

- **Use your POOD**
  - Answer the questions in an order that makes sense. If you haven't read Scientist 2 yet, don't try a question that asks about him!
  - If the Fighting Scientists passage itself is too hard, cut your losses and move on to something that will get you more points.

Let's apply this Basic Approach to an actual passage.

Passage V

Comets originate from regions of our solar system that are very far from the sun. The comets are formed from debris thrown from objects in the solar system: they have a nucleus of ice surrounded by dust and frozen gases. When comets are pulled into the earth's atmosphere by gravitational forces and become visible, they are called *meteors*. Meteors become visible about 50 to 85 km above the surface of Earth as air friction causes them to glow. Most meteors vaporize completely before they come within 50 km of the surface of Earth.

The Small Comet debate centers on whether dark spots and streaks seen in images of the Earth's atmosphere are due to random technological noise or a constant rain of comets composed of ice. Recently, images were taken by two instruments, UVA and VIS, which are located in a satellite orbiting in Earth's magnetosphere. UVA and VIS take pictures of the aurora borealis phenomenon, which occurs in the magnetosphere. The UVA and VIS technologies provide images of energy, which cannot be seen by the human eye.

The pictures taken by VIS and UVA both show dark spots and streaks. Scientists debate whether these spots and streaks are due to a natural incident, such as small comets entering the atmosphere, or random technological noise. The layers of Earth's atmosphere are shown in Figure 1.

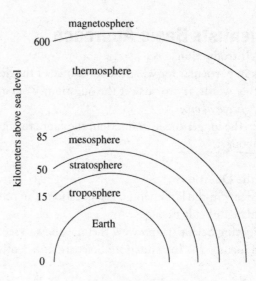

magnetosphere

thermosphere

mesosphere

stratosphere

troposphere

Earth

kilometers above sea level

600

85

50

15

0

Figure 1

Two scientists debate whether there is a constant rain of comets burning up in Earth's magnetosphere.

Scientist 1

Small comets are pulled into Earth's atmosphere by gravitational effects and burn up in the magnetosphere. They are about 20 to 30 feet in diameter and burn up in the magnetosphere because they are much smaller than the comets that become meteors. Comets with larger radii will burn up in portions of the atmosphere much closer to Earth. About 30,000 small comets enter the Earth's magnetosphere every day. The dark spots and streaks on UVA and VIS images occur when the small comets begin to boil in the magnetosphere, releasing krypton and argon and creating gaseous H_2O, which interacts with hydroxyl, OH^-, radicals. Images taken by these instruments at different points in time show the same frequency of dark spots and streaks and give conclusive evidence in favor of the Small Comet theory. If the spots and streaks were due to random technological noise, then the frequency of their appearance would fluctuate.

Scientist 2

The dark spots and streaks in the UVA and VIS images are due to technological noise, not small comets. If the small comet theory were true, and 20 small comets bombarded Earth's atmosphere per minute, there would be a visible bright object at least twice every five minutes. This is because, as objects enter the Earth's mesosphere, they burn up, creating large clouds of ice particles. As the ice particles vaporize, they have a brightness in the sky approximately equal to that of Venus. Because comets rarely enter Earth's atmosphere, such bright flashes are rare occurrences, far less than two times every five minutes, so the Small Comet theory cannot be correct. Further, since comets originate from regions of space beyond the orbit of the farthest planet, they contain argon and krypton. If the Small Comet theory were true and Earth were bombarded by 30,000 comets per day, there would be 500 times as much krypton in the atmosphere as there actually is.

23. According to Scientist 2, which of the following planets in our solar system is most likely the closest to the region of space where comets originate?

A. Jupiter
B. Venus
C. Neptune
D. Saturn

MVEMJSUN

24. Based on Scientist 1's viewpoint, a comet that burns up in the thermosphere would have a diameter of:

F. 5–10 ft.
G. 10–20 ft.
H. 20–30 ft.
J. greater than 30 ft.

25. Which of the following generalizations about small comets is most consistent with Scientist 1's viewpoint?

A. No small comet ever becomes a meteor.
B. Some small comets become meteors.
C. Small comets become meteors twice every five minutes.
D. All small comets become meteors.

26. During the *Perseids*, an annual meteor shower, more than 1 object burning up in the atmosphere is visible per minute. According to the information provided, Scientist 2 would classify the Perseids as:

F. typical comet frequency in the magnetosphere.
G. unusual comet frequency in the magnetosphere.
H. typical meteor frequency in the mesosphere.
J. unusual meteor frequency in the mesosphere.

27. Given the information about Earth's atmosphere and Scientist 1's viewpoint, which of the following altitudes would most likely NOT be an altitude at which small comets burn up?

A. 750 km
B. 700 km
C. 650 km
D. 550 km

28. Suppose a study of the dark holes and streaks in the UVA and VIS images revealed krypton levels 500 times greater than normal levels. How would the findings of this study most likely affect the scientists' viewpoints, if at all?

F. It would strengthen Scientist 1's viewpoint only.
G. It would strengthen Scientist 2's viewpoint only.
H. It would weaken both Scientists' viewpoints.
J. It would have no effect on either Scientist's viewpoint.

29. Scientist 1 would most likely suggest enhanced imaging technology that can take pictures of objects in the atmosphere be used to look at what region of the atmosphere to search for small comets?

   A. The region between 15 km above sea level and 50 km above sea level.

   B. The region between 50 km above sea level and 85 km above sea level.

   C. The region between 85 km above sea level and 600 km above sea level.

   D. The region above 600 km above sea level.

Read the Introduction

The core of the disagreement comes in the second paragraph: *The Small Comet debate centers on whether dark spots and streaks seen in images of the Earth's atmosphere are due to random technological noise or a constant rain of comets composed of ice.*

We may not quite know what any of this means, and it's actually not that important. We could sum the disagreement up like this: *What's with these dark spots? Where do they come from?*

Preview the Questions

Let's see who is more popular.

Question 23 – Scientist 2
Question 24 – Scientist 1
Question 25 – Scientist 1
Question 26 – Scientist 2
Question 27 – Scientist 1
Question 28 – Scientists 1 and 2
Question 29 – Scientist 1

Scientist 1 is the favorite by a few questions, so let's read Scientist 1 first.

Do One Hypothesis at a Time

When reading Scientist 1, look in particular for his answer to the central question of the fight (*What's with these dark spots? Where do they come from?*).

Scientist 1's answer to this conundrum comes in the middle of the paragraph: *The dark spots and streaks on UVA and VIS images occur when the small comets begin to boil in the magnetosphere, releasing krypton and argon and creating gaseous H_2O, which interacts with hydroxyl, OH^-, radicals.*

Although Scientist 1 doesn't believe the theory of "technological noise" producing the dark spots, he's certainly given us a lot of noise here! The important thing to draw from this statement is that the dark spots occur *when the small comets begin to boil in the magnetosphere.*

Once we've answered this central question, we can move on to the questions themselves. These questions will help us to know what else in the passage is important.

Use Your POOD

Let's reorder the questions as we've always done (easiest to hardest), but let's also be mindful of the fact that we want to use our time and knowledge efficiently. We've read only Scientist 1, and his ideas are relatively fresh in our minds, so let's do ONLY the questions that deal with Scientist 1 first.

Question 24 has numbers! Let's start there.

---

24. Based on Scientist 1's viewpoint, a comet that burns up in the thermosphere **would** have a diameter of:

   F.   5–10 ft.
   G. 10–20 ft.
   H. 20–30 ft.
   J.   greater than 30 ft.

Here's How to Crack It

Let's use the information from the question to find the relevant part of the passage. It comes in the first to third lines: *Small comets are pulled into Earth's atmosphere by gravitational effects and burn up in the magnetosphere. They are about 20 to 30 feet in diameter and burn up in the magnetosphere because they are much smaller than the comets that become meteors. Comets with larger radii will burn up in portions of the atmosphere much closer to Earth.*

Use the Figure. The magnetosphere is the region furthest from Earth, so any region closer to Earth will need comets that are larger than the comets that burn up in the magnetosphere. In other words, comets of 20 to 30 feet burn up in the magnetosphere, and comets in any other region shown on the figure will have radii of greater than 30 feet, as (J) indicates.

Question 27 has numbers in it also. Let's go there next.

---

27. Given the information about Earth's atmosphere and Scientist 1's viewpoint, which of the following altitudes would most likely NOT be an altitude at which small comets burn up?

   A. 750 km
   B. 700 km
   C. 650 km
   D. 550 km

Here's How to Crack It

As we saw in the previous question, small comets burn up in the magnetosphere. According to the Figure, this is any region with an altitude greater than 600 km. Therefore, if we are looking for a place where small comets will NOT burn up, it must be outside the magnetosphere, or less than 600 km, which only (D) is.

Question 29 seems to draw on these altitude values as well. Let's try that one next.

---

29. Scientist 1 would most likely suggest enhanced imaging technology that can take pictures of objects in the atmosphere be used to look at what region of the atmosphere to search for small comets?

   A. The region between 15 km above sea level and 50 km above sea level.
   B. The region between 50 km above sea level and 85 km above sea level.
   C. The region between 85 km above sea level and 600 km above sea level.
   D. The region above 600 km above sea level.

Here's How to Crack It

From the previous two questions, we have already seen that Scientist 1 is primarily concerned with the *magnetosphere* and that that region is 600 km above sea level. This conclusion is echoed in this statement: *The dark spots and streaks on UVA and VIS images occur when the small comets begin to boil in the magnetosphere.* In fact, Scientist 1 does not mention any –spheres other than the magnetosphere, so he is most likely concerned with the region above 600 km above sea level, or (D).

Question 25 is the last remaining question that deals only with Scientist 1.

———————————○———————————

25. Which of the following generalizations about small comets is
most consistent with Scientist 1's viewpoint?

   A. No small comet ever becomes a meteor.
   B. Some small comets become meteors.
   C. Small comets become meteors twice every five minutes.
   D. All small comets become meteors.

Here's How to Crack It

Each answer choice seems to draw on Scientist 1's view of the relationship between
comets and meteors. The parts of the passage that we've looked at so far contain
the answer: *[Small comets] are about 20 to 30 feet in diameter and burn up in the
magnetosphere because they are much smaller than the comets that become meteors.*

In other words, small comets are simply not large enough to become meteors, and
this is why small comets never become meteors, as (A) suggests.

———————————○———————————

Rinse and Repeat

Let's take the same approach with Scientist 2 that we took with Scientist 1.

When reading Scientist 2, look in particular for his answer to the central question
of the fight (*What's with these dark spots? Where do they come from?*).

Scientist 2's answer to this conundrum comes in the first sentence: *The dark spots
and streaks in the UVA and VIS images are due to technological noise, not small
comets.*

Scientist 1 is the small-comet guy, and Scientist 2 is the technological-noise guy.
Once we've answered this central question, we can move on to the questions themselves. These questions will help us to know what else in the passage is important.

Question 23 is short, so let's start there.

---○---

23. According to Scientist 2, which of the following planets in our solar system is most likely the closest to the region of space where comets originate?

　A. Jupiter
　B. Venus
　C. Neptune
　D. Saturn

Here's How to Crack It

This question requires a bit of outside knowledge because not all these planets are mentioned in the passage. The passage says, *comets originate from regions of space beyond the orbit of the farthest planet.*

The outside knowledge you will need to summon here is this: of the four planets listed, which is the furthest from the Sun? Now that Pluto is no longer considered a planet, Neptune is the outermost planet in our solar system. If you have trouble remembering the order of the planets, remember this: My Very Excellent Mother Just Sent Us Nachos (Mercury, Venus, Earth, Mars, Jupiter, Saturn, Uranus, Neptune).

---○---

Question 26 looks difficult, but it's the only one left that deals only with Scientist 2.

---○---

26. During the *Perseids*, an annual meteor shower, more than 1 object burning up in the atmosphere is visible per minute. According to the information provided, Scientist 2 would classify the Perseids as:

　F. typical comet frequency in the magnetosphere.
　G. unusual comet frequency in the magnetosphere.
　H. typical meteor frequency in the mesosphere.
　J. unusual meteor frequency in the mesosphere.

Here's How to Crack It

We will need to draw upon a few parts of the passage to answer this question. First, we should determine in which –sphere Scientist 2 is particularly interested. We know that Scientist 1 is interested in the magnetosphere, and Scientist 2 is interested in the *mesosphere*, where objects *burn up, creating large clouds of ice particles.* Given Scientist 2's interest in the *mesosphere*, we can eliminate (F) and (G).

Scientist 2 continues, *Because comets rarely enter Earth's atmosphere, such bright flashes are rare occurrences, far less than two times every five minutes.* The question mentions a time in which "more than 1 object burning up in the atmosphere is visible per minute." According to the quotation from Scientist 2, this rate of visibility is exceptionally high, or *unusual*, as (J) suggests.

———————○———————

Question 28 deals with both scientists, so we've saved it for last.

———————○———————

28. Suppose a study of the dark holes and streaks in the UVA and VIS images revealed krypton levels 500 times greater than normal levels. How would the findings of this study most likely affect the scientists' viewpoints, if at all?

F. It would strengthen Scientist 1's viewpoint only.
G. It would strengthen Scientist 2's viewpoint only.
H. It would weaken both Scientists' viewpoints.
J. It would have no effect on either Scientist's viewpoint.

Here's How to Crack It

This is not a subject we have seen so far, but let's use our time efficiently. The question seems to be largely about *krypton*, so here's what each Scientist says about it:

Scientist 1: *The dark spots and streaks on UVA and VIS images occur when the small comets begin to boil in the magnetosphere, releasing krypton and argon and creating gaseous H_2O, which interacts with hydroxyl, OH^-, radicals.*

Scientist 2: *Further, since comets originate from regions of space beyond the orbit of the farthest planet, they contain argon and krypton.*

In other words, for Scientist 1, there's extra krypton when comets boil in the magnetosphere, but for Scientist 2, krypton is just always there. The situation posed in the question would therefore support Scientist 1, who says krypton goes to abnormal levels, and only (F) can work.

———————○———————

FIGHTING SCIENTISTS 2.0

We've seen ACT change things up a bit on some recent tests, and one of the big changes has been to the occasional Fighting Scientists passage. While most of the passages still operate on the two-scientist model, some more recent Fighting Scientists passages have had as many as five scientists engaged in theoretical fisticuffs and some charts and figures to back up the arguments of each.

Our Fighting Scientists approach applies just as much to these weird passages as it does to the more traditional ones. Let's recall that Basic Approach.

Fighting Scientists Basic Approach

- **Read the Introduction**
  - Look in particular for what the substance of the disagreement is. In other words, try to answer the question: *What are these scientists fighting about?*
  - Note: The longer the introduction, the more the questions will ask about it.

- **Preview the Questions**
  - As we saw in the last chapter, the questions can often help to elucidate difficult passages.
  - In Fighting Scientists, preview the questions to see where most of them focus—the Introduction? Scientist 1? Scientist 2?

- **Do One Hypothesis at a Time**
  - Fighting Scientists is long: don't take it all in one gulp!
  - Pick the more popular Scientist from the previous step, and read his or her theory first.

- **Use your POOD**
  - Answer the questions in an order that makes sense. If you haven't read Scientist 2 yet, don't try a question that asks about him!
  - If the Fighting Scientists passage itself is too hard, cut your losses and move on to something that will get you more points.

Let's keep this in mind as we go to our next, bizarre Fighting Scientists passage.

Passage II

Recombination of genes is usually associated with the sexual reproduction of cells, or meiosis. However, it can also occur when cells that undergo asexual reproduction, or mitosis, need to be repaired, such as after radiation exposure. This repair process, known as *homologous recombination*, aligns two copies of the same double strand of DNA, one with the error and one without. As seen in Figure 1, correct genes are transplanted from the correct strand to the one with errors (genes with errors are represented with a *).

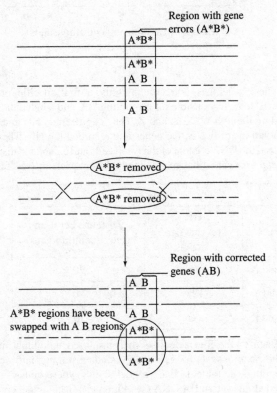

Figure 1

The activities of some genes have been found to promote homologous recombination (HR). In an experiment to quantify the genetic control over HR, four scientists measured the frequency of HR per hour over a 24-hour period in isolated connective tissue cells from rats placed in growth media. They then lysed the cells, separated out the entire protein content, and used gel electrophoresis to count the amount of protein present in the cells (see Figure 2).

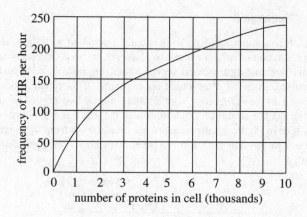

Figure 2

These scientists noticed that only a few specific proteins appeared to be responsible for promoting HR, and labeled the genes encoding them as W, X, Y, and Z. They engineered cells to express combinations of two active genes and recorded the HR. They then analyzed the DNA content of the lysed cells and calculated distances between four genes that encoded the relevant proteins (see Table 1).

Table 1		
Genes	HR (events per hour)	Distance between genes (centimorgans)
W and X	75	20
X and Y	125	30
W and Z	60	15

Each of the four scientists then proposed individual models for the positions of the genes they studied, taking into account the findings in Table 1. Each model shows where genes may be located along a strand of DNA (see Figure 3). Each model correctly assumes that the lengths of the genes are insignificant compared to the length of the DNA.

Scientist	Model			
1	Z	W	X	Y
2	W	Z	X	Y
3	ZY	W	X	
4	Y	W	ZX	

Figure 3

A final experiment showed that rat connective tissue cells in which genes W and Y were active had an HR frequency of 45 times per hour.

What a bizarre-looking passage! But now that we've seen all the ways around doing the most difficult and confusing parts of the Science Test, let's bring those to bear on this one.

And remember, even though Fighting Scientists is a little different from the other types of passages, our basic mantra still applies: *Don't understand the science. Just get the points.*

Read the Introduction

This "Introduction" is essentially the entire passage, so remember what our central task is in reading the introduction: *What are these scientists fighting about?*

The substance of the fight actually doesn't come until we get to Figure 3, where *Each of the four scientists then proposed individual models for the positions of the genes they studied, taking into account the findings in Table 1.*

As with any confusing figure, we'll wait for the questions to provide clarification of what we need to know.

In the meantime, there are figures in this particular passage, so let's do what we can with them. Figure 1 and Figure 3 are very confusing and don't seem to represent any "trends," so we'll ignore them for the moment.

Figure 2 and Table 1, however, show fairly consistent trends.

Figure 2

The variables are "number of proteins in cell" and "frequency of HR per hour."

The relationship between these variables is direct: as one increases, the other does as well.

Table 1

The variables are "HR (events per hour)" and "Distance between genes (centimorgans)."

There doesn't seem to be a relationship here, but if you reorder the Genes according to their HR, you will see a direct relationship: as HR increases, distance between genes increases as well.

Preview the Questions

Since we have more to work with than usual here, let's preview the questions to see if the relevant information is concentrated in any particular place.

Question 6 – Figure 3 (all four Scientists)
Question 7 – Figure 2
Question 8 – Scientist 2
Question 9 – Figure 3 (all four Scientists)
Question 10 – Passage
Question 11 – Figure 3 (all four Scientists)
Question 12 – Figure 1

Do One Hypothesis at a Time

While the hypotheses are not as distinct as we might like, we can see clearly from previewing the questions that we should begin with Figure 3, about which three of the questions ask.

We'll go first to Question 6.

---

6. All four models agree on the distance between which of the following pairs of genes?

    F.   Genes W and X
    G.   Genes W and Y
    H.   Genes X and Z
    J.   Genes Y and Z

Here's How to Crack It

This question gives us a simple indication of how to read Figure 3. Look at the distances between the letters. Let's use POE to figure out which pair of genes has the most consistent distance across the four models.

Genes W and X are nearly identical in models 1, 2, and 4. In model 3, the distance is the same, though the pair has been moved the left.

Genes W and Y are very far apart in models 1 and 2 but very close in models 3 and 4.

Genes X and Z are relatively far apart in models 1 and 3, but they are right next to each other in model 4.

Genes Y and Z are farther apart in model 1 than are any of the genes anywhere in the rest of the figure.

It would seem that the only pair with any consistency is that of Genes W and X, as (F) indicates.

––––––––––––––––○––––––––––––––––

The next question that deals with Figure 3 is Question 9.

––––––––––––––––○––––––––––––––––

9. The result of the final experiment studying the distance between Genes W and Y is consistent with models proposed by which of the following scientists?

   A. Scientists 1 and 3
   B. Scientists 2 and 4
   C. Scientists 2 and 3
   D. Scientists 3 and 4

Here's How to Crack It

This question draws on Figure 3, but it also requires that we read about the "final experiment" below Figure 3, where we learn that Genes W and Y had an HR frequency of 45 times per hour.

"HR (events per hour)" is shown in Table 1, where we have already seen that "HR" and "Distance between genes" have a direct relationship. Therefore, if the HR of Genes W and Y is 45, its distance between genes will be smaller than any of those shown in Table 1.

Because the figures are inexact, we will simply have to compare the different models. This comparison is relatively simple when we see that Scientists 1 and 2 have Genes W and Y farther apart than most or all of the other genes. Scientists 3 and 4 have W and Y a bit closer to one another, so (D) is the only possible answer.

Remember what we've been saying: *Don't understand the science!* The more willing you are to take the figures and tables at face value, the less likely you are to get caught up in things that may confuse you.

––––––––––––––––○––––––––––––––––

The last question that deals with all the scientists is Question 11.

––––––––––––––––○––––––––––––––––

11. Which scientist's model proposes that Genes Y and Z are separated by 65 centimorgans?

    A. Scientist 1's
    B. Scientist 2's
    C. Scientist 3's
    D. Scientist 4's

Here's How to Crack It

The distances between genes are not listed in Figure 3, but in Table 1, the largest distance listed is 30 centimorgans, the value given for the distance between genes X and Y.

Because we have nothing else to go on, we will need to find a model in which the distance between Genes Y and Z is nearly double that of Genes X and Y.

We don't have to look too carefully, as only Scientists 1 and 2 seem to give models in which the distance between Y and Z is larger than the distance between X and Y. Then, between these two, only Scientist 1's model shows a distance that is clearly more than double. Therefore, the correct answer must be (A), which gives Scientist 1's model as the correct one.

Question 8 seems to deal with many of the same topics, so let's go there next.

---

8. If Scientist 2's model is correct and an additional gene, Gene V, is 10 centimorgans from Gene X and 15 centimorgans from Gene Z, then Gene V is most likely between:

   F. Genes W and X.
   G. Genes W and Z.
   H. Genes X and Y.
   J. Genes X and Z.

Here's How to Crack It

As with any of the questions we've seen that deal with Figure 3, let's use POE as aggressively as we can. We're looking only at Scientist 2 in this question, and the question has told us that Gene V and Gene X are 10 centimorgans apart and Gene V and Gene Z are 15 centimorgans apart.

From Table 1, we know that the distance between W and X is 20 centimorgans. There's not enough space between W and X for V and Z to be 15 centimorgans apart, so eliminate (F). The same applies to (G) and (J).

This leaves only (H), which would place Gene V between Genes X and Y.

None of the remaining questions look easier than any others, so let's work them in order.

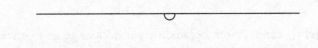

7. According to Figure 2, if some of the connective tissue cells had a protein count of 3,500 molecules per cell, the HR of these cells is most likely closest to which of the following?

   A. 50 events per hour
   B. 100 events per hour
   C. 150 events per hour
   D. 200 events per hour

Here's How to Crack It

What a refreshing question! Let's pull the information directly from the graph. The *x*-axis gives the number of proteins in thousands, so we will need to look between 3 and 4. At 3.5, the frequency of HR per hour is approximately 150, leaving (C) as the correct answer.

10. Based on the information provided, HR would occur when connective tissue cells are exposed to:

   F. growth media.
   G. sexual reproduction.
   H. asexual reproduction.
   J. X-rays.

Here's How to Crack It

Use lead words from the passage. Choices (G) and (H) both appear in the first paragraph, but they disappear in the discussion of HR that begins in the second paragraph.

HR stands for *homologous recombination*, which is a *repair process* that occurs *after radiation exposure*. Therefore, the closest answer of those given is (J), which is a form of radiation.

12. Genes A and B are separated by 10 centimorgans on a chromosome. An organism has alleles A and B* and 1 chromosome and alleles A* and B on the homologous chromosome. If a single HR event occurred between these 2 genes as shown in Figure 1, the genotype of Genes A and B for the 2 chromatids involved in the crossover would be:

F. AB and AB
G. AB and A*B*
H. A*B and AB*
J. A*B* and A*B*

Here's How to Crack It

This is a very difficult question that asks about a very difficult figure. But there are ways to keep it simple. First of all, there are four genes involved: A, B*, A*, and B. However, we end up rearranging them, so those four genes will still need to be there at the end.

Choices (F) and (J) cannot work because they introduce genes that were not present in the initial scenario.

Then, we can see that the * refers to a gene error, and the crossover process is used to fix pairs of genes that have errors. In other words, the whole process is done to eliminate the *. Choice (H) doesn't eliminate the *; it just moves the *. Choice (G), at least, creates one error-free pair out of the genes that were available at the beginning, so the correct answer must be (G).

Conclusion

Fighting Scientists passages can be very difficult, but if you rely on the basic principles of ACT Science along with the Basic Approach we've outlined in this chapter, you will be able to handle any pugnacious scientist that comes your way.

Let's recall the basic principles of ACT Science:

- Don't understand the science.
- Use POE.
- Let the questions teach you what you need to know about the passage.

Now try these strategies on your own. Go online to your
Student Tools and answer the Chapter 26 Drill.

Chapter 27
Science Test

SCIENCE TEST

DIRECTIONS: There are seven passages in this test. Each passage is followed by several questions. After reading a passage, choose the best answer to each question and fill in the corresponding oval on your answer document. You may refer to the passages as often as necessary.

You are NOT permitted to use a calculator on this test.

Passage I

Lean body mass (LBM) is an indicator of overall health. Low LBM increases the risk for heart disease, hypertension, diabetes, and other chronic health conditions. Scientists have established that LBM is linked to caloric consumption. Two studies, one with humans and one with mice, examined the effect of consuming high-calorie foods on LBM.

Study 1

A food-and-beverage questionnaire was given to 1,215 adult men and women with an average age of 42.2 years. Each individual was assigned to 1 of 5 groups according to his or her average daily caloric consumption. The average LBM for each group is illustrated in Figure 1.

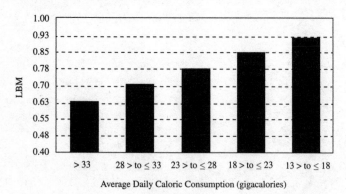

Figure 1

Study 2

Sixty 12-week-old mice were divided into 4 groups: Groups A and B consisted of 20 male and 20 female mice, respectively; Groups C and D consisted of 10 male and 10 female mice, respectively. Each mouse in Groups A and B was provided with drinking water, an unlimited supply of a solid, high-calorie food, and an unlimited supply of a solid, low-calorie food for 60 days. Mice in Groups C and D were provided with drinking water and an unlimited amount of solid, low-calorie food, but no high-calorie food, for 60 days. Figure 2 illustrates, for each group, the average daily weight of high-calorie food consumed per mouse, the average daily weight of low-calorie food consumed per mouse, and the average daily weight of total food consumed per mouse.

Note: Bars are stacked

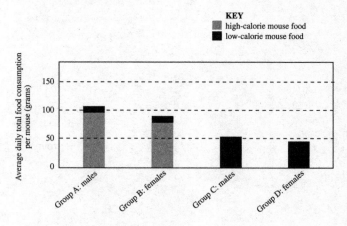

Figure 2

Figure 3 illustrates, for each group, the average LBM on Day 60.

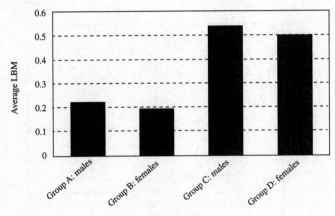

Figure 3

1. Based on the results of Study 2, on average, did male mice or did female mice consume less high-calorie food per day?

   A. Male mice; Group A mice, on average, consumed less high-calorie food per day than did Group B mice.

   B. Male mice; Group B mice, on average, consumed less high-calorie food per day than did Group A mice.

   C. Female mice; Group A mice, on average, consumed less high-calorie food per day than did Group B mice.

   D. Female mice; Group B mice, on average, consumed less high-calorie food per day than did Group A mice.

2. Which two groups of mice served as the control groups in Study 2?

   F. Group A and Group B

   G. Group C and Group D

   H. Group A and Group C

   J. Group B and Group D

3. In Study 2, the average daily total food consumption per mouse for Group C was approximately half that of the average daily total food consumption per mouse for Group A. Which of the following statements gives the most likely reason for this difference?

   A. The average daily total food consumption per mouse was lower for Group C because these mice were provided high-calorie food, and mice do not consume high-calorie food.

   B. The average daily total food consumption per mouse was greater for Group A because these mice preferred high-calorie food over low-calorie food.

   C. There were half as many mice in Group A as there were in Group C.

   D. There were half as many mice in Group C as there were in Group A.

4. In Study 1, the greatest number of people were assigned to the group with what average daily caloric consumption?

   F. > 33 gigacalories

   G. 18 > to ≤ 23 gigacalories

   H. 13 > to ≤ 18 gigacalories

   J. Cannot be determined from the given information

5. The LBMs of the subjects in Studies 1 and 2 were determined by average body composition scans. Based on Figures 1 and 3, was the average LBM for any group of mice greater than or less than the average LBM for any group of humans?

   A. Less; a mouse's body is less lean than is a human's body.

   B. Less; a mouse's body is leaner than is a human's body.

   C. Greater; a mouse's body is less lean than is a human's body.

   D. Greater; a mouse's body is leaner than is a humans' body.

Passage II

In an experiment to study the effect of the addition of various solutes on the freezing point of water, two identical, insulated containers without lids (Tank A and Tank B) were each fitted with a thermometer and a stirrer (Figure 1). Each tank was filled with 5 L of 15°C water. Both tanks were then placed in a freezer with a constant temperature of –35°C. The temperature from each thermometer was recorded every 30 minutes for 3 hours. During a second trial, 750 grams of sodium chloride (NaCl) was added to Tank A, and 750 grams of magnesium chloride ($MgCl_2$) was added to Tank B. The temperature from each thermometer was recorded as in the previous procedure (see Figures 2 and 3).

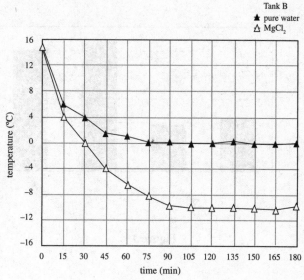

Figure 3

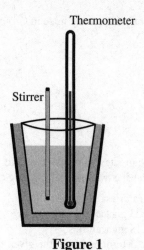

Figure 1

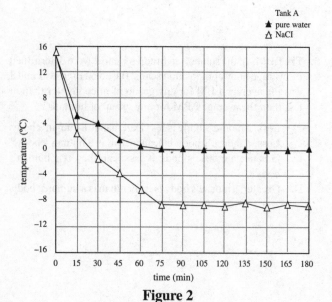

Figure 2

6. Over the 3 hours of the experiment, the temperature of the NaCl solution in Tank A:

F. decreased, then fluctuated up and down.
G. increased, then fluctuated up and down.
H. decreased, then remained constant.
J. increased, then remained constant.

7. Compared to the pure water in Tank B, the $MgCl_2$ solution took approximately how many more minutes, or how many fewer minutes, to reach 0°C?

A. 105 fewer minutes
B. 45 fewer minutes
C. 60 more minutes
D. 30 more minutes

8. Two bodies of water, Body A and Body B, are identical in all respects, except that Body A contains NaCl, and Body B contains $MgCl_2$. Based on the results of the experiment, during a prolonged period of –5°C weather, water in which body is *less* likely to begin freezing, and why?

F. Body A, because Figures 1 and 2 indicate that water containing NaCl freezes more slowly than does water containing $MgCl_2$.

G. Body A, because Figures 1 and 2 indicate that water containing NaCl freezes more quickly than does water containing $MgCl_2$.

H. Body B, because Figures 1 and 2 indicate that water containing NaCl freezes more slowly than does water containing $MgCl_2$.

J. Body B, because Figures 1 and 2 indicate that water containing NaCl freezes more quickly than does water containing $MgCl_2$.

9. Suppose that during the second trial, Tank B had been filled with NaCl rather than with $MgCl_2$. At 30 min, the temperature of the solution in Tank B would most likely have been:

A. greater than or equal to 0°C.
B. less than 0°C, but greater than or equal to –4°C.
C. less than –4°C, but greater than or equal to –8°C.
D. less than –8°C.

10. Suppose that when filled with pure water, both tanks were left in the freezer until the H_2O in each reached thermal equilibrium with the air in the freezer. Based on the passage, the temperature of the H_2O in each tank would most likely have been?

F. –15°C
G. –10°C
H. –8°C
J. 0°C

Passage III

When an object floats in a liquid, a portion of the object remains above the liquid's surface, while the remaining portion is submerged.

Seven objects with different specific gravities, ratios of the densities of these objects to the density of water at a given temperature, were placed in containers of 4 different liquids. Table 1 lists the objects and their specific gravities at 20°C.

Table 1	
Object	Specific gravity
A	0.200
B	0.300
C	0.400
D	0.500
E	0.600
F	0.700
G	0.800

Table 2 lists the 4 liquids and their specific gravities at 20°C.

Table 2	
Liquid	Specific gravity
Benzene	0.86
Butane	0.94
Water	1.00
Bromine	2.90

Figure 1 shows, for each liquid, a graph of the fraction of each object submerged below the liquid's surface versus the object's specific gravity.

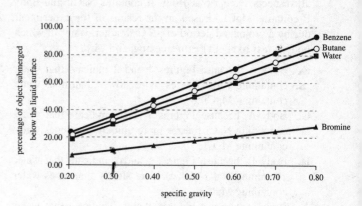

Figure 1

11. Based on Figure 1, for each liquid, as an object's specific gravity decreased, the percentage of the object submerged below the liquid's surface:

   A. increased only.
   B. decreased only.
   C. varied, but with no general trend.
   D. remained the same.

12. Based on Table 1 and Figure 1, the percentage of Object B submerged below the surface of the bromine was closest to which of the following values?

   F. 10
   G. 20
   H. 30
   J. 40

13. A cube is composed of a material with a specific gravity of 0.700 at 20°C. Each side of the cube is 10 cm long. The cube floats in a container of benzene. Based on Figure 1, what volume of the cube, in cm³, will be submerged below the surface of the benzene?

    A. 200 cm³
    B. 400 cm³
    C. 800 cm³
    D. 1,000 cm³

14. Suppose an object with a specific gravity of 1.00 floats in a container of water, and both the object and the water are at 20°C. If the temperatures of both the object and the water are raised to 85°C, and if the object neither expands nor contracts with the increase in temperature, will the object be more likely to sink or remain afloat?

    F. Remain afloat, because the water will become denser than the object.
    G. Remain afloat, because the water will become less dense than the object.
    H. Sink, because the water will become denser than the object.
    J. Sink, because the water will become less dense than the object.

15. What is the meaning of the value for the specific gravity of bromine that is given in Table 2 if the density of water at 20°C is 1 g/cm³ ?

    A. One cm³ of bromine has a mass of 2.90 g.
    B. One cm³ of bromine has a volume of 2.90 g.
    C. One g of bromine has a mass of 2.90 cm³.
    D. One g of bromine has a volume of 2.90 cm³.

Passage IV

Ceruloplasmin is a copper-carrying protein in the blood. When in the presence of copper ions (Cu^{2+}), each ceruloplasmin molecule will bind with Cu^{2+}. *Copper chelators* are used to remove excess copper in the blood because they can bind with and remove Cu^{2+} from ceruloplasmin.

Ceruloplasmin bound to Cu^{2+} strongly absorbs light at a wavelength of 560 nanometers (nm), but unbound ceruloplasmin and unbound Cu^{2+} do not. Three experiments were done using a *spectrophotometer* (a device that measures a solution's absorbance of light) to study the removal of Cu^{2+} from ceruloplasmin by copper chelators.

Experiment 1

Several solutions (Solutions A–G) were made all with an initial unbound ceruloplasmin concentration of 1 mole per liter (M), but each with a different initial unbound Cu^{2+} concentration. The solutions were incubated at 37°C for 60 min. A test tube containing a sample of Solution A was placed in a spectrophotometer. The spectrophotometer was adjusted such that the absorbance reading measured at 560 nm for Solution A at 37°C was 0.00. The absorbance at 560 nm of each of Solutions B–G at 37°C was then measured (see Table 1).

Table 1		
Solution	Initial unbound Cu^{2+} concentration (M)	Absorbance
A	0	0
B	0.25	0.25
C	0.5	0.45
D	0.75	0.56
E	1.00	0.60
F	1.25	0.60
G	1.50	0.61

Experiment 2

For each of 4 trials, 0.1 mL of solution that contained 100 millimoles of 1 of 4 copper chelators was added to 1 mL of Solution F. The absorbance at 560 nm was then monitored at 37°C over the next 60 minutes (see Figure 1).

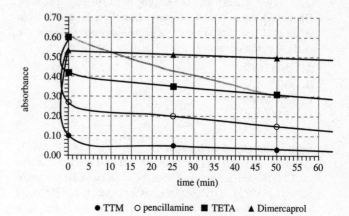

● TTM ○ pencillamine ■ TETA ▲ Dimercaprol

Figure 1

Experiment 3

The TTM trial in Experiment 2 was repeated twice, except that one trial was carried out at 20°C and the other trial was carried out at 35°C (see Figure 2).

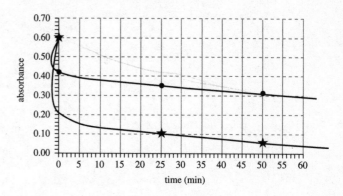

★ 35° C   ● 20° C

Figure 2

16. When a spectrophotometer is used, a solution called a *blank* is first placed in the spectrophotometer to establish a baseline value against which other solutions will be measured. Which of the solutions served as the blank?

    F. Solution G
    G. Solution D
    H. Solution B
    J. Solution A

17. In each trial of Experiments 2 and 3, how many absorbance measurements were recorded?

    A. 5 measurements
    B. 10 measurements
    C. 13 measurements
    D. 18 measurements

18. Based on the experiment, as the concentration of Cu^{2+} bound to ceruloplasmin in a solution *increases*, the absorbance:

    F. increases only.
    G. decreases only.
    H. varies, but with no general trend.
    J. remains constant.

19. Based on the results of Experiments 2 and 3, the average rate of change in the absorbance during the TETA trial was closest to that observed during the trial with what other copper chelator and at what temperature?

    A. TTM at 20°C
    B. TTM at 35°C
    C. Dimercaprol at 25°C
    D. Dimercaprol at 37°C

20. Suppose that in Experiment 1, 20 mL of Solution B had been mixed with 20 mL of Solution D after the solutions were incubated. If the absorbance of a sample of the resulting solution had been measured at 37°C, it would most likely have been closest to which of the following?

    F. 0.00
    G. 0.25
    H. 0.45
    J. 0.60

17:35

Passage V

In order to produce pharmaceuticals that are ready for administration, drugs are passed through *microfiltration membranes* to aid in the removal of bacteria and viruses from the products. This process is called *microfiltration*. These bacteria and viruses tend to counteract the health benefits of drugs. In pharmaceutical drugs, a bacterial content at or above 300×10^{-7} colony forming units (cfu)/cm^2 is considered unsafe.

Three studies investigated how filter pore size, *filtration time* (the length of time over which the drug products were cycled through the microfiltration membrane at a constant rate), temperature, and irradiation of the drug products affected the removal of bacterial content.

Study 1

Three 100 mL samples of a liquid drug product were prepared, all having the same temperature but each passing through one of three filter pore sizes: 100 µg/L, 250 µg/L, or 350 µg/L. Each sample was passed in a repeating circuit through the microfiltration membrane at the same rate of 100 mL sample/hr for 60 min. At various times during the microfiltration, a small amount of drug product was taken out of each container and analyzed for bacterial content (see Figure 1).

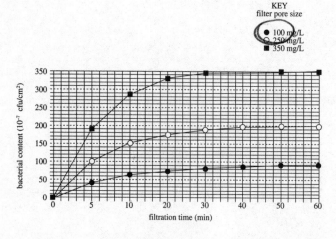

Figure 1

Study 2

Three 100 mL samples were all prepared passing through the same filter pore size of 250 µg/L but each heated to a different temperature: 100°C, 200°C, or 300°C. Each sample was then analyzed for bacterial content as in Study 1 (see Figure 2).

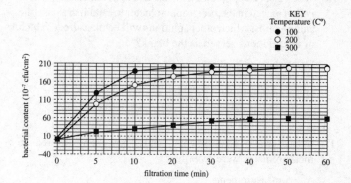

Figure 2

Study 3

Two 100 mL samples were prepared, both passing through a filter pore size of 250 µg/L and heated to a temperature of 100°C. One of the samples was irradiated prior to filtration. The other sample was not exposed to radiation. Each sample was analyzed for bacterial content as in Study 1 (see Figure 3).

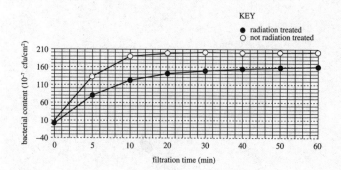

Figure 3

21. According to the results of Study 1, for a filter pore size of 100 µg/L or 250 µg/L, as filtration time increased, bacterial content:

   A. increased only.
   B. decreased only.
   C. decreased, then increased.
   D. increased, then decreased.

22. Suppose that in Study 1 a 100 mL water sample passing through a filter pore size of 200 µg/L and the same temperature as the other 3 samples had also been tested. At a filtration time of 10 min, the bacterial content for this sample would most likely have been:

   F. less than 75 cfu/cm^2.
   G. between 75 cfu/cm^2 and 150 cfu/cm^2.
   H. between 150 cfu/cm^2 and 200 cfu/cm^2.
   J. greater than 200 cfu/cm^2.

23. According to the results of Studies 1–3, from 0 min until 60 min, how often was a small amount of drug product taken out of each container and its bacterial content recorded?

   A. Every 5 sec
   B. Every 30 sec
   C. Every 1 min
   D. Every 5 min

24. According to the results of Study 3, for filtration times after 0 min, how did the radiation treatment on the drug product affect its bacterial content, if at all?

   F. At all times after 0 min, the bacterial content was greater with the radiation treatment than it was without the radiation treatment.
   G. At all times after 0 min, the bacterial content was the same with the radiation treatment as it was without the radiation treatment.
   H. At all times after 0 min, the bacterial content was less with the radiation treatment than it was without the radiation treatment.
   J. At some of the times after 0 min, the bacterial content was less with the radiation treatment than it was without the radiation treatment; at other times after 0 min, the bacterial content was greater with the radiation treatment than it was without the radiation treatment.

25. What variable had the same value for all the drug products in Study 1 but did not have the same value for all the drug products in Study 2?

   A. Bacterial content
   B. Filter pore size
   C. Sample temperature
   D. Radiation exposure

Passage VI

In two studies, students recorded the viscosity changes that occurred in different liquid polymers when polymer chains were *cross-linked*, or linked together, by one of three different methods.

For each trial in the studies, the students prepared a set of solutions of polyvinyl alcohol (PVA) and a set of solutions of polyacrylamide. The polyacrylamide solutions were prepared by the addition of 50 mg of acrylamide to 50 mL of water at 4°C. Both solutions were allowed to sit overnight for 12 hours. The samples were then cross-linked. An example of cross-linking using a chemical agent is shown in Figure 1.

Figure 1

At a temperature of 120°C, the students stirred the cross-linking agents with the samples of PVA and polyacrylamide. Over a period of 20 hours, the students observed and computed the velocity of a small metal sphere as it fell through the various substances. The density and velocity of this sphere was used with the densities of the various substances to calculate the values of η, viscosity, for each of the substances.

Study 1

The students computed the PVAs viscosity at each of several selected percentages of cross-linking, first with 60 micrograys of gamma radiation, then with maleic acid, and finally with glutaraldehyde. Plots of the PVAs η versus the percentage cross-linking for this study are shown in Figure 2.

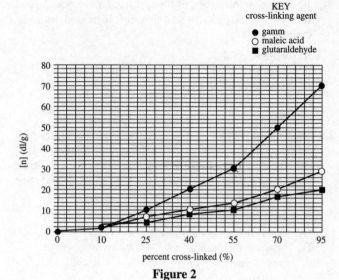

KEY
cross-linking agent

● gamm
○ maleic acid
■ glutaraldehyde

Figure 2

Study 2

The students computed the polyacrylamide's viscosity at each of several selected percentages of cross-linking. They conducted trials with 60 micrograys of gamma radiation, then with maleic acid, though the glutaraldehyde was replaced with 100 micrograys of gamma radiation. Plots of the polyacrylamide's η versus the percentage of cross-linking for this study are shown in Figure 3.

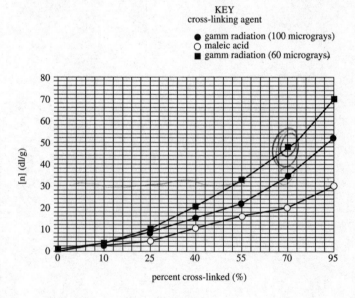

KEY
cross-linking agent

● gamm radiation (100 micrograys)
○ maleic acid
■ gamm radiation (60 micrograys)

Figure 3

26. According to the results of the studies, for a given cross-linking agent and a given substance, as the percent of the substance that was cross-linked increased, η:

F. increased only.
G. decreased only.
H. remained the same.
J. varied, but with no general trend.

27. Based on the results of the studies, to obtain the *highest* η at 55% cross-linking by the process diagrammed in the passage, the students should select which substance and which cross-linking agent?

substance	cross-linking agent
A. polyvinyl alcohol	gamma radiation (60 micrograys)
B. polyvinyl alcohol	glutaraldehyde
C. polyacrylamide	gamma radiation (60 micrograys)
D. polyacrylamide	maleic acid

28. The students stirred each substance for which of the following reasons?

F. To encourage a higher percentage of cross-linking
G. To prevent the small metal sphere from contacting the cross-linking agent
H. To prevent the temperature of the substance from fluctuating
J. To ensure that the cross-linking agent was equally distributed throughout the substance

29. Suppose that, in Study 1, the students had also tested a fourth cross-linking agent, Agent A, at 55% cross-linking, and determined that the substance's η was 22 dl/g. Based on Figure 2, if the students had next tested Agent A at 70% cross-linking, η would most likely have been:

A. less than 10 dl/g.
B. between 10 dl/g and 20 dl/g.
C. between 20 dl/g and 50 dl/g.
D. greater than 50 dl/g.

30. Based on Study 2, when polyacrylamide was 70% cross-linked with 60 micrograys of gamma radiation, its η was how much greater than when it was 70% cross-linked with 100 micrograys of gamma radiation?

F. 15 dl/g
G. 20 dl/g
H. 35 dl/g
J. 50 dl/g

Passage VII

Supergiant stars are much brighter and more massive than Earth's Sun. Supergiant stars form within *stellar nurseries*—dense regions of rotating clouds of gas and dust in space. Star formation begins when a cloud of gas begins to collapse under its own gravitational attraction, radiating energy and forming a *protostar*. Two scientists discuss how supergiant stars like Deneb initially form from protostars in stellar nurseries.

Scientist 1

A protostar continuously emits energy in the form of hydrogen, gradually reducing the amount of hydrogen in its core. If a protostar's core is depleted of hydrogen and that star is at least 10 times the mass of the Sun (M_s), it can expand and form helium and other elements within its core. The formation of a $0.5\ M_s$ protostar requires between 1 and 5 million years. The time required for a $0.5\ M_s$ protostar to grow to exceed $10\ M_s$ and thus become a supergiant star like Deneb, must occur in at least 100 million years. Because the conditions of the formation of a supergiant star, such as Deneb, are so particular, supergiant stars are relatively rare in our galaxy.

Scientist 2

less time

Supergiant stars form in stellar nurseries if gas pressure produced by a molecular cloud causes a collapse of the protostar, which then forms *actively accreting disc jets* (AADJ), which can form only if the protostar's mass does not exceed $5\ M_s$. An AADJ forms in less than 5 million years. After formation, the AADJ quickly forms the supergiant star. Through AADJ-forming, the entire process from protostar to supergiant takes less than 5 million years.

Supergiant stars like Deneb would not have time to form as described by Scientist 1. Observations indicate that active molecular gas clouds do not stay in existence for longer than 30 million years after the beginning of gravitational collapse. Also, protostars that exceed $10\ M_s$ and do not form AADJs are torn apart by their own rotational momentum, fusing with material accumulating in regions surrounding other growing protostars. Supergiant stars are not rare. Hundreds of supergiant stars as large as or larger than Deneb have been detected in our galaxy.

31. What are the two scientists' estimates of the mass of a protostar that later becomes a supergiant?

	Scientist 1	Scientist 2
A.	at least $10\ M_s$	at most $5\ M_s$
B.	at least $5\ M_s$	at most $10\ M_s$
C.	exactly $10\ M_s$	exactly $5\ M_s$
D.	exactly $5\ M_s$	exactly $10\ M_s$

32. Based on Scientist 1's discussion, which of the following statements gives the most likely reason the Sun is not a supergiant star? At the time the Sun was forming in a stellar nursery, the:

F. stellar nursery did not contain a dense enough cloud of gas or dust to produce any supergiant stars.

G. stellar nursery contained a dense enough cloud of gas or dust to produce only 3 supergiant stars.

H. protostar that became the Sun was not massive enough to begin to produce helium and other elements within its core.

J. protostar that became the Sun was massive enough to begin to produce helium and other elements within its core.

33. The discovery that some active molecular gas clouds remain in existence for more than 50 million years after their gravitational collapse would *contradict* a statement made by:

A. Scientist 1 only.

B. Scientist 2 only.

C. both Scientist 1 and Scientist 2.

D. neither Scientist 1 nor Scientist 2.

34. Suppose a protostar has, over the course of 75 million years, grown to 8 M_s in mass. Would Scientist 1 be likely to claim that this protostar that has grown to 8 M_s is a supergiant star like Deneb?

    F. Yes, because Scientist 1 claims that a protostar must grow to over 10 M_s or more in order to become a supergiant star.

    G. Yes, because Scientist 1 claims that a protostar cannot grow to over 10 M_s in order to become a supergiant star.

    H. No, because Scientist 1 claims that a protostar must grow to over 10 M_s or more in order to become a supergiant star.

    J. No, because Scientist 1 claims that a protostar cannot grow to over 10 M_s in order to become a supergiant star.

35. The discovery of which of the following objects would provide the strongest support for Scientist 2's viewpoint?

    A. Very few supergiant stars, formed from molecular gas clouds that have been collapsing for more than 50 million years

    B. Many supergiant stars, formed from molecular gas clouds that have collapsed in under 25 years

    C. Very few supergiant stars, formed from molecular gas clouds that have collapsed in under 25 years

    D. Many supergiant stars, formed from molecular gas clouds that have been collapsing for more than 50 million years

Chapter 28
Science Test:
Answers and
Explanations

ANSWER KEY

Passage I	Passage II	Passage III	Passage IV	Passage V	Passage VI	Passage VII
1. D	6. F	11. B	16. J	21. A	26. F	31. A
2. G	7. B	12. F	17. C	22. G	27. C	32. H
3. B	8. J	13. C	18. F	23. D	28. J	33. B
4. J	9. B	14. J	19. A	24. H	29. C	34. H
5. A	10. J	15. A	20. H	25. C	30. F	35. B

$$\frac{33}{35}$$

SCIENCE TEST EXPLANATIONS

Passage I

1. **D** Figure 2 shows the amount of food that each group of mice has consumed. The high-calorie mouse food is shown by the bottom, gray portion of the bars of Groups A and B. According to these bars, male mice (Group A) consumed approximately 90 grams, and female mice (Group B) consumed approximately 75 grams. Choice (D) correctly identifies the group that consumed less and gives the correct reasoning.

2. **G** This experiment seeks to understand how much high-calorie food the mice will consume if given a choice between high-calorie and low-calorie food. Groups C and D are given only low-calorie food as a baseline against which Groups A and B can be tested. Groups C and D are therefore the control groups in this experiment, as (G) suggests.

3. **B** The major difference between Groups A and C is that Group A is given both low- and high-calorie food where Group C is given only low-calorie food. The number of mice is the same in both groups, eliminating (C) and (D). Then, (A) can also be eliminated because the data show that mice *do* consume high-calorie food. Only (B) remains: the data show that when mice are given a choice between low- and high-calorie foods, those mice eat more total food.

4. **J** While the group that consumed an average of 13 > to ≤ 18 gigacalories has the largest bar in the graph, this bar represents LBM, not number of people in each group. In fact, the number of people in each group cannot be determined from the graphs or the passage, leaving (J) as the only possible answer.

5. **A** According to Figure 3, the maximum LBM for mice (as shown in Groups 3 and 4) is approximately 0.55. According to Figure 1, the minimum LBM for humans is approximately 0.65. Therefore, mice have a lower LBM, eliminating (C) and (D), and a lower LBM means less lean body mass, eliminating (B). Choice (A) correctly reflects the data in the figures.

Passage II

6. **F** According to Figure 1, the temperature of the NaCl decreased from 0 min to 75 min, after which point it fluctuated until the 180-min mark. This trend is described in (F).

7. **B** According to Figure 2, the $MgCl_2$ solution reached 0° after 30 min, and the pure water reached 0° after 75 min. Therefore, the $MgCl_2$ solution took 45 fewer minutes to reach 0°, as (B) indicates.

8. J   Given the data in the table, Body A will act in a way similar to that of the NaCl solution in Figure 1, and Body B will act in a way similar to that of the $MgCl_2$ solution in Figure 2. According to Figure 1, the NaCl solution takes between 15 and 30 minutes to reach 0°, and according to Figure 2, the $MgCl_2$ solution takes 30 minutes. The NaCl solution freezes more quickly than the $MgCl_2$ solution, which means that Body B is *less* likely to begin freezing than Body A, as (J) suggests.

9. B   Tank B, shown in Figure 2, contains no NaCl, but if the $MgCl_2$ in Tank B is replaced with NaCl, then the solution will behave identically to the NaCl solution in Figure 1. In Figure 1, after 30 min, the NaCl solution has a temperature between 0 and −4°C. It can be inferred that these results would carry over to Tank B in this situation as well, making (B) the correct answer.

10. J   Although the freezers are set to a constant temperature of −35°C, Figures 1 and 2 indicate that the temperature of pure water never goes below 0°C. Therefore, once the water reaches thermal equilibrium with the much colder freezer, it will have a temperature of 0°C, as (J) indicates.

Passage III

11. B   Figure 1 shows a direct relationship. As the object's specific gravity decreases, the percentage of it that is submerged in the solution decreases. There are no exceptions in the figure, meaning that (B), decreased only, is the correct answer.

12. F   According to Table 1, Object B has a specific gravity of 0.300. According to Figure 1, an object with a specific gravity of 0.300 will be approximately 10% submerged in a bromine solution, as (F) suggests.

13. C   If a cube has three sides of 10 cm, the cube will have a volume of 1,000 cm³ because the volume of a cube can be found by cubing one of its sides. The rest of the relevant data can be found on the chart. The cube in this question has a specific gravity of 0.700. According to Figure 1, because the cube is floating in benzene, approximately 80% of it will be submerged. The cube has a volume of 1000 cm³, which means that 80% of that, or 800 cm³, will be submerged, as (C) indicates.

14. J   This question requires a bit of outside knowledge. As the water heats up, it will become less dense. Think of it this way: it's easier to dissolve sugar in a hot drink than in a cold one because the hot drink is less dense than the cold one. In this question, as the water heats up, it will become less dense, leading the object (whose density will be unaffected) to sink rather than continue to remain afloat.

15. A   According to the introduction, specific gravity is the ratio of the density of an object to the density of water at a given temperature. According to Table 2, bromine has a specific gravity of 2.90. Given the specific-gravity ratio, then, for every 1 g/cm³ of water, there will be 2.90 g/cm³ of bromine. Use the units to answer the question: there are 2.90 g in each 1 cm³ of bromine, as (A) indicates.

Passage IV

16. **J** Without using the word, this question is essentially asking for the control of the experiment. Solution A seems like a reasonable candidate with its value of 0.00, and the introduction confirms it: *A test tube containing a sample of Solution A was placed in a spectrophotometer. The spectrophotometer was adjusted such that the absorbance reading measured at 560 nm for Solution A at 37°C was 0.00.* Solution A is thus the standard against which others are judged, making the correct answer (J).

17. **C** Count the dots. There are 13 measurements in each graph, or (C). While it may seem like there are twelve because measurements are made in 5-minute increments for 60 minutes, don't forget that 0 minutes is also a measurement.

18. **F** According to Table 1, as the concentration increases, the absorbance does as well. The correct answer is (F).

19. **A** Match the curves. Figure 1 shows a variety of chelators at 37°C. On this same graph, dimercaprol does not decrease as quickly as does TETA, thus eliminating (D). Figure 2 shows TTM at two different temperatures: 20°C and 35°C. Select a few points to see that the TTM curve at 20°C matches almost identically with the TETA curve at 37°C. The best answer is therefore (A).

20. **H** Given that Table 1 shows the values of different 20 mL solutions at 37°C, we can ignore the initial concentration and temperature values and simply work with the numbers on the chart. Solution B has an absorbance of 0.25. Solution D has an absorbance of 0.56. If the two were mixed, the new solution's absorbance would be between these two values, as only (H) is.

Passage V

21. **A** Figure 1 shows a direct relationship. For all variables, as the filtration time increases, the bacterial content increases as well. Choice (A) accurately describes this trend.

22. **G** Figure 1 shows a direct relationship. For all variables, as the filtration time increases, the bacterial content increases as well. The bacterial content values also increase with filter pore size (described in the Key). Therefore, a filter pore size of 200 µg/L will have bacterial content values between those of 100 µg/L and 250 µg/L. At 10 min, the 100 µg/L filter pore size has a bacterial content of approximately 75 cfu/cm², and the 250 µg/L filter pore size has a bacterial content of approximately 150 cfu/cm². The bacterial content for a 200 µg/L filter pore size should fall between these values, as (G) suggests.

23. **D** Pay attention to the units on the axes and the frequency with which the data points occur. Each of the x-axes gives filtration time in minutes, and the data points occur in intervals of 5 minutes, as (D) indicates.

24. **H** Figure 3 shows a clear relationship between radiation treatment and bacterial content: the sample treated with radiation had a consistently lower bacterial content than the sample that was not radiation treated. Choice (H) accurately describes this relationship.

25. **C** This information can be inferred from the graphs: the filter pore size changes in Study 1 and the temperature changes in Study 2. Based on this information alone, the answer is (C), as the temperature in Study 1 would have remained constant to test the bacterial content of various filter pore sizes. This inference is confirmed with the following information from the passage: *Three 100 mL samples of a liquid drug product were prepared, all having the same temperature but each passing through one of three filter pore sizes: 100 µg/L, 250 µg/L, and 350 µg/L.*

Passage VI

26. **F** Both figures show a direct relationship. As the % cross-linked increases, so too does η. In this question, the only answer that reflects this relationship is (F).

27. **C** Work with the substance first. According to Figures 1 and 2, the η for polyacrylamide is consistently higher than that of PVA. This eliminates (A) and (B). Then, the η is higher for polyacrylamide when gamma radiation is used than when maleic acid is used, making (C) the correct answer. The η with this combination when 55% cross-linked is just over 30 dl/g, which is higher than any value of PVA at the same cross-linkage.

28. **J** Stirring is typically done to ensure some kind of consistency, to make sure that substances combine in an even way. There is no indication that stirring would encourage cross-linkage, eliminating (F). If the small metal sphere does not touch the cross-linking agent at all, then no viscosity reading would be possible, eliminating (G). According to the introduction, the temperature was held at a constant 120°C, so the stirring (which is mentioned earlier) would not have ensured that this temperature remained consistent, eliminating (H). Only (J) remains: the students want to ensure that the substance and the cross-linking agent mix as thoroughly as possible to gain the most accurate possible readings of viscosity.

29. **C** In Figure 1, at a cross-linking of 55%, Agent A would fall between the 55% readings of maleic acid and gamma radiation. It can be assumed, then, that Agent A's reading would also fall between these cross-linking agents at 70%, or between 20 dl/g and 50 dl/g, as (C) suggests.

30. **F** When polyacrylamide is 70% linked with 60 micrograys of gamma radiation, its η is 50 dl/g. When polyacrylamide is 70% linked with 100 micrograys of gamma radiation, its η is approximately 35 dl/g. Its η at 60 micrograys is therefore approximately 15 dl/g greater than its η at 100 micrograys, as (F) indicates.

Passage VII

31. **A**   Scientist 1 writes, *The time required for a 0.5 M_s protostar to grow to exceed 10 M_s and thus become a supergiant star like Deneb.* The word *thus* indicates that the mass of *10 M_s* is essential to become a supergiant. As such, (A) is the only answer that can work, because it is the only answer that gives a correct value for Scientist 1.

32. **H**   Scientist 1 writes, *If a protostar's core is depleted of hydrogen and that star is at least 10 times the mass of the Sun (M_s), it can expand and form helium and other elements within its core.* This then leads to the formation of supergiant stars. The Sun cannot be a supergiant star because it is not massive enough, and it therefore cannot expand and form helium and other elements within its core, a concept reflected in (H).

33. **B**   Scientist 2 writes the following: *Observations indicate that active molecular gas clouds do not stay in existence for longer than 30 million years after the beginning of gravitational collapse.* If there were new information suggesting that molecular gas clouds could stay in existence 50 million years after the beginning of gravitational collapse, this would contradict Scientist 2, as (B) suggests.

34. **H**   For Scientist 1, a protostar must grow to 10 M_s in mass before it can be considered a supergiant star, so Scientist 1 would *not* consider the star in this question a supergiant star. This eliminates (F) and (G). Choice (H) gives the correct reason as to why Scientist 1 would disagree.

35. **B**   There are numerous POE opportunities within this question, and the most straightforward actually comes in the first part. While Scientist 1 claims that supergiant stars are extremely rare, Scientist 2 claims, *Supergiant stars are not rare. Hundreds of supergiant stars as large as or larger than Deneb have been detected in our galaxy.* Therefore, Scientist 2 would be supported by the existence of "many supergiant stars" rather than "very few supergiant stars," thus eliminating (A) and (C). Scientist 2 adds, *Observations indicate that active molecular gas clouds do not stay in existence for longer than 30 million years after the beginning of gravitational collapse,* so a number indicating a post-collapse time of over 50 million years could not work, eliminating (D) and leaving us with (B).

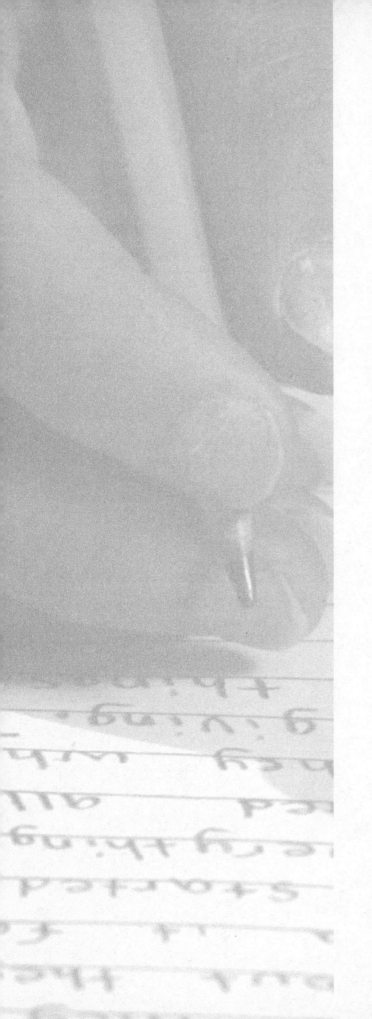

Part VI
ACT Writing

Chapter 29
Writing

The ACT includes an optional Writing Test. The Writing Test is optional because some schools want it, and some don't care either way. That said, the most competitive schools nearly always want the Writing Test, and you can't take it on its own if you later find that you need it (you'd have to take the whole ACT again), so you should probably take it. That's annoying, we know, but here are some tips to help you get a great score on the essay.

THE OPTIONAL-ISH WRITING TEST

The ACT Writing Test is optional, but unfortunately, the "option" is not exactly yours. After all, few of us would voluntarily take an extra forty-minute section. But many of the schools you're applying to require the Writing Test. Even if you're not sure, we still recommend that you take this additional essay, for the following reasons:

- Many schools require that you take the Writing Test. You wouldn't want to have to take the entire test over again because you opted out of the Writing Test.
- A Writing score can make your college application more attractive, even to those schools that don't require it. Your essay score will appear on every score report you send to colleges. Every school you apply to will see that you took the initiative to opt in for the Writing Test, which is a good thing. Think of it like Honors or AP classes. You don't have to take them, but it looks good if you do.

Not yet convinced? The biggest reason of all is that it's just not that hard to get a good score on the Writing test. An impressive score is an impressive score, optional or not.

ALRIGHT, YOU CONVINCED ME... NOW WHAT?

The ACT Writing Test consists of a single essay, which you are given 40 minutes to write. The big question will have to do with something ACT deems socially relevant. The question will not be relevant only for high-school students ("Are school uniforms the best?") nor so grandiose and abstract as to be basically unanswerable ("Is it always cruel to be kind in the right measure?").

A typical prompt will look something like this:

Education and the Workplace

Many colleges and universities have cut their humanities departments, and high schools have begun to shift their attention much more definitively toward STEM (Science, Technology, Engineering, Mathematics) and away from ELA (English, Language Arts). Representatives from both school boards and government organizations suggest that the move toward STEM is necessary in helping students to participate in a meaningful way in the American workplace. Given the urgency of this debate for the future of education and society as a whole, it is worth examining the potential consequences of this shift in how students are educated in the United States.

Read and carefully consider these perspectives. Each suggests a particular way of thinking about the shift in American education.

Perspective One	Perspective Two	Perspective Three
ELA programs should be emphasized over STEM programs. Education is not merely a means to employ-ment: ELA education helps students to live more mean-ingful lives. In addition, an exclusively STEM-based program cannot help but limit students' creativity and lead them to overemphasize the importance of money and other tangible gains.	ELA programs should be eradicated entirely, except to establish the basic literacy necessary to engage in the hard sciences, mathematics, and business. Reading and writing are activities that are best saved for the leisure of students who enjoy them.	ELA and STEM programs should always be in equal balance with one another. Both are necessary to provid-ing a student with a well-rounded education. Moreover, equal emphasis will allow the fullest possible exposure to many subjects before stu-dents choose their majors and careers.

Essay Task

Write a unified, coherent essay in which you evaluate multiple perspectives on the issue of how schools should balance ELA and STEM subjects. In your essay, be sure to:

- analyze and evaluate the perspectives given
- state and develop your own perspective on the issue
- explain the relationship between your perspective and those given

Your perspective may be in full agreement with any of the others, in partial agree-ment, or wholly different. Whatever the case, support your ideas with logical rea-soning and detailed, persuasive examples.

Here's How to Crack It

Your job is to write an essay in which you take some sort of position on the prompt, all while assessing the three perspectives provided in the boxes. ACT has hinted at the larger significance of the prompt, but you should also, if possible, give some indication of how you understand that significance.

This may be unlike essays you've written in your English classes. You're probably more used to answering some big question about a book or some ethical question. This time the question is, in a sense, already answered, so you need to be the moderator of the discussion. The idea behind such an exercise is that, in college, you will be required to take a variety of perspectives on some issue, assess those perspectives, and add your own. This is good practice: as you'll find in your college writing classes, essays are much less about coming up with the single correct answer than they are about *contributing to the conversation.*

Even if you have had to do something like this before, you probably haven't had to do it in 40 minutes. That's really not a lot of time, so throughout this chapter, we'll give you some tips for how to get a great score even with the time constraints.

A Note on Arguments

You'll notice that ACT has placed a very explicit emphasis on the terms *argument* and *perspective.* These are terms that you assuredly already know, but the way these terms are used in everyday speech differs a lot from how they are used among English teachers and academics.

It's important to note that ACT is very careful to ask for your *perspective* rather than your *opinion.* That careful choice of language is there for your benefit. An argument can be a difficult thing to construct because it doesn't just take into account what you think: it requires a more complex understanding of the topic at hand.

The crucial thing about arguments is this:

> In order for a statement to be an *argument*, it must be possible to disagree with that statement.

Think about it this way. As you were reading the prompt above, you might have been thinking, "Great! I hate my English class!" or "Bummer! I hate my math class!" So you might think it would be good to center your essay on this kind of statement:

I don't like to read, so I like the idea of having to take fewer English classes.

That is an opinion, but it's not an *argument*. In order for it to be an argument, it would have to be possible to disagree with it. And go ahead and try to disagree with the italicized sentence. What could you say? "Yes, you do like to read!" or "No, you don't like the idea!" This isn't a real argument, and that's because the statement that started it (the italicized one) isn't a real argument itself.

The same goes for statements that are too large, like this one:

The question of how to balance ELA and STEM classes is an interesting one.

Or this one:

All three of the perspectives provided are interesting.

Think about what kinds of conversations these statements begin. How would you respond? Probably something along the lines of, "Um… yep" or "Okay." Not much of a conversation, is it? That's because it hasn't started with an *argument*.

If you can find a way to anchor your essay with some argument, some unique perspective of your own that can be defended and debated, you are already in the upper echelon of scorers. Although it may seem like a minor point, the quality of the *argument* at the center of your essay will go a long way to predicting your score.

WHAT THE GRADERS ARE GRADING

If you think you have a tough job writing an essay in only 40 minutes, have some sympathy for the graders. They have to grade each essay in a matter of minutes. Imagine how you would feel if you spent an entire day grading thousands of essays on the same topic. By essay number 50 or so, you probably wouldn't care much if a student used "except" instead of "accept."

ACT graders focus on the big picture. Your essay will be read by two graders, each of whom will assign it a series of four subscores, each from 1 to 6. Their scores will be combined and then scaled into a score of 1–36. The scores will be based on how closely the essay adheres to the standards shown below.

Given the complexity of this grading system, it's best to think about these graders as grading *holistically*. In other words, they grade the essay as a whole, rather than keeping tabs on every little success or failure within the essay itself. To give one simple example, if you've got a few misspellings in the essay, that won't hurt you that much, but if your grammar and spelling are so messy that the grader doesn't know what you're saying, your Language Use and Conventions score will suffer.

ACT Graders vs. English Teachers
The graders who grade for ACT aren't like your English teachers. They don't have the time to focus on the little details of each essay, and frankly, they don't care about your grade the way your English teacher does. So don't sweat the small stuff! Focus on the big picture for the ACT: strong argument, engagement with multiple perspectives, solid examples, and neatness.

According to the ACT guidelines, essay graders give scores in the following four categories.

1. **Ideas and Analysis:** Above all else, graders want to see that you can handle complex ideas. This essentially refers to how skilled you are at constructing an argument and assessing the arguments of others. You won't be graded on whether you pick the "right" answer (there isn't one). Instead, you'll be graded on how complex and sophisticated your answers are.

2. **Development and Support:** It's tough to make an argument without citing some examples. Graders want to see that you can justify the positions you're presenting in a given essay. This applies to how you assess the three given perspectives as well: nothing damages your interlocutor's argument like a killer counterexample.

3. **Organization:** In order to make sure that your graders can see the complexity of your ideas and the quality of the support you provide for them, you need to make sure your essay is organized in a way that makes that easy. Your essay should be a vehicle to help your readers see how freakin' smart you are. If you don't organize the essay well or effectively, your readers won't be able to see your brilliance in its full and effervescent luminousness.

4. **Language Use and Conventions:** Writing is all about *communication*. If your use of the language is coated with grammatical errors and misspellings, your writing won't communicate the way that it should. Graders will forgive a few stray errors, but if your grammar and spelling get in the way of what you're trying to say, those mistakes could cost you.

HOW TO GET A GOOD SCORE

Give the graders what they want! You may be a great writer, but the ACT graders are only concerned with a few very specific things.

The way to get a good score on the Writing Test is to make the graders' job easy. Show that you understand the perspectives and can generate one of your own. Show that you can support your ideas with examples, real or hypothetical. Show that you can arrange your essay in a way that makes sense. Show that you can use the English language correctly. This may seem like a tall order, but in the next few pages, we'll talk about how to write an essay that is most pleasing to your graders.

It can be very intimidating to think that you have to keep all of this in mind as you write a 40-minute essay. It helps, though, if you remember that this essay is part of the ACT, and what do you typically have to do on the ACT? Fill in bubbles. Think of this essay as just another one of those bubbles: all the pieces should basically be in place before you even get to the test.

THE APPROACH

You may not know what the prompt will ask about, but you can at least go into the test with a consistent approach. You can approach each prompt the same way, and your essay can look very similar each time.

Just remember these four basic steps:

The Basic Approach for the Writing Test

1. Work the Prompt
2. Work the Perspectives
3. Generate Your Own Perspective
4. Consider Context

In what follows, we'll use each of these steps to break down the given prompt.

Step 1: Work the Prompt
Let's have another look at the prompt.

> Many colleges and universities have cut their humanities departments, and high schools have begun to shift their attention much more definitively toward STEM (Science, Technology, Engineering, Mathematics) and away from ELA (English, Language Arts). Representatives from both school boards and government organizations suggest that the move toward STEM is necessary in helping students to participate in a meaningful way in the American workplace. Given the urgency of this debate for the future of education and potentially society as a whole, it is worth examining the potential consequences of this shift in how students are educated in the United States.

In order to work the prompt, we'll need to clarify a few things.

First, we should identify the major *terms* of the prompt. Give this a try.

_____

_____

_____

The answers you came up with are probably some version of these terms: *education, schools, STEM, ELA,* and *workplace.*

The next task is a little more complex. Figure out the central relationship in those terms and identify the possible points of *tension* within those terms. In other words, what in the prompt requires you to weigh in? Why is this relationship still the subject of debate and not a done deal?

_____

_____

_____

This task is a little tougher, but it's essential. Try to pick two or three of the terms you identified as key and write a sentence describing their relationship.

You may come up with something like this:

If schools *prepare students for the* workplace, *what should students be learning in schools?*

Or like this:

Schools *should weigh* ELA *and* STEM *differently depending on what those schools care about teaching.*

You may have come up with something different, and that's fine. The real test will come in the next step when you read the three perspectives provided. If those seem to address the central tension you've described, you're in good shape.

Step 2: Work the Perspectives

Typically, the three perspectives will be split: one *for*, one *against*, and one *in the middle*. Your job in Step 2 is to identify these perspectives and to try to figure out what they have to say to each other.

> It doesn't matter whether you agree or disagree with the perspectives. Assess them *as arguments* first and foremost.

Let's have another look at the perspectives before we get started:

Perspective One	Perspective Two	Perspective Three
ELA programs should be emphasized over STEM programs. Education is not merely a means to employment: ELA education helps students to live more meaningful lives. In addition, an exclusively STEM-based program cannot help but limit students' creativity and lead them to overemphasize the importance of money and other tangible gains.	ELA programs should be eradicated entirely, except to establish the basic literacy necessary to engage in the hard sciences, mathematics, and business. Reading and writing are activities that are best saved for the leisure of students who enjoy them.	ELA and STEM programs should always be in equal balance with one another. Both are necessary to providing a student with a well-rounded education. Moreover, equal emphasis will allow the fullest possible exposure to many subjects before students choose their majors and careers.

Which perspective is *for* emphasizing STEM programs over ELA programs? What does this perspective consider? What does it overlook?

_____

_____

_____

Which perspective is *against* emphasizing STEM programs over ELA programs? What does this perspective consider? What does it overlook?

_____

_____

_____

Which perspective is *in the middle* on the question of emphasizing STEM programs over ELA programs? What does this perspective consider? What does it overlook?

_____

_____

_____

You may have come up with something like this:

For (Perspective 2): This perspective takes fully seriously the idea that education leads to employment, and as a result, it sees no value in ELA programs at all because those programs do not have any tangible benefits in the workplace. What this perspective misses, however, is that ELA could have some applicability to the world of work (in marketing, for instance, or in other creative spheres). Nor does it give any serious consideration to the idea that education could be good on its own.

Against (Perspective 1): This perspective is absolutely against the idea of allowing STEM programs to take over, even if those programs do lead to more employability. Perspective 1 says that education should be independent of the workplace and should be more about how to live life. What this perspective misses, however, is that de-emphasis of STEM programs is not practical in the contemporary world, which privileges STEM and technical knowledge. Perspective 1 also severs the link between education and employability too definitively: they must have something to do with each other!

In the middle (Perspective 3): This perspective is in favor of the status quo, which has STEM and ELA programs in equal balance with one another. It says that only a variety of exposure will allow students to find their niches within the workplace. What this perspective misses, however, is that if there is a link between education and employment, this variety is potentially irrelevant. It also overlooks the idea that there is a crisis in education, which is the whole impetus for the previous two ideas.

Your working of the perspectives may not look exactly like this, but that's okay. As long as you've identified where each perspective stands (*for, against,* or *in the middle*) and then identified at least one shortcoming of each perspective, you're in good shape for the next step: generating your own perspective.

Step 3: Generate Your Own Perspective

Now that you've outlined the prompt and the perspectives, it's time to generate your own. You'll draw from each of the perspectives, and you may side with one of them, but your perspective should have something unique about it.

> Come up with your own perspective! If you merely restate one of the three given perspectives, you won't be able to get into the highest scoring ranges.

Start by describing your perspective.

_____

_____

_____

Just so you have a sense of how to build this perspective, we've included one of our own. This is not to say that this perspective is correct—remember, there is no correct answer! It's just an effective argument that would generate a high score.

In my view, the question of how education and the workplace are related to each other misses the point. The cause and effect is wrong, and the very fact that we can ask this question shows that a significant change has already taken place. The prompt asks us to explain what the most effective link between school and workplace is, but that already presumes that there is a link between school and workplace, which is not necessarily universally true. Before we can answer the question of whether STEM programs should be emphasized over ELA programs, we should first wonder whether we'd like to proceed with this linkage between education and workplace. Understanding this linkage is essential because if we find that social prejudices are shaping education without seeming to do so, we will likely find that the potential for innovation and creativity shrinks, and all the technical knowledge in the world won't save us.

Now that you've generated your own perspective, check it against the perspectives already given.

How does your perspective compare to Perspective One?

_____

_____

_____

My perspective is probably closest to Perspective One, but it differs from Perspective One in that it refuses to engage in the question of employment. Perspective One is limited because, especially at the end, it tries to make a case for ELA as employable skills, which is not particularly viable.

How does your perspective compare to Perspective Two?

_____

_____

_____

My perspective is furthest from Perspective Two, though the disagreement is not so explicit as to say, "Perspective Two, you're wrong!" Instead, my perspective shows that Perspective Two is wrapped up in all kinds of assumptions and prejudices of which the author of Perspective Two is seemingly unaware.

How does your perspective compare to Perspective Three?

_____

_____

_____

My perspective has a different aim from that of Perspective Three. Perspective Three is interested in maintaining a balance, but only because he or she sees that balance as advantageous in determining one's eventual employment. In my view, Perspective Three is the worst of both worlds: it has a loose grip on the status quo while at the same time accepting premises that there is no good reason to accept.

If you were able to differentiate your view from all three perspectives while your view remained intact, congratulations! You're on your way to a great score! There's just one more thing... the bigger picture.

A Note on the Best Arguments

While there is no correct answer to the prompts that ACT gives, there is a bit of a failsafe formula for coming up with a complex argument. This is not to say it's easy to do so, but you bought the *Elite* book because you're not all about the easy stuff.

The best arguments are the least obvious, and the good arguments are often not obvious because they are *counterintuitive*.

Think about it this way. Let's say that you've got a prompt that asks whether there should be Internet-blocking software on school computers. There are two obvious sides to this position:

Yes, there should be blocking software on school computers because students can't be trusted to stay away from bad stuff.

And

No, there shouldn't be blocking software on school computers because that limits students' freedom to explore the Internet's full resources.

Either of these would be fine, but a higher-scoring essay would probably do something a little extra. Look at these claims, which are not quite *Yes* and not quite *No*. They're somewhere in between.

Yes, there should be Internet-blocking software. This software would not be constricting for students, however. Instead, such blocking software would be liberating because it would require students to get out of their traditional comfort zones. Students may believe that Facebook and other social-media sites open their minds, but we've all seen how teens are glued to these sites as if under some strange compulsion or addiction. Blocking software would force those students to have interactions that they would not have otherwise, and all students would benefit from such interactions.

Alternatively:

No, there should not be Internet-blocking software. Instead, schools should become more serious about exposing students to the true wonders and capabilities of the Internet, so as to positively motivate students to stay off prohibited and damaging sites. The average teacher uses the Internet for frankly pretty mundane purposes. If we had teachers and administrators who were tech savvy enough to point students toward more fulfilling uses of the Internet, blocking software would be a moot point.

These arguments are both a little on the long side, but notice that each one has a seeming contradiction at the heart of it. The first one says, essentially, *Blocking software is not limiting but liberating.* The second one says, in essence, *If students knew how to use the Internet with real freedom, they wouldn't waste their time on frivolous sites.*

If you can force yourself to come up with a counterintuitive argument, you'll be on your way to a really high score. If you need a little push in the right direction, isolate the Pro and Con arguments from a particular prompt. For the prompt we've been looking at in this chapter, those Pro and Con arguments are as follows:

1. ELA programs should be emphasized over STEM programs. Education is not merely a means to employment: ELA education helps students to live more meaningful lives. In addition, an exclusively STEM-based program cannot help but limit students' creativity and lead them to overemphasize the importance of money and other tangible gains.

2. ELA programs should be eradicated entirely, except to establish the basic literacy necessary to engage in the hard sciences, mathematics, and business. Reading and writing are activities that are best saved for the leisure of students who enjoy them.

One says *All ELA all the time because ELA teaches us how to live.* The other says *All STEM all the time because STEM is what matters in the workplace.* The middle perspective advocates a *balance* between the subjects because students should be allowed to decide.

Now try to generate a counterintuitive perspective of your own. Is there a way that you can use the answer from the Pro side but the reason from the Con side? Or vice versa? We've come up with a counterintuitive argument, but can you come up with another? Perhaps the counterpoint to ours?

Step 4: Consider Context

As you build your argument, remember that the graders are looking to see a complex mind at work. Examples are important, but they mainly exist to help you structure and discuss your perspective and *why* you have that perspective. Examples can come from anywhere, but they should be reasonable, and they should have a clear application to your argument.

To start, list the examples you'll use to make your argument and identify *how* they will help you make that argument. Try to come up with at least two.

_____

_____

_____

_____

I'm going to use one example that has a direct application to what's being discussed in the prompt: Albert Einstein. I'm going to use another that shows why the discussion may be irrelevant: the question of human happiness.

Now describe the order in which you'll discuss your examples and why:

_____

_____

_____

_____

_____

I'm going to discuss the examples in the order I've given above. That way, my essay will start by discussing the prompt directly and will then broaden out to show the larger question of which the prompt is part.

A Push Toward the Big Picture

As you may have noticed, ACT Writing is all about flattering your graders by basically showering them with gifts. That flattery doesn't have to stop with you fulfilling the basic expectations. You can also flatter them by telling them what a great question they've asked.

As you try to think about the bigger picture, ask this question: *Why is ACT asking this question in the first place?* If the only answer you can come up with is, *Because they need us to write about some garbage in this essay,* try again!

How about this prompt that we've been talking about so far? Why does ACT want to know where you fall on the ELA-STEM debate? Why would this be an important question for you, or your parents, or your teachers, or your government representatives to discuss? Here's an idea: *Because the future of education determines the future of society as a whole.* That's a big deal! And now it seems like this might be a question worth answering.

If you can attach your argument to this larger context, it can show not only that you can think beyond the limitations of this standardized test but also that you recognize the potential linkage between the small questions of life and the big ones.

THE TEMPLATE

You've done a lot of pre-work, and now it's time to put it all in essay form. Remember, though, that you are taking a *standardized test,* so it will help you to be as *standardized* as possible in your presentation. If you come in knowing basically what your essay will look like, you'll have a much easier time saying all you need to say.

If you already know what your template will look like, great. The best essays always reveal something personal about the writer and his or her complex mind.

If you're not sure what your essay will look like, never fear! Below, we outline a basic template that will have space for all the good stuff you just did in your pre-writing.

Introduction

A good introduction will lay out the terms of the *conversation* in which the writer is planning to participate. It will give the reader a preview of what is to come and will, hopefully, encourage the reader to keep reading. In roughly three to five sentences, try out the following:

1. Identify *why* the question posed in the prompt is important.
2. Present your perspective on the question posed in the prompt.
3. Preview how you intend to give support to your perspective.

Based on the pre-writing we did above, here is an example of an effective introduction.

"We want our students to have the best education possible." We've heard enough politicians say it to know that this idea is more or less a truth universally acknowledged. The problem comes when we start to think in a real way about what that "best" education could be. Recently, the rhetoric surrounding educational policy has been all about the importance of STEM programs—improving them, foregrounding them, and making them more attractive to all students. The idea motivating this rhetoric is economic. School is preparation for the workplace; therefore, students should become best educated in the subjects that will make them most employable. This seems like sound logic, but as I will show, both by citing some new examples and by showing the limitations of the three perspectives given in the prompt, this is not the only possible conclusion, nor even necessarily the best one. The more essential task, in my view, is to clarify what a "good education" is and, in a much larger sense, what we want from our lives.

This introduction is effective because it shows the broader context into which the prompt fits: that of education reform in the country as a whole. The introduction then goes on to show a potential problem with asking the question itself: the not-so-universal agreement on what a "good education" is. Then, the introduction is particularly effective at stating the essay's goal: to analyze the three perspectives, to show their limitations, and to show why a different question may get more squarely to the root of the problem.

Body Paragraphs

Body paragraphs provide your reader with the details and examples of your discussion. Try to generate one body paragraph for each example you discuss (usually two or three). Make sure that your body paragraphs do the following:

1. Provide a transition from the previous paragraph and a topic sentence that describes the new one.
2. Assess at least one of the perspectives given in the prompt as a way to strengthen your own perspective.
3. Use an example to develop your perspective or analyze one of the given perspectives.
4. Relate your discussion back to your position and the larger topic.

Based on the pre-writing exercises, here's an example of an effective body paragraph.

You may ask, then, which do I think is better? ELA or STEM? The idea that one would need to choose is part of the problem. Albert Einstein said, "Imagination is more important than knowledge." Now, you'd think that Einstein (the father of twentieth-century STEM, basically) would love the idea of turning all students into little scientists and mathematicians. What Einstein believed, and what his life showed, however, are far different. Einstein understood that all knowledge was valuable but that the imaginative things one does with that knowledge are even more valuable. One would be hard-pressed to find a great mind that was not richly educated across the subjects, from ELA to STEM and beyond. As a result, Perspectives One and Two both miss the point in suggesting the overemphasis of one subject group over another. As Einstein's example shows, what one learns is less important than how one applies that knowledge, and one's possibilities for breadth and imagination necessarily increase with the acquisition of many types of knowledge.

This is an effective body paragraph because it analyzes two or three perspectives given in the prompt. The paragraph gives an example, Albert Einstein, to show the limitations of both of those perspectives while supporting the author's own perspective.

The paragraph also contains an implied transition to the next paragraph, especially because the reader may now believe that if the author is neither *for* nor *against*, he or she must be *in the middle*. As we know from the introduction, however, this may not be the case, and we should read on to find out.

If you want to know what the author's next body paragraph says, good! That means we've got your interest. Think about some of the ways that has happened. What do you want to know? What questions have we left unanswered? What else do you want to contribute to the *conversation*?

Try your own paragraph. Even if our perspective doesn't match yours, try to think along with us here. You'll find it's a useful exercise: ACT Writing is not the place to express your deepest thoughts but to develop your most complex argument.

_____

_____

_____

_____

_____

What did you do well in that argument? What could you have improved? Do you need a third paragraph before you hit the conclusion?

_____

_____

_____

Conclusion

Even though you may be running out of time, it's important to write a conclusion. It gives your essay a completeness that it might not otherwise have. An effective conclusion will usually do the following:

1. Recap your discussion as it has related to the prompt and perspectives.
2. Restate your perspective and arguments.
3. Provide a final overarching thought on the topic.

Here's an example of an effective conclusion:

In short, this prompt forces us to ask an even larger question. What is education? Is it job training? Is it life training? Education reform creates larger changes than many of us realize, and it therefore requires more reflection. While we are comfortable in the idea that education creates members of society, we should also see that society creates a certain type of education. Before we implement these changes, we need to be very certain what our goals are, especially in the very long term.

This conclusion is effective because it summarizes what the author has said without restating it outright. It also pushes the discussion toward a different, larger question, showing that the author has a broader understanding of what is going on in the prompt.

Now, here's the full essay in all its glory:

"We want our students to have the best education possible." We've heard enough politicians say it to know that this idea is more or less a truth universally acknowledged. The problem comes when we start to think in a real way about what that "best" education could be. Recently, the rhetoric surrounding educational policy has been all about the importance of STEM programs—improving them, foregrounding them, and making them more attractive to all students. The idea motivating this rhetoric is economic. School is preparation for the workplace; therefore, students should become best educated in the subjects that will make them most employable. This seems like sound logic, but as I will show, both by citing some new examples and by showing the limitations of the three perspectives given in the prompt, this is not the only possible conclusion, nor even necessarily the best one. The more essential task, in my view, is to clarify what a "good education" is and, in a much larger sense, what we want from our lives.

You may ask, then, which do I think is better? ELA or STEM? The idea that one would need to choose is part of the problem. Albert Einstein said, "Imagination is more important than knowledge." Now, you'd think that Einstein (the father of twentieth-century STEM, basically) would love the idea of turning all students into little scientists and mathematicians. What Einstein believed, and what his life showed, however, are far different. Einstein understood that all knowledge was valuable but that the imaginative things one does with that knowledge are even more valuable. One would be hard-pressed to find a great mind that was not richly educated across the subjects, from ELA to STEM and beyond. As a result, Perspectives One and Two both miss the point in suggesting the overemphasis of one subject group over another. As Einstein's example shows, what one learns is less important than how one applies that knowledge, and one's possibilities for breadth and imagination necessarily increase with the acquisition of many types of knowledge.

This is not to say, however, that I find Perspective Three especially compelling either. While I do agree that there is some value in maintaining a balance between ELA and STEM subjects, Perspective Three's reasoning seems wildly misdirected. While it is to be hoped that all adults will be gainfully employed once they leave school, the idea that school should be all geared towards employability is disappointing. As Einstein's example shows, there is more to learning than employability, and even if STEM programs were somehow foregrounded, the lack of ELA programs would limit how imaginatively and creatively students could interpret their data. And let's not overlook the biggest problem of all: if all knowledge acquisition is geared toward how much money it can make us, then to what have we reduced the meaning of our lives? This rhetoric of schools as training sites can lead to only one place: five-year-olds who believe that the only purpose anyone could have on this earth is to get a good job and make money. Is that a world you'd want to live in? Consider yourself lucky to have the capacity to imagine such a world!

In short, this prompt forces us to ask an even larger question. What is education? Is it job training? Is it life training? Education reform creates larger changes than many of us realize, and it therefore requires more reflection. While we are comfortable in the idea that education creates members of society, we should also see that society creates a certain type of education. Before we implement these changes, we need to be very certain what our goals are, especially in the very long term.

A CONCLUSION OF OUR OWN

We know that this can seem like a lot to do in forty minutes, especially for something that won't count toward your composite. We can't help you with the composite part, but we can say this: the essay becomes easier with practice.

And now that you're an expert at the ACT Writing section, here are a few other things to keep in mind.

1. **Length.** ACT graders tend to reward longer essays. Make sure you get onto the second page and the third, if possible. If your writing tends to be small, you may want to practice writing larger, especially because it will also make your essay a bit neater and easier to read. If your handwriting is large, make sure you write an extra page to compensate.

2. **Sentence structure.** Varying your sentence structure helps to improve the rhythm of your essay. If you write a really long sentence with lots of modifiers and dependent clauses, it sometimes helps to follow it with a shorter, more direct sentence. It really works. Don't try to be too fancy, though. The longer the sentence is, the more opportunity there is to confuse the reader or to make a grammatical mistake.

3. **Diction.** Diction refers to word choice. You certainly want to sprinkle some nice vocabulary words throughout your paper. But make sure to use and spell them correctly. If you're uncertain about the meaning or spelling of a word, it's best just to pick a different word. Using a big word incorrectly makes a worse impression than using a smaller word correctly.

4. **Neatness.** Make sure you indent each new paragraph. Align your essay using the lines on the paper. Don't go over the lines or write down the side of the page. Avoid messy cross-outs. Although the grader should not take these kinds of things into consideration when determining your grade, a neat, legible essay will be easier to read. Your grader will read hundreds, if not thousands, of essays. A neat essay will make the grader happier.

PRACTICE ESSAY PROMPTS

Here are a few more sample essay prompts that you can use for practice. After you finish each essay, read it over—or better yet, have someone else read it—and see how well your essay conforms to the ACTs grading standards. When you practice writing the essay, it's best to limit your time to 40 minutes to experience how short the allotted time really is.

Prompt #1

Proper English and Text Speak

Because students today are so fluent in the language of "text speak," the spelling and syntax used in text messages, some schools have begun to allow text speak on tests and in essays. Such a move can be helpful to students, say these schools, because it does not allow archaic grammar conventions to block students' expression of their knowledge of certain topics or ideas. Because this move points toward larger questions about the meaning of communication in the modern world, it is worth examining whether this allowance of "text speak" in schools is a help to students' educations.

Read and carefully consider these perspectives. Each suggests a particular way of thinking about the shift in American education.

Perspective One	Perspective Two	Perspective Three
While there is no problem with students writing in shorthand in some instances, proper English should still be taught in English and other humanities classes because students may need to know how to use proper English in some later circumstances.	The purpose of language is communication, and if "text speak" communicates, there is no reason that it should not be used. It may not have the same rules that grammarians know, but it does have its own set of rules and communicates just as effectively as, if not more effectively than, standard English.	Students already know how to write "text speak," so schools should continue to teach them standard English, which is still the privileged way of speech in all formal written documentation outside of personal conversations.

Essay Task

Write a unified, coherent essay in which you evaluate multiple perspectives on the issue of how schools should balance "text speak" and standard English. In your essay, be sure to:

- analyze and evaluate the perspectives given
- state and develop your own perspective on the issue
- explain the relationship between your perspective and those given

Your perspective may be in full agreement with any of the others, in partial agreement, or wholly different. Whatever the case, support your ideas with logical reasoning and detailed, persuasive examples.

Prompt #2

Technology and Experience

Technology surrounds us everywhere now, and from very young ages, children are using technology and building their mental lives around it. Some companies boast that their technologies are so easy that children can use them. However, some traditionalists suggest that new generations are being denied authentic experiences by being so tied to technology from such a young age. These traditionalists suggest that children should not be allowed to use smart technologies until those children are of a mature enough age to appreciate the benefits of those technologies. Because technology is so prevalent in today's society, it is worth examining whether some authentic experience has been lost in such a techno-centric world.

Read and carefully consider these perspectives. Each suggests a particular way of thinking about technology and authentic experience.

Perspective One	Perspective Two	Perspective Three
Children may have early experiences with technology today, but that does not make those experiences inauthentic. Children learn about the world in a different way today, and to give them experiences without technology would be to force a version of the world upon them that no longer exists.	Parents should require their children to use technologies within moderation. While it is important that children learn to use these technologies, it is also important that they learn the more traditional face-to-face interactions that predate these technologies.	Young people's ability to interact in a meaningful way has changed for the worse. This is because they are better at interacting with technology than with other people. As a result, young people should be kept away from these technologies for as long as possible.

Essay Task

Write a unified, coherent essay in which you evaluate multiple perspectives on the issue of whether children should be permitted to interact with technology before they have matured. In your essay, be sure to:

- analyze and evaluate the perspectives given
- state and develop your own perspective on the issue
- explain the relationship between your perspective and those given

Your perspective may be in full agreement with any of the others, in partial agreement, or wholly different. Whatever the case, support your ideas with logical reasoning and detailed, persuasive examples.

Summary:
An Essay Checklist

Now look at your essays and see if you applied the strategies presented in this chapter.

○ The Introduction
Did you
- start with a topic sentence that paraphrases or restates the prompt?
- clearly state your position on the issue?

○ Body Paragraph 1
Did you
- start with a transition/topic sentence that discusses the opposing side of the argument?
- give an example of a reason that one might agree with the opposing side of the argument?
- clearly state that the opposing side of the argument is wrong or flawed?
- show what is wrong with the opposing side's example or position?

○ Body Paragraphs 2 and 3
Did you
- start with a transition/topic sentence that discusses your position on the prompt?
- give one example or reason to support your position?
- show the grader how your example supports your position?
- end the paragraph by restating your thesis?

○ Conclusion
Did you
- restate your position on the issue?
- end with a flourish?

○ Overall
Did you
- write neatly?
- avoid multiple spelling and grammar mistakes?
- try to vary your sentence structure?
- use a few impressive-sounding words?

NOTES

NOTES

NOTES

NOTES

NOTES

NOTES

International Offices Listing

China (Beijing)
1501 Building A,
Disanji Creative Zone,
No.66 West Section of North 4th Ring Road Beijing
Tel: +86-10-62684481/2/3
Email: tprkor01@chol.com
Website: www.tprbeijing.com

China (Shanghai)
1010 Kaixuan Road
Building B, 5/F
Changning District, Shanghai, China 200052
Sara Beattie, Owner: Email: sbeattie@sarabeattie.com
Tel: +86-21-5108-2798
Fax: +86-21-6386-1039
Website: www.princetonreviewshanghai.com

Hong Kong
5th Floor, Yardley Commercial Building
1-6 Connaught Road West, Sheung Wan, Hong Kong
(MTR Exit C)
Sara Beattie, Owner: Email: sbeattie@sarabeattie.com
Tel: +852-2507-9380
Fax: +852-2827-4630
Website: www.princetonreviewhk.com

India (Mumbai)
Score Plus Academy
Office No.15, Fifth Floor
Manek Mahal 90
Veer Nariman Road
Next to Hotel Ambassador
Churchgate, Mumbai 400020
Maharashtra, India
Ritu Kalwani: Email: director@score-plus.com
Tel: + 91 22 22846801 / 39 / 41
Website: www.score-plus.com

India (New Delhi)
South Extension
K-16, Upper Ground Floor
South Extension Part–1,
New Delhi-110049
Aradhana Mahna: aradhana@manyagroup.com
Monisha Banerjee: monisha@manyagroup.com
Ruchi Tomar: ruchi.tomar@manyagroup.com
Rishi Josan: Rishi.josan@manyagroup.com
Vishal Goswamy: vishal.goswamy@manyagroup.com
Tel: +91-11-64501603/ 4, +91-11-65028379
Website: www.manyagroup.com

Lebanon
463 Bliss Street
AlFarra Building - 2nd floor
Ras Beirut
Beirut, Lebanon
Hassan Coudsi: Email: hassan.coudsi@review.com
Tel: +961-1-367-688
Website: www.princetonreviewlebanon.com

Korea
945-25 Young Shin Building
25 Daechi-Dong, Kangnam-gu
Seoul, Korea 135-280
Yong-Hoon Lee: Email: TPRKor01@chollian.net
In-Woo Kim: Email: iwkim@tpr.co.kr
Tel: + 82-2-554-7762
Fax: +82-2-453-9466
Website: www.tpr.co.kr

Kuwait
ScorePlus Learning Center
Salmiyah Block 3, Street 2 Building 14
Post Box: 559, Zip 1306, Safat, Kuwait
Email: infokuwait@score-plus.com
Tel: +965-25-75-48-02 / 8
Fax: +965-25-75-46-02
Website: www.scorepluseducation.com

Malaysia
Sara Beattie MDC Sdn Bhd
Suites 18E & 18F
18th Floor
Gurney Tower, Persiaran Gurney
Penang, Malaysia
Email: tprkl.my@sarabeattie.com
Sara Beattie, Owner: Email: sbeattie@sarabeattie.com
Tel: +604-2104 333
Fax: +604-2104 330
Website: www.princetonreviewKL.com

Mexico
TPR México
Guanajuato No. 242 Piso 1 Interior 1
Col. Roma Norte
México D.F., C.P.06700
registro@princetonreviewmexico.com
Tel: +52-55-5255-4495
+52-55-5255-4440
+52-55-5255-4442
Website: www.princetonreviewmexico.com

Qatar
Score Plus
Office No: 1A, Al Kuwari (Damas)
Building near Merweb Hotel, Al Saad
Post Box: 2408, Doha, Qatar
Email: infoqatar@score-plus.com
Tel: +974 44 36 8580, +974 526 5032
Fax: +974 44 13 1995
Website: www.scorepluseducation.com

Taiwan
The Princeton Review Taiwan
2F, 169 Zhong Xiao East Road, Section 4
Taipei, Taiwan 10690
Lisa Bartle (Owner): lbartle@princetonreview.com.tw
Tel: +886-2-2751-1293
Fax: +886-2-2776-3201
Website: www.PrincetonReview.com.tw

Thailand
The Princeton Review Thailand
Sathorn Nakorn Tower, 28th floor
100 North Sathorn Road
Bangkok, Thailand 10500
Thavida Bijayendrayodhin (Chairman)
Email: thavida@princetonreviewthailand.com
Mitsara Bijayendrayodhin (Managing Director)
Email: mitsara@princetonreviewthailand.com
Tel: +662-636-6770
Fax: +662-636-6776
Website: www.princetonreviewthailand.com

Turkey
Yeni Sülün Sokak No. 28
Levent, Istanbul, 34330, Turkey
Nuri Ozgur: nuri@tprturkey.com
Rona Ozgur: rona@tprturkey.com
Iren Ozgur: iren@tprturkey.com
Tel: +90-212-324-4747
Fax: +90-212-324-3347
Website: www.tprturkey.com

UAE
Emirates Score Plus
Office No: 506, Fifth Floor
Sultan Business Center
Near Lamcy Plaza, 21 Oud Metha Road
Post Box: 44098, Dubai
United Arab Emirates
Hukumat Kalwani: skoreplus@gmail.com
Ritu Kalwani: director@score-plus.com
Email: info@score-plus.com
Tel: +971-4-334-0004
Fax: +971-4-334-0222
Website: www.princetonreviewuae.com

Our International Partners

The Princeton Review also runs courses with a variety of partners in Africa, Asia, Europe, and South America.

Georgia
LEAF American-Georgian Education Center
www.leaf.ge

Mongolia
English Academy of Mongolia
www.nyescm.org

Nigeria
The Know Place
www.knowplace.com.ng

Panama
Academia Interamericana de Panama
http://aip.edu.pa/

Switzerland
Institut Le Rosey
http://www.rosey.ch/

All other inquiries, please email us at
internationalsupport@review.com